D1349833

Brenton pinxit   J. A. Vinter lith.   Day & Son, Limited, Lith.

Sincerely yours
Geo Bell
Colonel Royal Regt.

1855

SOLDIER'S GLORY

being

'Rough Notes of an Old Soldier'

by

MAJOR-GENERAL
SIR GEORGE BELL
arranged and edited
by his kinsman
BRIAN STUART

LONDON
G. BELL AND SONS, LTD
1956

First published 1956

PRINTED IN GREAT BRITAIN AT
THE UNIVERSITY PRESS
ABERDEEN

FOREWORD

SOLDIER'S GLORY, as its name implies, is a story of courage. In all our military annals, I know of none more moving. From the March day in 1811 when seventeen-year-old George Bell left his parents' home on the shores of Lough Erin and boarded the royal mail-coach at the end of the avenue to join his regiment in Spain, to the day, forty-four years later, when a colonel of sixty-one, wracked with ague and fever after a winter in the Crimea, he sailed for England on enforced sick-leave, his tale is one of repeated hardship, cheerfully borne. The key-note to his book is epitomised in an incident of his campaign, when marching under 'Daddy' Hill on Arroyo-Molinos—that most brilliant of surprise attacks—and bivouacking in torrential rain on flooded ground, he was asked by a comrade how he had slept. 'Slept like a fish,' he replied, 'I believe they sleep the best in water.' 'Bravo,' said the other, 'you'll do.'

The young ensign, then eighteen, was in the assault on Badajos—one of the most remarkable of all feats of arms—and has left a description of it unrivalled by Napier.

'Let any one picture to himself this frightful carnage taking place in a space of less than a hundred yards square. Let him consider that the slain died not all suddenly, nor by one manner of death; that some perished by steel, some by shot, some by water, some crushed and mangled by heavy weights, some trampled upon, some dashed to atoms by the fierce explosions, that for hours this destruction was endured without shrinking, and that the town was won at last. Let any man consider this, and he must admit that a British army bears with it an awful power.'

He fought at Salamanca and Vittoria, in the Pyrenees, at Nivelle, St. Pierre and Toulouse, and, before he was twenty-one, was a veteran soldier with three years' continuous fighting behind him under one of the great captains of all time. He was justly indignant when, at the end of the 1812 campaign, an anonymous private of the Connaught Rangers passing with his Regiment on the march—'merry as larks, singing and cracking their Irish jokes, regular bronze fellows, hard as nails'—observed in an audible voice to a comrade, 'I think that young gentleman would be better at home with his mother.'

After the Napoleonic Wars George Bell, like many another fine young officer without influence or private means, was retired on a half pay pension of 4s. a day. In 1825, through the kind offices of that friend to all good soldiers, the Duke of York, he was gazetted once more in a Regiment of the Line. The hardships that he and his wife endured, on transports, in India, in the dreadful first Burma War, in Canada, in the West Indies, in Corfu, even in England as a poor regimental officer—'in two wretched little rooms not fit for a dog kennel, fitted up and finished with four rickety old chairs, . . .

three rusty fire-irons of great antiquity and an old iron candle-stick' — make painful, yet strangely heartening, reading. For he was never defeated by anything, like the 'seasoned old bricks' — 'the ragged pack of red-coats' — he loved and served so well, as they 'marched cheerily down the hills, singing the old song:

> "Merrily, merrily march away,
> Soldier's glory lives in story,
> Our laurels are green, if our locks are grey . . .".'

His account of the Crimea War is an epic of British valour and endurance under almost unbelievable sufferings, caused by the grossest mismanagement. Yet somehow the ultimate effect left on the reader is not so much of waste and tragedy, of which there was plenty, as of the power of heroism and brotherhood to triumph over the worst that can befall. As with Dr. Johnson's friend who tried to be a philosopher, in the writer and hero of this book, 'cheerfulness was always breaking through'.

George Bell was not only a fine soldier, who, in an age which rewarded merit and not merely birth and wealth, would have risen to be a full General long before his seventy-ninth year — the age at which, at last and in retirement, he attained that honour. He was also a brilliant writer. To him we owe the wonderful story of how that valiant little Irishwoman, as broad as a turtle, 'Mrs. Commissary-General Skiddy, carried her sick husband, Private Dan Skiddy of the 34th' and his firelock and knapsack on her back for many a weary mile during the retreat from Burgos. To him we owe, too, one of the finest of all our pictures of Wellington's relationship with the rough men he led. 'He never came near us without a cheer that made the woods ring. When he appeared, the men would say, "There he comes with his long nose, boys; now you may fix your flints." ' Bell had a natural gift, almost Dickensian in his range and humanity, for delineating character. His book is full of magnificent character sketches, like that of Maurice Quill, the 'saw-bones' of the 31st who won a bet that he would borrow ten dollars from Wellington and dine with him too, or Colonel Brown of the old 'Slashers' — the fighting 28th — whose longest speech to his men was, 'There they come, boys; if you don't kill them, they'll kill you; fire away!' He so clearly loved the men whose likenesses he delineated and whom he led during his long career with such understanding and humanity. 'At what an easy rate', he wrote of the days when he carried his spare bottle of rum round the frozen trenches before Sebastopol, 'you may win the affection and respect of your men in the Army. They never forget a kindness, and any officer may be popular if he has common-sense and the feelings of a Christian.'

Smedmore, 1955   ARTHUR BRYANT

HABEBIS QUOD CONTRAXIS

Edmonton Sculpt

LIEU.T COLONEL BELL,

Royal Reg.t

BOOKPLATE (*Slightly enlarged*)

PUBLISHERS' NOTE

THE author of *Rough Notes of an Old Soldier* belonged to an Irish branch of the widespread family of Bell. A genealogical tree, 'certified by Francis Townsend Esqre., Windsor Herald, etc., etc., etc.', in 1818, was compiled by Henry Nugent Bell, the well-known genealogist and author of *The Huntingdon Peerage*. It traces the family back to Edward the Elder, but shows that it must have been settled in Scotland in the early Middle Ages, for the falcon and supporters shown in the copy of the bookplate commemorate a grant made by King Robert Bruce to George Bell, or the 'Burley Laird', as he was called, in the fourteenth century as the result of the feat of venery described in *Debrett*, 1870.

Among Sir George's better known ancestors was Sir Robert Bell, Speaker of the House of Commons and Lord Chief Baron of the Exchequer, who died in 1577, and the line was continued through his eldest son Edmund, by his third wife Dorothy Beaupré of Wells in Norfolk.

It was probably in the last quarter of the seventeenth century that a later ancestor, Walter, settled in Fermanagh, and his grandson George, of Belle Vue on Lough Erne, was the father of the family of which Henry Nugent was the eldest, and George the second, son. Other sons were Tom, William, and Alexander, and there were four daughters, Martha, Mary, Catherine and Charlotte.

The grant of arms displayed and blazoned on page x, made to Walter Bell of Gortadrate, which had been registered in Dublin Castle, received 'confirmation of user' at the College of Arms on 12th July 1819.

Sir George, who was born on 16th March 1794, was twice married, firstly to Alicia Scott, heiress of James Scott of Ecclesjohn and Conniston, and secondly to Margaret Addison, daughter of Thomas Dougal, Banker of Montrose. He left a daughter by each wife, and descendants of both daughters are living today.

His death took place on 10th July 1877 at 156 Westbourne Terrace, London, and he was buried in Kensal Green Cemetery.

It is evident that the branch of the family to which Major Brian Stuart belongs had settled in Ireland at an earlier date, for it is recorded that in 1599 Elizabeth I sent a General Darragh to Ireland to help Lord Mountjoy quell the O'Neill Rebellion, and that one of his daughters married a John Humphrey Bell; it is from this union that Major Brian Stuart traces his descent. As the genealogical tree is incomplete, it is difficult to trace the relationship between him and Sir George.

The Publishers are indebted to Miss Caroline M. Maitland, great-grand-daughter of Sir George Bell, for the information she has provided regarding Sir George's family, and for kindly allowing them to inspect the genealogical tree.

CONTENTS

MAPS

Coat and Crest of
Major-General Sir George Bell, K.C.B.

ARMS : Azure, a fess ermine between
2 bells in chief & 1 in base or.

CREST : On a ducal coronet or a
falcon rising proper, collared gules,
belled or.

I join the 34th Foot

IN an account of his career, published in 1867, George Bell begins with the words:

The *London Gazette* of the 11th March 1811 proclaimed 'George Bell, gentleman, to be Ensign in the 34th Regiment of Foot, by command of His Majesty King George the Third'. On the 11th of March I was at a public school, when some one came and gave me the above information.

So soon as I collected my senses, I jumped up, broke my way into the presence of the great Dominie, bid him a hasty farewell, shook hands with my class companions, and bolted out of the house, no one seeming to know what it was all about until I was clear away, and sent back a newspaper with the Gazette, which fully explained my hasty retreat from thraldom.

Six days after the 11th of March I was just seventeen years of age, an independent military gentleman, let loose upon the world with the liberal pay of 5s. 3d. a day, less income-tax, which has never been increased from that day to this.

I had an official letter very soon to join my regimental depôt without delay, signed HARRY CALVERT, Adjutant-General.

So I went off that night by the mail a hundred miles' journey, to bid them farewell at the beautiful paternal residence on the banks of Lough Erin. Here I only remained two days: there was weeping and lamentation over-much at my departure; but it was the tender custom in Ireland long ago. The family circle saw me off, at the end of the long avenue, all pretty cheery until we heard the mail-coach horn in the distance, when the ladies began a fresh lamentation, which set me going until I nearly cried my eyes out.

I was now fairly off, and with my pocket full of money, so I began to brighten up by the time the coach stopped for the night, for this hundred-mile journey occupied two days.

This royal mail-coach was horsed with a pair of old Irish hunters, carried four passengers inside, and two guards in royal livery behind, with a box of blunderbuss firearms and pistols, to protect themselves and the mail-bags; the roads in those days being swarmed by highwaymen. We had no adventure.

After being well furnished with a good kit, and supplied liberally with everything I required, I sailed in the mail-packet for Liverpool, which I reached the third day, after a stormy voyage. It was then the custom for each passenger to carry his own prog; my hamper never was opened, I was so desperately sea-sick, consequently the steward came in for nearly all the good things, and might have set up a cookshop for many a day afterwards.

Safely on English ground for the first time, I enjoyed myself for a couple of days, and then took coach with four spanking horses for Beverley, in Yorkshire, where I joined my depôt, and went to drill under the command of an old Sergeant, who used to say that he was preparing me for a great General some day, if I didn't fall on the bed of honour before my time.

I now mounted my uniform for the first time, and when full dressed was ashamed to appear in the streets. I fancied all the people would be laughing at the raw Ensign, with his cocked hat and feather, jack boots, white breeches, sword, and belt; then the sword was always getting between my legs, trying to trip me up as I cautiously went along, not daring to look at any one. I thought myself the observed of all observers, being just bran-new out of the tailor's shop. We were encumbered with many sorts of regimental useless dresses, such as long black cloth leggings, with about two dozens of bright buttons up the outside of each leg! Then, for the evening, tight-fitting white kerseymere pantaloons, and Hessian boots with black silk tassels in front; and, when on duty, a gorget hanging under one's chin.

I was a right jolly fellow when I got all this toggery off my back, and enjoyed myself to the full. We had no mess, lived in lodgings, no restraint on us young fellows, and had, with the 5s. 3d. a day, 6s. a week lodging money, to provide ourselves with respectable quarters.

I found the pretty town of Beverley a most agreeable residence, and never dreamt of leaving it, until one fine morning we heard of the battle of Albuera, in which my regiment was engaged and suffered severely: the gaps of death must be filled; I was one of the number ordered out to fill a vacancy.

The route came upon us all of a heap, in the midst of fun and frolic, to march for Portsmouth, and embark for Portugal. It was twenty-two days' march; and away we went, thoughtless jolly dogs, living at hotels on the road, which astonished the 5s. 3d. a day! The marches were long at times, and many a day I almost dropped footsore and weary, which I never confessed. We always had breakfast at the half-way house, ordered by one of our men sent in advance; halted and formed up in military order before we marched into the town or village, swords drawn, and our drum and fife playing martial music. We had all the little boys and girls half a mile round pressing into the ranks to hear the band, as they said, and see the soldiers. After one hour's halt, and 2s. worth of a first-rate morning meal, leaving the jolly landlord very little profit, we continued our march, the same orderly going on to announce our approach at the billeting town, and to order dinner for the army! The march from Brigg to Lincoln I shall never forget — twenty-four miles of a straight line, the steeple that held Big Tom always in front — only one other march in all my campaigns knocked the life so much out of my feet, and that was a forced night march to Madrid, which I may record hereafter.

The landlords of the hotels always waited personally on us, to know our pleasure about the dinner hour, and what wines we liked best, etc. For my part, I would have been perfectly satisfied with a beef-steak and a pint of ale, but dared not express anything so *infra dig* with a red coat on my back; so left it all to my superiors, and paid my share of the bill with the best grace I could, not being a wine drinker, and finding the 5s. 3d. only about equal to satisfy the servants and some minor things by the way. At Oxford we were met by another detachment of different regiments on the same route, going to the wars; here we amalgamated and had a great jollification dinner-party. I could only consent to any proposal, having no voice of my own in the matter, paid three times the amount of the usual bill, and had a crashing headache next morning to cheer me. I was astonished to see what some of those fellows could drink, and not seem to feel the worse; one lad of my own age and standing got screwed every night — but he did not last long! I gave him many a lecture, being his senior officer by one week, but could not make any impression on a lad that sucked the money, i.e. going to bed with a bottle of brandy.

We had charming weather all the way — old women came toddling out by the wayside as we passed, crying out — 'There goes a few more lambs to the slaughter, poor things!' which only caused some merriment amongst the soldiers, who were the most thoughtless set of dogs I ever saw since or before—not one of them ever returned to England!

We finished our march at Portsmouth, and were billeted at an hotel called the 'Blue Posts'. I was very tired and very green in those days; I went to bed early, left my door unlocked, threw my clothes on a chair, and was soon in my dreams. I had £25 with me—all I was worth in the world; my pocket-book contained this treasure—it had many folds, in which my money was divided. When I turned out in the morning, I was nervously horrified at seeing my clothes scattered about the floor. I approached the examination with dread and saw at once the shadow of, to me, a great calamity. Some very unkind but thoughtful person had entered my bedroom while asleep, to count my money and square my accounts, extracted a ten pound Bank of England note, for the trouble and risk, and left, but perhaps overlooked, the balance of £15 which lay in another part of the book, so that I was not altogether bankrupt. I had a very good guess who this wretched robber was, and might have put my hand upon him, but I had no proof. I made my report to the commanding officer of our party; but he seemed to doubt my tale; nor would he make any inquiry, which nettled me more severely than the loss I sustained.

A week in Portsmouth reduced my £15. I had £7 10s. to pay for my share of sea-stock; the balance I changed into dollars, and embarked, in light marching order, on board the *Arethusa*, a rotten old transport of 300 tons. We had a gale of wind, of course, in the Bay of Biscay-O, and put back to Falmouth for some little repairs and more prog. We all subscribed and laid in a few sacks of potatoes, flour, and fresh meat. I took a Sunday walk in the country, strolled into a farm-house, while the jolly fat landlord and his dame were at their roast beef dinner and ale; they looked a little surprised at seeing a young fellow in a red coat at the door in that part of the country, but asked me to come in and taste their roast beef. I was always hungry in those days, and took my seat at the little round table, in the neat, clean, well-furnished kitchen; there was an air of comfort about it one hardly ever sees in any other country; they asked me a great many questions, every one then being interested in the war. I told them all I knew; and when I was going, they both shook my hands with some interest. I gave them thanks, bid them good-bye, left half-a-crown on the table, and went back to my den upon the waters. Our commanding officer had a cabin about the size of a coffin to himself; thirteen of us commissioned officers of different corps messed and slept in the cuddy, a sort of dog-kennel, where we washed by turns in the morning. One very lazy fellow, a Lieutenant of the 39th Regiment, who swung in a cot over the table, never could be got up in time to have the saloon swept and garnished for breakfast. I told him that the next time I was on duty as the orderly officer, if he was not up at the first bugle sound I would cut him down. The weather now was very warm, and this Paddy from Cork slept without any shirt, whether from long habit or economy I did not inquire. However, as usual, he could not be roused up, so I cut the head-rope of his cot, and down he came whop on the table; he was furious, grasped a knife and chased me up on deck. I ran into the rigging like a cat. He flourished his knife, the people stared and thought him deranged. I explained in four or five words: 'I cut down Mr. Lazybones.' Then there was a general yell of laughter; he dived below. I had only obeyed orders, so he dared not dispute the matter, and was never late again.

The voyage was a long one, owing to a convoy of all sorts of small craft going to Lisbon. 'What have you on board?' said our skipper to a wretched-looking tub from Cork. 'Fruit and timber,' says Pat. 'What sort are they?' 'Birch brooms and praties, admiral,' speaking through an old tin pot with the bottom knocked out of it, and then a roar of a laugh on the potato barge. We were on short commons before we made the land, and our potatoes were counted out every day until we entered the Tagus. A joyful day it was to get out of prison. Ten miles up the river, and we anchored off the Block Horse Square. The scenery all around the country is beautiful — very beautiful. The city stands on the north bank of the Tagus, here nine miles wide, and could shelter ten thousand ships. No end to the multitude of churches, chapels, convents, and monasteries. What a good people these ought to be, with so many friars, priests, and nuns scattered amongst them to look after their morals!

We landed under a broiling sun. The men were sent into an old monastery, and bivouacked in the corridors. The officers got billets in different parts of the city; mine was in a very ugly quarter of the town, and had a cut-throat-like entrance, through a long dark vaulted passage. I made my way up a long flight of dark stairs, knocked at an iron portal very like a prison, presented my billet, which was examined by a Portuguese nigger, with a grin. The door closed until 'Massa see ticket', when, after some delay, I was admitted, and shown into a small room with a wee sleeping-cot in the corner, and there left in solitude. Not knowing three words of the Portuguese lingo, and no one coming to pay me a visit or give me a welcome, I went out for a ramble, lost my way, and wandered about until ten o'clock at night, when I most fortunately met an officer going to our ship, who took me on board for the night. Next day I found my quarters, took the bearings, and went in search of my party, but could not find one of them. The weather was broiling hot, the market full of the choicest fruits—oranges, grapes, melons, peaches, greengage, an abundant supply of all sorts, enough for an army. Like a very imprudent young spoon, I went right at them all, and feasted too freely; then made my way out of the town into the country, about half a league, to enjoy the breeze. Seeing a fine vineyard, and the gate open, I went in without ceremony. The señor was there, recumbent in a beautiful arbour, while his people were busy making wine. He very politely asked me to be seated, talked a great deal, I suppose about the army of England. All I understood were a few words, as Wellington, and the *guerre*, and Marshall Soult. I felt myself very small, not being able to speak to this gentleman; but there was no remedy, so I resolved at once to learn the language, and thus quieted my mind. He ordered one of his men to present me a goblet of wine, which I drank off to his health. He returned the compliment, only tasting his cup, and we parted, my host accompanying me to the gate, hat in hand. I found my home, went to roost early, was taken seriously ill in the night, and lay there for many days. No one of my party knew where I was; I could not speak, and the only person I saw was a little black maid, who brought me some rice-water daily, and put it down by my bedside. The fruit and the wine nearly finished me. Had I been in the hands of a doctor, he would most likely have put me under the sod—particularly a medico of this country, who are celebrated for their ignorance in the profession. Ditto in Spain, where they continue the old Sangrado system, phlebotomize nearly to death, shut you up tight in a dark room without breath of fresh air, and give you plenty of hot water to drink. The patient dies, of course!

When I was able to crawl, I went out in search of the monastery, met one of my men, who conducted me to it, and there found all my people. Some thought I was kidnapped, others that I had deserted, and many were the surmises what had become of G.B. The old captain, our commanding officer, never troubled himself about me. I found out for the first time now, that we were all entitled to rations, and the Captain B—— had been drawing mine and making use of them like an honest fellow. He was our Paterfamilias, an old soldier who had been at home on sick leave, and knew the country and its ways and means, up to every dodge, and how to take precious good care of himself. He told us many stories about his former campaigns, and how he leathered the French.

Subsequently we were informed it was but his playful way of amusing 'Johnny Newcomes', as he had never yet had the good fortune of slaying a Mounseer in battle. He had the soubriquet in the regiment of 'Bloody Mick, who killed all the French with his great big stick'.

I went back to my billet with my servant to take away my few traps, and settle down in the old monastery with my companions. I was met by the padrone, who inquired after my health, and asked me to dinner at two o'clock with his family. This was done by the aid of a Portuguese and English dictionary. I made my appearance, and got Benjamin's portion, the first course — that was, a plateload of rice and oil, chopped onion and garlic, too savoury for an invalid. I put it gently aside, which rather astonished the landlady, who was evidently taken aback that I did not relish this part of her dinner. However, there was something else without that most delicious flavour of Portuguese garlic — good bread and palatable wine and fruit; and so I finished my first and last meal in the house of a Portuguese gentleman.

I gladly embraced the opportunity of housing myself now in the monastery amongst the monks and friars — a lazy, indolent crew, with their bull-necks, bare shaven crowns, sandals, cowls, and white rope girdles and rosary. They lived in their cells, or very comfortable little rooms, while we occupied the corridors and galleries. I slept on the flags with my martial cloak around me! It was all the bed and bedding I had; the climate was blazing hot, and the broad flags kept me cool.

We had a camp-kettle in which we cooked all our rations together; there was an abundance of the finest vegetables, very cheap, so that, with some rice in addition, we turned out excellent soup and *bouilli*. Each of us had a tin dish, an iron spoon, knife and fork, without any other incumbrance of this kind. Sometimes we got a bullock's head to add to the rations, which when cold also gave us a breakfast.

I joined another lad in the purchase of a *boura* to carry our baggage, i.e. in English, a donkey. My camp equipage was small when the broadside of a donkey carried it all. This purchase cleared me out. I had not a dollar left, and had no opportunity of seeing any of the sights, or enjoying any of the pleasures of a Lisbon life. I became a sort of a monk myself, visiting those old crows every day. They supposed me a good Roman Catholic, because I spoke a little Latin to them, and confessed myself an Irishman. One question they never forgot to ask, 'Are you an Irishman?' They consider all Irishmen Roman Catholics; regarding myself, they were quite out of their reckoning, for there never was

B

a more staunch, loyal Protestant subject of the Queen of England than G.B.

The route came for us at last, and all the convalescent men from Belem depôt joined us for the march, and away we went in the middle of the night, to get it over before the burning early sun of the morrow. It was weary work ploughing through the deep sands all the way. How I looked back to home, sweet home! and to the noble horses I used to ride there at pleasure. Any money now for 'Billy Button', the orderly pony, always ready saddled in the stable for general use.

The marches were sometimes very long and dreary, and provoking. No one knew the distance; meeting a solitary peasant now and then we would ask, 'Quantas leaguas, señor, a Sacavem?' Answer, 'Dos leaguas e pokito, señor' (two leagues and a bit); march on another league and meet pizano the second, and ask the same question, 'O señor, Sacavem, *tres* leaguas e no mas' (just three leagues)! No milestones, no hotels, inns, or refreshment houses; we knew, however, that there was a town in the distance somewhere, and that we must reach it. Our Captain, commanding officer, was well mounted and always had some grog, etc., in his haversack, which he seemed to enjoy at the usual halting-place half-way, under a shady tree, all alone! Sergeant Bolland, a fine old soldier of our regiment, returning from Lisbon, aided us in many ways, gave us good advice in the arrangement of our future campaign and as to how to take care of ourselves, for as he said, 'this is all pleasure to what is before us, if I may judge of the past' — he had been wounded at Albuera.

We went merrily on for many days, living on our rations, until we arrived at Portalegre, the headquarters of the 34th, and such a nice handy well-disciplined corps, with high-caste officers, all well seasoned and experienced in the late campaigns.

I had letters of introduction to Colonel Fenwick and other officers of note and standing, all of whom received me cordially, and I was no longer a stranger. The Colonel asked me to breakfast on arrival, when I gave him my history from the starting-point, and a sample of such an appetite that must have astonished him, and I feared would prevent him from showing me any more such attentions; but he was always kind—an amiable man, a good and gallant soldier, decided in character, just and impartial.

I was appointed to the company of 'Moyle Sherer', then a Lieutenant, a gentleman, a scholar, an author, and a most zealous soldier.

I now settled down in my billet, commenced my orderly duties, and endeavoured to make myself comfortable and to prepare for the storm of war, then sweeping over unhappy Spain. I had nothing to trouble me but a big appetite, for which my ration was quite insufficient; three-quarters of a pound of lean beef, half bone at times, a pound of brown bread or biscuit, and half a gill of rum; I often finished the whole dish at a sitting, and got up from the noble repast very hungry. The beef or the bread never was weighed; a certain quantity was served out to each company; say the company was fifty strong, the meat was cut into fifty pieces, and spread on the turf. One man turned his back on the rations not to see them, another called out, 'This—say Tom Johns,' and Tom picked up his morsel of beef; 'This—Jack Simmons,' and there was a great roar of a laugh, for it was nearly all a marrow bone! 'This—Mr. G.B.,' and so on, all fair play between officers and men.

I had a chair and a table, and a sort of a bed in my little room on which I slept soundly—dogs always go to sleep when hungry!

I had no books and was very idle; it was not customary in those days in the army to read the Bible; I don't think that I saw one for three years, so that Portugal or Spain had no fault to find with us on this score! However, there were some good and pious men to be found, who were not ashamed to

> Kneel, remote, upon the simple sod,
> And sue, in formâ pauperis, to God.

We Subs were a sociable class of bipeds; we had dinner parties, and evening parties, and dancing parties, and horse-racing parties all very simple in their way, and not attended with any expense; for instance, 'Come to dinner tomorrow in camp fashion', that means, send your rations, your servant, chair, knife, fork, spoon and plate (not plates); three or four rations of beef made better soup than three-quarters of a pound with a bone in it; then there might be a bit of liver and bacon, and some roast tatties, and roars of laughter and fun; so much for subaltern dinner in service fifty years ago.

Those who could afford an evening party had brandy and cigars, or wine and crackers for their guests, plenty of chat about the past, the present, and the future; and some comic songs. The bottles being all drained, the evening closed, and good night was said; some one of the guests adding, 'You will all come to me tomorrow night.'

The girls were very fond of dancing; we sometimes all joined for a ball, and invited young ladies and their mammas to look after them. We had no band; a flute and guitar filled the orchestra; there was some lemonade and cakes—to refresh the señoritas—all they wished for; all they expected. The priests were always reluctant and jealous to see any of their fair flock mixing with heretics; the ladies quite differed in opinion!

The Derby never created more fear or excitement than our race-ground on the olive plain. All the Tats in the garrison went to the post very smart, and ready to win the bag of dollars hanging on the big olive-tree; first away often last in the race—the real winner sometimes losing his race by dismounting before coming to the scale to be weighed—one or two disappearing as bolters amongst the trees. A jockey with perhaps a red night-cap going right off to his stable in the town, and knocking down two priests in the gateway. Then the donkey race; every Jock sitting with his face to the tail, a smart fellow running in front with a bunch of carrots, and so we passed our time.

I had a letter from home now, and no little sympathy expressed for my loss at Portsmouth. I might draw for my allowance in advance; it was enough for me—more than I deserved; but far away less than the young gentlemen of the present day in the army receive, or demand, or cannot do without! I never went into debt in all my life—I knew that it was dangerous; and, not being able to pay, dishonourable. I had recourse to my old commanding officer, Captain B——, for some money—he was the only one who seemed to understand those pecuniary affairs with advantage. He charged me 6s. sterling for every dollar he gave me, a dollar being worth 4s. 2d.! I was now rich for the present, and fared well, and had an evening party—no very great enjoyment to me, for I detest brandy and cigars.

I made myself happy in a way until October, when there was a flare-up with the French.

General Girard made too free with our side of the country, and began to poach on our guard. The 2nd Division, commanded by Lieutenant-General Sir Rowland Hill, was let loose to hunt him out of our district. The rainy season had commenced, and the weather was dreadful. We marched all the day, and lay down on the wet sod by night, which rather surprised and alarmed me, expecting to be under cover in some civilised way after our day's work, instead of herding with the beasts of the field. I had an old boat cloak and a blanket for my bed and bedding. I never had more, but sometimes less, for the next three years. 'We have made a raw and rainy beginning of our campaign,' said Richardson, my chum; 'how did you sleep?' 'Slept like a fish,' I said; 'I believe they sleep best in water.' 'Bravo!' said he; 'you'll do.' I thought in my own mind I might do for a night or two more, but I would soon be done in a bivouac in such weather; however, I kept that secret to myself. David Richardson was an old soldier, and had passed through a campaign. 'Come over to my quarters,' he said, 'and have a cup of tea; it will take the chill out of your old bones; you look blue in the face.' Near at hand his kettle was boiling under an olive-tree, and a pork chop in the frying-pan—very savoury. 'Shake a little pepper on it, Ned, and be quick; the bugle will sound directly, and get the other plate.' 'There's only one, sir,' replied Ned; 'You know we left in light marching order.' 'You have the advantage of me, Davey,' added I, 'having seen service, and knowing how to forage. As for me, I am indeed in light marching condition, and have nothing but my haversack, containing my three days' rations cooked— but where in the world did you fall in with this savoury meat?' 'Well,' he said, 'my man Ned there has a sharp eye and a sharp bayonet, and if those pigs will intrude upon us at night, it is at their own risk; you will learn more about these little private affairs time enough.' Bugle sounds. 'There, Ned, get your breakfast quickly, and throw that leg of pork into the bag, and load the donkey.'

We continued our march in this way for a week. Our ration of rum at night kept the life in us. There were no tents in the army in those days; it was all bivouac, pleasant enough in hot weather and dry ground; but this was an exceptional case, and not meant to continue. The rain kept along with us. I was never thoroughly dry, yet there is nothing that keeps out wet like a blanket; there was no such thing as an india-rubber or a macintosh A.D. 1811, and as for anything else called waterproof, it was all fudge. We never undressed of course, but just pushed on, apparently having the right scent, as the men would constantly say, 'I smell those *crappos*, they can't be far off.' They had been keeping one day ahead of us, and left behind them a perfume of tobacco, onions, etc., that could not be mistaken. On the evening of the 27th of October we got close to their heels; it rained all the day, and in the dusk we halted on ploughed ground. 'Pile arms; keep perfectly quiet; light no fires; no drum to beat; no bugle to sound', were the orders passed through the ranks. I was very tired; threw myself up against the side of a bank ditch, dived into my haversack, where I had in reserve a piece of cold bullock's liver and salt, some biscuit, and a very small allowance of rum, so I was not so badly off. All was still, and cold, and cheerless, until about two o'clock in the morning of the 28th, when the word was gently passed through all regiments: 'Stand to your arms!' The whole division was now in silent motion, and moved on to the plain some few miles, pretty close to the enemy, who were quartered and encamped in and about the little town of 'Arroyo-Molino'. The division was now divided into three brigades, cavalry on flanks and centre. It

was just the dawn of day, with a drizzling rain.   We could just see
our men to call the roll.

Our gallant and worthy General, riding along our front, said,
'Are you all ready?'   'Yes, sir.'   'Uncase your colours, and prime
the load.'   All this looked very serious, and I began to have a queer
feeling of mortal danger stirring my nerves.   As I took the king's
colour in charge, being senior ensign, the Major said, 'Now my lads,
hold those standards fast, and let them fly out when you see the
enemy.'

Away we went across the plain to be baptised in blood.   Our
skirmishers in advance had come upon the French outlying pickets,
and had begun operations.   A cannon-shot came rattling past,
making a hissing noise, such as I had never heard before.   Four
sergeants supported the colours in battle; my old friend Bolland
from Beverley was one of them.   I said, 'What's that, Bolland?'
'Only the morning gun, sir; they're just coming on them now.'   A
little onwards, and I saw two men cut across by that last shot, the
first I had ever seen killed.   I was horrified, but said nothing.

The French were getting ready to be off again when our advance
got up to their pickets and began the quarrel.   Their horses were
saddled and tied to the olive-trees, infantry gathering from different
points for their alarm-post — artillery taking up position — all getting
on the defensive, when they were skilfully hemmed in on three
sides; behind the little town the 71st and 92nd Regiments brought
up their left shoulders, and came pouring into the streets with a
destructive fire; the French were now falling by fifties, but fighting
and struggling hard to maintain their ground.   We had lined the
garden walls, and kept pitching into their ranks while our cavalry
cut off their retreat; they formed squares, but our artillery mashed
them up and the cavalry gave them no time to re-form; a thick mist
rolled down the craggy steep mountain behind the town; there was
a terrifying cheer, such as is not known except amongst British
troops on the battleground; it drowned the clatter of musketry,
while the driving storm carried with it the enemy up this sierra, the
28th and 34th Regiments at their heels.   We pressed them so closely
that they threw off their knapsacks, turned round, and fired into us;
still our men pushed on until this body of Girard's brave army
dropped their firelocks, dispersed, and as many as could got clear
away over the mountains.   Below, the 50th and 39th Regiments
were tormenting the unfortunate French with the bayonet and
making prisoners; the 13th Dragoons captured their artillery as they
made a dash for escape, which was simply done by shooting a mule
in each gun; the 9th Dragoons and German hussars charged and
dispersed their cavalry with great loss, taking many prisoners;

Prince D'Aremberg, making his escape in a light carriage, was followed by a few of our dragoons; one of them rode up to the door and desired him in English to halt; the reply was a bullet through his head—a useless and rather cowardly endeavour to save his liberty, for instantly one of his mules was shot, which brought him to a single anchor, as the sailors say. He was then handed out of his coach, not by a powdered footman, but at the point of an English broadsword, and his comfortable nest immediately plundered, the soldiers being exasperated for the untimely death of a comrade while doing his duty. Girard was wounded, but fought nobly until he saw that any further resistance was useless; then, having given his men the order to disperse—*Sauve qui peut*—fled and saved himself; 600 men, the remains of 3,000 of the most valiant and chosen troops of France, saved themselves by flight.

Our trophies this misty morning were General Le Bron, the Prince D'Aremberg, 40 officers, 1,500 men, all their artillery, baggage, and commissariat stores. I was very proud of having unfurled the colours of my regiment before the French for the first time, and cheered loudly with the rest when I saw them run! Our loss did not exceed 70 men left *hors de combat*—not many killed.

The Horrors of War

IT was a little remarkable that the two regiments—34th English and 34th French—happened to meet face to face in mortal combat. The *Parley Vous*, as our men called them, had no chance against the old Cumberland infantry. We took very many of them prisoners, with all their band and drums and the drum-major and his long cane. They are still, or part of them, in possession of the regiment. I know of only one officer now alive who was present on that day, and he bought from a soldier a very valuable diamond crescent for three dollars, taken out of the Prince D——'s carriage. There were many valuables for sale at a low figure that day! I had not a dollar left, or would have given it cheerfully for a loaf of bread, little expecting that I would soon have one for nothing. Our Commissary bought plenty of flour at the mill, 'Arroyo-Molino', and set all the bakers to work to give the troops a ration of fresh bread and an extra ration of rum after their morning's amusement. I was drying my wet duds in the village when my eye caught the sight of a cart-load of bread going by, and a Portuguese soldier behind in the act of stealing a loaf. I watched until he performed the successful operation, when I gave such a yell and a rush, he thought me the Provost-Marshal, dropped the loaf, and ran for it. I continued the cry of 'Halt, Ladrone', until he was too far gone to see or know what use I made of it!

Lieutenant Strenowitz, an Austrian officer on General Hill's staff, always too dashing, was made prisoner. He was brave and enterprising, useful, and very clever in reconnoitring the enemy at any time. He had been dodging the movements of Girard all along, and was well known, having abandoned the French army in Spain to join the Patidas, and liable by the laws of war to death. Sir Rowland, anxious to save him, frankly applied to General Drouet, who, although smarting under his late disaster, released him. A noble generosity, worthy of being recorded in letters of gold.

The 34th now took charge of all the French prisoners, officers and men. The former accepted parole; the latter we locked up in the church, a goodly congregation for the old padre. Yesterday, perhaps, they were robbing his hen-roost, and today certainly teasing his church-toggery — indeed, before the day was closed, they had arranged a theatrical troop, and were performing a play, all rejoicing in the expectation and hope of being escorted to their future banishment by British troops, being under bodily fear of the Spaniards, who would, as they well knew, have bayoneted every man of them that fell out of the ranks; for they had a long account to settle with these French marauders. The following day we had a rest, and the prisoners opened a bazaar in the church to dispose of, perhaps, all their unlawful gains. It was a great day for the church and for the priests when those fellows departed; every one of them seemed to have a watch for sale, gold or silver, and a great variety of bijouterie. There were some great bargains going, but I had not a dollar to get a single kind remembrance of those dear departing friends! My regiment escorted them down to Portugal. By the way they were very cheery, and went to church every night for safety!

On a pinch we always turned the churches to useful and good account. The commissariat, mules, and stores of biscuit and rum were lodged there for nights, weeks, and months, as required, the padres looking in now and then, crossing themselves right-centre and left, with a wailing sort of grunt, seeing their confession-boxes filled with sacks of barley and kegs of rum, the mules picketed on one side, big cooking-fires on the other, and a pleasant smell of fried pork and garlic! The only priestly sound left in the temple was the bell-ringing, every mule having a dozen or more of them as part of his trappings; and pleasant music it was to us many a starry night on the lonely march to hear the muleteers coming along through the cork woods, singing plaintive strains, accompanied by the light guitar. The muleteer is a fine, honest, independent fellow, well made, quaintly dressed, always gay, strong, and active, and very fond of music and dancing when time admits. But he never neglects his work, carries his guitar, sits between two bags of biscuit,

both legs on one side, singing a serenade, and twitching his own
heart with something plaintive, or perhaps with a fandango, the
Castilian Maid, or a bolero.

The French officers, being all on parole, conducted themselves
with great propriety. They messed with the Colonel, Major, and
one or two of the senior officers who had means of adding something to the rations. They were under no restraint, and their old
soldiers were very careful in not attempting to straggle or fall out by
the way, knowing what a sharp look-out the Spaniards had after
their liberty. We delivered them all over in safety to another
escort in Portugal, returned to Estremadura, and took up quarters
in the old town of Albuquerque, with the 28th Regiment, or
'Slashers'. Every regiment and division had its cognomen; the 2nd,
Lord Hill's Division, was called 'the Surprisers', after the affair of
Arroyo de Molino; 3rd, or Buffs, 'the Resurrection Men', so many of
them returned to the ranks after Albuera. They had been returned
missing, but the truth was having taken a brilliant part in that
day's big fight, and finding the French retreating through the woods
and forest, they pursued them until night, and many of the old
Buffs who lost their way in the dark, bivouacked, and came care-
lessly back to their old ground the next and following days, sat
down upon the sod, and went to work to clean and polish up their
old flint firelocks for another day; and then inquired after yesterday's rations; for they were very hungry after hunting 'them frog-
eaters through the woods — bad luck to them!' The 50th always
went by the name of the 'Dirty Half-hundred' — they had black
facings; 34th, 'the Cumberland Gentlemen'. We had certainly
some of the most select and high-caste officers I ever met in the
army — such brave and zealous men too; such as Colonels Maister
and Fenwick, Willett, Wyat, Fancourt, Egerton, Sherer, Baron,
Worsley — Jolliff, the most liberal paymaster, and the clever surgeon, Luscombe; Sullivan and Eccles, bravest of the brave; Norton,
Day, *cum multis aliis*. I love to record their honoured names,
being myself, I believe, the last man of that generation that
I know of living, unless it be Captain Norton, the inventor of an
exploding shell, about which he hoped to gain a name and some
emolument, after many years of incessant toil. Not being in
the dress circle, I believe all his labour was in vain, and his talent
pooh-poohed.

At Albuquerque we got the English newspapers with an account
of our exploit at Arroyo-Molino, and wasn't I proud to see Sir
Rowland Hill's despatch in print, with the few words, which never
escaped my memory, viz. 'where the 28th and 34th Regiments
eminently distinguished themselves'?

Albuquerque was a very old town, at one period of some importance. It was walled all round, and had a castle of defence, crumbling away like the old walls. In the castle, which stood high, there was a square tower standing still much higher, commanding a most extensive view of the country on towards Badajos (pronounced by the Spaniards Badahos). On the top of this tower there was always an officer on the look-out from before daylight until ten o'clock, with telescope in hand, to watch any movement of the French coming over the plain, a duty not very agreeable to early risers! On many a cold morning I have got up to take this duty for one of my own brother officers better off and more provident than myself, with the understanding that I was to breakfast with him when relieved; for the truth may be told, I had not myself a breakfast to eat, and really nothing at this time but my one scanty meal per diem, and that was my bit of ration beef, which I fried in a pan with water for want of a spoonful of oil. My money was all expended long ago. Our pay was months in arrears. My time was not come to draw for my home allowance, and I would not ask for a penny in advance, although I knew it would have been cheerfully granted.

About this time, Drouet came down to forage the province with 14,000 men, and to throw supplies into Badajos. We left our dry quarters, and sallied forth to meet him, Sir Rowland Hill intending to give him battle. On our way to Merida we fell in with a battalion of French infantry in a fog, who were out foraging. We could see nothing. They felt our advance guard as we came up, and left some few wounded prisoners, who told the tale. As the fog rose, we saw them retiring over the plain in the greatest order. Having a good start of us, our cavalry were called to the front, and slipped at them; the French retiring double quick in quarter-distance column. On the near approach of the 14th Light Dragoons, they formed square, and waited the charge, which was repulsed by a volley, leaving some empty saddles. While the cavalry were reforming for another charge, the French again formed quarter-distance column, and went off at the double. The 14th went at them again on two sides; for they whipped into square in a moment, but as unsuccessfully as at first. This play was repeated three times without any success, when our guns came up from the rear, unlimbered, and sent a few round shot into their ranks, which left them short forty men; but the rest got clear away into Merida. I don't remember our loss; but I saw many of our men and horses killed and wounded as we passed by. Nevoux, which was the name of the brave French colonel who commanded, was decorated with the Legion of Honour for his gallant conduct on this occasion.

Honourable retreats in war, they say, are in no ways inferior to brave charges, as having less of fortune, more of discipline, and as much of valour.

We marched on and took possession of Merida, driving the chief and headquarters of his army out of this fine old town. It stands on the Guadiana, had a bridge of sixty arches, said to have been built by the Romans, as well as the town, which was partly of very great antiquity. Here we were quartered for some time amongst pretty girls and burly priests, who kept a sharp look-out upon their intimacy with British heretics. This was all jealousy; for I think I had cause to see and believe they were the most immoral and irreligious part of the community. Lazy, indolent, useless cowls, and their name was Legion. The señoritas were generally very pretty, very graceful, ladylike, and extremely correct in manner, morals, and conduct, although at times there was an elopement with some wild handsome young fellow who knew the soft language, which cannot be surpassed in love-making. How many of those poor girls were forced into convents by the aid and advice of crafty priests, where their young hearts were blighted for ever! I often had conversations with them through their iron grating, hearing them wailing and lamenting their unhappy fate, and pining for liberty. 'We are here,' they would say, 'like birds with clipped wings, powerless'; then a little noise perhaps, and they would fly like a chamois, with an 'adios, adios, caballero. Otro tiempo.'

Monsieur le General Drouet gave us a great deal of bother at this time, marching and counter-marching across that great plain to Almandraleho, a little town some five leagues distant. There he assembled his army, took up position, inviting a quarrel, but always declining to fight. When we got within reach of a nine-pounder gun, he was off in retreat, leaving no chance of giving him a checkmate. Here we halted, generally for a couple of days, and returned to Merida. This game was played so often, I was thoroughly acquainted with every big tuft of grass and swampy pool over that dreary plain ploughed up by wheels, cavalry, and baggage animals. The object of the French was to harass our troops as much as possible, and to keep us away from Ciudad Rodrigo, a great fortress, which he knew would be attacked by Wellington before we could advance up country.

Settled down once more in Merida, *pro tem*, we tried to be happy. I was now pretty well broken into harness, learned something, and began to like my trade, seeing all my comrades as jolly and fearless as if they were foxhunters. We were soon, however, on the trot again. Our division was separated, and placed in different towns and villages near Rodrigo.

In January 1812, Wellington (as I may now call him with great respect) laid siege to Ciudad Rodrigo (city of Rodrigo), and now for the horrors of a siege, and the double horrors of another near at hand; this one lasted twelve days, the city being stormed on the 19th January. Wellington's morning order on that day was laconic and to the point, understood, and nobly responded to; it was this, 'Ciudad Rodrigo *must* be stormed this evening'.

All the troops reached their different posts after dark; the storming-parties — volunteers and forlorn-hope — foremost; as they advanced they were ravaged with a tempest of grape from the ramparts, which staggered them; however, none would go back, although none could get forward, for men and officers falling fast from the withering and destructive fire choked up the passage, which every minute was raked with grape-shot. Thus striving, and trampling alike upon the dead and wounded, these brave fellows maintained the combat. The stormers of another division, who had 300 yards of ground to clear, with extraordinary swiftness dashed along to the glacis, jumped into the ditch, eleven feet deep, and rushed on under a smashing discharge of musketry and grape, gaining the ascent; the foremost were blown to shatters, their bodies and brains plashing amongst their daring comrades behind, which only stimulated their determined exertions and doubled their strength. Supports came forward, all the officers simultaneously sprang to the front, when the herculean effort was renewed with a thrilling cheer, and the entrance was gained. The fighting was continued with fury in the streets, until the French were all killed, wounded, or prisoners; the town was fired in many places; many were killed in the market-place; our soldiers were desperate, really mad with excitement, furious; intoxication, disorder, and tumult everywhere prevailed; discipline and restraint disregarded, the troops committed most terrible deeds. They lighted a fire in the middle of the great magazine, when the whole town would have been blown into the air but for the courage and immediate exertions of some officers and soldiers who were still in their senses, and sensible of the awful gulf around them.

Our loss was, I think, 1,400 soldiers and 90 officers — 60 officers and some 700 men fell in the breach. Generals McKinnon and Crawford, two noble and gallant soldiers, were killed; and along with them many stoutly brave fell that day, who feared no danger, and whose lives were more precious than fine gold.

The great obstacle in the advance of the siege was caused by the useless and most disgraceful tools furnished by the Storekeeper-General's office in England. The contractor's profits seemed to be more attended to and respected than our chances of success in taking this fortress; and so it has been the case, again and again, even on to the siege of Sebastopol forty-two years afterwards, to my knowledge.

Three hundred French had fallen, we had 1,600 prisoners, immense stores of ammunition, 150 pieces of artillery, and Marmont's battering train. On the following day, when the escort with the prisoners were marching out by the breach, somehow or other an explosion took place and numbers of both parties were blown into the air!

Wellington was now created Duke of Ciudad Rodrigo by the Spaniards, Earl of Wellington in England, and Marquis of Torres-Vedras in Portugal. Thus ended this chapter of the war.

From this time until the middle of March 1812, we were kept roving about the country to pot the French, kill them, and cook them in our own fashion. All was lawful in war, but they were very sharp and always slept with one eye open: we had to do the same. It was like deer-stalking at times—a glorious thing to whack in amongst a lively party with their flesh-pots on the fire of well-seasoned wood. A chest of drawers, perhaps, or the mahogany table of some *Hidalgo* in the middle of the street blazing away, and the *crappos* calling out, 'Bonne soupe, bonne soupe'. 'Bone soup,' says Paddy Muldoon one day, 'those vagabonds live on bone soup: I blive they would make soup out o' an owl gridiron that once fried a red-herrin'. But we're purty near them now, I think, to have a crack at their bone soup.' Paddy, a front-rank man of the Light Company, was in advance as we cautiously moved along under cover of some of the evergreen olive-trees and stone walls. He was brave, but nervously irksome to be at his work whenever he smelt a Frenchman; and here he spoiled our fun and a capture. As we approached the head of the village, Paddy let fly a shot into the middle of a covey who were in reality cooking their dinner, as I have said. Then a general rush on both sides; one party to grapple their arms and run, the other to pursue, slay, or capture. But the French Light Infantry run very fast when there's powder and lead at their heels, and no blame to them. Paddy was called to account for breaking the peace without orders. 'I couldn't help it, sir, you see, for I had a fine rest for my firelock on the wall, and was sure of one on 'em, bein' in line sitting so close; but they've left their kittles behind, and o' course their bone soup, packs and all.' We gave them chase a little way, and captured a few, who Paddy said had corns, for the rest got into a wood and cleared out of sight in no time. The kettles were left and examined: some contained bits of pork and vegetables, or a gallina or old hen, but no fresh meat. ''Pon me conscience,' says Muldoon, 'that's the cook I knocked

over, for there's the bullet-hole right through his pot, and I'm sorry
for him; but he kept a bad look-out.'

This was merely a small advance picket of the French. Such
things happen almost every day, and there was nothing more
about it.

War for three years was spread over unhappy Spain; battles
were fought, men were slaughtered, the country ravaged, houses
robbed and burned, families flying to the mountains to escape the
horrors of licentious soldiers. The terrors of a marauding army
are little known. Legions of low-caste, vulgar men, all loose
amongst the people — always for evil, never for good. Then the
guerilla bands for ever watching the French, intercepting their
convoys and detachments, and pouncing into them from the rocks
and mountain passes, dealing fearful death to every victim; and this
continued for six years in a charming country, amongst a formerly
happy, contented, and amiable peasantry. I have been at the heels
of a French party as they escaped from a sweet little country
town, leaving their camp kettles on fires in the street, lighted (as I
have said) by household furniture, and sometimes one or two mem-
bers of a family lying murdered on their own hearth-stone! This
was but too common a tragedy, and repeated very often to my own
personal knowledge.

We again returned to our quarters at Albuquerque early in
March, and I made my acquaintance once more with the look-out
tower, where the order was vigilance from dawn to dark.

The British army now began to concentrate their forces in
Estremadura. A great battering train was moved up from Elvas, a
large fortified town in Portugal, about three or four leagues from
Badajos. This was a laborious, slow-coach affair, the great guns
were moved slowly along, with only a cavalcade of bullocks the
whole length of the natural road that never felt a stone on its soft
surface; hundreds of the Spanish peasantry were employed carrying the shot and shell. All the engineers, sappers, and miners were
called to attention. Groups of officers at every corner with unusual
solemnity talked of the coming storm, when ground would be
broken, who were to lead the way, what divisions to be chosen,
and who would describe the fall of Badajos to friends at home.

No one doubted the success of the enterprise, but no one ven-
tured to say that his life was his own after the first gun was fired.
There was a terrible day approaching, but nobody afraid, even bets
being frequently made on the day and hour of the opening ball.

I had no particular nervous feeling now. Men stand together
and encourage each other in the hour of danger, but I can't understand the man who would openly express himself callous to all

feeling under a shower of lead, or before the mouth of a cannonade. A common saying was, 'every bullet has its billet', and all seemed outwardly serene.

Badajos, which stands on the river Guadiana, in a plain, is about the strongest fortress I had ever seen; but there was nothing proof in those days against British valour. Here were two of the most warlike nations on earth armed against each other in deadly strife. 'Vive Napoléon! vive L'Empereur!' was the exciting cry on one side; on the other, 'Hurrah for old England'. A flourish of drums, with the 'British Grenadiers' or 'Garryown', set our fellows wild for a dash at any time. Both were so badly armed that I wonder how we killed each other at all. But the distance was very short at times, and the bayonet did a great deal of the work. The French never liked the steel, still, they were brave, very brave.

The days rolled away quickly as they do at present. We got a small advance of pay. The 17th was my birthday, and if I had no salutations, gifts, or a home jollification, I had a good loaf of Spanish bread, a pork chop, and a bottle of country wine, all alone in my billet, and was content. The battalion was so scattered, that few of us Subs could form a little mess to put our rations into the same pot to make some bone soup. My billet was on a very respectable family—the patrone, his señora, and two daughters, both 'hermosa'. We sat of an evening over the *brazero*, or brass pan, filled with charcoal, red cinders, which kept life in our fingertips. It was renewed occasionally, and we conversed about the coming storm, for they had many friends in Badajos. I had picked up the language pretty well for my time, which was a great advantage; it is a sweet and expressive language and easily learned.

The Duke had now arranged his plans. Patrick's day came round as usual, and on that fighting festival-morning the band and drums enlivened all Patlanders with the national tune. The same night 1,800 men broke ground 160 yards from the out fort of Picurina, protected by a guard of 2,000; so that some of the Irish soldiers were not altogether disappointed in having a bit of a shindy before they went to sleep. There was a call for some volunteer officers for the engineer department, and to superintend the work in the trenches—two from the 34th—Lieutenants Masterman and George Bell. I was very much attached to poor 'M'; he did me a service once, and I never forgot the smallest kindness in all my career, which has been a long one. The trench work was as dangerous as it was arduous—all those who served before Sebastopol will understand this—and now the work of death began in reality.

Generals Picton, Colville, Kempt, and Bowes, commanded alternately in the trenches. All the arts of war then known were

brought into play on both sides, for the attack and defence. Every
man carried his life in his hands; hope lived in the hearts of all.
Many were our difficulties. Torrents of rain at nights poured upon
the working parties, shot and shell continually striking down the
men, provisions scarce, our pontoon bridge carried away, artillery
and engineer officers being killed and wounded every day, but no
suspension of the fiery trial.

About nine o'clock on the night of the 24th the assault was
made on Fort Picurina. The distance was short and the troops
quickly closed on their game—black and silent before—now one
mass of fire. The depth of the ditch baffled them, also the thickness
of the poles. The quick shooting of the enemy, and the guns from
the town, rendered the carnage dreadful. Rockets were thrown
up by the besieged; the shrill sound of the alarm-bells, mixing with
the shouts of the combatants, increased the tumult. Still Picurina
sent out streams of fire, by the light of which dark figures were
seen furiously struggling on the ramparts, fighting hand to hand
with the enemy. None would yield until but 86 men of the fort
and the Commandant were left. Our loss was 18 or 20 officers and
some 300 men killed and wounded. This was only clearing the
way a bit. A frightful and destructive havoc was carried on inside
and outside (in particular) the town until the 4th of April. Time
being now a great object, and Soult advancing with a large army to
relieve the city, the breach being reported practicable, 18,000 of
our daring British soldiers burned for the signal of attack.

The assault was arranged and ordered for the next evening, and
eagerly did the men make themselves ready for a combat so fiercely
fought, so terribly won, so dreadful in all its circumstances, that
posterity can scarcely be expected to credit the o'er true tale; but
many are still alive who know that it is true.

C

CHAPTER 3

The Fall of Badajos

THE night was dry and cloudy, the trenches and ramparts unusually still—lights were seen to flit here and there—while the deep voice of the sentinels proclaimed 'All well in Badajos'. The British, standing in deep columns, as eager to meet that fiery destruction as the French were to pour it down, were both alike, gigantic now in terrible strength and discipline, resolute, and determined to win or die. The recent toil and hardship, the spilling of blood, the desire for glory, an old grudge and a dash of ferocity, not omitting the plunder, the thirst for spoil, and pride of country and arms, caused our men never to doubt their own strength of arms to bear down all before them, and every obstacle opposed to their furious determination. At ten o'clock the Castle, the San Roque, the breaches, the Pardaleras, the distant bastion of San Vincente, and the bridge-head on the other side of the Guadiana, were to have been assailed at the same time. It was to be hoped that the enemy would quail and lose some of their strength within this girdle of fire. But many are the disappointments of war, and it may be taken as a maxim that the difficulties are so innumerable that no head was ever yet strong enough to forecalculate them all.

An unforeseen accident delayed the attack of the 5th Division, as at first intended. A lighted carcass, thrown from the castle, falling near, rendered it necessary to hurry on the attack about half an hour before the time which was subsequently arranged. So, all being suddenly disturbed, the 4th and Light Divisions moved swiftly and silently against the breaches, and the guard of the trenches rushing forward with a cheer, encompassed the San Roque with fire, and broke in so violently that little resistance was made there; but a sudden blaze of light and the rattle of musketry indicated the beginning of a frightful conflict at the castle.

General Kempt fell here wounded; General Sir Thomas Picton took his place. The men dashed forward under a terrible fire, spread and raised their ladders against the castle walls, and with unexampled courage ran up under a shower of shot and shell, stones and small arms, while a fearful fire was kept up on the red-coats from flanks and centre. The leading men on the ladders were met by pikes, bayonets, and musketry, and their ladders pushed from the walls. Now the deafening shouts, crashing of broken ladders, and the shrieking of the crushed and wounded men, became loud amongst the din of war. Excited to madness, the comrades of the undaunted brave below, who swarmed again round the ladders, swiftly ran up, and were tossed over from the enemy above, who cried, 'Victory!' and 'Why don't you come into Badajos?'

The brave Colonel Ridge, with a voice like thunder, called to his men to follow, raised a ladder to the wall a little further off, and met but little opposition until he got in. Another ladder was raised, and our men went pouring in, took the enemy in the flanks, and delivered a volley which very much astonished and staggered them. Here another fight commenced, and here poor Ridge fell—no man died a more glorious death in battle, although multitudes of brave men fell who deserved great military glory.

The frightful tumult at the main breach all this time, the incessant roar of cannon, musketry, bursting of shells, yells of the wounded, and cheering of those who had so short a time to live, rent the air in a fiery lava of exploding shells and barrels of powder.

Every flash showed the French ready and prepared on the ramparts; showed their glittering arms, dark figures, heaps of live shells, and an astonishing amount of artillery, every man having three loaded muskets beside him. Yet our men leaped into the ditch, of whom 500 volunteers, being foremost, were dashed to pieces with shot, shell, and powder barrels. The Light Division stood for a moment in horror at the terrific sight; then, with a wild shout dashed with one accord into the fiery gulf, and, with the light of a blaze of fire-arms from above, the 4th Division followed in an excited fury. One hundred men were drowned in the inundation (for at this time the sluices were opened, and the water let into the ditch from the river). They now turned off to the left, seeking for the main breach, and got crowded and mixed together. The

only light was that of the flashing guns, pouring death and destruction among them. The confusion was great, but all cheered like
thunder; the French cheers also were loud and terrible. The bursting of grenades, shells, and powder-barrels, the whizzing flight of
blazing splinters of barrels, the loud voices of the officers, and the
heavy groans of the dying, were sufficient to create a terror indescribable. Now they found the way, and went at the breach
like a whirlwind. Sword-blades, sharp and pointed, fixed in
ponderous beams, were in their front as they ascended; planks, too,
filled with iron spikes; while every Frenchman had three or four
loaded muskets at his feet, with leaden slugs over the usual bullet.
Hundreds of our men had fallen, dropping at every discharge, which
only maddened the living. The cheer was for ever on, on, with
screams of vengeance and a fury determined to win the town.
The rear pushed the foremost into the sword-blades to make a
bridge of their bodies rather than be frustrated in their success.
Slaughter, tumult, and disorder continued. No command could be
heard; the wounded struggling to free themselves from under the
bleeding bodies of their dead comrades; the enemy's guns within a
few yards, at every fire opening a bloody lane amongst our people,
who closed up, and, with shouts of terror as the lava burned them
up, pressed on to destruction. Officers, starting forward with an
heroic impulse, carried on their men to the yawning breach and
glittering steel, which still continued to belch out flames of scorching death.

About midnight, when 2,000 men had fallen, Wellington, who
was looking on, sent an order for the troops to retire and re-form
for another attack. In the retreat from the ditch there was great
confusion and terrible carnage under the continual fire of the
French. The groans and lamentations of the wounded trampled
on, and expecting to be left to the mercy of an exasperated and
ferocious enemy, were awful. Who could explain their feelings?
The bitterness of death to them was past. The 3rd Division had
gained the Castle. The 5th Division also was engaged at another
point. The town was girdled with fire; General Walker's brigade
was escalading—the Portuguese troops were unnerved, and threw
down the ladders. Our men snatched them up and raised them
against the walls nearly thirty feet high. The ladders were short,
yet the men clambered up. The fire of the French was deadly; a
mine was sprung under the soldier's feet, live shells and beams of
wood were rolled over on them with showers of grape; man after
man dropped dead from the ladders. Other points were attacked
and won. The French fought like demons. A death struggle of
fiery antagonists took place at every corner, while our men most

thoroughly maddened with rage and excitement, dashed at the breach with wild resolution: for is it not recorded, 'Who shall describe the martial fury of that desperate soldier of the 95th, who, in his resolution to win, thrust himself beneath the chained sword-blades, and there suffered the enemy to dash out his brains with the ends of their muskets'.

Here now was a crushing and most desperate struggle for the prize; the bright beams of the moon were obscured with powder-smoke. The springing of mines, powder-barrels, flashing of guns and small arms, rendered our men marks for destruction. Death's grasp was just on the remnant of the brave, a total annihilation of humanity on our side, when the troops who had escaladed the Castle made a dash at the breach, and, with one loud cheer for England, and a sweeping volley, and another mad shrieking yell, rushed on with the bayonet, and cleared the bloody gap for those below, who now rushed in, driving the French from every point — and Badajos was won!

Let any one picture to himself this frightful carnage taking place in a space of less than a hundred yards square. Let him consider that the slain died not all suddenly, nor by one manner of death; that some perished by steel, some by shot, some by water, some crushed and mangled by heavy weights, some trampled upon, some dashed to atoms by the fierce explosions, that for hours this destruction was endured without shrinking, and that the town was won at last. Let any man consider this, and he must admit that a British army bears with it an awful power. No age, no nation ever sent forth braver troops to battle than those who stormed Badajos. When the extent of the night's havoc was made known to Lord Wellington, the firmness of his nature gave way for a moment, and the pride of conquest yielded to a burst of grief for the loss of his gallant soldiers.

For two days the town was in possession of the victorious, and it may be as well to draw a veil over the misdeeds of men stained with the blood of their comrades, now excited to very frenzy. A siege is always terrible, but the sacking of a town is an abomination. Here the inhabitants suffer the terrible vengeance of all the ferocity of the human species.

I remember two sisters, beautiful daughters of Spain, who made their escape from the town when the soldiers spread for plunder and mischief. They made their way into our camp outside, and threw themselves on the protection of the first British officers they met (two of the —— Regiment). One of those ladies married her protector. I knew them both: he became a distinguished general officer, and now lies in Westminster Abbey; she is still living. The scenes that took place in the town were frightful, not fit to be recorded. The priests took refuge with the fair sex in the great church for safety, and barricaded the doors. There was no safety anywhere, the maniacs, for the time, loaded their firelocks and let fly a volley into the lock of the door, which opened it quickly enough, and then——

The wine-shops were all in demand. If the men were not all drunk there were none of them quite sober, but very able to go on with the plunder. One fellow might be seen with a bag of dollars; another cove would take him into a wine-house, make him stupidly drunk, and carry off the *douros*; one or two more working in concert would knock this chap down, and rob him of his treasure. They brought all sorts of things into the camp, until the tents were supplied with furniture such as was never seen in a camp before. One fellow with a tattered red coat, grasping his firelock, was groaning under an old-fashioned eight-day clock; while another had a broad looking-glass on his back; chairs and tables, priests' vestments, ladies' dresses, beds, blankets, and cooking-pots, with sausages, and pig-skins of wine. 'Stop, Jack, and give us a dhrink ov that wine', some fellow would say (dressed in his half-bloody uniform, and on his head the *sombrero* of an old priest). 'Devil a drop, now; it's going to the camp.' 'Faith an' I'll tapt it for myself, then', and slap goes his bayonet into the skin and out flows the wine. Then there is a wrangle, then they are friends, and both get jolly drunk and lie there helpless long enough. There were watches amongst them, gold and silver, some valuable ornaments, doubloons, and dollars; they were fond of parading their treasure, and more fond of drinking to excess; consequently these articles changed hands frequently as they got drunk, and the sober ones saved them the trouble of looking after their stolen goods. But still the truth must be told: the besieging army were promised the sacking of the town when taken, and, notwithstanding all the devotion and bravery of the British soldier, this promise of pillage adds to his courage and determination. Therefore it became their reward, and as all the Spaniards in the city had timely notice of the siege, and were offered a free and safe escort away to any place of safety, those who chose to remain stayed at a fearful risk. Very many went away at the beginning, but many who favoured the French party remained to their cost. There was no discipline as yet amongst the stormers; all was riot, confusion, and drunkenness. The officers had no control over their late devoted and obedient soldiers; they were mad, and went about with loaded muskets and fixed bayonets, to the terror of each other and everybody else. The Duke rode into the town with his staff, on the evening of the second day, and was immediately recognised. 'There he comes, with his long nose,' said one old warrior who knew him well; 'let's give him a salute.' A dozen or so of halfdrunken fellows collected, fired a volley of ball cartridge over his head, with a cheer, saying, 'There goes the owl chap that can leather the French!' and then they all cut away and hid themselves out of his sight. It was rather a dangerous *feu-de-joie*, for the commander-in-chief, who did not seem to like it, went off directly and gave orders for a gibbet to be erected in the great square, and had it proclaimed in camp and through the town that any man found in Badajos the next day would be hanged! This seemed to sober the drunken and curb the passions of all. Fatigued almost to death with fighting and excitement, riot and drunkenness, they were glad of some rest, and, gathered in now to the camp, became obedient to orders, and got ready for any future emergency. Many a bloody, hard-contested battlefield was still before them which I intend, in my poor insignificant way of writing, to record, but only what I saw and shared in.

Badajos had now fallen, and with it 5,000 of our bravest men; and, to the discredit of the English Government, no army was ever so ill provided with the means of prosecuting such an enterprise. The ablest officers trembled when reflecting how utterly destitute they were of all that belonged to real service; without sappers and miners they were compelled to attack fortresses defended by the most warlike, practised, and scientific troops of the age. The best officers and the finest soldiers were obliged to sacrifice themselves in a lamentable way, to compensate for the negligence and incapacity of a Government always ready to plunge the nation into a war without the slightest care of what was necessary to obtain success. The sieges carried on by the British in Spain were a succession of butcheries, because the commonest materials, and the means necessary for their art, were denied the engineers. This liberal and generous Government and their noble successors took thirty-six years to consider whether the men of Badajos and those who fought their way from Torres Vedras to Toulouse, in victorious conquest for six long years, were yet worthy to wear a medal!

Napoleon's troops fought in bright fields, where every helmet caught some beams of glory, but the British soldier conquered under the cold shade of aristocracy. No honours recognising his daring, no despatch gave his name to the applause of his countrymen; his life of danger and hardship was uncheered by hope, his death unnoticed. He endured with surprising fortitude the sorest of ills, sustained the most terrible assaults in battle unnerved, overthrew with incredible energy every opponent, and at all times proved himself to be a soldier worthy of England.

I was greatly surprised at the size of the guns and mortars used in the fortress—some of the latter were wide enough to admit my head and shoulders. Often when the shot and shell fell and exploded in our lines, they left holes wide enough to bury a horse.

The wounded, amongst whom was my friend Masterman, were sent to the hospital at Estramos, in Portugal, established there as the grand depôt for sick and wounded; and now we all broke up from before the shattered town, and went our different ways. Soult had made a forced march down country with a great army to relieve Badajos, and got as far as Merida to be just too late, for our people had blown up two arches in the fine old bridge to delay his progress, and on finding, while within hearing of our guns, that the place had fallen, he retired. Lord Hill went back to Merida. We crossed the bridge, it being repaired in a temporary way by our own engineers, the men passing over by files, the baggage animals one at a time, while great caution was used in getting over the guns. It was melancholy to see the two centre arches had gone, but still there were left fifty-eight in glory.

The French army had divided, and so we had to give them chase. We had a variety of marching and counter-marching, stopping here and there in nice Spanish towns, billeting for a week or two, and then off like a shot when in full enjoyment of rest and peace. Zafra, Fuente del Maistre, Malpartida, Caceres, and *otras pueblas*, were familiar to us all, having visited them so often; but still it was a weary and hungry time with most of us. The army was long unpaid, and our credit low. I found favour in the eyes of the brigade butcher, himself a private soldier of my own regiment, who gave us tick for a bullock's head, heart, or liver—sometimes a sheep's head and pluck—until we got our pay. These, to us luxuries, were his perquisites, for three of us were now messing together, adding any little additions that fortune might throw in our way into the camp kettle. There was a positive general order against plunder, and of course no officer would be guilty of such an act. Our rations were short at times, yet we fed the Spanish troops; and their generals purloined the English gold, robbed and plundered, and sold the very arms supplied them by England for their own defence. Yet if a soldier of ours was caught picking up an old hen or duck, or a stray goose, he was at once tied up, and got six dozen. If a very grave offence—such as robbing the person —he was tried by court-martial, and, if found guilty, hanged upon a tree, and no mistake. I remember seeing three soldiers hanged one morning, on the long projecting arm of a cork tree, for robbing some muleteers; men who would have fought to the death in the battlefield. It was a most melancholy and touching sight, as we marched away, to see three red-coats dangling in the air, awaiting the vultures which generally followed on the army.

The Spanish muleteers were the very life and sustenance of the Peninsular war; we could not have existed without them. Everything was conveyed by them for the army—provisions, ammunition, rum, etc. Their patience, hardiness, and fidelity to the British army were remarkable; but, on the contrary, the men high in rank, generals, governors, diplomatists, hidalgos, the Spanish Junta, and Portuguese leaders, such as the ambitious and intriguing Bishop of Oporto—commonly called the Patriarch—the Sousas—were contemptible, selfish, cowardly, ignorant, fraudulent, faithless, and cruel. These were the worthies Wellington had to contend against while fighting their battles—always contentious and deceptive.

Our next exploit was to take and destroy the stronghold of Almaraz, a fortress held by the French on the Tagus. General Sir Rowland Hill assembled his corps of the army in and about the fine old town of Truxillo in the middle of May 1812. My regiment happened to be billeted in this city of Pizarro. His birthplace, his house, still a noble building, gave good cover to our soldiers; altogether a likely place to look at for one's dinner; but there was no hospitality. So we determined to get up a big mess dinner for the whole regiment once for all, to celebrate the battle of Albuera! A celebrated sutler, one Tamet, a Turk, always followed our division with a supply of good things, such as English hams, tea, sugar, pickles, and a variety of other luxuries, all at famine prices; but Señor Tamet was a good-natured fellow, and gave some people tick until the next issue of pay, and continued to give credit to those who paid according to agreement. He now furnished our regiment with what we required for our banquet. We selected a pretty spot outside the town, under some cork trees, marked out the size of our table on the green sod, and cut a trench all round. Our legs in the trench, we sat on the ground, with the table in front, but without a table-cloth. This was our arrangement.

We were like schoolboys about Christmas, looking out for a jollification dinner; but all was rough, and nothing at all smooth in these days. However, the 16th of May was to be a day of festivity.

There had been a great many auction sales of late, so many officers being killed at Badajos. It was usual to sell their effects, and remit the amount of sale to the agents at home. In this way most of us got our supply of clothing. I bought a pony saddle and bridle. Always fond of horses, being light in weight and a good horseman, I was now a sort of mounted officer, and a great don in my own estimation. I was in demand for riding races, too, an amusement manly, cheerful, and always present where there is a British army. While preparations were being made for the 16th, which was the following day, we got orders to cook three days' rations, and march the same night! A sad disappointment—no baggage to accompany the division, so that our return was pretty sure, at least that of the living; but of course we were obliged to postpone our dinner *sine die*. Three of us jolly Subs messed together, called the 'Tria juncta in uno'; and our motto was, 'Toujours prêt'. I gave up my pony to carry our three days' prog, tied up in our haversacks, and slung across the saddle, with three distinct orders to my servant to be careful and follow the column and not lose sight of the troops.

We marched away by moonlight; the men slung their arms, to prevent the enemy seeing our line of march and calculating our numbers, for the barrels were bright in those days and might be seen glistening a long way off by moonlight. The daily polishing of the old flint firelock gave the men an infinity of bother and trouble. Rainy days and night dews gave them a rust which was never permitted on parade, as we were more particular about clean arms and powder dry than anything else. We moved on all quiet, the muleteer alone singing a serenade to beguile the passing hour. We marched through rugged mountain passes nearly all the night, halting about every quarter of an hour, in consequence of the many obstacles in front; and at every halt I was fast asleep on the sod, and everybody else also perhaps.

About four o'clock in the morning my regiment was ordered to halt, the rest of the division pushing on, and now Colonel Fenwick explained our plan of attack in a few words. On the top of a mountain, just above, stood the castle of 'Mirabete', garrisoned by 1,000 French soldiers and eight guns, with a rampart twelve feet high; to storm this place by *coup-de-main*, by an escalade in the old style, and as quickly as possible, was our part of the night's amusement. Volunteers were called for the forlorn hope, and they jumped to the front in a minute, with an officer, Lieutenant Sullivan, at their head. Being myself orderly officer for the day, I was detailed to go in front with the scaling-ladders to place against the walls, a position I considered at the time equal to a wooden leg; but it never can be too often repeated that war, however adorned by splendid strokes of skill, is commonly a series of errors and accidents. We crawled up this steep ascent with great caution and silence; but just as we approached the tower, a solitary shot was fired at the foot of the hill, and the next moment the castle was in a blaze. Luckily for us it was not yet daylight, and that a cloud of mist hung over the castle top. We could not be seen, but the garrison kept up a random fire, all their shot passing over our heads as we lay on the heather. It was now too late to surprise our friends, as they rather surprised us with their *feu d'enfer*, and so we retired a little way down and got under cover before dawn. There we lay all day waiting for fresh orders. General Hill, too, was discovered, and lay *perdu* with 6,000 men until nearly day-light on the morning of the 19th, when he let loose his troops upon Forts Napoleon and Almaraz. Sharp work and severe loss in the escalade, but our men went there to win, the forts were taken and destroyed, guns spiked and sunk in the Tagus, and all material rendered useless. We lost 2 gallant good officers and 180 men, captured 17 officers and 250 men of the French, besides the number killed, one stand of colours, a large amount of ammunition, stores, etc.; opened the passage of the Tajo, and went back to Truxillo. When the day closed, my regiment retraced their steps, and joined the main force all safe and sound. A little thing deranges the best-laid plans. When leaving Truxillo, as I have stated, I gave my servant his orders; he dallied, and kept too far in rear of the column, in company with a groom of General C——, who was leading a spare horse. They missed the turn in the road, dawdled on until they popped on the sentry of an outlying picket, who popped on to them at once. The General's groom was killed, my fellow was unhorsed, the pony ran away and kicked off saddle, haversacks, prog, and all. That single shot awoke up the garrison above, the whole expedition was deranged, and many lives were lost in con-sequence; but many, too, were saved, for we left the tower and its garrison for another day, and I cannot say that this grieved me very much!

My pony was found, with his bare back. After having counter-marched, three of us found ourselves likely to starve for two days, unless that other coves could spare part of their common cold ration. Colonel Fenwick kindly spared me a bit of his cold beef and biscuit to keep me alive, just at a time when a quartern loaf, a pound of ham, and a quart of brown ale would have tempered my appetite while dinner was being prepared! However, we looked joyfully forward to the coming big dinner at Truxillo. We did return victorious, but not to the banquet. Alas! in our absence a foraging party of French dragoons entered the town and carried off all our larder, with all the baggage they could grasp. The wines were overlooked, and, fearful of another foray, our doctor, who had been left behind unwell, got up a ration dinner with a few other friends, took the chair, represented the whole corps, drank to the success of the war, the memory of the brave who fell at Albuera, a safe return to the regiment, and other toasts, until he got so merry he bolted off to a convent to release the nuns like a gallant knight! Many of the fair señoritas he knew were there pining for liberty; but the watchful and wily priests came to the rescue. There was a shindy of course, a few officers of the baggage-guard, who had shared in the toasts, collected their forces and joined the medico. They assailed the convent again, and had nearly forced an entrance, when the second in command received a wound on the head and tumbled down the stairs. The doctor called off his troops to see after the wounded, and dressing the *cabeza* of the only one, made an awkward incision on his *corona*. The *sangre* began to flow, and the holy priests made their escape, satisfied in preserving the dark-eyed maidens from the hands of such heretics, and keeping *perdu* lest they might get into a scrape for wounding one of H.M.'s officers in uniform. After this quixotic deed the dinner-party retired to their siesta, and I believe all got up sober.

Great ferocity existed at this time amongst the guerilla chiefs, and indeed at all times. Mina was cruel and revengeful. The curate Merino, too, was revolting in cruelty; he took some hundred French prisoners on one occasion, and hanged fifty or sixty of them in cold blood, deliberately butchering them in order to avenge the death of three of his men, although he had no proof of their being killed at all. Then there was counter-retaliation, and so the blood work went on continually, both parties to be condemned. Yet, make the case our own, and ask, if an enemy landed on our shores, killed, burned, and destroyed all before them, what would we do? How would we feel towards such an enemy? The poor Spaniards had very great provocation; but still no one could approve of the ferocious conduct on either side.

There was at all times a chivalrous feeling between the English and French in all their quarrels. We respected each other when prisoners of war, and sometimes in deadly strife I have known some instances of such generous conduct. For example: at Elboden there were some days of hard fighting, and some brilliant examples of skill and bravery. In a cavalry charge, a French officer, in the act of dashing sword in hand at the gallant Lieutenant-Colonel Felton Harvey, of the 14th Light Dragoons, saw, just in time, that he had but one arm, and with a movement as rapid as his horse brought down his sword into a salute, and passed on. Nothing on military record more manly, or more beautiful than this!

About this time I was ordered away, in charge of a convoy of sick and wounded, to the grand dépôt at Estramos, in Portugal. I sold my pony to raise the wind and pay my debts, and prepared for my long journey. I had about ten dollars over, and my donkey, which was now all my own. I bought him out and out; he carried all my world's treasure on his broadside, and might have carried myself at times, for he was not overloaded. An old leather trunk containing my kit on one side, balanced by a sack on the reverse, which held the frying-pan, camp-kettle, reaping-hook, and some odds and ends, with my servant's knapsack, a privilege which he claimed when away from the regiment. Tom Tandy, who was a good forager, always left room in the sack for anything Providence might send on the way, as he said, 'to help the rations'. He drove the willing donkey before him, and we commenced our journey.

My troop were all mounted on commissary mules, one muleteer having charge of three or four. Taking sick and wounded down to the depôts, they always returned to the army with a cargo of rum and biscuit. They were constantly employed.

My companion, the assistant-surgeon in charge, was a joyous fellow, full of Irish wit and humour, and all sorts of quaint sayings and drollery. His name was Maurice Quill. Any old soldier still in the land of the living, who served in Spain, would remember something about Dr. Quill and his exploits. We marched away from Truxillo without much regret. Quill stated that he had never had a decent dinner since he came into the country, and could not be worse off on the line of march, although he did not consider it his turn of duty for such practice. The weather was very hot, and the marches sometimes long to some town or village, where, according to route, there was to be cover for the night. A billet, with fire and light, was all that we could demand. If the people were kind, and gave us a welcome, we were soon very good friends, and gave them no trouble. This was generally the case; but they seldom attended to one's appetite, and we really had to forage a bit privately about the roadside, it being considered no man's land, not that I remember personally breaking the law, but I believe I may have said to my Sancho, 'How nice one of those ducks, or that little pig, would fit into the sack, and roast for supper at our next billet'. Somehow or another Tom had a magic knack of inviting these innocents in a playful way into his big wallet, for a ride on the outside of a donkey never agreed with them!

We always called a halt about a mile or so from our next resting-place for the night, to look about us and do a little business, to save our patrone any trouble. Tom took out his reaping-hook, stepped into the next field of standing green corn, and bundled up a ration for the gentleman who carried his knapsack. Never forget the poor dumb animal, he must live as well as his master. As for the muleteers, they were at home, and took good care of themselves, and so we snailed along until we came to Badajos, the mutilated and battered old town. They were building up the walls

and ramparts, and cleaning away the debris out of the ditches as we
passed in. All the tools were laid down as they scanned the
cavalcade with sympathy, and with a 'Viva los Engleses' and 'Via
vm. con Dios'. Having first housed my troops and left Quill to
look after their health, I went in search of my billet, and to arrange
for our dinner. The great event of the day is a good dinner, here
and there and everywhere, with cheerful company, and we fared
very well. A gallina and sausages, salad, bread, and good country
wine, formed no bad repast after a march of seven leagues. The
Spanish bread is the finest in the world, the pork in its season most
excellent, and the sausages, with the little tinge of garlic, the best I
ever tasted. Quill was very tired with his long tramp, as he called
it, and retired early. I was fairly knocked up myself with the
march, and a broiling sun beaming on my head all the day. I had
comfortable quarters in the square—two rooms and a decent kind
of bed. The windows below were all guarded by iron gratings.
My bedroom was decorated by an iron balcony, from which I
looked out on the poor, desolate, shattered city, hardly a house
visible without a smash. Spaniards were still coming in looking
for their old habitations, others mending, patching up temporary
dwellings, and looking patiently bewildered.

The seven-league march sent me early to roost. Tom picked
out a soft plank for himself on the floor outside my door. I left
my window wide open to see the dawn and be early away, tumbled
in amongst the fleas, and was soon insensible to their claws. I will
back Spain and Portugal against the world for the breed of this very
lively creature. Like the dogs in Constantinople, I believe they are
encouraged to live and multiply. Always early, I jumped up about
five o'clock, rather late for me, and to my horror found nothing
in my room but an old shooting-jacket, a pair of trousers to match,
my cocked hat and feather, my sword and shoes! I opened the
door and found Tom Tandy asleep, gave him a kick to open his
eyes, and then asked if he had been in my room. 'No, sir.' The
whole thing now flashed before my eyes, the open window invited
some ladrone to walk in and inspect my kit. It was easily done,
like crawling up a ladder—everything valuable was gone: my trunk
and its contents, red coat, boots, trousers, and all—with the few
dollars I had in reserve for hard times coming—all this to me just
now was a great calamity. I flung myself into the tattered garments left, and ran off to tell the medico, still hoping it might be
some trick of his; but, soon undeceived, I related the sad tale, of
which he knew nothing, but kept saying, 'I'll get your traps for
you.' When dressed he said, 'Now, come along, and show me your
Patrone' (landlord). I saw that he was screwing himself up for a

charge at the Patrone. I said, 'He knows nothing of the robbery;
Tom was asleep, with his head to my door, all night.' 'Never mind,
I must see him.' I sent Tom down for the señor. As soon as the
poor gentleman appeared, the doctor made a spring, and fastened
in his collar, saying, in his own native language and excitement,
'If — you — don't — get — this — officer — all — his — things —
which — you — stole — I'll — cut — your — (Spanish) — throat'.
laying an emphasis on every word, that the Spaniard might not
misunderstand him! The poor man was dreadfully alarmed.
There was a noisy row. His daughter, a pretty black-eyed maid,
rushed in to the rescue, at the time the doctor was making signs of
an incision across her father's throat. I tried to drag him off; the
young lady screamed, but the medico declared it was all sham, and
he would have my traps restored. However, I got the señor
released from an iron grasp, and his daughter in tears took him
away. Quill at the same time took his leave, saying, 'If I chose to
submit to be robbed at every billet in Spain, not to call upon him
for any advice or assistance!' He could not speak a word of
Spanish, and was much prejudiced against the whole race, believed
every man in the country to be a public robber, and looked sharp
after his own kit. He was not very far wrong, but still there were
honest men and women too, and plenty of them, who loved 'los
Engleses' as well as their own bright land.

Time being nearly up, I ran off to the office of the Alcalde to
report my misfortune, not expecting much redress there. 'Give me
a list of your losses,' he said, 'and I will make inquiry after them.
You must wait the result here.' I gave him the list in writing, and
my address, name, regiment, and division of the army, and there it
ended. Going back with all my dander up and a melancholy phiz
to move off my traps, I heard a sweet voice from a balcony call
out, 'Señor George'. I looked up, and saw a fair lady whom I had
known formerly in my old quarters at Albuquerque. She called
me up, and, quite rejoiced to see me again, asked a hundred questions all at once. Where was the regiment? How were all the
officers? How came I here in this queer dress? And where I was
going? When she gave me time to speak I told her all, which
greatly distressed her. 'To be robbed,' she said, 'amongst my own
people'; and, 'Dios mio, yo siento mucho,' etc., and 'I'm grieved that
I cannot help you. I am only here to see some friends who stood
out the siege; we are all poor now. Our property destroyed and
pillaged, and Spain ruined. You must have some chocolate and
something to eat by the way, and two of my brother's shirts,
and——.' 'Oh, no,' I said, 'I can't take anything. I must be off,
my people are waiting.' But the chocolate came in with some

toast, the almuerzo (breakfast) of all the better class of Spaniards.
I parted from her with great reluctance, and with what is called a
tender good-bye too.   She saw me to the door, slipped two dollars
into my hand, and ran upstairs with a 'povorasito' on her lip, and
a 'viva mil años, caro amigo, á-Dios, á-Dios.'   Dear, sweet, gentle,
kind-hearted Leonora!   I never saw her afterwards to return a
hundred-fold her generosity.   I would have walked a long day's
journey to have met her again to show my gratitude — so much was
I touched with this disinterested loving-kindness.

I found my troops all present, and in the saddle — 'a pack-saddle'.
'Nobody dead, sir,' said the medical officer and took his usual place
in front.   Away I went from Badajos in very light marching order,
never to see it again.   The doctor was as mute as a tombstone for
two leagues, when I called a halt, and sat down by the side of a
clear nice fountain, while the mules had their refreshing beverage.
Quill now came up and sat down beside me, with a laughing face
and admonition for not permitting him to 'choke that rascally
Spaniard who stole my traps'.   'I hope he didn't steal the frying-
pan.'   'I have all the cooking traps,' says Tom, who was sitting
beside his donkey at the fountain, gnawing a bone.'   'All,' says the
doctor — 'a tin pot and an ugly frying-pan.'   'All we want, sir,' said
Tom, 'where nothin's to be got without money, and I haven't seen
a dollar of my pay for five months, and nuffin' to eat but the
rations.'   'What are you eatin' now, then?' said Quill.   'Just
pickin' a sheep's wag, sir, I got at the last billet.'   'Or the hotel, say,
where you paid for everything, and two sheep and a pig into the
bargain.'   'Sir, you're hard upon the patrone.   He couldn't get into
master's room, yer see, the door being shut and my head up again
it all night.   It was some ladrone that climbed up and got in at the
window, which was wide open and easy as a stair.   They're not bad
people the Spaniards, sir, if you could speak to them like me, sir,
and not meddle with anything about their doors.   You see, sir,
when the old fox wants a goose or a duck, he always goes away
from home to forage, and never touches a chicken near his own
den.'   'Vamos, señor,' said the leading muleteer, and we moved on.
The doctor came up to me and said that he had a few dollars in
his pocket, and would divide with me the last pisetta (1s.), and made
himself very agreeable until we crossed the border and entered the
little kingdom of Portugal, put up at Elvas, a strongly fortified town.
We met an officer, Lieutenant Bowers, of the 50th stationed there,
an old acquaintance, and passed the day with him.   I had no
occasion, I said, to lock my door tonight, for all my wardrobe was
on my back, which astonished a well-dressed military officer of the
British army, until I explained the cause.   'Why,' he said, 'if you

were not so very young, you would be taken for some guerilla chief, and all the convoy for prisoners of war, only that the guerillas are on our side.' 'Just so,' I said, 'and that makes all the difference.'

We passed on our way without any adventure until we sighted Estramos, the end of our journey. It was a bright sunny day, hot as you please. About noon, as I headed my long line of mules bearing the lame, and the sick, and the sore, the battered trunks of brave men representing many corps, a general officer and his staff, with their cocked hats and fine plumage, stood in the middle of the square and caught my eye at once, as I marched in at the head of my troop. With open mouth and eyes they all turned towards this spectacle, particularly the commanding officer in the fancy dress. Up comes an aide-de-camp directly from the General, to inquire who I was, where I came from, my name, 'and about your dress, sir'. I thought I would have a rise out of the well-dressed gentleman, so sleek and so well fed. 'Just from the fighting army above,' I said. 'We are not over particular in dress; hard times too, little to eat, and plenty of field exercise in the fire-away-style; here's a sample of our trade behind me.' He went off to make his report to his master, who sent him back for a more direct reply, particularly about my uniform. I then told him the whole story, and my duty being discharged when I had delivered my troops at the general hospital, requested permission to proceed to Lisbon to get a new rig out.

The General gave me two months' leave at once, but forgot to ask me to dinner! Quill wished me a safe return through Badajos, and desired me to be sure to call and apologise to my old patrone! And ask him for my toggery, particularly the *douros!* We shook hands and parted mutual good friends—more of him again.

I went in search of my good friend Masterman who had been wounded in the siege; he was nearly recovered. I passed the day with him. He gave me an old military blue coat and two dollars, all he could spare, and with this I began my journey over a whole kingdom on foot. Tom had his red coat, so we could not be mistaken for any other than true British soldiers. I knew that there were bandits on the road, but consoled myself with the truth that they would not disturb a couple of English red-coats, driving an empty donkey before them. Tom had his brown bess, and sixty rounds of ball cartridge. He kept his flint well fixed and his powder dry. We had a ride on the donkey, and carried the gun turn about. I was commanding officer and Tom as respectful as on parade, while sober. The first night on our new line of march he got right jolly on wine. He had no money nor credit, but a winning way at the

D

wine-house, and a singular way when he lost his balance.   I found
him in heavy marching order, firelock in hand, when I thought him
in bed for the night.   'Ho, Tom,' I said, 'where are you going?'
'Back to the regiment,' he said.   'I go no further: no service on this
road.'   I gave him a punch that floored him right into his little den,
where he lay as quiet as a turtle until I took away his gun, knapsack, and ammunition, then locked him up a close prisoner till
morning, when he turned out quite fresh and as penitent as priests,
who'll never do it again until the next time!   And so Tom worried
me all the way, but only at night, when I usually locked him up.
I had no other adventure on this line of march.   Rations were
provided by the head man of the village to all who had a route to
show, and were paid afterwards by our Commissary.

CHAPTER 4

Toledo and Salamanca

IT was a long, weary, hungry walk over a little kingdom, but I had a stout heart then, a pair of very active legs, an iron constitution, an appetite too big for my means, a devil-me-care way of my own, always merry and ready for any sort of fun or frolic. I rejoiced to see 'Aldea Gallego'. Here I crossed the Tajo, nine miles to Lisbon, and made my way to Belem, the English depôt, where an officer of my own regiment was stationed. Lieutenant R——n was a kind, hospitable fellow, glad to see me and to give me a room in his quarters, as well as a hearty invitation to be his guest while I remained in Lisbon. I did enjoy myself full measure here; very opportunely, too, a box of clothing had just arrived in the river for me from home, with a permission to draw for the ready; in addition, I was now all right again, and went to work quietly to equip myself out like a campaigner for rough days before me. I got up a canteen, bought a silver spoon and fork, a new frying-pan, tin plates and dishes, and tins for salt, pepper, tea and sugar, etc. A tailor made up my uniforms, riding-jacket, and cap for racing, and other habiliments. All this was going on while I was enjoying myself. I had a good horse to ride, and dined out often; old starvation ration days were forgotten, and I became a great swell. At this time our old friend, Dr. L——, who played the part of Don Quixote at Truxillo, arrived in bad health, with a home certificate for six months' leave. He came out to dinner with us one day, when we observed by his singular manner that he was not just all right in his pericranium. Dinner was being prepared and wine on the table. He walked in, and was helping himself to a goblet of sherry, when I interposed and requested him to wait a little. He put down the decanter, took up a carving-knife, and made a rush at me. I ran round the table, he after me, when I jumped out of the window, which fortunately was open, and made my escape. I turned round and spoke to him. He flourished his *cuchillo* and told me not to come back, or he would stop my promotion! We found that the poor fellow had gone a little crazy. He had cut half the tail off his red coat, and had played some queer pranks in Lisbon. We had him carefully looked after, and I saw him safely on board a ship and placed under the special care of the captain, who took him safe to England. He was considered a very clever man in his profession. He never rejoined the regiment, but we shall meet him again.

Major B—— of ours was promoted into the 77th Regiment, now only seven miles from Belem. He asked us to dine at the mess which they had established. We rode over to have a jollification, for it was almost necessary at that period to drink wine for three hours after dinner; then supper, and finish off with spiced wine and stirrup cup. I saw that my friend R—— was getting top-heavy, very loquacious, speaking like a senator, and getting very valiant. He was invited to a shake-down for the night. Oh, no! his gallant grey was at the door and would take him home in no time; so we mounted and rode away quietly about one o'clock in the morning. We had not gone far when my companion fancied he saw a regiment of French Dragoons in his front, and ordered me to charge. He dashed away at full speed, swaying from side to side in the saddle, so that the right or left spur was always in the flank of the poor horse. The moon was bright, and the perfume along the hedges sweet as honey. Such a climate at that hour was meant for the thoughtful, the gentle, thankful, weary traveller on some errand of mercy, not for Don Quixote and Sancho. I am sure if R—— had met a windmill in his flight he would have made the fatal charge; as it was, I found him in a ditch by the roadside about a mile on, and his horse standing gently beside him. I jumped off my nag and roused him up. Finding no bones broken, I got him once more into the saddle after a great struggle, for people in their cups are always very wise and very obstinate! No sooner firmly seated than he gave one wild whoop and was off again, full speed. No use in following, I thought; it would only urge on his horse the faster. I rode on quietly, watching both sides of the road for this wild fellow, but never saw him or his horse. I arrived at home about six o'clock in the morning and sent his servants in search of him along the road that we came; but no tidings until mid-day, when he came riding home quite jolly, as if nothing had happened, and blew me up for leaving him alone in a quinta! Poor R—— was a very sober fellow at all times, but addicted to gambling, which ultimately ruined him.

I had no desire to dine out again with such-like hospitable friends. A simple repast under a tree suited me better, and I do not remember being at any sort of a mess dinner again during the war.

I saw a good deal of Lisbon this time and the beautiful country around it. As for the city itself at that period, it was the most filthy town I had ever seen: it was dangerous to walk the streets by night. No end to the slops coming from the top windows whop into the gutters below. The dogs were ever on the alert at night, prowling and fighting—a community of scavengers without owners, rejected and kicked about; existing in mangy wretchedness, and dying in the streets. As for beggars, they were as plenty as paving-stones. Lazy, indolent, and filthy, they lay on the hot flags, stretching out the long bone of an arm for an alms, but would not rise for it. They lived in the sun, half-naked; but as a shirt and trousers were quite enough for any señor Englese, they required few garments—it was awfully hot.

My time was now up, and we started—a large detachment of many corps—to join the army. I got charge of a spare horse going up to a field officer of the 2nd Division, so I was in luck. Tom and the donkey in good feather and high condition for the road. Tom was two months under garrison discipline, and sober as a judge; and very glad, as he said, to go home again. We halted at Elvas en route. I called on the Commandant, and found that officer dressed in part of my late wardrobe. I said to him, 'Might I ask who is your tailor?' 'Why do you ask?' he said. 'Oh, just because he made for me as well, and my things fit you so nicely. That silk riding-jacket is mine; I had it for riding races. I can't swear to the trousers, but the vest I would know anywhere.' He seemed very much taken aback, and explained how he had bought several things ready-made from a travelling pedlar, which no doubt was the fact. When I explained the Badajos tale, it was all clear that the pedlar was the ladrone (thief), and he had purchased stolen goods, not knowing that they were stolen from Ensign G. Bell, when in the performance of his duty in the service of King George III, of gracious memory. He offered to restore all he had at half the price he paid for them, but I declined his offer, saying that I had a full kit, and really wanted for nothing. Between this little unexpected surprise and excitement he forgot to ask me to dinner, so we parted, and never met again. I was satisfied that I did not awake when the wretched thief was in my room, or I might have felt the plunge of his cuchillo under my fifth rib, to keep me quiet. I got home safe, and was welcome. There was no fighting in my absence, so I lost nothing.

I found my young friend P——, who used to drink more than his allowance of grog on board the *Arethusa*, missing, and was informed that, on one unlucky morning for him, the brigade was roused up suddenly to disperse some advance troops of the enemy, who were poaching upon our grounds. They were being followed up close by the infantry when the word was passed to the rear to send up the guns, as they were rattling past, and our men closing to the left, poor P—— lost his balance, tumbled over, and a gun-carriage ruffled his legs, with one of the colours in hand. There was an inquiry, and it could not be denied that he had been indulging as usual in too much of the strong waters, so he got leave to go home for an indefinite period, which meant to say that his military career was at an end.

The other gentleman, Lieutenant S——, was found one night while on duty mortal drunk, and got leave to quit also. It was this unfortunate fellow who chased me up on deck with knife in hand for cutting him down on board the old transport.

Commanding officers had almost unlimited power in those days to dismiss officers without court-martial for grave offences like the above. It saved a great deal of trouble and inconvenience, and kept young fellows and old ones *in terrorem*. The men were being flogged every day for drunkenness, and it was right that there should be no partiality between officer and soldier for this crime.

Wellington about this time ordered Sir Rowland Hill to give battle to Drouet, Count D'Erlong, who was roving about our part of Spain with a large army, feeding and foraging upon the unhappy Spaniards, who received nothing but blows and abuse for feeding their enemies. We hunted them all over the country, and from town to town, but they would not have our acquaintance on any terms. We drove them from Toledo and Valladolid, two cities of Spain celebrated in story. I did so enjoy a short stay in the former. The French were hardly gone when we marched in, and the same evening a ball was given at the Palace in honour of the English General and his officers, the first British troops that had been here. These Spanish balls and parties are not attended with any expense beyond the refreshment of country wine, lemonade, and cakes. The Bishop was present. Many grandees, poor and proud, assembled there, and the gentle señoritas, so neatly and so simply dressed, looked pensive and beautiful. They move about in the dance so gracefully, while generally their feet and figures are perfect. There is a very fine cathedral here, and a magnificent organ, on which I helped to perform a grand piece of church music in the way of blowing the bellows—a simple process. 'Tis not done by hand, but by the feet. You walk up and down the great double bellows behind the organ. As one exhausts, the other fills, and so 'tis a walk up and down hill while the music lasts. Toledo was celebrated for sword-blades, as it is now for priests and friars. It stands on the Tagus, in New Castile.

We started in chase once more, and they led us a dance at their heels into Leon, declining to enter into any personal gun-powder quarrel with us for the present. We had very long marches and very hungry soldiers, no money and no credit, six months now in arrears of pay, the muleteers twelve. What could one expect in the trail of a French army? I paid 6s. for a loaf of bread, my daily pay being 5s. 3d., less income-tax! Soldiers without money become robbers almost everywhere; but our men behaved admirably. Bad ones were to be found in every corps, because we got the sweepings of jails at home to fill up our ranks, recruits were so scarce at eighteen guineas bounty. But they were all game cocks at fighting; never was such an army, and Wellington knew it.

At this period, our noble Duke and the French General Marmont were dodging each other, and manoeuvring about Salamanca both on the *qui vive* some days before the 22nd of July 1812, on which day the great row began. The battle was fought and won by the noble army of Old England—a day of victory garnished by the blood of thousands. Many a time that day did the battle change its very doubtful position. Wellington was here and there and at every point at the right time. The men went down by hundreds, but won their way by desperate courage through such a fire as British soldiers can only sustain. Onwards they pushed through gloom and blood and powder smoke, which rolled along the field, and clothed the scene in partial darkness. In sounds of terror, the battle raged, volley following volley with deafening rapidity, while charges of cavalry and the booming of great guns swept off the warriors, on both sides brave and bold. They fell in sections, crying victory before the fight had half begun. The French reserve came quickly on upon our front and flanks; their great masses closed on us in clouds of smoke and stream of fire. The hill-side was soon covered with the dead and dying. The battle-ground was shaking like an earthquake, for the French rapidly followed up their advantage, and their fire sparkled along the line with terrible effect, as the many gaps in our ranks clearly showed. The crisis was at hand, and victory awaited the general who had the best and largest reserves.

The 5th Division now met the enemy with a shower of leaden hail in their teeth, a cloud of dust blinded their vision, and in that cloud a tremendous charge of cavalry, swift and sure, sword in hand, broke in upon them in full tilt, trampled and cut them down. They lost both nerve and courage, and upwards of 1,000 men threw down their arms, while the glittering swords of our heavy dragoons, all powerful, cut down all before them; but not before a hundred saddles or more were emptied by a flank fire. The French left was now broken, Marmont was wounded, and some of his Generals, amongst others Desgraviers, killed, the batteries still ploughing through each other's ranks. On our side a sheet of flame advanced in front, men only thinking of victory. A few more desperate conflicts took place along the lines. The French, drunk with excitement, staggered, were beaten, and having lost 2,000 prisoners, retreated in the dusk of evening. With our dragoons at their heels, they made for the Tormes, and crossed that river by night. The Duke, always wide awake, left the Spanish General Carlos d'España at Alba de Tormes to intercept the French in case of retreat; but, as usual, he paid no respect to his orders. He left his post, and so let the defeated enemy escape across the ford! Trifling actions often mar great combinations. If this valiant Spaniard had obeyed his orders, at least a third of the fugitives would have been captured. As it was, the victory was great and decisive. Many stories might be told of noble deeds of valour done that day, every tale a true one—of how the gallant soldiers of 1812 fought for Albion, and sent their laurels home. A 43rd man, shot through the thigh, lost his shoes in the marshy ground. Refusing to quit the battlefield, he limped on under fire with naked feet and blood streaming from his wound, and thus marched on for several miles over a country covered with a small flinty stone. Kit Wallace, a private in my company, a simple sort of fellow, who had no friends, and was always a butt, and often called a coward in joke, said, 'I'll not fire a shot, a single shot in the rear rank' (his proper place), and rushed to the front, expended his sixty rounds of ball-cartridge, and calling for more, said, 'Now, am I a coward?' A man who fought beside Wallace was struck with a ball that passed through his body on the right side: you might have put a ramrod complete through the hole. He deliberately took his last shot, walked to the rear, lay down under a tree, and went to sleep in death.

The delicate and beautiful wife of Colonel Dalbiac braved the dangers and privations of two campaigns with the fortitude and patience of her sex. In this battle of Salamanca, forgetful of herself, supported by strong affection for her gallant knight, irresistibly impelled forward, trembling at the fear of death, she rode amidst the enemy's fire, exposing herself to imminent peril. There was no man present that day fighting the battles of his country that did not fight with more than double enthusiasm seeing that fair lady in such danger on the battlefield.

Wellington was hit by a spent shot in the leg, but pushed on early next day after his friends, when there was another row and some slaughter. Poor General Forey had died of his wounds, and was buried by the roadside. The brave Spaniards found the spot, and tore up his body from his humble grave to mutilate and dishonour the shattered shell, when our soldiers came up, and rescued it from their unholy grasp, buried it afresh, and covered it over with large stones for greater safety. The French lost in this day's sport 1 Field-Marshal, 7 Generals, 12,500 officers and men killed, wounded, and taken prisoners, 2 Eagles, several standards, and many guns (when we talk of guns we always mean cannon). We lost 6,000 killed and wounded, with 4 Generals. Our troops marched 150 miles in twelve days, just before the battle. Some regiments suffered severely; but the 11th and 61st could not muster at the end of the fight over 150 or 160 officers and men—all that were left to tell of noble deeds done on that hot day. Some 6,000 men lying in the hospitals of Salamanca, besides French prisoners also suffering from their wounds, rendered it the abode of extreme misery. Officers sold their horses and what they could get a few dollars for to sustain life, and many died of want and wounds—in plain language, starved to death from neglect, the reward of devotion and courage unequalled in the annals of Great Britain!

There was no getting quit of these Frenchmen. They multiplied and formed new armies, always on the trot, like locusts, eating up all before them. The order of the day with them was free quarters. They paid for nothing, and it was always an unlucky time for us when we got in their wake, for they cleared out the whole country as they went along, the poor Spaniards hiding out of sight all they could put away. Supposing a brigade of French troops on the march to a certain town, where they would arrive on the next day: they sent an armed escort in advance to the alcalde, or head man there, desiring rations to be ready for, say 500 or 1,000 men next day. There was no alternative but that of providing for these plunderers, or taking the chance of their being let loose to help themselves. 'Ye gentlemen of England, who sit at home at ease', how would you like such visitors along the coast of Kent, or in your snug little country towns?

We passed nearly the month of September in the pretty town of Yepes. It was the vintage season, and all were busy gathering in most delicious grapes and making their wine. The people were very kind, simple, industrious, and happy. My regiment and the 28th were the first British troops that had ever paid a visit here, and we were welcome. The town was divided between the two corps for their separate quarters in this way: the Quartermasters went on in advance, looked into each house, and chalked upon the door, 'Grenadiers, 34th, ten men', more or less according to size and convenience, and so on until the whole corps was disposed of. All this was done without asking the proprietors a single question. The best of the houses were marked for the officers, one or more in each house, as there was room. The commanding officer had the best quarters, of course, and went there at once. When the men were put up, all the officers assembled to choose their quarters by seniority. They were not particularly choice when my turn came. Once in possession, good or bad, no one's senior could turn you out if you selected your house according to regulation.

I had an excellent quarter (that had been overlooked) as far as rooms went. My patrone was one of those old grandees of Spain, advanced in age, as well as his señora. I very seldom saw them, but the servants had orders to look after my comfort, which they did in their own way. My table was served with grapes and sweetly-preserved melons. A loaf of bread and a big sausage would have been more in my way, but I fared better than usual. There were many pretty girls in the town, all fond of dancing, in which we often indulged of an evening, until we became almost as one family. In fact, every young fellow had his sweetheart. The young ladies were charming, barring education. The priests took care to keep them in ignorance, and free from the trammels of over-much learning, so that they were generally very idle, but fond of music, dancing, gossiping, and eating grapes and chocolate. However, we thought our fair friends here of a superior race, and indulged them in every way we could. It was a terrible blank to those who could not speak their beautiful language.

Our little evening dancing parties were not expensive; lemonade, fruit, and cakes was the usual refreshment—all that we could afford, all that was expected. I was a great don in the dance; knew all the figures and all the bonitas.

The weather was beautiful, and after morning parade we had nothing to do but enjoy life in this paradise. With my rations and half a cow's head once a week I made out a living.

I walked into the coach-house one day to look at two curiosities in the shape of the Spanish carriage of the olden times. I found on the seat of my host, the grandee, a hen's nest with seven eggs, which I put by for breakfast, leaving a white stone in their place, which the good old hen was kind enough to consider sufficient security, and called there every second day.

Wellington all this time was laying siege to Burgos, and although not so strong as Badajos or Rodrigo, he was obliged to abandon it after thirty-three days' pounding and five assaults, with a loss of more than 2,000 men, thanks to the home mis-government not supplying him with the guns he asked for and required. Surprising difficulties met this great warrior at every corner in his every-day arrangements, while straining every nerve to accomplish the very work cut out for him by an English Cabinet. He was always active, vigorous, firm in all his arrangements, with a wonderful foresight and conception, admirably formed for success. But he must have found a certain bad Government a scourge with a double thong. What a man of patience and perseverance!

This failure at Burgos knocked all our charming little arrangements to bits. We thought we had taken root in Yepes, being nineteen days undisturbed.

An unexpected order came to 'march tomorrow'. It came as an order never came before—most unwelcome. All was now hurry and bustle, to get the donkeys ready, and go and see our hermosa Castilian maids, and feel there was a farewell to peace and pleasure whilst a Frenchman remained in Spain. My washwoman, Mrs. Skiddy, came in with my two shirts, etc. 'No money yet, Mrs. Skiddy. I owe you a long washing bill.' 'Och, never mind that, jewil, if you never paid me. Sure, you're always mindful of Dan on the march, and carry his firelock sometimes a bit when the crather's goin' to drap wid all the leather straps on his back, and nearly choked wid that stock round his thrapple.' 'Well, we march tomorrow, and so go and get ready.' 'O worra-worra, march the morrow, and not a shoe on me wee donkey. The curse o' the crows be on the French; may they nivver see home,' and away she went, storming agin the French.

When the unwelcome news spread over the town, the young ladies seemed to feel it most, and many of them, indeed, sadly grieved. However, we got up a dance the same evening, as a farewell party. I well remember it was not so joyous as usual. Before the evening was over, many a sigh and gentle tear was heard and seen sliding over pale cheeks. I passed very little of my time in the house of my grandee patrone. I was welcome in another quarter, and my comrade and self promised our fair friends to come back and see them from Aranjuez (pronounced 'Aranwhays').

In the early morning the windows were crowded with our sweet young friends. 'Adios, señores! adios, Vi vm. con Dios!' was heard till far away. I believe there were some very tender partings, for we never left a town in Spain with such regret. Our march was over a plain, about six leagues, to the nice town of Aranjuez, on the Tagus, where the country palace of Spanish kings has stood for centuries. Fine gardens and pleasure-grounds, and fishponds and statuary adorned this royalty. Inside the palace all those charms in which kings and queens luxuriate. We had permission to see everything. One room was occupied by mirrors from top to bottom, in which, if any person was shut up, he could never find his way out, so curious was the construction. Another room had its walls entirely covered with paintings — the exploits of Don Quixote, and so on.

A few days passed here, when three of us young fellows agreed to go over to Yepes next morning at daylight, to pass the day, and see our young lady friends once more, according to promise. I was at my post in good time. There was a rumour of a move, and so my two coves backed out of the trip to Yepes. Nothing daunted, I started off alone, and found a joyous welcome after my long walk across a burning plain. My dress was a scarlet jacket and white waistcoat — the Spaniards liked it, and I did not care a rush who did not. I made for the Caza Don Chaves, and ran upstairs without ceremony. There was a great welcome, and, I believe, some kisses, and a hundred questions about Señor S. and twenty others, and why they did not come, etc., etc. I was almost swallowed up with kindness. Maria sat before me, with her raven hair so nicely turned back from her snow-white forehead, her ivory teeth seen through her smiles, and her beautiful speaking eyes, listening to all I said so imperfectly. All the people in the town seemed to be attached to our men, who behaved so well amongst them. They understood each other by a few words and more signs. An early dinner was being prepared, I was in the midst of enjoyment, and going to pay another visit, when some one came rushing in, in great fear, saying, 'Los Franceses! los Franceses! O. per Dios, Señor George, via vm.' (The French are coming! For God's sake, escape for your life — we are all ruined). Another messenger — 'La caballeria, la caballeria viene!'

All was now hurry, scurry, and excitement in the house to secure valuables, and hide themselves. I tried to compose the ladies by an assurance that they were safe, but their fear of the French, of whom they heard so much, gave them great alarm, and they would not be comforted. I have found ladies in general everywhere much alike in this respect, and I might add that the civillest person I ever met was a woman in a fright. A hasty 'Adios, caras amigas', and I bolted out of the house — just in time, for the advance guard of a cavalry regiment sounded a halt at the top of a long street leading down to my friend's caza. In any other dress than a red jacket, I might have approached near enough to count their numbers and make a report, but my object now was to run for it and escape. I went off at a good round trot for a league or so, and then, wet as a sponge, broke into a smart walk. I might be seen at any distance on this wide plain, and kept both eyes open. Here I met a pizañno going to Yepes with a mule laden with wine. The wine in Spain is carried in pigskins, tanned, dried, and prepared for the purpose, as in days of old Bible history (Matthew ix. 17). The bottles might have contained ten or twelve gallons each. I stopped to tell him the news, which seemed to stagger him exceedingly. He knew very well that the French were not in the habit of paying for their wine, nor drinking to the health of the Spaniards. The salutation of our allies, I well remember, was always, 'Viva los Engleses'. He said, 'Is there any of your army in Yepes?' 'None,' I said, 'I am the last to leave,' and explained as well as I could. 'Lo siento mucho, señor,' he said, and began to open a bottle, the mouth of which was a leg of the skin, tied by a string. He had a tin measure, and filled me a bumper. 'Drink', he said, 'you seem hot and tired.' I did with gusto toss off a pint of his *bueno vino*, and bid him God-speed.

I got home just in time to join my regiment crossing the Tagus —one bridge on fire, and the other about to be blown up—a little later, and I should have been on the wrong side! The two bridges had not been destroyed more than an hour or so when the French cavalry approached and sent their videttes down to the river to look after our locality. It might have been very inhospitable, but they received a very ugly discharge of musketry from our riflemen, who lined the banks under cover of the evergreen shrubs and bushes. I was in no good humour with them myself for routing me out of Yepes. So I paid into them some shots from a rest which, I fear, told what I intended at the time, although of all the sports in the field that of man-shooting I like the least. There was a good deal of pot-shooting across the water from our amateurs out of sheer spite, for we were all very angry at being disturbed from our royal quarters. Our troubles were only beginning, but we were in happy ignorance of all before us. When night came on, we all moved off silently from before Aranjuez, across some newly-ploughed lands, wherein I sank to the ankles until my short boots got full of sand and dirty water. When we did get into the Camino Real, or 'royal road', there was a halt to let all stragglers come up. Fires were soon lighted and blazing bright. I pulled off my Wellingtons and my socks to get them quickly dry, and fell asleep, so dreadfully tired as I was after the long day's work. I never awoke until the whole army had moved away, and there I was all alone in the darkness of solitude. The fire had nearly burned out. My socks were pretty dry but the boots very damp. I pulled one on after a painful difficulty—the other foot would not go home on any terms. Half on and half off, I limped on until I came up with my regiment at the next halt, fairly knocked up, but continued on till morning, when we pulled up at Madrid. There, on the bridge leading into the great city, I dropped like a stone, where I lay for two hours unable to move, footsore and weary. The day was fine, and a general rush was made into the town, when the bugles sounded the assembly. A general order was issued to serve out three days' rations and have them cooked immediately, and then to be ready to march at a moment's warning. The butchers were very expert at their trade. The oxen and fatlings (without any fat) were slaughtered, cut up, divided, served out, and in the camp kettles in less than two hours. I dragged myself down to the river, got off my boots, washed my socks, got up a fire, and fell asleep. Tom roused me up with, 'The rations, sir.' 'What have you got, Tom?' 'Somewhat of three pounds of beef with a big bone in it, orders to cook and be off again—sharp. I suppose them *Franceses* are coming after us—the d—l's luck to them!' If my feet sometimes failed me my appetite never did. The dinner was not at all inviting when turned out on a tin plate, but it was all gone in twenty minutes, barring the bone, and I got up rather hungry, and put two pounds of the biscuit into my haversack for the next two day's subsistence.

Fancy being in Madrid without a dollar in one's pocket to buy a loaf of bread or a sausage—all that I desired or cared for at that moment. However, I was now refreshed. The bugles sounded, I rolled my blanket, strapped it on my back, and waited for the assembly call. when the 88th Regiment, or Connaught Rangers, passed by as merry as larks, singing and cracking their Irish jokes. They were regular bronze fellows, hard as nails, and as ready for a fight as for a ration of rum. One fellow took a side glance at me and said, not in a very undertone, 'I think that young gentleman would be better at home with his mother!' I was very indignant at this remark and kept it to myself. I knew they were a crack regiment, and esteemed them for their remarkable bravery at all times.

Retreat from Madrid

In Madrid was a junction of the whole British army. Soult and his best Generals were at our heels with 58,000 fighting men, 84 guns, and 8,000 cavalry, a sad turn of affairs as we all thought at the time. So began the grand retreat from Burgos and Madrid; a frightful scene of misery and death, continual slaughter, privation, and cruelty. Men, women, and children crowded around us, bewailing our departure, moving along with us in one great mass for some miles.

We passed the Escurial, that celebrated palace, built by Charles V, where his bones and those of so many kings of Spain were deposited with regal pomp. The great passeth away in his greatness, and a bit of a churchyard fits everybody!

Many peasants lay dead by the roadside, murdered, but by whom we did not know, and I doubt if any one cared, for death was so familiar in all shapes at that time. We crossed the Guadarama mountains, and a splendid sight it was to see so grand an army winding its way zig-zag up that long pass, as far as the eye could see from the top step, in the far distance. The old trade was going on, killing and slaying, and capturing our daily bread. When we got on to the plains on the other side, and crossed the Tormes, we expected some rest, a bit of sleep, and better rations, or some improvement in the foraging department, but things got worse and worse. I had been feasting the last few days on some bullock's liver without salt, and hard biscuit, abominable feeding until people

come to know what hunger really is.   We got near to Salamanca,
and bivouacked in a cork wood.   The oak trees too were large and
numerous, and the acorns ripe and dropping from the branches.
We were gathering, and roasting, and eating them all day, for the
Commissary failed in issuing our common ration of biscuit.   He
served out instead a quarter pound of raw wheat to each man; this
we pounded on a stone, and threw into the camp kettle with our
beef, which thickened the soup!   There was a little bit of growling
now and then, much laughing and joking, but no complaint.   Queer
music it was to see and hear an army sitting on the sod, each man
with two big stones grinding his dinner, but everything was sweet
that came out of a camp kettle.   It must be remembered that the
British army had no tents, it was all bivouacking, i.e. lying out on
the sod in all weather, like any other wild beasts, and always up
and armed ready for anything one hour before daylight, and never
dismissed until we could see a white horse a mile distant.   This
was always a very long hour, just unrolled from one's blanket to
stand shivering in the early chill of a drizzly morning.

We had to be always ready for a move, or a march, or a change
of ground, or a fight, as the bugle sounded.   Always on the *qui vive*,
night and day, and much need too, for we expected the army of
France to be upon us at any moment.   I bought a pony on tick
just now, i.e. to be paid for by instalments as we might get our pay.
This was the practice, and the price I paid was eighty dollars, being
glad of anything to get my feet off the ground, I was so much
knocked up.   As for forage, my caballo was not entitled to forage,
or anything but what he could pick up for himself.   He would eat
acorns like a pig, and lie down by the camp fire like a Christian at
night.   'Yonder they come', is echoed by a hundred voices.   The
bugles sound, and the old word runs along, 'Fall in'.

The French now are seen in dense dark columns, crossing the
Tormes by the fords.   The train of artillery miles long, cavalry in
front and on the flanks—all move on quietly towards us for a
while, when they bring up their right shoulders and sweep along
the base of the Aripiles out of our sight, but right under the eye of
Wellington and his guns.   From this point he offers to deliver battle
to the French Marshal, but that crafty General will not accept the
challenge.   He had made an effort to get us into his net by a com-
bination of movements, but would not fight.   It is a great thing to
fight an important battle against such a General as Wellington, and
such troops as the British, and to win.   But Soult might have been
excused, if he thought twice before putting the life and fame of so
many thousands upon the event of a day, for here, on this very
ground, three months before, General Marmont was beaten, and his

army nearly destroyed. Wellington now courted a battle on the Aripiles, or on the Tormes. He opened a cannonade, did all he could to invite them on, but no go, they declined to quarrel.

My regiment was formed in quarter-distance column on the breast of the hill ready for action, all the French on the other side out of our sight. Anxious as we were to get a peep at those ugly customers, we could not see one of them. An aide-de-camp came riding down the hill now, and asked our Colonel if he had a mounted officer. 'Yes, I believe there is one.' 'Please send him up to the crest of the hill there, where the Duke is with his staff, and let him report himself to the Quartermaster-General.' 'Always in luck,' said a few of my comrades, as I jumped on my dirty white steed. 'Yes,' I said, 'but there is bad as well as good luck at one's heels everywhere.' 'Never mind, come down and tell us, if we are going to fight today, for it is getting late.'

When I got up and swept my eye over the plain below, what a grand spectacle! The massive dark columns of the whole French army standing at ease or with arms piled; dragoons alongside their horses, and the guns limbered up, our artillery pounding at them without provoking a return shot. I saw they were beginning to move, so asked for my orders at once. 'Go off,' he said, 'as fast as you can to Algiho, and order the baggage of the 2nd Division to push on to Ciudad Rodrigo.' 'I don't know the way, sir. How am I to find the place? Nor do I know the distance.' 'Right in that direction,' he said, pointing with his glass, 'and the first village you come to ask for a guide: now be off, quick.' I could now see that instead of a fight we were likely to continue our retreat; so I jogged on to the first village to get my guide. The town was empty and pillaged, inhabitants all gone, night was on me, I got bewildered, but rode on in the direction I was told as well as I could remember. As the dark clouds left the bright moon clear, I got a glimpse now and then of the skeletons of man and horse lying where they fell in the great battle of July, looking grim and ghastly.

How soon one loses his way if he shuts his eyes for a hundred yards! I ought not to have been here at all, the first hours of darkness put me all astray, and so I wandered on, not knowing where I was or where I was going, until I saw in the distance a corps of cavalry coming towards me. There was no cover on the plain where I could hide. My pony was white so I had no chance of escape; I could not evade the enemy. To France I must go a prisoner of war, and no mistake, if they thought me worth catching for the pony. As to my pockets, they were empty. I had not a dollar and was altogether nothing of a prize. I kept edging off on the flank, when I heard a loud English laugh. Oh, what a relief,

E

how cheering—a regiment of our own cavalry! 'Where are you going?' I said. 'Up to the army. Where are you bound for?' 'Can hardly tell; to look after baggage in some forest, perhaps ten leagues off. You'll find the army in retreat from the Aripiles—good night.'

I went on my lonely way until I fell in with a Portuguese regiment in bivouac, close to a large town. I asked the name. 'Salamanca, señor.' Prodigious, entirely out of my line of march. However, I thought I might be still in luck, for our kind and generous paymaster I knew was here, and having been to see him a week before, I remembered his quarters and made my way there in the middle of the night, made a thundering noise at his door with a big stone. He popped his nightcap out of the window in alarm, with 'que quiera vmd?' 'Oh, never mind talking Spanish to me, dear Señor Pagadore, let me in, for I'm half dead and my pony ditto.' Kind, amiable, good fellow, he came down directly, in amazement to find me so far away out of my place. I soon told him all. The pony was brought into the house and got some provender. 'And now,' he said, 'go off to the alcalde and get a guide for tomorrow, while I am getting your dinner, tea, and supper ready, for you look starved.' There was a great stir in the city, of course, and the chief office of police open all the night. I asked for a guide in the name of Wellington. The chief man present, an uncouth-looking savage, said 'Take that fellow beside you,' pointing to a pizaño in the dirty crowd. 'I don't know the way, señor.' 'Take him away,' he said, 'he's a ladrone, and knows the country well.' So I drew my sword, and walked him off to the paymaster's, and locked him up for the rest of the night. I had a most excellent feed, and had my haversack stored for the march next day. I lay down for three hours' sleep, my very kind friend keeping watch to have me up in time, and not letting me go without a few dollars in my pocket. I was away early with my guide, who was very loquacious and very hungry, as he said, and I believed him, but declined allowing him to go home just for ten minutes, to *comer* (to eat). I gave him a piece of bread and beef out of my wallet, and we became great friends until we arrived at the next village, when he gave me the slip. He doubled round a corner with an 'Adios, señor', and I saw no more of him!

I got another vagabond guide here, a piece of pork, four potatoes, and two loaves of bread, and took my journey onwards without the slightest knowledge of where I was going. It appeared that this fellow was taking me to his own native village, and when we got there he bolted off like a shot, and left me on the road. On foot I might have kept him beside me, but on horseback I had no chance. So it is between cavalry and infantry; vain and fruitless

to match the sabre with the musket, to send the charging horsemen
against the foot-soldier. I have seen the squadrons cheering on
loudly, and at full speed closing on the infantry squares, when they
were instantly scorched and scattered by the peal of musketry.
As the smoke cleared, the British bayonets glittered and the regiment came forth unscathed as from a furnace.

I rode on a few leagues farther in a mysterious jumble of
thought about responsibility, and the wild orders I had received.
I met a multitude of the peasantry, men, women and children, all
laden with their little household goods and traps, the matrons
marching erect with babies in little cork baskets balanced on their
heads. 'Where are you all going?' I said. 'O, señor, come back
with us to Salamanca. The French are behind us, our town pillaged, the English all killed, and you will be a prisoner.' Poor
people, I was sorry for them, but thought I would not give up my
wild-goose chase upon this report, and rode on. I soon met another
batch with the same tale, and turned back with them, being satisfied that I really was on very dangerous ground. As it happened
I met with my old regiment crossing my path, and joyfully did I
fall into my old place, after making a full report of my journey to
the good Colonel Fenwick. My haversack was soon lightened by a
few of my hungry comrades, but still I held on to the pork and
potatoes with a loaf of bread in reserve!

The whole British army was now in full retreat. The rains had
set in, the weather had become dreadful, and we were sorely pressed
by the enemy; all dreary and desolate, marching and fighting all
day, tired and hungry but not desponding. My regiment being in
its turn one day on the rear guard, we halted by the edge of an oak
wood to cook, and I rode over to a cottage a little way off very
wet. I asked the patrona, a poor old woman, to make up a good
fire, and give me a little pot to cook my dinner, which being done
con amore, I then pulled off my boots and socks, and put them to
the fire. 'And your coat, señor', said the good woman. I made
room for that too, put the piece of pork and the potatoes in the
one pot, and sat there in great luxury. Everything was going on as
nice as in a restaurant and getting so dry. My landlady was heap-
ing on sticks and the pot boiling, when she came bustling in, greatly
alarmed, with 'O, señor, los Franceses—los Franceses!' I heard a
distant shot and looked out. Sure enough, and to my horror, there
was a French cavalry corps feeling their way up to the wood, where
the smoke of our fires told them a tale. A few more stray shots;
I looked out. The bugle sounded; there were men falling in after
upsetting their half-cooked rations and shoving the beef part into
their haversacks; all hurry-scurry and long shots at the cavalry. I

got on my toggery, pretty well dried, and bolted out of the cabin just in time to fall in while my corps was forming square against those bold dragoons. They were very plucky, but great spoons to match themselves against a regiment of infantry without support. We emptied some of their saddles, when they retired to re-form, and wait for their advance-guard of foot-soldiers coming up. In the meantime we got into the wood and continued our course. I lamented all the day for the loss of my dinner, which I carried so far and left at last to be devoured by a Frenchman. How the men did swear at them! 'If the vagabonds had come on after dinner, sure they'd be welcome, but just as our pots were on the boil—O, bad luck to them, and may they niver see home!'

The enemy followed, and pressed us hard until night, when they bivouacked. We did the same, after a good start in advance. It rained hard, and the ground was in one great swamp. We had no baggage, it being all in front, as is usual in retreat. I got up into a cork tree, amongst the thick branches, and balanced myself there until we moved on, about four o'clock in the morning. This was a hard day upon the men, from the heavy rains. Many fell out, some sick, others disabled and footsore. Hundreds broke down, overcome by the great weight they had to carry, in addition to the wet clothes on the back—viz. a knapsack, heavy old flint firelock, sixty rounds of ball cartridge, haversack with sometimes three days' rations, wooden canteen, bayonet, greatcoat, and blanket—half-choked with a stiff leather girdle about the throat, and as many cross buff belts as would harness a donkey. It was wonderful how they moved along, and more surprising that they were not all left on the line of march. As it was, the French were picking them up in scores as they dotted the cheerless route.

We gained our bivouac at a late hour, made our fires, and pre-pared for supper—a hard biscuit and the remnant of a carrion ration of beef, no rum. We finished the little we had by the way. Our Commissary (Brook) came up now with the mules and stores, pitched his tent beside us, and looked so comfortable, that three of us cast lots as to who would go on a sort of forlorn hope and ask or beg of him to give us a ration of rum to keep in life till morning. I braced up all my courage, went forth, and demanded an audience. 'Hard times, Brook (no preface), three of us here beside you, famished. Will you give us a drop of rum?' 'And then,' he said, 'I will have the whole camp on the top of me, and my supply short already.' 'Honour bright,' I said, 'close as a pill-box.' He called one of his people and told him to fill my flask. My flask happened, luckily for me, to be my wooden canteen, which held about three pints, and the generous muleteer filled it up to the brim, and away

I went joyful. Little as this trifle may appear, it was more than gold could purchase, and raised our barometer amazingly. Our luck was not yet over, the moon came peering through clouds of rain, when a herd of innocent, friendly swine wandered in amongst the men. This was tempting beyond all endurance. Thousands of hungry soldiers by fires blazing bright, hundreds of well-fed pigs at the very point of the bayonet, the camp already yielding in anticipation a perfume of pork chops, who could let these wanderers of the dark forest pass away without further acquaintance? It would not be etiquette; but now, against all military discipline, a hundred shots were fired almost simultaneously. The mudlarks were knocked over right and left. The bivouac was all in alarm, the drums beat to arms, bugles sounded the assembly, the men groped their way to their alarm-posts, every one supposing that the enemy were upon us (barring the pig-shooters). The general officers kicked up a frightful dust about this unaccountable midnight row. Nobody did it, it was all the fault of intruders. However, before morning there was a savoury smell of roast pork about our fires, and no further inquiry. I found a small joint beside me, left there by the fairies, not over nicely dressed, the bristles like porcupine quills, but well fed.

The Duke made a great fuss about all this insubordination. But it is to be remembered that the line of march from Salamanca was through a flooded and flat clay country, that the troops, ankle-deep in mire, mid-leg in water, had lost their shoes; and with strained sinews had heavily made their way upon two rations only in five days, feeding on acorns, when Wellington supposed that the Commissaries were supplying the army with their usual rations.

The great Commander, in whom we had the firmest reliance, was unrivalled in skill, vigour, and genius, but could not see at once into the wants and necessities of 70,000 men. The pursuing enemy captured much of our stores and baggage, and our loss of seasoned British soldiers on this retreat, in killed and wounded. and prisoners, according to the returns, came up to 8,000 men. War tries the strength of military framework and hunger will not resist a porkchop fried on the top of a ramrod. 'The pigs,' men said, 'had no right poaching on our grounds, and we had a right to our ration of acorns.'

When we came to rivers, there was no halting or hesitation. The men walked in and over, as if on parade; when pretty deep, they linked together to break the stream. In fording the Duero, near Toro, we found it so deep and rapid, that the men slung their ammunition on the back of their necks to keep it dry. Our baggage being in advance, it made one wince to think of the chance of

the poor little donkeys crossing this gulf with all our treasure on
their back, and it was many a long day before we heard the fate of
our respective quadrupeds. Many were lost with their precious
load, and there was no compensation.

A multitude of soldiers' wives stuck to the army like bricks.
Averse to all military discipline, they impeded our progress at times
very much, particularly in this retreat. They became the subject
of a general order for their own special guidance. They were
under no control, and were first mounted up and away in advance,
blocking up narrow passages, and checking the advance of the army
with their donkeys, after repeated orders to follow in rear of their
respective corps, or their donkeys would be shot. 'I'd like to see
the man that wud shoot my donkey,' says Mrs. Biddy Flyn, 'faith
I'll be too early away for any of 'em to catch me. Will you come
wid me, girls?' 'Aye, indeed, every one of us,' and away they all
started at early dawn, cracking their jokes about division orders,
Wellington, commanding officers, and their next bivouac. Mrs.
Skiddy led the way on her celebrated donkey called the 'Queen of
Spain'. She was a squat little Irishwoman, and broad as a big
turtle. 'Dhrive on, girls, and we'll bate them to the end ov this
day, at any rate,' says Mother Skiddy. 'An' the morrow, too,' says
Mrs. Flyn. 'An' the day after,' cried Betty Wheel, and then a
chorus of laughter by the whole brigade (those three industrious
women will be remembered by any old 34th man still alive). Alas!
the Provost-Marshal was in advance—a man in authority, and a
terror to all evil-doers. In his department the Habeas Corpus Act
was suspended throughout the war, and he was waiting here in a
narrow turn of the road for the ladies with an advance guard, all
loaded. He gave orders to fire at once on the donkeys, killing and
wounding two or three, *pour exemple*. There was a wild, fierce,
and furious yell struck up at once, with more weeping and lamentation than one generally hears at an Irish funeral, with sundry
prayers for the vagabond that murdered the lives of these poor,
darling, innocent crathers! As we came up, the cries of distress
echoed in the hollow trunks of the old cork trees. It was 'Oh, bad
luck to his ugly face—the spy of our camp—may he nivver see
home till the vultures pick his eyes out, the born varmint,' and so
on. They gathered up what they could carry, and marched on
along with the troops, crying and lamenting their bitter fate, with
not a dry rag on their backs. It was wonderful what they endured; but, in spite of all this warning, Mother Skiddy was foremost
on the line of march next morning, as she said, 'We must risk something to be in before the men, to have the fire an' a dhrop of tay
ready for the poor crathers after their load an' their labour. An'

sure if I went in the rare, the French, bad luck to them, wud pick
me up, me an' my donkey, and then Dan would be lost entirely.'
She was a devoted soldier's wife, and a right good one, an excellent
forager, and never failed to have something for Dan when we were
all starving. Dan Skiddy was not much bigger than his wife—
short and stumpy, but with great bone and pluck, and of good character. I carried his firelock for him at times many a mile, when he
was ready to drop, as he said, with rheumatiz pains.

Our long and weary wet march of seventeen days came to an
end at last. During all the time I don't think I was perfectly dry
for twenty-four hours. Our Brigadier, General Wilson, an old man
with a grey head, who rode a blind horse, was always very plucky
in showing the men how to cross a stream. When they hesitated
on its brink, he would dismount, walk in with the greatest nonchal-
ance, and remount with his boots full of water. But this practice
did not agree with his years or constitution, 'and he died'. The
French did not get fat on our trail. Heaps of heavy baggage and
broken-down soldiers fell to their lot, but little to eat. Our good
paymaster, J——, offered a poor peasant one day a doubloon (sixteen dollars) for a loaf of bread. He said, 'Señor, I can't eat your
gold; I am starving myself' — so hard were we pressed at times for
food. But these little incidents in a campaign were soon forgotten,
and never entered into the columns of an English newspaper.

We got into the mountains bordering on Portugal, and the army
was soon distributed amongst the towns and villages in Estremadura, very celebrated for fever and ague. The little village of
Caza-don-Comez sufficed to give covering to my regiment; bad as it
was, we rejoiced at the change. I lodged with a very poor peasant
in a very humble dwelling. He herded goats all day on the hills,
was dressed in sheep-skins, and returned at night to the family meal,
which he always prepared himself. It never varied; a loaf of
brown bread sliced into a wooden bowl, some olive-oil poured over
it, then some hot water, and mixed up. He and his wife and
children sat round with their spoons and kept time till the dish was
cleared out. None of the party ever spoke a word until the evening meal was finished. In this humble way they lived and seemed
contented. In their simplicity and poverty there was a courteous
hospitality, such as never sitting down without asking me to partake of their supper. I had a little sort of a bed in a recess in the
kitchen, near the fire, where we all sat of an evening by the light
of some sticks, a very taciturn party. I was hardly domiciled here
when I was taken ill of a fever, accompanied by total prostration
of strength and physical power. I don't remember how long I lay
in the corner. The regimental surgeon came daily to see if I was

dead or alive. He had nothing to give me but a kind and encouraging word. Men died here by the score for want of care and medical comforts.

Poor Robert S—— and I were very great friends, but he had nothing but his carving tools, blue pill and salts, and his good name, which carried him through an honourable life with success. I met him accidentally long afterwards in India in a *choultry* by the wayside, and years after I returned from the Burmese war we were stationed in the same beautiful cantonment at Bangalore.

We got a little of our back pay on account at this time, and I was able to provide some tea, sugar, and bread for myself—all that I cared for. I got some of the goats' milk for my tea, which I considered a perfect luxury. The rough edge was wearing off the winter, brighter days shining through dark clouds. Change of quarters and returning health cheered me up a bit when I thought I was left here forlorn to die in a hovel, but I was never forsaken. There was a bright star above to guide and protect even the thoughtless and unworthy, and so far strength of frame and energy of mind had borne me scatheless and uninjured through scenes of fatigue, and danger, and blood, and death. I had been pining after home in my long illness, but as health came gradually rolling back, and rousing me up, I soon forgot the feeling.

I had sold my pony to pay for himself, and was again on my pins, a foot-soldier. There never was any objection to an officer keeping a horse and riding on the line of march, but he got no forage beyond the usual allowance—that is, two Subs were allowed forage for one baggage animal. When we came to a scrimmage on the line of march at any time, we quickly dismounted and sent our steeds to the rear. If they were killed in action we bore the loss, besides having a better chance of being killed also.

My regiment moved to another little village, just able to hold us all, and no more. So we had it all to ourselves and a pretty, cheerful little place it was. The people were poor, but very simple, honest, and kind in their way.

We got clear away from the Spanish army for a time. They were incapable of any dexterous movement. No master spirit was amongst them, and they continually worried our great chief with their apathy, intrigue, and dogged habits of indolence, faction, and violence. Their insolence and ferocity at Salamanca were infamous. One instance is well known: a horse, led by an English soldier, being frightened, backed against a Spanish officer, commanding at a gate. He caused the soldier to be dragged into his guard-house, and there destroyed him in cold blood with bayonet wounds! There was nothing for it but counter-violence.

Another Spanish officer wantonly stabbed at a rifleman, who shot him at once. A British volunteer slew a Spanish officer at the head of his own regiment in a sword fight, the troops of both nations looking on; but here there was nothing dishonourable.

Our kind, good, and amiable soldier chief, General Sir Rowland Hill, had a little pack of hounds sent out from England at this period to afford some field sport to his division. There was no lack of the sly fox; plenty of red-coats in the field, and good horsemen too. Crossing a plain one day in full chase, Reynard disappeared all at once. The foremost horseman had but just time to pull up at the edge of a rocky precipice, when they discovered poor Reynard and nine of the hounds below, all dead!

The General's headquarters were at Coria, about two leagues from us. He encouraged any amusement likely to afford pleasure to his officers, and now he patronised an amateur theatre, which was very well got up. We had amongst so many regiments capital actors, scene-painters, and really a first-rate company. The delicate-looking, pale-faced, slim Ensigns distinguished themselves in petticoats, and right well they played their parts. All we wanted was an audience! We had some very handsome Spanish señoras, who looked on and laughed through their bright eyes, but understood nothing. There was one fair and beautiful Englishwoman always present, joyous and happy, a charming representative of those bright stars of Albion, whose presence was always cheering amongst so many red-coats, the only lady at headquarters, wife of Colonel C——, Hill's first aide-de-camp, who afterwards fell at Waterloo.

After the play we all went in our stage dresses to the General's supper table, where we did enjoy ourselves to the full, a singular-looking group of painted actors and actresses. I can now see his good, honest, benevolent face shining with delight at the head of his table, enjoying the scene and the songs that went round until a late hour. He was the man who never could say an ill word to anyone; the Duke's favourite and most successful General. His sobriquet was 'Farmer Hill', while another was called Tiger C——, and so on. Every General, as well as regiment, had a nick-name. But there was a mutual confidence that could not be shaken between the parties, and they, one and all, had the firmest reliance on Wellington. He never came near us without a cheer from the men that made the woods ring. When he appeared, the men would say, 'There he comes with his long nose, boys; you may fix your flints'.

My Captain, Egerton, or, as the girls called him, 'Señor quatro-ojos', or four eyes, as he wore spectacles, was a fine specimen of a Cheshire gentleman and a brave soldier. He had gone on General

Hill's staff as chief aide-de-camp, and was always my friend, until he finished off his campaign, a general officer on his native ground.

1813. We were very busy with parades and drills and field-days, and some little horse racing in April. Large reinforcements of cavalry and infantry arrived from England, and the whole British army was being reorganised by the great chief for the coming struggle. Our ranks were filled up by officers and men, all 'Johnnie Newcomes' of course, but were soon drilled into a new form of discipline, which rather astonished some of their backs. They were men, chiefly volunteers from the Militia, who seemed to have had a leetle too much of their own way. But that was soon drilled out of them, and they were taught that the first duty of a soldier is 'to obey orders'. Amongst the officers, a nice-looking lad named Phillips, about seventeen, with June roses on his cheeks, stuck to me, and we ran in couples very happy during his brief campaign, which ended on the battlefield in less than four months. I grieved after this lad very much, so young, so brave, so full of life and joy.

Since we finished off the retreat from Burgos and Madrid there was great mortality amongst the troops, fever and ague prevailing. I caught both and suffered severely. There was no cure. All the charms the doctors got from the medical department at home was some rotten old bark intended to be mixed with some country wine, to dose the soldiers. Some fusty sawdust would have had the same effect! Lives were held cheap, but they cost money, nobody cared: 'things will last my time', and the national debt will probably last a while longer!

On the 1st of May Wellington mounted his gallant steed, took a last look across the hills, and saying, 'Farewell, Portugal!' headed his grand army to do or die in this campaign.

Three of us young fellows clubbed up a little mess. I was the best provided of the party with everything, as my baggage got safe over the retreat. I bought another donkey on the strength of all Subs being allowed forage for one animal. Our kind and generous paymaster made me a present of a very pretty Spanish jennet, and now I was all right and ready for the road, barring the ague, which left me prostrate every second day. The cold shivering fit first came on, nothing would warm me, then after a few hours the hot or burning fever fit succeeded, with a splitting headache that nearly drove me crazy. The next day I was quite well and fit for anything.

We now broke up from our cantonments, and the very first day was my ague day, and somehow doubly severe. I suffered dreadfully. Unable to keep my saddle, I tied my horse to a tree, lay down beside him until the last fit passed away, and then followed my corps to the camping ground. I was sometimes detained until long after dark, when my messmates were sure to have something for me along with the tea, always a stand-by and a luxury.

We commenced this campaign with tents for officers and men. The mules that formerly carried the camp kettles now carried the tents. The old large iron cooking-kettles were put *hors-de-combat*, and replaced by smaller tin kettles which were carried by the men in addition to their usual load. Captains had a mule allowed to carry a tent (and some company books, etc.) for himself and his Subs. I had the fortune, good or bad, to be once more in the company of 'Bloody Mick' of former days. He had the politeness to say at the start that I might occupy a corner of his tent at night. I knew very well I had as much right there as himself, but the invitation was not so hospitable as to induce me to sleep in the same house with my gallant Captain. I preferred the outside, and slept under a tree on the sod for two months, when I was transferred to the Light Company, one of the Subs thereof being taken prisoner in a scrimmage with the French. My Captain (Fancourt) was a first-rate fellow, a fine and gallant soldier, always generous, hospitable, and kind. I never left him afterwards. He was the best dressed man in the army, very fond of horses, and always well mounted. Joking one day with our Commissary Barlow, he said, 'I wish you would give me a little barley for my horse, I am very hard run over for a feed.' 'Do you see that sack-full there? It contains rations for three mules for ten days; if you will carry it to your quarters on your back you may have it—mind, no help.' Fancourt peeled off his red coat, made one great effort, got under the sack and carried it out of the store, through the town, to his quarters amidst hurrahs and 'Well done, old fellow, you have done the Commissary'. He dropped his burden at his stable door with a face as red as a peony with laughter and exertion! He would have shared his rations with his horse at any time if hard pressed. Commissary Barlow never made him a similar offer, although they were ever good friends.

The weather was very fine and very dry. It was rather agreeable sleeping under the trees at night although the dews were heavy. To keep dry I generally cut a bundle of fine branches to lie on, rolled myself in my blanket, put my saddle under my head, tied my bonny black jennet to a tree, gave him the length of his tether to feed, and went to sleep myself until the bugle sounded before dawn, when I had the night dew shaken out of my blanket, placed it as usual under my saddle and marched away. The men were generally cheerful and full of mirth for the first few leagues,

when they began to labour along in silence until they reached the
next lodging-ground to shake off their load for the night.

Wellington led on his brave army with confidence to a succession of victories. We crossed the Douro and the Ebro in our line
of march, the army divided into many columns, and were not long
in scenting out the enemy. I went on the Burgos road with General
Hill. His orders were, I believe, to fight there or take the fortress.
It cost us 2,000 the last visit, and here we fully expected another
slaughter, but King Joseph Bonaparte had not the master-spirit of
Soult, whom he disliked. As we advanced, he retreated from
Burgos. The castle had been prepared for destruction, and I was
not sorry at being awoke one night out of my tired slumbers on the
green sod by an awful explosion, like an earthquake. I drew myself up, half-asleep, into a sitting posture and said, 'Thank God!
there goes Burgos,' and lay down again to finish my slumbers. But
with the castle 300 souls were blown into eternity! At the moment
I cared little for that; such is war! From hurry or neglect, the mine
exploded before its time, several streets were laid in ruins, thousands of shells ignited and exploded and rolled about with destructive power. And so this great impediment in our way was finally
removed, just as we could have wished, except the terrible death
of 300 of our enemies. In war, nothing so bad as failure or defeat,
and this must have damped the King's courage a bit. His brother,
the great Napoleon, they say, used to tell him that if he would
command, he must give himself up entirely to business, labouring
day and night: just the thing he never was cut out for, as will be
found recorded in his history. Indeed, his cognomen was 'Roi de
Bouteille'. He had a fine command, a great and brilliant army, an
obedient army; but that soul of armies, the mind of a great commander, was wanting. It was all on our side, in Wellington's
knowledge-box! and nothing now retarded his progress. With an
eagle's sweep he poured his columns through all the deep narrow
valleys and rugged defiles, gullies, ravines, and passes, amongst the
rocks. Nothing even retarded the march of the artillery : where
horses could not go nor draw, the soldiers did their work; and when
the wheels could not roll, guns were let down or lifted up with
ropes. Bravely did our rough veteran infantry work their way for
six days, with unceasing toil, through those wild and beautiful
regions.

Our army, swelling in numbers, came rushing in from hill and
vale and valley, like roaring streams from every defile, foaming
into the basin of Vittoria. When the King was conjecturing about
the quickest way to put the English army *hors-de-combat*, and at
what hour he might consistently partake of the banquet he had

ordered in Vittoria, Wellington was making his arrangements to cook him before sunset. The 20th of June was my ague day. I was wearied and worn with this horrid complaint persecuting me every second day for the last two months, but I was not singular. However, I stuck to my trade and resisted being left in hospital at any of the depôts formed in our rear—perfectly well today, tomorrow in torture, dejected and cast down. I lay under a tree, seeing my comrades pass away over the plain. Night came on, I rose like one from the dead and followed in their wake. My chums had some tea ready for me, with something in the frying-pan, when I got into camp.

We knew little or nothing of what was to come off the following day, except from our men, who were fixing their flints, chaffing and talking of the 'frog eaters' who could not be far off. They said they nosed them from their backie and inions! I declined the tent accommodation, and slept soundly on the sod. We were all under arms right early in the morning, the rolls were called, all present, and nobody afraid! It was a bright, warm, and beautiful day—the longest day—and a long day's work was before us, before the sun was to set on so many of the brave. We had scarcely advanced a league across the plain when we heard the riflemen on our left beginning the work of the morning; cheers through the ranks, many jokes and quaint sayings. There was great hilarity, buoyant spirit and cheerfulness, a determined resolve to fight to the front, and never say die. When the British soldier is let loose in the field with all his steam up, the difficulty is to keep him in check, to stop his onward rapidity. When he sees the enemy in his front, he fights for his Queen, fights for Old England, fights for victory, and always wins. The British soldier is a queer sort of biped, fierce in battle, full of a child's simplicity and kindness when over. He will tear the shirt off his back to bind up the bleeding wounds of his fallen foe, carry him away on his back to some quiet spot for medical care, lay him gently down, and divide with him the contents of his flask.

CHAPTER 6

Vittoria

TWENTY soldiers may give a descriptive account of a battle, all different, yet all correct. It is impossible for one man to see the entire of a battlefield ten or fifteen miles in extent, even on the swiftest horse. One intelligent, active mind can gather in a great deal from personal observation, and collect from other sources much information and truth, and unless a truthful narrative is recorded in a journal like this, it is not worth the printer's ink. There was no man of our day could give a more thrilling descriptive account of a battlefield than the brave and gallant veteran Sir W. Napier.

The river Zadora ran through the whole line of the battleground for many miles, and was spanned by seven bridges. It was about ten o'clock before we (2nd Division) got into action. General Hill had 20,000 men, and moved them on the left of the French position, when we began with a sharp skirmish, and renewed the old quarrel. We soon began to warm to the old work, and matters looked serious. We won a hill on which the enemy were strongly posted, but at a severe loss. The Hon. Colonel Cadogan, commanding the 71st Regiment, was killed here, with many other valuable officers. We were gaining ground along the side of the mountain, when we met with a biting fire, and the battle here remained stationary for some time, until our General sent us more aid. Then, passing the Zadora, we won the village of Subijana-de-Alava, in front of General Gazan, and maintained our ground in spite of all opposition. There was a good deal of fighting in the churchyard, and some open graves were soon filled up with double numbers; indeed, churches and churchyards were always a favourable resort for this peculiar amusement. They were places of strength, and contended for accordingly; and here our battle raged with more violence and contention. We had possession — nine-tenths of the law in battle — but, hardly pressed front and flank, I thought we had killed more of our French neighbours here than was needful; but as they cared little for life in their excitement, they would be killed. As Colonel Brown said, 'If you don't kill them, boys, they'll kill you; fire away.'

There were three great battles going on. The curling smoke in the far away distance and booming of guns showed that our comrades were deeply engaged with all the destructive power at their disposal. Our wretched old flint firelocks would not burn powder at times until the soldier took from the pocket in his pouch a triangle screw, to knock life into his old flint, and then clear the touch-hole with a long brass picker that hung from his belt. Many a fellow was killed while performing this operation. But the French had no better fighting tools than ourselves, so in this respect we were not unequally matched. However, the red-coats got impatient and excited to be at them with the bayonet, and when the word was delivered 'Prepare to charge', the very hills echoed back the mighty cheer of thousands with an overwhelming terror, for the charge was irresistible.

Upon all favourable occasions our men were let loose in this way to complete a victory. Our opponents never liked the steel, it was so indigestible, and at this part of the play the *En avant* was never heard, but rather *Sauve qui peut*.

It was now about one o'clock. The whole line of the battlefield was in a blaze — guns, mortars, cavalry, and infantry displaying double exertion and courage to win the day. Seventy thousand brave men, not fearing death nor danger, on each side were contending for a kingdom that must be lost or won this day. Yes, this 21st day of June 1813 must decide the fate of Spain.

'Morillo's' Spaniards displayed unusual courage, and fought well, himself wounded. But 'Longa' would not move his troops when they were required at a very critical moment, just like the old mule. Our troops plunged into the village of Arinez amidst a heavy fire of musketry and artillery. This was an important post. Fresh French troops came pouring down to the bloody work. The smoke, dust, and clamour, the flashing of firearms, the shouts and cries of the combatants, mixed with the thundering of the guns, were terrible. The continuous cries of the wounded for water were piteous, while

the horses, distracted and torn with cannon-shot, were hobbling
about in painful torture, some with broken legs, and others dragging
their entrails after them in mad career.   It was indeed a sickening
sight I never wished to see again, but my heart and eyes were since
in time to be tortured with more dreadful scenes.   As we gained
this village and advanced, many guns were captured.   It was a
country of high corn, vineyards, wood and plain, ditches, villages,
hamlets, and the river winding right away down to the Ebro.   We
had now fought over about six miles of country, yet the French
were not quelled nor beaten.   General Reille maintained his post
on their last high ground, and made his muskets flash like lightning,
while fourscore pieces of artillery, nearly all fired together, made
a furious uproar that shook the earth, and ground our men to pulp
before they had time to make the dash.   Amidst the fire and smoke,
the dark figures of the French artillery were seen bounding about,
and serving their guns with frantic energy.   This terrible cannonade and fire of small-arms checked our troops until the 4th Division
came up; they needed no introduction to General Reille.   With
one long loud cheer, an electric shock to Frenchmen's nerves, this
important position was won at a rush.

In other places the battle was waged with fury and great energy
on both sides.   The day was not yet won; it was the longest, and
in every respect the most bloody day that many of us had ever seen,
but I had little time to think about it.

A Spanish pisaño told Lord Wellington that one of the bridges
was undefended, and offered to lead any troops to it.   A brigade
was immediately sent forward, and while passing over it at the
double, the poor fellow at their head was killed by a cannon-shot.

About six o'clock the whole of the French army was beaten
back to their last defence, about a mile from Vittoria.   Behind
them was the plain, and beyond the city.   Thousands of non-
combatants, carriages, men, women, and children belonging to the
host of the great army, were crowded together in wild terror.   Our
cannon-shot went booming over their heads, which threw them into
a convulsive movement of distress.   They swarmed together,
swerved, looked about for safety; but there was no hope now for
the multitude or the army.   They lost the day.   It was now the
wreck of a nation—of a great army in all its power and pride and
glory, led by a King and the most efficient and accomplished
Generals of an Emperor.   Twelve hours ago the balance of military
power on the plains of 'Old Castile' was about equal; but there was
a confiding reliance throughout our ranks in the skill of our great
chief that never was shaken, and defeat was never named.   Yet we
did, if truth must be told, get rather a severe kick in one month

after this by these very well-beaten Frenchmen, or by some of their relations or friends.

The British army closely pursued the flying and shattered columns of the French, now broken and dispersed, until night stopped the chase. Never was there a more complete victory, and, as General Gazan said, 'They lost all their equipages, all their guns, all their treasure, all their stores, all their papers—so that no man could prove how much pay was due to him.'

Generals and subordinate officers were reduced to the clothes on their backs, and most of them barefooted. The trophies were very numerous. Marshal Jourdan's bâton, a stand of colours, 140 brass cannon, all their stores, carriages, and ammunition, their treasure, and prisoners too many to enable us to pay attention to their wants and safety. They lost 6,000 men. Our loss was nearly equal, 5,176; of these, according to returns, 1,049 were Portuguese, and 553 were Spaniards, our loss being more than double that of our two friendly powers. In fact, the red-coats were always expected to do the real fighting business. British troops are the soldiers of the battle.

The spoil was very great; it may be said that the fighting men were marching and fighting upon gold and silver, without helping themselves. Five million dollars, abandoned by the French and left upon the ground, were picked up by non-combatants and camp followers. There were little barrels of doubloons and Napoleons in gold, for the picking up, but rather heavy to put into one's haversack. The chase was so swift, and the men so excited, that but a few just stumbled over this treasure, nor would any man be permitted to stop a moment if observed, yet a great many did fill their pockets and haversacks, and holsters with loose treasure just *en passant*, and kept on blazing away like fun. Not a dollar ever came to our treasury as prize money, which the Duke complained of; but, as for this, it was no great loss to us Subs, for we were always cheated of all but one-tenth of our share, and received that six years after the Peninsular war, and fourteen years after the first Burmese war. However, I only speak for myself. I know the time, and place, and amount I received, and the sum total did not come up to £20! My losses were more than five times as much.

But to continue our pursuit: the wreck of the army was in full retreat, their contest ended. The allies being now advancing on every point caused their confusion to increase, the guns were abandoned, the drivers rode off the horses at speed, the soldiers pressed wildly through a road half choked-up with the unfortunate refugees from the capital, and the vast number of vehicles which moved

F

along with them in their flight. A scene of the most frightful disorder ensued. The sun now began to sink below the western hills, and the last rays of golden light fell upon a spectacle not easily described. Red columns of infantry were advancing steadily over the plain. The horse artillery were galloping to the front to open a fresh fire into the fugitives, the cavalry charging along the Camino Real; while the 2nd (Hill's) Division, which, overcoming every obstacle, had driven the enemy from its front, was extending along the heights and lower ground, on the right of the British army, its arms flashing brightly in the fading sunshine of this ever-memorable day. (Our arms now are brown: in former days they were bright and glittering in the sun or moonlight march.)

Never was a victory so complete, nor an army so very well thrashed and disorganised as this great French host. The bright and warm sun of a June morning rose on three united grand corps, all speaking the same language, perfect in every arm, admirably combined, and placed in a position of battle well selected and defended with batteries and breastworks, a river in their front, and all the chances of war in their favour. Night closed upon a pitiful and helpless, broken-down, dislocated, and shattered rabble, hurrying away from the fatal field of their defeat. The day was ours, but one could not help feeling deeply for the helpless multitude when our cannon-shot plunged amongst such a crowd of humanity trying to escape. 'Like the Scottish monarch at Flodden (just three hundred years ago, 1513), King Joseph remained to witness the ruin which his rashness wrought, but not to expiate his folly with his life.' He effected his not very glorious retreat with difficulty. Our dragoons overtook and fired at his carriage, out of which he escaped by jumping, mounting a horse, and riding, harder than ever John Gilpin did, for life and liberty, guarded by a strong escort. He made Pampeluna that night without the value of a horn spoon of all his treasure.

I happened to be marching along in his track, and came upon his carriage upset in a ditch, and also seven waggons loaded with his personal baggage jammed up in a heap: the mules all gone; soldiers excitingly engaged, their muzzles black with powder from biting the cartridges, and perspiring like hunters, all busily employed stripping the carriage even of its lining in search of something portable in the shape of the image and superscription of Napoleon. I never saw such handy fellows. So expert were they that the whole contents were laid before the public in about fifteen minutes for selection, or, as a Paddy of a Grenadier said, 'Come, boys, help yourselves wid anything yes like best, free gratis for nothing at all! The King soon made his will and left all you see behind him for our day's throuble. He's away to France, an' the de—l's luck to him! Who'll have a dhrink o' wine?' And so they cracked their jokes at the expense of His Majesty. Another party were actively engaged unloading the waggons, pitching into the whole contents—trunks, boxes, great bundles of papers, letters private and confidential, charts, pictures of great value, which had been cut out of their frames, best French wines, brandy, beds and bedding, portable furniture, a whole library of books, everything in the cuisine department, camp equipage, and lots of grog corked and ready for this fatigue party; with skins of Spanish wine, and a multiplication of other things which had belonged to this robber king, too tedious to be inserted in this bill of fare! I picked up hastily a big sack, a cold fowl, a few maps, and a flask of wine, the sum total of all the plunder I touched that day, and rode on.

Wellington went back to Vittoria about nine o'clock, still daylight, where all was panic and confusion. Every door was closed, every lattice darkened, the streets funereal and deserted, where two nights before all was brilliant and gay. The game took an unlucky turn for all Spaniards of the French party, many of whom went off with the retreating robbers. The loyalists now began to crow, and received Wellington with welcome cheers. During the progress of the battle, over three leagues of difficult country, the long summer's day was spent in an unremitting succession of laborious exertions to attain this great end. It was not generally a night of repose. There was a grand general auction in the camp of every brigade. The great variety of articles for sale was far beyond anything ever heard of, and if one was to attempt to enumerate them, would be beyond belief. How they were picked up so quickly by fighting men, who kept their fighting place, would astonish the reader. But when an army finds itself beaten and receives the word *sauve qui peut*, away they go, d—l take the hindmost, and as 'light marching order' is the swiftest retreat, they cast away everything as they run, arms, ammunition, firelocks, knapsack, and accumulation of plunder, which our men picked up in their advance. When they stumbled over a cask of dollars, in went the head with a punch from the butt-end of a firelock; the cask then rolled over, an inviting spread, and everyone helped himself and pushed on.

At this great night fair dollars were sold eight or nine for a guinea, or a Napoleon—too heavy to carry! In Spain the British army were paid in old English guineas and dollars. The 21st was my good day. I had no ague, but felt tired and excited after such a fight and a chase, for my horse was in the rear until the grand retreat began. It being now late, we halted for the night. I rode into a field of corn, so very high I could not be observed. Here I dismounted, sat down and ate my supper, provided by the cook of His Majesty or some of his people! I tied my gentle little horse to my leg, gave him a long tether, lay down upon my sack and fell asleep, *tout de suite*. Now and then 'Sancho' would get too far nibbling at the corn and give me chuck. I pulled him in by the rope close to my bed, and soon fell over again in dreams of peace and home. I was very early astir, and found my companion, *cheval noir*, lying beside me. He was a great pet and a handsome fellow. Saddled, mounted, and away to look for my regiment which was scattered about without any regularity in bivouac. But Freeman's bugle, so well known to every 34th man, soon brought us all together—no, not all, the prison of many a soul was broken up.

My servants were generally in great luck, having their legs and arms broken by musket-shot, and none of them killed outright except Tim Casey, and he was only *kilt*. But he made a most horrible whilalaloo about it, crying out, 'Oh, *murdher*, I'm kilt entirely. I'll never see home—I'm ript up!' holding his bloody hand to his stomach. 'Let me see where you're kilt, Casey. There is no murdher here, everybody kills everybody—that's the order.' A ball struck one of his buttons, turned off, and ripped open the surface of his bread-basket from right to left without in the least spoiling his appetite.

Andrew Orrell, one of my chums, was playing 'hide-and-seek' with a French voltigeur amongst the trees. I told him he would get a lump of lead that would stop his rations if he exposed his long legs to this rifleman any longer (he was all legs and a long Lancashire tongue), and very soon was he hit something like poor Casey. The ball broke a trousers' button, turned off its course, which was intended for the 'bull's-eye', went through his flank, and lodged at the backbone. I took out my penknife to cut it out, but he made such an oration, I knocked off surgery, and went to my own business. He was carried away, and came back all right in three months.

Lieutenant Ball had a narrow escape. A ball meant to go right through his head, was turned by the scale of brass on his cap, opened a furrow across his forehead, baring the bone and passing away on the other side. Poor A. B. C. (Allen Bellingham Cairns) was wounded, not badly; yet he died afterwards. I got his watch and key—the latter as a remembrance—no reminder like a watch-key. I have used it ever since, upwards of fifty years, and it is as good as new still and, I may say, it has ever since been a nightly remembrance of my old comrade.

It was wonderful the multitude of extraordinary wounds that men received. I felt a curiosity in their examination, attending with the surgeons at times (it was the profession that I was first intended for, so many of my name being eminent men in Scotland). Wounds in the feet and in the groin were the most painful and dangerous. Lieutenant G—— had both his eyes shot out. Lieutenant C—— narrowly escaped the same dreadful calamity; the ball passed close under the eyes, breaking the bridge of his nose, and spoiling his beauty. I have seen men wounded in every part of the human frame—some wounds most extraordinary and severe—and yet the men recovered. I should hardly get credit for the relation, if I enumerated them here.

The morning of the 22nd of June displayed the extent of the spoil which the runaway Frenchmen left behind them. There was a scene rarely to be equalled, for many leagues about Vittoria—the wreck of a mighty army, and plunder accumulated for years, torn with rapacious and unsparing hands from almost every province in Spain.

Waggons, and cannon, and caissons, tumbrils and carriages of all descriptions, upset and deserted, a stranger *mélange* could not be presented to the eye. Here the personal baggage of a king—there the scenery and decorations of a theatre—war stores and china ornaments, all sorts of arms, drums, trumpets, silks, jewellery, plate, and embroidery mingled in strange disorder. Here were wounded soldiers, deserted women and children of all ages imploring aid and assistance and seeking protection from the British—here a lady upset in her carriage—in the next an actress or a *femme de chambre*; sheep, goats, and droves of oxen roaming and bellowing about, with loose horses, cows, and donkeys—everything in lamentable confusion.

Camp followers were dressed up in the state uniforms of the King Joseph's court; the rough class of women-kind, drunk with champagne and Burgundy, and attired in silks and Paris dresses – once envied, perhaps, in a palace. The pride of France was, indeed, levelled with the dust after this signal defeat.

The greatest part of the enormous baggage and plunder was grabbed by the people who had the best right to it, viz. the Spanish peasantry following up our army. The sword of the King was secured, and a marshal's bâton was sent by Lord Wellington to the Prince Regent, who returned the compliment by sending him a bâton of a marshal of England. Oceans of women—wives, actresses, and nuns—were captured, but no padres that I heard of. All of them were treated with respect, and allowed to follow their husbands and sweethearts as they found opportunity.

A week or ten days were wholly occupied collecting the wounded and burying the dead, in a fashion, just as they fell. Men were found alive on the wild field the ninth day, where they dropped in obscure places. Having crawled to some waterpool they existed, but they were few. Carts were in constant motion carrying away from the hospitals dead men and amputated limbs—a scene of anguish to look on—the pale, shattered, desolate, bloodstained, helpless forms of soldiers, so very lately in fine health, marching along for six weeks in joyful glee to meet a sudden death and no grave. Our saw-bones were not prepared for so much practice coming on them all of a heap, and hundreds died for want of medical care and hospital comforts. No fault due to our medicals; they worked away day and night at their trade like good ones.

When the battle began, my old friend Dr. Maurice Quill was in his proper place in the rear of his regiment. He deposited his carving tools under a tree in charge of his hospital sergeant, and crept along in rear of the troops until he saw the men begin to fall, when he ran away back as hard as he could tear to bring up his mule and the apparatus. Doctors wore at this time cocked hats and feathers, and were not easily distinguished at a little distance from the general staff. As he went at speed on one side of a hedge, a general officer with his aide-de-camp came galloping up the opposite way. The General cried out, 'There's an officer running away, stop him. Halloo! sir, where are you going to?' No answer. Both wheeled about their horses, and called loudly to stop. 'Stop, sir!' cried the General, 'and give an account of yourself and your name.'

'No, no,' said Quill. 'I'm off; seen enough fighting for one day,' and ran on. The General got furious. A court-martial at least crossed his mind as he pushed on after the fugitive, the stiff fence between them.

'Give your name, sir!' 'Oh, never mind my ugly name, everybody knows me. Your life's not worth a dollar this blessed day. Go to the front and be killed if you like—everybody's being killed but myself—oh, such slaughter!' speaking all this time over his shoulder and running like blazes. On he went at full speed, pursued by his enemies till he came up to what he called his tool-box (the hospital panniers), told his hospital sergeant to load the mule and move up quickly to the front, while he got out a few things for immediate use, and then right about face and away back as hard as he could tear.

'Oh, I see it all now!' said the aide-de-camp, "tis that wild fellow Maurice Quill—always up to some drollery in camp or quarters'; and with a hearty laugh they galloped away.

At early dawn on the 22nd, our bugles sounded the assembly. Men and officers might be seen emerging from ripe wheat-fields nearly as high as one's head, and from behind hedges and ditches and trees, until all the living got under arms to pursue the retreating enemy. About mid-day, as we were marching over the hills, there commenced a fearful thunderstorm. I was riding alongside of my friend Masterman (who gave me the two dollars at Estramos when I was so hard up on my way to Lisbon). Poor fellow! he was struck dead in a second of time by the lightning—his horse was also killed, the hair of his head was scorched, his watch-chain cut in two, and the little steel screws inside were extracted. The full force of the forked thunderbolt passed right through him. I was so electrified that I lost all power of holding my horse, which ran away with me downhill in fright. My knees shook and trembled, my hands were useless. I lost all power of holding or guiding my little jennet, although I managed to keep the saddle, and gradually recovered. The glittering arms of so many men, no doubt, was a great conductor for the lightning—several were knocked down, but none killed. The regiment halted for a melancholy hour, the pioneers dug a grave under a big olive-tree. Poor dear Masterman was rolled up in his blanket, and left behind! Awfully sudden: on this summer's morning to lose his hold of life, and pass away!

Alas! poor Masterman, so kind, so gentle—such a favourite with all of us; mourned for and deeply regretted; escaped from the battle of yesterday, today snatched off in a moment. But in those days nothing more sure than 'battle, murder, and sudden death'.

We followed after the runaways, leaving the great fortress of Pampeluna blockaded by the Spaniards. It was the key of the kingdom. It had a garrison of 3,000 men and an able commander, but was not victualled for a very long siege. When the French got well into the hill country, they gathered up some pluck, rallied, and contested every mile of ground. By this time they had lost all their guns, 150 brass cannon. We had many sharp affairs with them, so very unwilling were they to leave Spain. But we never let them out of sight until we drove them right over the Pyrenees. They robbed and plundered everywhere *en route* to make up their losses; but murder and even worse crimes were combined with plunder. Our own men were very expert at times, just looking into houses along the way for a *parlez-vous* or a loaf of bread. On one occasion, opening a press, the poor man of the house fell over on the top of a big grenadier, quite dead. Perhaps he had taken refuge in the press from the marauders, who, as they looked in, found the poor fellow hid there, and ran a bayonet through him.

Women and young girls were found on their own hearth-stone, outraged and dead. Houses were fired and furniture used for hasty cooking, as our army passed along. Such is war! We had the last brush with these vagabonds on 30th June, i.e. on the Spanish side of the Pyrenees, while skirmishing in the wood up the hills, General Sir William Stewart, a brave and gallant officer, who had been wounded in the leg at Vittoria, was at our head, with a pillow between his leg and the saddle. He was here wounded again, for there was no keeping him out of fire—just like Picton, that old hero, always foremost in the fight—and so he now passed us, going reluctantly to the rear, held on his horse by two soldiers. 'Sorry to see you wounded again, Sir William,' we said. 'Never mind—never mind me, gentlemen. Take the hill—take the hill,' was his reply. He had a lisp, and spoke quick. I can see him now, distinctly the bravest of the brave, cool and collected. He was always cheered by the men when at any time riding through the camp. We took the hill, of course. In doing so, Brigadier Sir William Pringle was badly wounded, shot right through the body, but he ultimately recovered. Our Major (Worsley) tumbled over. Some wag cried out, 'There goes a step in the regiment'; but he was out in his reckoning, for the gallant Major was on his legs *tout de suite*. His horse was shot in the head and dropped like a stone; a bullet ruffled one of his epaulets, but left him all right for another day.

One of our sergeants, a fine young fellow, said 'We must not leave the Major's saddle and bridle behind, I would rather carry it on my back.' While stopping to unloose the girths, a French rifle-bullet hit him in the mouth, and took away his lower set of teeth quite handy. No dentist could have done it in half the time. It was an ugly wound, and deprived him of all acquaintance with hard biscuit for many a long day. I do not know what forty or fifty thousand of our men were doing at other points on our left. They may give an account of themselves, or some clever cove may do it for them. I must stick to my own people, General Hill and his division and endeavour to immortalise myself by writing a book. There are, I believe, different ways of leaving a name in remembrance, and I honestly confess that I have no talent for book-making, and am one of the least qualified for such an attempt. I am therefore ready to be 'kicked, cuffed, and disrespected' by the press and by the public for such presumption.

At sundown, on the last day of June, we fired our last shots into the skirts of the *Parley Vous*, as we slashed them over the hills into their own country, while they carried along with them the curse of a whole kingdom!

We went down and encamped in the beautiful valley of Bastan
to have some rest after our two months' frolic across the country.
The men wanted washing, and shaving, and patching, and darning,
scrubbing up, and a bit of polish for the next fight.   I continued
to sleep under a tree; my bed was the royal sack filled with ferns,
dried grass, chopped straw, or anything soft that came to hand.
In my good days I rode about the country, into the town of Alizondo, and made my acquaintance with the mountain passes, hamlets, and houses of the Basques—a quiet, primitive, honest people,
like the Swiss, fond of their native hills, and speaking a language
distinct from Spanish or French.   They were very active and intelligent, detesting their French neighbours, who plundered them as
they did everyone else.   They wore wooden shoes, and a facsimile
Kilmarnock bonnet.

Three of us chummed together.   Having a horse, I was considered the grand forager for the mess.   I sometimes got a loaf of
bread for a dollar, some milk and honey.   The chestnuts were
large and ripe, they flourished on great shady trees above head.
My horse ate them raw; we preferred them roasted or boiled; they
filled up chinks, and were a good stand-by, better than the acorns
in bivouac at Salamanca.   The Basque lingo was most difficult to
get hold of.   The only word I could retain in memory was 'housequack', i.e. the bellows, which I often borrowed to blow up our
fire under the chestnut tree.   I drilled our servants to be very civil
to these people; they would lend us anything they had.   'Well,
Tom, what did you say to the lady of the house?'   'O, sir, I just
seyd, plase mam, yill you lend us the housequack, an' she handed
it out at onst; but I forgot the name av the fryin'-pan, ours is goin'
in holes, an' beint of any much use.'   In fact, Tom was always
brushing the bottom of this old frying-pan with a sprinkling of
water to burnish our shoes, which had a wonderful effect on leather,
and was a tolerable substitute for Day and Martin.

A chaplain was now in reality sent out from England, and
attached to Farmer Hill's division.   My regiment was here alone,
and his reverence came to perform Divine Service; twenty minutes
was the regulation time.   A square was formed, the big drum
placed in the centre to do the duty of a reading-desk   The parson
entered, made for the drum at once, got one leg up, when the big
drummer made a rush, caught him by the tail, and pulled him
nearly over, saying, 'You'll be through it, sir; the only parchment in
camp.'   The poor padre thought, he said, it was to elevate him in
reading the service.   No one, of course, could keep his gravity
during this scene.   I remember the text very well—in St. Luke iii.
14.   There went a buzz through the ranks.   The men knew very

well they were six months' pay in arrears, and their daily bread
was killing and slaying their neighbours!

The 7th of July was one of my very worst ague days, but turned
out afterwards a day of rejoicing, thanks to our enemies. I was
lying under an apple-tree in the beautiful valley, *hors-de-combat*, in
a hot fit, my head splitting open, as I thought, with pain. The day
was extremely hot, which only aggravated the malady, and increased my sufferings. All of a sudden the drums beat to arms, the
bugles sounded the assembly, and the men hastened to the alarm-
post, and the order of march was—up the mountain as fast as we
could go. I joined my company, and dragged myself along with
difficulty, faint and weary with pain and debility. There was in
those days a chivalry, an *esprit de corps* amongst officers and men
never to be absent if possible when there was a chance of a brush
with the enemy. It was a point of honour not to be detained by
any trifling illness, and so I stuck to my trade as usual. When we
got up to the tableland, we met the French advanced skirmishers,
and renewed our acquaintance in a very unfriendly way, by knocking over a few of their riflemen. The compliment being returned,
both sides went to work, and the matter was who would live
longest under a shower of lead. Their supports came rapidly up,
swelling their ranks, while our brigade, 28th, 34th, and 39th de-
creased in numbers. We fired kneeling, to take down all the birds
we could. Still, so overmatched were we, that the combat became
extremely doubtful. Plenty of help was coming to us, but never
came. A whole division of ours was lost in a fog, crawling uphill
in another direction to take the enemy in flank. Wellington and his
staff came up, but the fire was so brisk and the heather about their
horses' heels so torn up with musket-balls, he said, 'This won't do,
we must get away. These regiments will be sacrificed.' The fog
saved us. It came on so thick we were all soon rolled up in a cloud
of darkness. The fire continued at random, the French still grop-
ing their way. We heard them distinctly talking and getting nearer
and nearer. Being formed in line, both ranks kneeling, we gave
one loud cheer and a volley, which took the shine out of them for
half an hour, when they commenced another fire at a greater distance, all their shot passing over our heads. This waste of powder
and ball lasted till eleven o'clock, but we never arose from the sod
until daylight next morning. The fog then cleared away, and we
saw the strength of our opponents far below, going home to breakfast!

When the fog rose in the morning under a bright sun, we discovered the extent of our loss. Lieutenant Ball, who was hit on the
head at Vittoria, was here badly wounded. Some fellows were

always being hit, while others—a few others—went through all the war without a scrape. The wounded were groaning on the heather all night, and not a drop of water within our reach. They always suffer extremely from thirst, and their cry is, 'Water for God's sake!' I remember drinking more water on an occasion of this kind than I had done for a month previous. My servant followed me yesterday to the fight, seeing I was rather shaky at the start, and got his arm broken by a musket-ball; my two left-hand men had their legs broken. We had many wounded; the dead were left where they fell, and being myself first for escort duty, I got charge of all wounded in the brigade to take them to the hospital at Alizondo. The only conveyance for these poor cripples with broken legs and arms and shattered shells, were some mules sent up by the Commissary. Two men were placed on each mule, with their broken limbs bandaged up in a way and dangling down. No help for it; no cart-roads in the Pyrenees, and the poor fellows were groaning with their sufferings all the way. When night came on I got my cavalcade under cover of an old cattle-shed I happened to spy out a little out of my way. The assistant-surgeon got them dismounted as quietly as possible, and laid some upon dry ferns. We had nothing to eat or drink; not a spoonful of water for the dying men. I could not sleep for their moaning and groaning all night. I could not see them nor help them in the dark. When the morning was welcomed in, I found that many had passed away to the promised land; the mortal part was left where the spirit took its leave. We had no means here to bury the dead. We got to Alizondo on the second day of torture and suffering, and glad I was when I delivered over my charge to the chief saw-bones and was allowed to depart for my home, which I always considered to be under the colours of my gallant corps.

On the 7th I was roused up in a fit of ague. I went into fire unexpectedly; in the excitement I forgot everything. I lay out under a cold damp fog all night; the ague took flight and never returned during the war! Some fellows said that it was frightened out of me! Maybe so. I wish it had been frightened out of me sooner. I have had some severe shocks of it afterwards in the East and West Indies, and other climates, but I know how to treat it without any medical advice—quinine!

I found my old corps with the flags flying on a tableland half-way up the Pyrenees, and they were here 8,000 feet high.

CHAPTER 7

Crossing the Pyrenees

GENERAL HILL settled his headquarters in Alizondo. I was invited to dine with him by my old Captain Egerton, his chief aide-de-camp. A great day for G. B.! I had a better dinner with him afterwards in Belgrave Square! But he was always so kind and hospitable, so desirous to make one at home and talk over the old campaign, it doubled the agreeable pleasure of meeting him when Commander-in-Chief, with Egerton as his private secretary. I lost two good friends when they finished off their campaign.

The 2nd Division was encamped in the valley of Bastan, detaching a brigade in advance up the hills; from this brigade a regiment went forward a long way up (relieved weekly). This advanced corps gave the pickets and outposts, which were planted on the very tip-top of the Pyrenees. The view was very grand, and and the climate up there charming. France lay right in our front, and as we looked down below, there was the French army in camp quite visible, and their drill going on as in a barrack-yard. 'Plenty on 'em (as one man said) arter all the whackin' of late.' To the left the sea and the ships—a glorious sight once more. On the extreme right the *magnum mare*, but quite out of view.

The 34th, being the advance corps for the week, gave the pickets on the 24th July, commanded by Captain Moyle Sherer, a vigilant and distinguished officer. He had three Subalterns, H——n, R——l, and P——s. On Sunday morning, the 25th, at dawn of day, the picket and outposts were suddenly attacked by an advance of French sharpshooters. The signal-gun was fired, when we got away up hill as fast as we could (the men never went on a parade at any time but in heavy marching order, just as if they were never to return to the same spot). But the pass up was narrow, steep, and tiresome, the loads heavy, and the men blown. We laboured on, but all too late — a forlorn hope; our comrades were all killed, wounded, or prisoners. The enemy had full possession of the ground. Some 10,000 men were there, nearly all with their arms piled, enough of them arranged along the brow to keep us back. It was death to go on against such a host; but it was the order, and on we went to destruction; marching up a narrow path in file, with men pumped out and breathless, we had no chance. The Colonel is always a good mark, being mounted and foremost. He was first knocked over, very badly wounded. The Captain of Grenadiers (Wyatt), a very fine handsome man, being next in advance, was shot through the head. He never spoke again. My little messmate, Phillips, was also killed. I thought at the time, what a sin to kill such a poor boy. Seven more of the officers were wounded, the Adjutant, severely hit, tumbled off his horse and was left for dead (more about him hereafter). We persevered, pushed on, and made a footing notwithstanding our disadvantage, for the men were desperately enraged and renewed all their exertions to be at them with the bayonet, but in vain. We kept our ground until we were minus, in killed and wounded, some 300 men and 9 officers; some slight wounds were never returned. We did not think it very warlike to notice every skelp one got when little harm was done. But this little point of modesty was a mistake, found out too late, for at the conclusion of the war every officer who had been returned as wounded, was compensated from a great fund raised by the usual liberality of the English people, and many were well recompensed for the loss of a little claret or broken bone.

Different regiments scrambled up the hills to our relief as fast as they could. The old half-hundred and 39th got a severe mauling. Then came a wing of the 92nd and opened a flank fire on the enemy, while we moved over to another hill, got our men left, and commenced a cross fire. The 92nd were in line pitching into the French like blazes, and tossing them over. They stood there like a stone wall overmatched by twenty to one, until half their blue bonnets lay beside those brave northern warriors. When they retired, their dead bodies lay as a barrier to the advancing foe. O! but they did fight well that day. I can see the line now of the killed and wounded stretched upon the heather, as the living retired, closing to the centre. Every regiment that came up lost its quota, and the French increased as the battle went on. We had two six-pounder guns up here for signal, to give warning. Richardson, self, and two other lads made an effort to turn them to salute the French, but a few rifle-shots stopped our play, so, for fear they should go over to the other side, we wheeled them round and at the word 'Let go' away they went rattling down the mountain with great velocity, perhaps never to be seen again. We 34th for the last hour had been amusing ourselves in comparative safety, picking off our friends in the distance, when a very large column came down upon us to stop our play. There was but one escape for us now—to run away, or be riddled to death with French lead. The officer commanding, a brave man, saw how useless it was to contend against such a multitude, gave the word to retire at the double, and away we went down hill at a tearing pace. I never ran so fast in my life! Here the French had another advantage, rather a cowardly one. They kept firing after us for pastime. Every now and then some poor fellow was hit and tumbled over, and many a one carried weight over the course, i.e. a bullet or two in the back of his knapsack.

We were now broken and dispersed. Our bugles sounded, few heard them—some too far way! The old corps was severely handled. We hoisted a flag at the bottom of the hill, Freeman blew his well-known blast, and all that heard the sound rallied here. Up another hill we scrambled, and passed the night among the heather. Hungry, cheerless, and thirsty, I would have given a dollar for a drink of water. Lieutenant Simmons had his horn full of brandy slung on his back going into action, and was about to rejoice over it just now, but alas, the bottle was empty. A musket-ball played one of those practical tricks one hears of after a big fight. One passed through the horn during the row, and let off the brandy without any notice. Simmons knew that he had been slightly wounded in the side, little knowing it was a cow's horn saved him! Our sergeant-major found his arm very stiff about the crook, as he said; no blood, nor mark of a shot-hole. He pulled off his jacket and found a ball lodged in his elbow-joint, which had run up his sleeve in this playful way. A young officer was shot through the nose, which, as he jocosely said, made him sneeze a bit! Every part of the human frame in one or other was riddled with shot, and many wonderful escapes were talked of that night—were there any thank-offerings?

In the middle of the night, a horseman nearly rode over me bawling out for a doctor. 'What's the matter now? Who's dead that you want a doctor in the dark?' 'Sir W. Stewart bleeding to death, they say.' 'Sorry for it, he's always getting bled by Frenchmen's lead. Call louder, all the saw-bones are asleep,' and he passed on. Soon after an orderly dragoon came thundering amongst

us in our feather—no, in our heather beds—calling out for a guide
(all such orders in the dark were circulated by a loud call). 'Where
to, France or Spain?' 'No, sir, Alizondo.' 'Well, I know the way,
I think, in the dark, if that will do.' 'All right, sir. Will you come
with me to the Quartermaster-General?' 'Yes, lead on, I want to
warm my legs, the dew is heavy, and I feel stiff and powerless. I
feel very like the Irishman's gun, that wanted a new stock, lock,
and barrel, all in rags, and my barrel empty. Have you got any
water in those holster-bags of yours?' 'Not a drop, sir. Not a
grain of barley for my horse all day, nor a pick of a ration for myself, being the whole day mounted and riding about with orders.
The men got a great slashing today, sir. I see them coming down
the mountains in hundreds wounded, forby what on 'em were left
behind doubled up, an' the whole country below like a mixed fair.
The Commissary, artillery, baggage, and wounded all jammed in
that narrow road, trying to get away; but we're near sir.' He
called out, 'The Quartermaster-General said that Sir Rowland Hill
wished to get his division out of the hills the very shortest way
into the valley by daylight.' 'Do you know any path?' 'O, yes,
I think I will steer the column out of this darkness,' and took my
place and led the way down curving goat-paths, clear away into
Baston before sunrise. I had the personal thanks of the dear
General, and moreover dined with him. We had a sheep's head
for dinner, the first I had ever seen decently cooked, a dish I have
patronised ever since, as it makes a first-class curry.

A month had only passed away since the battle of Vittoria, and
here the French stood triumphant on the Pyrenees, for all the passes
were forced on the same Sabbath day! The truth was, the Emperor
superseded his brother Joseph (it was but mockery to call him
King), gave the command of the army to Soult, with orders to re-
organise it, and, when prepared, force all the passes in the Pyrenees,
assault Wellington, drive him back into Spain, relieve Pampeluna
before it fell, and be quick about it! It can't be denied that his
first efforts were successful. We all felt it to the bone, and the
men were vexed and disappointed.

The French army came down after us very cautiously on the
26th, but declined battle, endeavouring to get round our flank, a
movement well matched by General Hill. We retired and took up
position on the 27th. They came on, looked at us, but would not
engage in any war game that day either. Our great chief was
engaged during all this row with the siege of St. Sebastian, which
he left in a hurry, and came up to us in the nick of time. He was
always the right man in the right place; all honour to his glorious
memory. He saw at a glance the object of his adversary, and put

his army in motion.   Soult was pushing on for a great victory to
restore the fortunes of France.   At a racing speed Wellington rode
for Sauvoren, and seeing the enemy close at hand, is said to have
dismounted, taken a look at Soult, as pointed out to him by a
Spanish spy, pencilled a note on the parapet of the bridge, despatched it by his only staff-officer present, the late lamented Lord
Raglan, then Lord Fitzroy-Somerset, and rode up the hill alone.   He
was at once recognised by our troops, who raised a triumphant
shout of gladness.   The cheering swelled out loud and long as it
ran through the line from corps to corps, and became that appalling
shout which the British soldier is wont to give upon the day of
battle, and which the army of France never heard unmoved!

Our Field-Marshal stopped in a convenient spot, conspicuous
enough to be seen by his troops, so as to let them know that he was
on the ground.   It is said that he fixed his eyes on his formidable
enemy, and speaking as to himself said, 'Yonder is a great commander, but he is a cautious one, and will delay his attack to
ascertain the cause of these cheers; that will give time for the 6th
Division to arrive, and I shall beat him.'

The Marshal Soult made no attack that day.   Nevertheless, there
was some hard fighting at different points between the detached
divisions of English, Portuguese, and the French, but now for
another battle, which caused mourning and lamentation, pain and
sorrow.

Early on the morning of the 28th July, our chief formed his army
in order of battle in front of Pampeluna, in the midst of rugged
hills, craggy rocks, and rivulets, and there waited the pleasure
of the French Field-Marshal, who sent on his legions with all
the ardour and determination of a warlike people, to win this day
and let his troops once more into Spain to regain their reputation.
Both sides were soon engaged, and under a biting fire.   Both fought
bravely, but nothing could stand against the ragged red-coats of old
England, when they met their late acquaintance on fair honest
ground, with any sort of equality.   Both armies were jealous and
vexed, the French having been whacked out of Spain, and the allies
having met with some reverses of late.   Now was the time, this
was the day to decide a great and final triumph — ay, for a kingdom.

For two miles and more a storm of fire raged along the line.
The ground was uneven, rugged, and hilly.   Strong posts were taken
and retaken with the bayonet.   It was what the Duke called
'bludgeon work'.   Charge succeeded charge; each side yielded and
recovered ground by turns, yet all the noble valour of French effort
was of no avail.

Wellington brought forward, at a critical moment and at full speed, the gallant Enniskillen and the Northampton regiments (27th and 48th), who came with a rush from the hills against the crowded masses of the French, rolling them backward in disorder and throwing them down the mountain side. With anything but child's play, these two regiments fell upon the enemy three separate times with the bayonet, and although their charge was irresistible, lost more than half their numbers. A great slaughter was going forward along the whole line of battle, the cannonade furious. Every man held his life in his hands, to dispose of it to the best advantage for his own country. A French brigade made a great dash up a connecting hill. Our gallant Somerset regiment (the 40th) waited in stern silence, and with unwonted patience, until the enemy planted their feet (with their *En avant*) on the very summit, when the war whoop of charge was given. The whole mass was almost completely broken to bits. Away they went at the double, a tempest of lead following their heels. Four times this assault was renewed, the French officers, caring for nothing but victory, dragging and driving on their weary and exhausted men to win or die! The thundering shock and cheer of the British soldier ever prevailed in these days, and, at last, with their ranks thinned, heartless and fainting, hopeless from failures, the French gave way, having lost two Generals, a great many brave officers, and 1,800 men in this part of the battlefield.

We had less sanguinary play against Count D'Erlong in another position. Every regiment drew a prize that day. The British soldier is a disciplined biped. Discipline is the sure means of conquering, without which bravery is useless, and ours was an army always ready to go into action, not to be driven. It was the difficulty to keep them back and restrain their impatience, game-cocks as they were, and as they proved themselves this day, and every day.

Soult was still very powerful, and kept up the ball day after day, hoping still to gain some advantage against Wellington. Of the danger and intricacy of this hill country, in manoeuvring and fighting an army, no one can form anything like a true idea. A formidable enemy might be concealed within a mile and the sharpest eye not know it. The great chief, with an escort, I believe it was said, of the 43rd, went out to reconnoitre in the hills, and dismounted to examine his maps. A sergeant, who was sent up the hill to look out, had not been there long when he discovered the French winding round the side of the hill, where our Welling*ton* was sitting. (The Spaniards always laid a weighty emphasis on the *ton*.) One of the men holding his *caballo* (horse), Sergeant Blood, as his name was recorded, came flying down the rocky hill

G

like a deer, calling out, 'The French! the French!' He might have called out, 'The Philistines are upon you, and what a prize!' But the Duke was mounted and away at full gallop in a moment, not without a shower of bullets after him by the disappointed Frenchmen. There were spies in both camps, and they well knew the whereabouts of the grand prize! There was hard fighting and plenty of broken bones on the 29th and the following day. Then Soult went off in retreat the way he came, the whole British army at his heels like terrier dogs, snapping at him round every corner.

When our Colonel was wounded on the 25th, shot through the knee-joint, the agony was so great he was put into a house by the roadside. His servant and the doctor (Murray) alone remained with him. The French advanced that day, and hearing that an English officer lay wounded there, Count D'Erlong, the General commanding, went in to express his regret and to assure him of protection and quiet. He placed a guard at the gate and a sentry at the door, with orders that no one should be admitted while his army was passing that way—a noble trait of generous feeling. But the Count was always a kind-hearted, good soldier, and respected his enemy. It was said at that time that he and Sir Rowland Hill, now in direct antagonism, had been at one time school-fellows.

It so happened that my regiment, in following up the retreating French army, passed along the same road over which we had retired, and coming to the little house in which the Colonel had been left, and hearing from his servant at the gate that he was alive, the men gave one unanimous cheer, which so unnerved him that the doctor came running out to stop a repetition of such kindly feelings. He said, 'The Colonel is doing very well; with the only help I had (one servant) I cut off the leg to save his life. The French behaved admirably, only asked the Colonel's parole, would not take mine, the Count saying I had only done my duty. And now keep quiet,' he said, 'he knew the cheer came from his own men, but another like it might destroy life, he is so nervously excited.'

In due time he recovered, went home, and was exchanged for a Colonel of the French. He was appointed Governor of Pendennis Castle, married a wife, and had three sons in the army, all Colonels.

We pushed on to the pass of 'Donna Maria', where the French made a stand, and we had a big fight, the 34th leading. A thick fog prevented our pursuit, there was a small victory, and a loss of 400 *hors-de-combat*. Soult kept on his retreat through the mountains, and Wellington kept his eye upon him like a hawk. But there is nothing certain in war—a great chance was lost, and here it is recorded. The French Marshal had got into a deep narrow valley and halted. The Duke gave strict orders to prevent fires being lighted, the straggling of soldiers, or any indication of the presence of our troops. He placed himself amongst the rocks, from whence he could observe every movement of the enemy. Our troops were ready to cut them off, when unluckily a few marauders entered the vale, and were instantly carried off by some French horsemen, when their whole column beat to arms and marched away. Thus a few plundering vagabonds deprived the great chief of the splendid success he had in his eye, and saved the French from a terrible loss. However, they were pressed hard, and although they got out of this prison, their chains hung round them. The pass was narrow, the beaten army was great, vast numbers of the wounded were carried by their comrades on their shoulders, while their baggage impeded the march, and all got mixed in extreme disorder. Prisoners and baggage fell at every step into our hands. Men fled from their broken and confused ranks up the hills for safety, being all sorely crippled before they got out of this trap, to fall into another where they were wedged in a narrow road with steep rocks on one side, and the river on the other. Indescribable confusion followed. The wounded, thrown down in the rush and trampled on by the cavalry, were calling out to our people for quarter, while very many were supported along, carried on branches of trees, on great-coats clotted with blood, and gory stained sheets taken from the cottages. Wretched sufferers! brave men would not, did not fire upon them, and so they straggled along out of this labyrinth. The Spanish General Longa, as usual, did not attend to his orders, or the retreat of this part of the French would have been entirely cut off—but the prize was lost.

General Hill pursued his old friend D'Erlong to the pass of Maya. Pitching into his people as we went along, we helped them over the hills here, 8,000 feet high, and halted on the old battleground on the 1st of August, being absent only eight days! Our dead lay there just as they fell, only most of them stripped naked, decomposed, and swelled up to a vast size. Some had the appearance of being dressed in fine white muslin shirts, the skin inflated and raised up from long exposure to the air—the medicoes may understand it, I don't. The vultures had been here, they always followed the armies—dirty birds of ill omen. They begin their feast with the eyes, and sometimes leave bare bones!

I was for picket, and had to pass the night in the midst of this loathsome company of horrible perfume and decaying humanity. Going my rounds, I was continually stumbling over old comrades, and would then roll my head up in my cloak, and lie down amongst them for half an hour or so, jump up, and tumble over another ghost!

Next day we had all the dead covered with sods; graves were impossible on that rocky ground.

The 2nd Division now encamped on the tip-top of the Pyrenees, along the ridge from Maya to Roncesvales. Sir Rowland Hill pitched his tent amongst us and kept a sharp look-out against another surprise, for a surprise it was in July, and no mistake. I lost two of my messmates for whom I was very sorry, particularly for the joyful, rosy-faced lad Phillips. But there was no real grief for any one beyond a week or two—all a shadow that passed away. Their effects were sold by auction. We bought their clothes and wore them, and they were sold again perhaps in a month, being once more part of the kit of deceased officers killed in action.

The mountain sides about the pass of Roncesvales were covered with thick woods; trees were felled, and log-houses built at every point where an enemy might approach, and we slept with one eye open. I formed a new alliance, got into another mess of three, our assistant surgeon, Robert Simpson, president! A fine, handsome, clever young fellow, and a general favourite in and out of the regiment. He was afterwards surgeon of the 13th Dragoons and 7th Fusiliers. I was still the active forager for the mess, being mounted. Our batman always took good care of my horse, which, with others, was always kept with the baggage when there was any fighting going on. Poor Tom Tandy, my old servant, was killed in one of the late battles. He knew my ways and winks, he knew how to forage in safety, and just the sort of fellow who, if hard up, could live on the smell of an oil-rag for a day or so. I got another intelligent sharp fellow, who knew a sheep's head from a carrot, was only sober when he could get nothing to drink, but never got into a scrape. Along with the rations, he sometimes had a present of a duck, or an old hen from the 'valley below'. Pigs were few hereabouts, but the fairies would be kind at times and shove a little joint under the walls of our tent after night!

I used to ride into Alizondo, and get back the next day with anything I could pick up. A dollar a loaf for bread was the usual price asked and given, sausages and pork were scarce and dear, and no wonder after a French army passing twice through this little pretty town. Every man in a French army has the organ of destruction just over his eye; what he can't use he will destroy from pure mischief.

The weather was charming. We had little to do, little to eat, no books, and led a monotonous life. We would pass hours rolling stones down the mountains; it sometimes occupied three or four of us for an hour engineering at a great rock to get him up on the right end for a start. Once in motion, nothing could stop its heavy velocity. It dashed through the forest trees amputating great limbs and branches, making such a row as it passed away, and leaving an echo which traversed the forest and deep glens even into France.

We had very advanced pickets posted in chain-links down the hills on to the French border within pistol-shot of the *Parley-vous.* I always led my horse down to keep me company, and get him some good grass feeding, when on this duty. There was a picket-house, where the men kept up a roaring fire. I took the sergeant out in the middle of the night to visit the outposts. One of the sentries was gone; we halted to listen for any sound or voice. We knelt down and put ears to the ground, when we heard voices in the distance and gradually approaching us. It was dark; they knew where our pickets were posted every night, and thought to catch us asleep. I said, 'They may make a dash. Fire at once in the direction, and alarm our men at the house.' 'Wait, sir,' he said, 'a moment. Let them come a bit nearer. Now, I hear them pushing through the bush'; and he fired. All the other sentries immediately fired at the moment. There was no other result that we could tell than the words, '*Ah, grand diable·*' and all was quiet. My horse lay down beside me at the fire amongst the men, like a Christian, and we had no other adventure that night.

At one of these outposts our sentries had disappeared in the night three times, and always at the same place. They were good intelligent soldiers, not at all likely to desert. Many surmises and opinions were advanced about this mystery. I recommended double sentries one night to be planted close to each other — one of them to have his ear to the ground frequently, to catch any sound or movement. The place was very quiet and retired, by the side of a goat-path amongst the rocks, and the night was dark and late. One of the sentries jumped up from the ground, where he had been most attentively listening, and whispered to his comrade that he heard a little rustling amongst the leaves and low brushwood. There was no wind, all else was calm and quiet. They now stood together a little more retired, round the edge of the rock breast high, and waited this coming ghost, as they said, with their flints fixed. The men's names were Murphy and Styles. 'Don't you hear a noise, now,' said Murphy, 'just like a pig smellin' for acorns?' 'I do, and I think I see something crawling up here, like a bear. Will you cover him, and fire? I'll keep my shot in re-serve — hush! It approaches slowly, on all fours, and crouches down.' 'I see it,' says Styles, 'it's a bear. Cover him well, and knock him over.' And over he went at the instant. Both men waited a little — one to reload, and then cautiously advanced with fixed bayonets. The game was dead as a door-nail — and what was it? A Spanish spy (perhaps) in the French service, dressed up in an old bear-skin, armed with a sort of tomahawk, short spear, and a *cuchillo* (Spanish knife). No doubt the same wild beast that carried off former sentries, who might not have been so watchful on their solitary outpost. We supposed this wild beast might have had a reward for every red-coat he caught alive. It is certain none of our men were found, dead or alive, after we missed them, and again, the French had too much of military honour to engage in anything so unworthy of their noble character. The advanced sentries were always doubled in future.

Twelve battles had been fought within the last seven or eight weeks, in which the French lost 15,000 men, and the allies 12,000. The streams of blood were deep, and everything seemed to recoil at death but the soldiers in this war. There were deeds of valour achieved by hundreds of British officers, within the last few weeks, that would astonish the soldiers of any other nation in the world. Wellington himself declared that 'he could go anywhere and do anything with the army that fought at Vittoria and in the Pyrenees'. Yet those officers were entirely neglected by the influence of cold aristocratic pride, injustice, and partiality. Promotion went too often by favour, Court influence, political intrigue, or Horse Guards' interest.

I remember riding sixteen miles one day, through slush and mud, over the fetlock at every step, for no other purpose but to get a real dinner at St. Juan de Luz, and bring home something for our mess. The posada was crowded, horses and mules stood jammed together in the stable as close as they could pack. I bought a good bundle of forage for my poor tired horse, but his neighbours right and left had eaten two-thirds of it, for they had nothing provided for them. I had myself a wretched apology for a dinner, and a corner of the floor to lie on, without bed or blanket. One would desire neither if he meant to have a snooze; a soft plank is preferable to a lively mattress.

This was the Duke's headquarters. My companion on the ride down to the coast was the senior Lieutenant of the 11th Regiment, a man of long and good service. There was a death vacancy, and so fearful was he of being passed over, that his object was to see the Duke and to present his letters of recommendation to secure him a step which was his legitimate right. Many brave men were driven out of the service by tyrannical injustice. They could not brook the system of being passed by and purchased over by boys from the nursery, who stayed at home and never smelt powder. Army tailors had wonderful interest in those days!

CHAPTER 8

Nivelle and Bayonne

ALL military men who have seen much active service have no doubt had many opportunities of witnessing the dash and courage of the British soldier. How, when the hour of danger approaches, his anxiety to meet it increases, and how, still more, he will court danger, although duty does not call on him to face it. I remember one striking example of the latter.

It was a practice permitted in regiments to send a steady non-commissioned officer down to the coast to bring up what good things he could purchase for the officers. He had his list, a bag of dollars, and a couple of mules, with a pass from the commanding officer. On one occasion, when the great siege and butchery was going on at St. Sebestian, a sergeant named Ball, belonging to the 28th or 'Old Slashers', was on his way with a party for this purpose. Hearing the guns, he pricked up his ears like an old hunter, persuaded his party to follow him, lodged his trust—some 2,000 dollars—with a Commissary, took a receipt, dashed on, joined the storming party, survived, reclaimed the money, made his purchases, and returned to his regiment without any boasting or bravado. Insensible to fear or danger, this was the stuff our men were made of!

We changed our quarters or camp from Maya to Roncesvales. It was late when we pitched our tents in a beech wood. All tired, we lay down upon the sod, and were soon asleep. The first object that caught my eye in the early dawn inside our dwelling, close to my nose, was the two feet of a dead man with his toes up.

'Hallo!' I cried, 'whose ghost are you, my friend? And how came you here?' 'O, begad!' says my comrade, 'here is a fellow's head under my pillow of ferns! We are in some graveyard where they don't bury the dead; we have pitched our tent in the dark on the late battleground, amongst the dead.' 'By Jove!' says Captain Darcy, a rollicking Irishman, 'I didn't pitch at all. I saw a fellow snug asleep in his blanket, and lay down quietly at his back to keep myself warm. When I cleared my eyes this blessed fine morning, who was it, do you think?—don't know? A dead man, sir, without rag on his back, enough to frighten a donkey!' Many of the old Buffs and 20th had fallen here on the 25th of July; we knew them by their buttons. They had not been buried; we had them all covered up and changed our ground.

We led a monotonous idle sort of life here. We had no fine view into France, as at Maya. It was a thick wood before and behind us, outlying pickets were our only amusement!

At Roncesvales, a very small town on the highway from Spain into France, there was a posada, a sort of inn or caravansera, full of muleteers and ladrones, followers of the army. I rode down there one day to dine at the *table d'hôte*, put up my horse and stopped an hour to regale the inward man on a sausage and some rice, oil, and *vino tinto*. I smelt strong of garlic for three days afterwards — so I was told. Going into the stable for my horse, he was there, but the saddle and bridle absent without leave. I called out the patrone, kicked up a dust, but the innocent landlord knew nothing about it. I persevered in my search, twenty or thirty fellows watching me. At last I discovered the treasure up in a loft, covered over with chopped straw. I saddled my jennet, rode away in triumph, but never to return to dine at Roncesvales.

Our brigade returned to the Maya pass, and we had the pleasure of looking down upon the French army in the distance becoming again organised and getting ready for action. We overlooked their camps and saw their drills going on. They could only see our flags flying above them, the old 'flag that braved a thousand years the battle and the breeze'. October came on, and with it the snow, which buried us all up for some time. We were frequently dug out of our tents of a morning by the pioneers. My old Captain, who never loved fighting, had gone away somewhere to take care of himself, and I had no one to cash a bill for me at 30 per cent.! My best donkey died in the snow, and my mule was stolen one night when I was on outlying picket. I sat down now in real grief, and could have cried with vexation. Misfortunes seldom come alone. Here was I in a fix; I had paid sixty dollars for the mule and forty for the donkey. There was no remuneration, a dead loss of one hundred dollars to be made up from my pay, 6s. 6d. a day, minus income tax, which was never forgotten to be deducted from our paltry pay, which was now again five months in arrear. I could not bear this double misfortune with a patient endurance, and fear that I was very stormy about it. But, *cui bono*, what can't be cured must be endured; it might have been worse. Had we got a sudden order to move, I should have had no choice but to leave my little baggage behind me, but the snow kept us fast. Provisions became very scarce; bread, six pounds, thirty reals, or about 6s. a loaf, when we could get one. Anything else to be had was equally dear, and no wonder when such a multitude of locusts were on the ground. Towns, and villages and hamlets of white canvas were to be seen everywhere, all alive and red-coats and blue. The Spaniards were not particular in their dress—a coat, like Joseph's, of many colours, seemed most in fashion—and with a ration of beef (raw), or any bit of plunder, stuck on the bayonet, they passed on in their own rollicking, independent way, more like banditti than soldiers.

There was always some officer being killed, or disposed of, which caused an auction sale of effects, and so I bought another stout baggage animal on tick. We always got credit until the next issue of money, or by a bill on home, which was more acceptable. Somehow, my money never lasted its natural time! As Paddy said who lost the despatch on the road, 'It eloped out of his pocket'.

We had many severe snowstorms at night, and one day in particular, a hurricane that floored every house in the town, church and all. The commanding officer's marquee was called by the wags the church, the rest of the tents the town. Huge branches were torn from the trees and whirled through the air like feathers. Thin streams swelled into torrents, and dashed down the mountain ravines, rolling great stones with a mighty clatter. The melting snows increased into rivulets and waterfalls, where so very lately we could not get so much as would fill a teapot. In the distance we could observe the sea, in terrible commotion about Bilboa and Santander, where many fatal disasters occurred. This very rough weather did not last long, and glad were we to see the heather green once more. I always had a good bed since I picked up the royal sack at Vittoria. Stuffed with leaves or chopped straw, it was invaluable; yet I was doubled up with rheumatism for nearly three weeks, and unable to run in a foot-race, sweepstakes, a dollar each, ready money, the second in to save his stake. Very few could beat me in this sport, and none with the pole.

Pampeluna was still holding out. Being the centre of a ring, no one could get out, no one get in. And so the question was only a matter of time, and many were the bets about its fall. The most common was, 'Give me ten guineas and I will give you a guinea a day until the town falls', or, as the case might be, five, six, or seven guineas.

Pampeluna, the key into Spain, did fall; not before the garrison had eaten up all the prog in the city, as well as every horse, dog, donkey, cat, rat, and mouse that they could catch. They held out bravely until starvation compelled a surrender, and no fortress being now in our rear, Wellington prepared to enter and visit our old friends in *la belle France*. We left our snow-capped mountain homes on the 9th of November, and descended the hills to cross the border, just to see what the *parlez vous* were doing there so long, and soon found that they had been very industrious since July last, fortifying an immense position on the Nivelle, extending all the way to the seacoast, about sixteen miles.

We were, under General Hill, on the right of the army, the Duke on the left, fighting in the mountains. For weeks past there was a continued struggle going on to dislodge the French from strong posts they had occupied in the intricacy and labyrinth of this hill country. Other Generals, brilliant and brave, commanded the centre, and there lay the promised land before our eyes. Who will cross the border and live?

Few people, I fear, ever thought of danger or death, heaven or hell. Death was too familiar to be looked on with terror, and made no impression. I never saw a Bible nor do I remember ever seeing anyone read the Bible, although that is *the* book, a sure guide on our way to eternal life. We never thought that the time was short and the soul precious, where the man spared in the battle of today was killed on the morrow. I don't say that men did not pray, but I never saw but one on his knees. Yet here was a palace for prayer—pray in the open air, "Tis God's palace'.

> To kneel remote upon the simple sod,
> And sue *in forma pauperis* to God.

What could be more acceptable? Or what place more appropriate for a soldier? But soldiers were not looked upon in those days as parts of humanity, although wasting their lives to keep the people of England in possession of their wealth, their homes, and firesides.

Corporal punishment went on everywhere the whole year round. Men were flogged for small offences, and for graver crimes flogged to death—a thousand lashes were often awarded by courts-martial. I have seen men suffer 500 to 700 lashes before taken down, the blood running down into their shoes, and their backs flayed like raw red-chopped sausages. Some of these men bore this awful punishment without flinching for 200 or 300 lashes, chewing a musket-ball or a bit of leather to prevent or stifle the cry of agony; after that they did not seem to feel the same torture. Sometimes the head dropped over to one side and the lashing went on, the surgeon in attendance examining the patient at times to see what more he could bear. I did see, with horror, a prisoner receive 700 lashes before he was taken down. This was the sentence of a general court-martial, carried into effect in the presence of a brigade, for an example.

We had certainly some very bad characters sent out to fill up gaps in the ranks of the army, sweepings of prisons in Great Britain and Ireland. But such punishments were inhuman, and I resolved in my own mind if I ever had the chance of commanding a regiment I would act upon another principle. The time did come, and I did command a gallant corps for eleven years, and abolished the lash. Kindness is the key to open the human heart, and with that key I reformed the worst characters. It does not always tend to reform a man by bullying and abusing him before his comrades. I often made a deeper impression by taking a bad character into my room privately, speaking to and admonishing him in a sort of friendly way, appealing to his better feelings, and with a promise to forget all the past. In this way I reformed one of the most drunken characters I ever met wearing a red coat. He became the Quartermaster of a militia regiment afterwards, a teetotaller, and a most intelligent, useful officer. His name was Murray.

On the evening of the 9th of November we bivouacked on the broadside of a heather brae (out of sight of the French outposts not far away) to eat our supper of whatever might be found in the old haversack. Little and good would have been acceptable, but it was generally less and bad. We lay in groups and talked of the morrow, and of a great battle sure to come off, for which the two game-cocks of England and France were long preparing.

'Now, Tom Eccles', I said, 'good night, and mind that if you run your jolly red nose into danger, as you always do at the first flash of fire, we will miss you tomorrow evening.' This was a most excitable, young, thoughtless Irish officer, who had fought through the whole way up to the present Lord Mayor's day. He had nearly lost one of the colours of the regiment in Albuera by running far in advance of the battalion while fighting in line. The staff of the flag was cut by a shot in his hand, while he was loudly cheering on the men. Nobody could hold him, he was always in the front of the battle. When the morning signal-gun fired for our advance, the whole army already being under arms, loaded and ready for action, we went forward by divisions, brigades, and regiments, according to the nature of the ground and previous arrangements. Skirmishers to the front. In ten minutes or so the dawn was lighted up by the flashing of great guns and small-arms. The fusillade ran down the line like wildfire. Poor Eccles, always foremost, was riddled to death with French bullets. We never saw him more.

Several points of the enemy's position were assailed at the same time, and some of their intrenchments and redoubts taken at the point of the bayonet; but these were minor works in advance, which were only taken after a sharp resistance and loss on both sides. They were beaten back to their stronger position, well defended and guarded by batteries, breastworks, and plenty of cannon, with brave men and gallant officers ready for death or victory. 'En avant' was their continual cry, and 'Vive Napoléon', 'Vive l'Empereur'. Our shells and round shot kept them uneasy on their ground, while our men were advancing in their old formidable way of renewing acquaintance with 'Johnny Crappo', as the soldier redcoats so often called them. It was hard work charging up these sloping hills, receiving a heavy fire in the face, and losing men at every step; but if a certain number were destined to fall, the survivors only got the more excited in strength, agility, and resolution, feeling determined to win, and never looking behind. Oh! how clearly I can look back and see that day and noble deeds of valour displayed on both sides. That gallant *chef de bataillon*, leading on his men, waving them forward with his cocked hat at arm's length high in air. He rode far in front and cheered them on, while our shot were rattling amongst their legs. Our men were saying, 'Well, I'm blowed if I like to knock him over, he's so plucky.' 'Ay, Bill, but you see he must come down, for he wants to be killed.' 'Faith, and I'll make him leave that,' says a big Irish grenadier, 'or he may be riding over us,' when down he tumbled off his charger as dead as a stone. I was really sorry for him at the moment, but he was madly brave. All this was but a preface to the great battle of the day then only beginning.

Ninety thousand of our troops, with ninety-five pieces of artillery, and 4,500 cavalry, descended to fight this great battle. I believe the French army were less in numbers. They had more cavalry. They were of one country and one language, while the allied army were a mixture of English, Spaniards, and Portuguese, the Spaniards never to be relied on in the moment of trial and danger. The French too were fighting in France, for France, and on a very strong position which they had been fortifying for three months, so they had no disadvantage.

The river Nivelle formed a semi-circle; both flanks of the French army rested on that river. In the centre of their commanding position many hills and mountains were strongly fortified with all the skill and ingenuity of Frenchmen. I believe such defensive posts could not be wrested from our old red-coats, but our fellows took them all that day under a most tremendous fire, and an avalanche of great stones which rolled down the hills amongst them and made them jump about like buck-goats, as they expressed it.

General Hill, with 25,000 men, threw himself on the left flank of the enemy, and made his attack. General Sir John Hope assailed the right, while the great Duke forced the centre after a most severe conflict. We had redoubts—batteries, abbatis, and deep intrenchments in our front, with a determined and most formidable foe well planted behind them, shooting fast and thickly as we advanced. Their skirmishers were all driven in by this time. The battle now thickened fast, but no one could see very much of this brilliant fight beyond his own regiment or brigade. Indeed, at times I could see nothing from the obscurity of powder-smoke.

As we advanced, the red-glare flash of the cannon, the bellowing of the guns, and the white puff far to our left, showed us that death and destruction were extremely busy, but that the fight was going on in our favour.

I was on the right, with Lord Hill, and when the moment arrived to make the grand *coup*, he made a flank movement, getting on the French left, while the centre of their position was penetrated by one grand and tremendous effort. The day was ours—they began to retire. Once the chain was broken, nothing could stop the current of their speed. Away they fled; d—— take the hindmost; nobody wished to stop them! Our fellows forgot their fatigue in the moment of victory, hurried on and after the enemy with a cheer and a volley, and many fell at the eleventh hour. I confess I was not sorry to see them give way, for we had enough blood and brains on the sod for one day, our loss being 2,690 officers and men, 2 Generals, the late Lord Strafford and Sir James Kempt, wounded. The loss of the French: 4,260 men and officers, 1,200 prisoners, 1 General killed, 50 cannon and their field magazines taken, to swell our triumph. And great swells we thought ourselves that day!

We passed on through their lines of defence, where they had been so long domiciled. Their huts were extremely neat and comfortable, many had their green blinds over their little lattice windows; their neat little fireplaces, bedsteads of green boughs, shelves for their prog, and arm-racks, so like the natty Frenchman

in camp. We found their rations uncooked, and plenty of onions
and other vegetables, which were transferred *tout de suite* into our
haversacks *en passant*. We pressed on with a running fire after
them until sundown. Then we gave up the chase, stretched our
weary limbs on the November sod. We turned out the contents
of our larder — a Dutch cheese, onions, biscuit, cold ration beef, and
a little rum — and finished off the breakfast, dinner, and supper all
at a go, went to roost, and thus ended another chapter of the war,
as recorded in history.

It was marvellous how quickly the dead, and often the wounded,
were stripped on the battlefield by the camp-followers of the two
great armies — an unhallowed trade, and no stopping it. I remember nearly stumbling over the bleeding body of a young French
officer rolling in the dust, speechless in agony, and stark naked! He
was very handsome, well formed, and from his light moustache he
had not numbered twenty years. A ball had passed right through
his body, poor fellow, and his end was near at hand. I had wished
him out of pain before I passed on. Close by him lay one of his
rough soldiers, also stripped naked, showing a terrible and fatal
wound, and rolling over and over in the dust, for the November day
was warm and the ground very dry.

Many young officers have an opportunity at times of distinguishing themselves in battle, while others are more careful of life,
or may not have the chance. Two or three I may name whose
memory will never die as long as the history of the Peninsular War
is read. Lieutenant-Colonel Thomas Lloyd was killed today at the
head of the 94th Regiment. He was a valiant officer, skilled in
knowledge and of great experience. He predicted his own fall, as
many often do before a battle, without any abatement of courage.
When he received a painful and mortal wound, he remained on the
ground watching the fight, and making his own observations, until
death closed his eyes where he fell, at the age of thirty years.

Another young fellow, a simple Lieutenant, about nineteen,
bearing many wounds, in person very slight, and so very handsome
that the Spaniards thought him a girl in disguise, fell on that day.
So vigorous, active, daring, and brave was he, that the old soldiers
watched his looks on the battlefield, and followed wherever he led,
and obeyed his slightest signal in any difficulty or danger. Edward
Freer was well known. One of three brothers, who all died in the
service, he had also that presentiment of death in the coming battle
so often felt and expressed by military men. He was pierced by
several balls in the early part of the morning while storming what
was called the Rhune rocks amongst the hills. Old soldiers wept
for him, even on the battleground, when they heard his fate!

After five hours' hard fighting about the above rocks, where poor Freer was killed, the Spaniards cowed, and hesitated to attack an outwork, or abbatis, behind which a very strong regiment of French were firing as hard as they could load. Lieutenant Havelock, of the 43rd, who was then on the staff, a young officer of a brave and fiery temper, could not resist this opportunity of showing the Spaniards the shortest way how to quench this murderous fire. He took off his hat, called upon them to follow him, and putting spurs to his horse, at one bound and a dash cleared the fence, and went headlong amongst the enemy. The Spaniards followed, shouting and hurrahing for 'El chico blanco'. This one shock broke the spirit of the French, and sent them flying down the hill, the Spaniards in their turn paying them off as fast as they could load, and crying out, 'Viva el chico blanco!' (Long live the fair boy) for he was very young, very fair, and very brave. The Spaniards would have fought well had they been led in this gallant style, but their chiefs were too haughty, proud, and selfish to admit English officers to command in their service. Not so the Portuguese. Every regiment, I believe, was commanded by an English officer, who obtained a step of rank as he passed from his own corps into the other. So a Captain in my regiment became a Major, with Major's pay in the Portuguese service, and his superior rank was confirmed after the war. The Portuguese army was always well and gallantly led, fought well, and ranked next to the English troops in all ways.

Marshal Beresford was their chief, and he sent his troops into the field well disciplined and well clothed, with an *esprit de corps* not so well understood amongst the Españoles. There was more genuine heroic pride amongst the ladies of Spain than in the ranks of the army. I remember a beautiful Castilian maid looking from the balcony of her house on to the square where some Spanish troops were again preparing to take the field after a severe defeat and a run for it. She said, 'Los Engleses son bravisimos, pero nuestro general es una vieja' (The English are very brave; but our general is an old woman), and concluded by saying or speaking through those bright expressive dark eyes, 'I will never marry a man who will not distinguish himself in the army of Spain and for the honour of his country!

'Bravo, señorita', I said, 'you are worth fighting for.' 'Gracias, señor', she replied, 'a-Dios! hasta la vista,' and she tripped lightly away.

I saw her afterwards enjoying the fashionable but barbarous delight of a bull-fight, in the square where all the beauty and fashion of the town assembled, seated in the balconies and eager as we are on our race-course to see the 'Derby'.

There were a multitude of people below enthusiastic for the sport. The different entrances into the square were secured by wooden bars fixed into the grooved stone sides. A bull was driven in, who faced the audience with dignified simplicity. He was hooted, jeered, pricked with spears, and taunted for his patient forbearance, but declined a quarrel with his adversaries on any terms, and was turned out in disgrace. Another of the tribe was driven into the arena, a very stout, fierce-looking fellow, with short, sharp horns, a fiery eye, and full of mischief. Some one gave him a prick of a lance behind, when he made a sudden rush forward, caught a fellow on his horn, and pitched him up in the air like a sheaf of corn, then stood with a defiant look, pawing up the ground undecided what to do next. I was in the crowd, expecting safety amongst so many, and, as I supposed, out of horn's length, when this wild beast made another charge, cleared all before him, and took a bit out of my best holiday white trousers behind with the tip of his horn. My conscience! if I did not run for it, and soon found myself high up in a balcony, never to be seen again amongst such wild beasts in a bull-fight!

This poor beast was now driven to utter madness by his tormentors. Several men were carried away wounded, perhaps dead. Two horses were killed, and dragged out of the square amongst the cheers of the people above, the ladies waving their handkerchiefs. This was quite delightful!

The square was now clear of all but two expert horsemen with spears and scarfs, and two or three regular professed bull-fighters on foot, armed and dressed in the same way. They were the most expert, active fellows I had ever seen. When the bull made a charge at one of them, he threw a red mantle over his head, and slipped aside. Now a horseman attacked him with his spear, and there was another rush head foremost, horns nearly touching the ground. It was surprising the dexterity with which the horses were managed so as to escape; however, they were occasionally ripped up! The poor beast was foaming at the mouth, with wild bloodshot eyes, but still powerfully strong, when the matador, the great leader in these games, jumped on his back while a mantle had been thrown over his head and horns, and gave him the *coup-de-grâce*, and 1,000 voices gave consent to this finale with no end of bravos, and the now happy bull was dragged away. This is the national sport of Spain; so enjoyed by all classes of the people, from the grandee to the pizañno, and is it less cruel than the cock-fighting of England, now happily abandoned?

Our supplies now became very scanty indeed, and there were symptoms of discontent in the camp, for it was reported that some Commissaries had a league with speculators down at Bilboa and St. Ander, and used the public mules for getting up luxuries for sale at a fabulous cost. But our great chief appealed to the military honour of the army to be patient and firm, and the supplies would come in as usual in a few days. The Duke had only to make an appeal at any emergency to his ragged red-coats, and they would go through fire and water for him, ay, to the death. It was hard on those fighting fellows to be so long in arrear of pay, and to have their rations cut short. I paid sixteen dollars myself for a pair of boots, brought up from the coast, and everything else was equally dear.

Sir Thomas Picton told his Commissary one day that if he did not find rations for his men, he would hang him on a tree. The Commissary became very indignant at this insult (as he termed it), and went off to Lord Wellington to complain. After hearing the whole story with wonderful complaisance, he said, 'Did Sir Thomas really say so?' 'Yes, my Lord, those were his very words.' 'Very well, you had better get the rations, or you may be sure he will keep his word. I can do nothing for you; good morning!' The Commissary returned and found the rations for his brigade.

Maurice Quill, joking on the parade-ground one day after the men were dismissed, said, 'Who will ride over to headquarters and smell out some prog? I used to get a sheep's head upon tick once a week from our butcher, but I never see head nor horns now.' 'O,' says Tom Higginbottom, 'I suppose you're going to dine with Lord Wellington.' 'Well, I might do that same and do worse. As for you, Mr. Higginbottom, you begin to crow very loud that you have got the use of your Irish pin again. The next time you get a crack on the leg perhaps I may give you the chance of a pension by taking it off! I am going over to headquarters, and if any of you sporting fellows are inclined for a bet, I'll stake ten dollars that I will see Lord Wellington and borrow ten dollars from him before I come back, and more than that too, I'll bet other ten dollars I will dine with his Lordship.' 'Done, done, done,' shouted (with loud laughter) many voices. 'Win or lose, my coves, the money to be paid the next issue of pay,' and the bets were booked.

Saw-bones, as the Subs called him, was full of adventure, and loved a joke whatever it cost, but this day's excursion and his bets would have shut up any common-place man in the camp. However, he mounted his mule in a most confidential cut, as they said, and we saw him really off; whistling along to bear his courage up, turning over in his mind, no doubt the sort of reception he was

H

likely to meet from so great a man as we all justly thought the
Grand Duke to be. Riding up valiantly to the quarters of his
Lordship, he gave a thundering knock with a big stick at the door,
and asked if the Duke of Wellington lived here. 'Yes, sir,' said the
orderly, 'here is an aide-de-camp coming. May I ask your business,
sir?' 'I wish to see Lord Wellington, if he is at home.' 'His Lordship is in the house, but too much engaged to see anyone today. I
will take your message to his Lordship.' 'No, I thank you, if I can't
see him today, I will wait until tomorrow.' 'Something particular,
perhaps, you wish to say in private.' 'Precisely so.' 'Well, step
in, and I will see what I can do for you.' Away he went and told
his Lordship that 'a Dr. Quill was below in a state of anxiety, and
would not take any denial, came a long way to see your Lordship,
and could not go back until he delivered his secret.'

'Well, well, show him up.' After some bowing and scraping
— 'My Lord,' he said, 'I am the surgeon of the 31st and have come
over to pay my personal respects, and to see your Lordship,
and——'

'Yes, yes (cutting him short), how are you all getting on in the
2nd Division, many men in hospital? You must get them out, we
will want them all by-and-by.' 'Indeed, my Lord, I was going to
say, that we are badly off for hospital supplies, and no money to be
had. I think I could get many restoring comforts for the invalids
that would put them on their legs if I might make bold enough to
ask your Lordship for a loan of ten dollars until the next issue of
pay, when I will return it with a thousand thanks.' 'Very well,
very well, Mr. Quill, you shall have it. How far have you come
today?' 'O, indeed, I have rode seven long leagues on an empty
stomach, and there's not a bit of an inn over the whole country
where a body could get a morsel of dinner.' 'O, well, if not too late
for you, stay and have some dinner before you return, we dine at
six. Good morning, Mr. Quill.'

Quill's eyes opened wide and joyfully at this invitation. He
was punctual to the six as he said. All his wit and humour came
to the surface. He kept the table in a roar of laughter all the evening until he retired with his ten dollars and his Wellington dinner,
got a shake-down with his friend the aide-de-camp, and his whack
of brandy and cigars. He got safe home next day and claimed his
bets. He told his story honestly and gave his reference. But there
was no question about it, everyone knew him to be as upright and
honourable as he was eccentric and surcharged with mirth and glee
when others were desponding.

Some impudent fellow asked him one day why he had exchanged into the 31st. 'O, just because,' he said, ' I wanted to be

near my brother, who was in the 32nd.' That man was shut up, and asked no more questions.

The weather became very wet and rainy about the end of November, but we happened to get under cover in some hamlets near the Nive, hard up too for provisions, and no money. The French had cleared the country of everything as they retired, like so many locusts. I had three articles that I could pawn, or pledge, or exchange, and they must go: an old half-crown, and the silver fork and spoon I bought in Lisbon. The half-crown had been given to me when a lad, by a kind, good old lady who said at the time with great simplicity, 'My dear, as long as you keep that, you will never want money!' She was right, but I thought I had kept it long enough, and exchanged it for an old hen, the mother of many a brood. The fork went for one loaf of bread, and the spoon followed in a few days. An iron fork was always my abhorrence, but there was a necessity. Bread was dear; when an old Spaniard said to our paymaster, 'I can't eat your gold, señor, I'm starving myself.' The money offered was sufficient to buy a baker's shop well stored.

The French crossed the Nive—it was now our line of demarcation. We planted our line of pickets along the left bank, while they did the same on the other side, with an understanding between us that there should be no hostilities without due notice. The river was narrow, but rapid in the rains. We kept watching each other carefully day and night, yet were good friends.

We conversed with the French officers across the stream. They told us of their many escapes in action, pointing to bullet-holes in their head-dress, and why they had retired just now, 'just to collect all their forces and be ready to return to Spain when the Emperor came down to take the command personally.' In reply, we told them how happy we should be to meet them all in Paris soon. This little badinage went on with good humour. We exchanged newspapers occasionally, rolling up a stone in one and throwing it over, and getting one in exchange.

On the very day that we entered France, the Spaniards lost no time in beginning their foraging excursions amongst the people and spreading themselves over the country, committing all sorts of villainy on their murdering excursions. They considered marauding, murder, and plunder their chief duty, now that they got into an enemy's country. The poor French people fled from their homes in terror after witnessing the frightful excesses of those wild and reckless fellows, whose country, no doubt, had suffered most fearfully for many years under the dominion of the soldiers of France —not from the peasants of Gascony.

Wellington marked his lofty character of justice in putting to death all the marauders he could grasp, and sent back into Spain their whole army, save that of Morillo's division. Thus confidence was restored, everything was paid for, and a friendly intercourse established—much to our satisfaction and advantage.

Our men made acquaintance, too, with the French soldiers across the river. This being a permanent picket station, they built a hut here, which was added to daily until it became a water-tight, snug little dwelling, and a shelter from the rains. It stood just opposite a ford, with the entrance facing the French picket on the other side. There were stepping-stones of large size across, which were used by the country people when the river was low. One day they were all dry above water, and the next covered, perhaps, by a torrent.

Our fellows knew there was brandy in France, but the matter was how to get it. They made themselves very agreeable to their neighbours, calling out at times 'Bono-frances', Fromage, Cognac, and Tabac, which seemed to be understood over the way, so they established a telegram when the river ran low, they subscribed their coppers, put them into a mess tin, gave it a rattle to draw the attention of the sentry, and without any arms in hand, one of the picket stepped down to the water, gave his tin another rattle, placed it on the centre big stone, calling out 'Cognac!' and retired. By-and-by it was taken away, and returned in the evening full of brandy (not likely of the best quality). The relieving picket was let into the secret, and the trade went on for a while, but not so smooth as the stream, for the brandy-pot forgot to come back one day. One Paddy Muldoon, a big Irishman—always very fond of a dhrop, as the boys said—was very indignant at this thratement, and watched an occasion to square accounts with the robbers acrass the wather. Seeing the sentry put down his firelock for a few moments to go into the hut, he dashed across, laid hold of his arms, and, as the rogue of a parlez-vous stepped out, he gave him a clout on the head and brought his firelock over to his own side in pledge for the brandy-pot.

Soon after this feat the French officer on duty came down to the bank and called over for the officer of our picket, told him the true tale, and requested that the firelock might be restored, or the young fellow, who was but a conscript, would be tried for leaving his post, and severely punished.

A search was made in the hut, the musket found and restored. The French officer returned thanks, and Paddy was sent back a prisoner to the camp, where he was tried for the offence, found guilty and sentenced to a corporal punishment. He was a brave, dare-devil soldier, and his defence was honest and truthful. He said, 'he only wanted back the money or the brandy, an' did not want to be done by any ov them frog-ating fellows, who he was chasing all over Spain for three years, and hoped the coort would consider his good service, and the next time he met this fellow, he might rely on it he would never see his firelock again.' The punishment was remitted, and the brandy trade stopped.

The weather was now mild, but very damp and rainy. The winter had really set in and kept us under cover until the usual time of turning out, one hour before daylight, when all the troops were on their respective alarm-posts until dismissed and we could see a white horse at a mile distant. This was the most disagreeable part of our war game. On the 8th of December there was a great stir of cocked hats and orderly dragoons galloping about—a sure indication of a move. The men dived into the secret at once, and began to fix their flints and look to their ammunition. In the middle of the night we received orders to be on our alarm-post earlier than usual in the morning. The women were all astir in a moment, lighting their fires 'to have a dhrop ov tay for their respective warriors, jist to warm their hearts before plunging into the river, bad luck to the French.' Well did they know our line of march, and were always in the way; but this intended advance bothered them. How were they to cross the river and follow the troops, against a positive general order? The ladies assembled around a big fire on a dark winter's night to discuss this point. Mother Skiddy, Brigadier-General of the Amazons, so called, addressed the meeting. 'I have the weeest donkey of you all, an' I'll take the wather if I'm to swim for it, and let me see who's to stop me, Bridget Skiddy, who thravelled from Lisbon here into France. If Dan falls, who's to bury him? God save us! Divil a vulture will ever dig a claw into him while there's life in Biddy, his laful wife. Now, girls, you may go or stay.' and so she began to saddle her ass.

The troops were now assembled in perfect quiet. No drum nor bugle was sounded—not a word was spoken—all as still as death, waiting the signal-gun to make the rush. The outposts on the river-side had their orders not to take any advantage of the enemy when, just at dawn, bang went the first cannon. The French were under arms in a moment. Our pickets on the river-bank gave them the signal to clear off. They took the hint, got out of the way a little, halted, and formed up on the defensive. Bang went another gun, and now the field-day began. Our men had slung their pouches behind their necks, resting on the pack, to keep their powder dry, as the river was swollen. The grand rush was now being made under cover of our guns. We took the stream; some killed and

wounded went away with the current, for the French kept up a
fire on us now, which was quite lawful. We made good our footing on the right side, fought on all the day, and calling the roll at
night, we found there were many widows.

The passage of the Nive being successfully made by our division
on the right, there was hard fighting along the left of the entire
position, and a desperate attempt made to repulse our whole army.
It was known at the time that Soult had written to the Minister of
War to expect good news very soon, Wellington's army being
divided by the river Nive. Lord Hill's division, being now situated
in an angle between the 'Nive and Adour', was cut off from Wellington. It was very unpleasant, to say the least of it, and required
great caution and brave hearts, resolute and determined, to keep
our ground. On the 10th Soult attacked Wellington in front of
Bayonne with 55,000 men and thirty-seven guns. The ground was
very unfavourable for fighting—ugly weather and swampy land,
rough and rugged—it was always cheery enough fighting over grass
fields and churchyards on a sunny day. The Light Infantry and
Rifles liked the tombstones, they said they were such a steady rest
for a pot-shot, and a good shield!

The great Marshal Soult got a thrashing today after all his
boasting and expectations, but it cost the Duke 1,200 men, 2
Generals *hors de combat*, and 300 prisoners. However, to balance
the account, the French loss was considerably more. Moreover, a
whole regiment of Nassau and Frankfort came over to us, their
Prince having abandoned the Emperor Napoleon in Germany. But
there was no end to this quarrel. We were all fighting again the
next day, when there was a trifling loss of some 600 men a side.
The 12th was also a bloody day in our army. Death was busy
from dawn to dusk, and that was only preparatory to the following
day, the 13th December 1813, when Soult tried his grand coup
upon General Hill.

Lord Hill at St. Pierre

ON the night of the 12th the rains swelled the Nive, carried away the bridges, and left us cut off from the rest of the army, between the two rivers, with less than 14,000 men and officers, and twelve guns. We had a front of less than two miles of ground, which was rather in our favour, the enemy not being able to deploy their overwhelming force. We (28th, 34th, and 39th), occupied a plateau on the left, the Château of Villefranche being just in our rear. The morning was ushered in with a wet, misty fog. We had no time for a mouthful of breakfast, shook the rain out of our blankets, and stood to our arms. The fog continued heavy, covering the vast masses of the French dimly seen. Now and then, they appeared in solid columns like black thunder-clouds, as the mist rose spreading over a mile of ground. Soult expected to trap our Farmer Hill and his little force by marching out from Bayonne and his intrenched camp with 35,000 fighting men, quite fresh, and forty guns, early in the day. The sparkling fire of the riflemen spread far and wide over the low grounds, and gradually crept upon us, while the thundering of parks of artillery shook the ground from river to river, but never shook the nerves of a British soldier. The French General Abbé pushed on his attack against our centre, with a force and determination difficult to resist, and gained upon us rapidly. The musketry and cannonade rolled for hours in our teeth. Regardless of all danger, the two armies now met each other. Neither would yield, and the artillery tore the ranks on both sides fearfully. We had hard work to keep our own against such long odds, 35,000 versus less than 14,000! Besides their forty guns against our one dozen of nine-pounders! Our brigade was let loose early, and we soon separated, on account of the ground, as we could thus do more work independently. Colonel Brown said to the old 'Slashers', 'there they come, boys; if you don't kill them they'll kill you; fire away.' This was the longest address he ever made to his men. He never had but one book, and that was the Army List. He was a great soldier, very popular, and survived the war.

The Château of Villafranche, which was in our rear when we commenced operations in the morning, was well in our front before twelve o'clock, i.e. we had to abandon it to a superior force, and this caused our fellows to get furious. It had been taken and re-taken several times today, but we held it at last. It was one of those fine old French family mansions that one sees sometimes peeping out of a wood elevated amongst the trees. It had been deserted, and left by its owners, well and substantially furnished in old style. The old ladies' armchairs, the library of the landlord, the young ladies' nicknacks, with all the beautiful china ornaments, etc., etc., were mashed up together. The feather beds, down pillows, mattresses and ottomans were stuffed into the windows for defence to resist incoming shot, and very sensible barricades they made. The cellars were not overlooked, and many thirsty souls were all ready to do full justice to the wines of Bordeaux, although preferring, as they always do, 'strong waters'. However, in this department they were generally disappointed, for some prudent officers were always at hand to knock the heads of wine and brandy casks and let them run.

We left this château now to camp-followers, the worst of all enemies (as it was no longer of use to us), and took ground to our right, to help a brigade of Portuguese who were fighting bravely. We were just in time to strengthen their hands to fight it out. Before we got up, we saw them twice charge their adversaries most gallantly with the bayonet. We pitched a flank fire into the parlez-vous and made them 'leave that', as Paddy said, when he fired at the French sentry. 'Did you hit him, Paddy?' 'No,' he said, 'but I made him leave that!'

The enemy now concentrated all their force towards the centre, to make the grand coup, and so we took that direction, keeping up the ball as we moved towards Saint-Pierre. This was a hamlet on the main road, leading from the bridge at Cambo (across the Nive) into Bayonne. The French now attacked this point with three strong columns—the very key of our position; whoever kept this key was pretty sure to be master. We formed in reserve, a couple of regiments behind the houses, with a battery of three guns and a howitzer. A good deal of pounding went on below, and on both our flanks. Every point was attacked to weaken our force and keep us separate, their guns keeping up a terrific fire, knocking the dust out of Saint-Pierre, and ploughing up the side of the hill, thinning our ranks, and playing Old Harry, having no regard for life or limb.

We were now on the highway for a retreat or a victory. The latter was the choice of the British army, and nobly did they win it. Facing Bayonne, and on our right, an old British regiment was firmly placed in a very strong position, the right of that regiment resting on the Adour. As the enemy's main column advanced up the hill to the hamlet, they were annoyed by a flank fire from our left; but they persevered and approached within pistol-shot of the key of our kingdom! Just then our little battery opened a fire of grape into their ranks, which made a lane through their column. A few volleys of musketry, in their confusion staggered them grievously, and sent them pell-mell on top of their reserve, our guns plunging their shot into their ranks until there was a flow of blood down the great road. Yes, the blood was running in a stream!

A tremendous fire of artillery now covers the advance of another great column of the French, who are determined to have Saint-Pierre at any cost. With a cloud of voltigeurs in front and on both flanks covering their deep and dark masses, they steadily move up the incline. We are prepared by order to be steady: 'Dead or alive, my lads,' said our chief, 'we must hold our ground.' Every eye is fixed on this deadly mass, every nerve is strung. Like the gallant steed as he champs the foaming bit, ready for the charge, so was every man of ours in pain to be let loose. A howitzer, with a double charge of grape, went slap into their foremost ranks; then one tremendous cheer, that only British soldiers can give with electric fire! 'Hurrah for old England!' 'Ireland for ever and the Limerick lasses!' 'Bonnie brave Scotland, hurrah!' 'Hurrah!' from a thousand voices, as they dashed with the cold steel bayonets into the solid mass of human flesh before them. Writhing and quivering humanity lay over each other now in mortal combat, steeped in blood. The cannon-shot from each side was crushing up the living with the dead and dying. It was a horrid sight, but not yet over. This broken column retired, and on the way lost considerably from our guns, which banged into them as fast as we could load. They went far away to the rear before they could reform, while another massive column took their place and came on. The French always attacked in column. I think they were wrong, but they know their own business best, and upon this occasion gave us an opportunity of showing them an error, which they never acknowledged to this day. This last black, dense, great body of troops came steadily on, encouraged by seeing our troops on their left give way, and losing their grand position, which might and ought to have been kept against very long odds. Lord Hill saw at once this alarming turn in affairs, and despatched part of his force to retard the progress of the enemy there or drive them back. We had not a man to spare. Another frightful and uncommon event occurred which nearly damaged our day's work. A brigade and a regiment were commanded by two nervous old officers who had no wish to be killed. They had most likely been reading that couplet in Hudibras—

> He that fights and runs away,
> May live to fight another day;
> But he that's in the battle slain,
> Will never rise to fight again.

Cowards die many times before their deaths—the valiant never taste of death but once.

They had a ticket of leave next day from the Duke, and were no more seen. I need not mention their names.

As this great column of French came up, they were first met by a discharge of shrapnel shells and canister shot, which did not slacken their pace over the dead bodies of their comrades that lay in their way. Saint-Pierre was the key, still in our hands; to lose it all was lost. The Highland Brigade was under cover, in waiting for them, headed by the gallant 92nd Gordon Highlanders, who led on the charge, colours flying, and their piper blowing out his national music to cheer them on. He was soon floored by a broken leg, but would not be moved, playing 'Johnny Cope' with all his might, while the blue bonnets, well supported, went into this mass with the bayonet and sent them back in utter confusion. This was to understand war.

We were also successful on our right and left. The French couldn't do it. They had enough for one day, and did not renew the attack. Two divisions which had been on the line of march since daylight now made their appearance in our rear, and formed in line of battle, but were not required. Our ranks were terribly wasted, nearly all the staff had been killed or wounded, as also three Generals.

Lord Wellington had been riding hard from the time he heard the first gun in the morning, and only arrived at the very close of the battle, and declared that he had never seen a field so thickly covered with dead. It was Lord Hill's own day of glory, and it was recorded by the celebrated historian, Colonel W. Napier, 'that five thousand men were killed or wounded in three hours, upon a space of one mile square'.

When the Duke rode up, he shook our chief by the hand, and said, 'Hill, the day's your own.'

Our men threw up their caps in the air, and gave one long loud, thrilling cheer, that echoed down the valleys amongst the retiring foe. And so ended the battle of the Nive, which lasted five days, from forcing the river on the morning of the 9th to the evening of the 13th.

The days were short, and night closed upon the saturated field of blood before we had time to light our fires and cook the wretched ration dinner. But still, with our half-gill of rum, after so long a fast, exercise, and excitement, it was an acceptable banquet. It came on now to pour rain like fury, and the bivouac was anything but agreeable, particularly to the wounded, among whom there was a multitude of hurts (as the doctors called them), great and small, from the amputation of limbs to the scalping of heads! I don't know if I was thankful enough for my escape. I was not hit very hard and got off cheap. Three inches taller and it was all up. An inch makes a wonderful difference they say in a man's nose—life or death was today in the height of many a British soldier!

14th December. We sent in a flag of truce to the French General to say they might carry away all their own wounded men from off our ground, and we would bury the dead. We had no hospitals nor medicos to care for them, and as prisoners of war they were not worth their rations.

All was friendship and politeness now. Our offer was accepted, and a line drawn out between us. Some trees were cut down and laid across the high road into Bayonne. Our men collected all the wounded of the French, carried them down in blankets to this point, and handed them over. The sentries of both armies were planted along the line, not over six or seven yards from each other, as quiet and gentle as lambs! The hillsides were perforated with cannon-shot, some places like a rabbit-warren, and dyed with blood. Our little hamlet of Saint-Pierre was knocked inside out; but if ever the French got a decided thrashing, they might have boasted of it yesterday, in sight of one of their own chief towns. This 'labour of love', in presenting so many disabled and useless soldiers to their country, lasted some days, and no end to groaning and moaning until we had them all removed. Two or three nights exposed to the rains left many of the unfortunates in a pitiable condition, for they had fallen in sand-pits, amongst brushwood, and in nooks and

corners out of sight.   The rains continued to overshadow the scene
of desolation all about us, and not a blink of the sun to cheer or
warm the bivouac for many days, our baggage not having yet come
up.   We had no feather beds; the old pound of lean beef, a hard
biscuit, and ration of rum our banquet; a cold sod and a shower-
bath our dessert; hard times.   But we survived them, to tell of yet
more battles.   Our sentries, and the French ditto paced at the distance of a few yards from each other, trying to converse a little in
their respective lingos.

The officers kindly proffered their services in sending into
Bayonne for anything for us that we required.   We took advantage
of their civility.   I got a piece of cloth to make up a new Sunday
pair of inexpressibles, very much required, and a bottle of brandy,
for which I invested the few dollars in hand.   The tailors were not
all killed, and so I turned out very respectably dressed, but rather
out of the fashion, in a week or so.   We paid in advance.   There
was no mistake, everything came to hand about the hour appointed,
and delivered at the outpost picket.   The officers showed us the
bullet-holes in their shakos and clothes; I believe we could do the
same.   They said we would all be back into Spain very soon.   The
reply was, 'Not before we see a little more of la belle France';
and really there was not the least animosity between us, and
I thought it very unkind and inhospitable to have any more of
a quarrel.   But the two great chiefs of the fighting cocks thought
otherwise.

The truce ended, sentries withdrawn, we gave our friends warning to be on their guard, as we intended to pursue our campaign.
They took off their hats with an 'Adieu, messieurs; au revoir!' and
it was not long before we met again in mortal combat.   My regiment was left in the shattered hamlet of Saint-Pierre, to take care
of itself and keep a sharp look-out to our front.   Bayonne was just
one league distant, full of French troops, and a whole army was
concentrated in and about the city, holding fast their intrenched
position, Sir John Hope in command.   Vieux Monguère, a little
town on our right, on a hill just above the Adour, where Lord Hill
quartered himself and his staff, all jolly fellows.   They were not
long there before they got up an amateur theatre, and the drama
went on as in Estremadura in Spain.   Our dear, rosy-faced Farmer
Hill entertained the whole *dramatis personae* at supper after the
play.   There was nothing about the war, except in some comic
songs composed for the occasion, of how 'He (Lord Hill) leathered
the French'.   I had to walk home in the middle of the night, up to
my ankles in mud, after the fun; but I had a pair of wonderful legs
for hard work day or night.   We had little to do now for a long

time, but listen to the attack and defence about Bayonne—bellowing of guns and waste of gunpowder.

We had quite gained the confidence of the people. Everything was paid for. They were permitted to go into Bayonne with their sheep or their cattle as they liked, and soon found that the English were as equitable as brave, and that the word of a British General was sacred. All we seemed to want now was money, and a dollar was worth 8s.

The battle of the 13th was hardly over, when Mother Skiddy came into camp, mounted on her wee donkey, calling out for Dan. 'Has any ov yer seen Dan Skiddy? He's not killed or wounded is he by them vagabonds, bad luck to them. Sure I'd been up two days ago, only I was drowned crassin' that bit ov a sthrame, an' sure I've niver been dry since?' 'O, then, you're welcome home, Misthress Skiddy, how did you lave all behind you?' 'Och, is that you, Paddy Muldoon? Avourneen, it's me that's glad to see ye on your two Irish legs; I'm thinkin' you paid them off for the brandy.' 'Bedad, we gave them a great slashin', and not many of us killed after all. Will you let me take ye off your charger?' 'Is our Captain safe, and our two officers?' 'O be gar they are, only Mr. B—— had a bit ov a scalp and a bullet through his cap in San Pierre there, but they can't touch him, or Mr. Norton in all the fights and scrimmages we have.' 'But where's Dan, tell at ons't?' 'O, indeed, he's run away wid a French lady he tuck in the battle.' 'An' he'll spake Irish to her,' says Mrs. Skiddy. 'But no more ov your blarney, where'll I find him?' 'Well, he's up there in the hospital tent wid a broken leg, and got off chape if they cure him; and there's Mr. Higginbottom wid another cropper beside him, and there's Sergeant——' 'O, worra, worra, that'll do, let me go, they're all kilt'; and away she went bellowing to the shambles.

We lost 300 officers the last five fighting days. Some of them had cut their way from Lisbon to be buried in France, but they were soon forgotten. They had their day of glory, and a bit of a churchyard fits everybody.

Wellington had his hands quite full. The intrenched camp before Bayonne was very strong, the weather rough and rainy for troops on the *qui vive* day and night close to a watchful enemy playing the sortie too often for one's comfort and patience, a game which ended by Sir John Hope being grabbed, wounded, and carried off to town quarters. A terrible slaughter of officers and men took place also on both sides, without any advantage being gained.

It was said, and I believe it was very generally recorded as true, that our patient, scientific, and gallant chief was abused and libelled by the Spanish Government, with all his army. Their hostility and growing enmity were no secret. We were all considered as invaders rather than friends. The insolence and duplicity of their Minister of War were obvious. All this ingratitude and savage conduct troubled the Duke's temper a bit. In fact, he had good reason to rebuke Morillo for allowing or permitting the Spanish soldiers to plunder in France, and to commit violence on the people, which he encouraged, from his savage, untractable, bloody disposition, hating English, Portuguese, and French equally. The poor French peasantry would have been entirely ruined without our protection. Sometimes they would take refuge in our camp or quarters with their bundles, even to escape from their own soldiers, and many of our own men were hanged for plundering them. I never could excuse our soldiers for committing any such excesses. But 'tis true that they never saw their pay, and were half starved at times. Morillo, of course, sent a sackful of lies by every post to his corrupt, imbecile, prejudiced, ungrateful Government in Madrid for the snub he got from his superior. Spanish pride was touched with the pen of justice and equity, and Spain is jealous and revengeful.

No one complained if the Duke was severe in our own ranks; it was never without cause. It was said that he was cold and careless of his officers. Some discontented men may have said so, but the truth was, no one expected reward for doing his duty, unless for some very gallant and extraordinary conduct—such as the leading a forlorn hope, when a step of rank was expected. But there were a hundred chances to one against the daring heart that tried this game, yet they were never wanting to lead the way when required.

I sold my only donkey to raise the wind, and bought two nice little horses, on tick, at the sale of the effects of officers killed in action. A bill on England was always acceptable payment, or the next issue of money the same. This traffic always went on briskly, and in this way we were supplied with second-hand clothes! I was now ready for the road. My head-gear had something of a warlike appearance all right for a five-foot-nine man—a six-foot fellow, and he was a gone coon.

We sent our wounded to Cambo, on the Nive, where an hospital was established. My poor friend Allen B. Cairns died there. He had been wounded, but not badly—what the doctors called 'a hurt' cost him his young life. I got his watch-key. I have had it, and that of another friend, in use for fifty years, and might say with truth that I never used them without thinking of the poor fellows.

On the 25th and 26th of February, our chief was examining Soult's position, which was a right good one as usual. It had the

bend of a reaping-hook, and it was difficult for cavalry to approach
from swamps and rocky ground. It was high ground above the
'Gave de Pau', and near to Orthes, where our friend Soult received
battle. He had a fine army, and his best Generals commanding
them, such as Drouet, Raille, Clausel, Villatte, Paris, Harispe, etc.
There was a very handsome old bridge across the river at the town,
fortified and mined. Above and below the bridge it was deep, and
full of jagged rocks, and altogether a very formidable and dangerous place to run one's nose into without leave. There was some
little fighting in the advance towards it, just to keep up the steam.
We lost 20 or 30 men, but that went for nil. Early on the 27th
the great row began. Wellington delivered battle (as old
chroniclers used to say) to his warrior antagonist Marshal Soult, the
favoured and favourite Lieutenant of the Emperor. There were
two valiant armies in the field, of some 40,000 men a side, besides
cavalry and guns. Our approach to the French position on the
heights was marshy and difficult, in some places our troops sinking
up to their knees, and the enemy above pounding at them in the
mire—painfully provoking. But still this only braced their nerves,
and made them more savage. Just now there was more swearing
than fighting, for this part of the force were struggling to get out of
the mud, unable to use their arms. The cannonade and flashing of
small-arms had now begun in earnest to echo down the river,
through the town, and over the hills. All was in full play about
nine o'clock, and continued all the day. The bold French rushed
upon our columns with a wasting fire, and forced back our inferior
numbers with unusually desperate valour, but our supports came
up and shattered their masses. The nature of the ground would not
permit very many to be engaged at this point; so that little progress was made, except in deadly slaughter, in which the French
had the best of it.

Soult put all his reserves in motion, to complete what he supposed must be a victory all but gained, and 'twas said that he
exclaimed aloud, 'I have him at last'. The moment, no doubt, was
very dangerous, but Wellington's head was clear, and he had the
most devoted hands and hearts to aid him, in the full assurance of
another victory for old England. Amidst all this thundering din of
battle, which shook the earth with violence, the Duke ordered Hill's
division to ford the river on the French left, and get on their flank.
It was deep to our loins. We slung the cartridge-boxes on top of
the knapsacks, to keep our powder dry. The men linked arm in
arm, to support each other in a very strong current. Some cavalry
formed in the river above us, to break the force of the stream.
And so we all passed over unmolested, and marched on without

halting for a moment, our shoes full of water, and our nether garments clinging to our bones, for none of us were very fat, but still in good working condition. The 4th Division gained ground and secured a good position in the church and the graveyard (all ready for its victims). The French Marshal now rallied all his forces to make the grand coup that was 'at last to have him'. The thunder of the guns on both sides made the very hills quake. Our grand chief was wounded, with two other Generals, Ross and Walker. After fording the river, we drove back the troops there, seized the heights, cut off the French from the road to Pau, and turned the town of Orthes, menacing the only line of Soult's retreat. When his troops began to yield, our army advanced with an incessant and destructive fire of musketry and cannonade, losing men very fast, for the French saw their own danger, and fought like devils. But, seeing their retreat being cut off by Lord Hill, we hurried on until both sides began to run. They ran for dear life, and we kept to their heels, until coming up pretty close, down went their arms, after that their knapsacks. They got into racing order in no time, and endeavoured to make good their escape. But our fellows got amongst a regiment with long greatcoats, and now Paddy Muldoon had fair play at last, as he said. I don't know how many of these *parley-vous* he had caught by the tail, giving each of them a crack on the lug, as he termed it, pulling him down upon the sod, and telling him to stay there while he was hot after another, but never firing a shot at those unarmed.

Sir Stapleton Cotton with his cavalry got amongst them in another quarter, and cut them down by scores. Upwards of 2,000 threw down their arms, and their whole army now dispersed, *sauve qui peut*, leaving nearly 4,000 killed and wounded on the field of battle.

When the French broke, they made a rush for the bridge, which was soon choked up with baggage, broken gun-carriages, waggons, dead men and horses, thousands pressing forward to this point of escape. Our troops were in full pursuit, and cheering them on to destruction, while a brisk fire of artillery mixed up the living and the dead upon it. Our guns soon got the range, and kept it up, tearing to shatters every living thing attempting to escape that way. The skeletons of late strong fine regiments dashed into the boiling river on both sides, amongst the jagged rocks (peeping above the current), hoping thus to escape; but they only met another grave, nearly all perishing. It was an awful sight, as we passed that fine bridge, to see it covered with dead bodies and the debris of an army; the wounded groaning in torment, supplicating for water, and it so very near. The Duke was so hurt, he could not ride without pain, and so the pursuit was relaxed at sundown, when we gave up the chase, and then, weary enough and nothing in the larder, lay down on the sod, to dream of weeping and lamentation in England and France, our loss being 2,500 killed and wounded! *Cui bono?*

Aire and Tarbes

AFTER the affair at Orthes the medicos had great practice in carving. Maurice Quill was engaged with the French wounded a good deal, and while extracting a ball from the left side of an old veteran, he said, 'I hope you don't feel much pain.' 'Ah,' he said, in deep emotion, 'cut deeper, sir, and you will find the Emperor; he's buried in my heart!' I was looking on while he was taking off the arm of another old soldier. When done, he laid hold of it, and tossed it up in the air, crying out 'Vive l'Empereur! Vive Napoléon!' Such was the enthusiasm of those brave men.

The Duke of Richmond (then Lord March) had served on Lord Wellington's staff during the whole war without a scratch. He was a Captain in the 52nd Regiment, and, like a good and gallant soldier, joined his corps the night before the battle, to be shot through the body at the head of his company, thus learning by experience the difference between the labours and dangers of staff and regimental officers, which are in the inverse ratio to their promotions! We never got a step but by a death vacancy. The cold-hearted, ungenerous, self-interested arrogant directors of military affairs at home threw a wet blanket over young officers, unless there was a handle to one's name, court interest, or a hat-full of votes for a Tory minister!

> What can ennoble knaves, or fools, or cowards?
> Alas! not all the blood of all the Howards!

The Duke of Richmond was ever the friend of the old Peninsular army. He was a true and gallant soldier, brave and generous, and to him the remnant of the officers of that unconquerable army, so glorious to the arms of England, were indebted for the distinguished medal, bearing on clasps the names of numerous battles in which we were engaged. He represented the tardy justice to our Queen, the fourth crowned head for whom this army fought so many battles. And this noble and generous sovereign, best of all monarchs that ever filled an English throne, granted the request for all those victories achieved before she was born! The Duke of Richmond himself had ten clasps, and we gave him a splendid piece of plate to keep in continual family remembrance our love and respect for his manly and soldierlike bearing in behalf of the just claims of his comrades in war.

The battle of Orthes added another laurel to Wellington's name. It was another Sabbath-day's slaughter; somehow, most of our quarrels happened on Sunday, but I do not think that one in a hundred knew Saturday from Sunday, or Sunday from Monday, when in the field.

We followed up our friends the next day as close as we could, sticking to them like a burr to a sheep's tail. They made every effort to shake us off with a forced march and in light order, having left their arms behind them.

We had something to do as well in tinkering up our own broken ranks for the next scuffle, which was not far off. I believe, to do the thing well, an army ought to march twelve miles, fight a battle, and follow up the fugitives twelve miles farther to gain a great victory! I think we accomplished this more than once. It was surprising to find how soon the French troops rallied and made another stand after being dispersed and scattered like frightened sheep all over the country.

The weather was now very fine, which was always cheery in the field, and we had some pleasant marching over la belle France, falling in at times with some of those domestic birds about barn doors and farmyards that will not get out of one's way. It was a serious matter to meddle with them or ruffle their feathers. A farmer did complain one day, after passing his gate, that he was minus a goose. A halt and a search was made, quite satisfactory to our honesty. But these gobblers make such a fuss when out of their own element, goosy was heard skirling and clapping her wings most violently, there was a tittering laugh amongst the men, and an oho! Another search-warrant, and the farmer's goose was discovered in a drum! A drumhead court-martial on the spot, and the drummer got goose without sauce for breaking the law, all the people about looking on in amazement with their mouths wide open at the severity and justice of our discipline in an enemy's country. Our military law was severe but necessary; hanging on to a tree for theft and violence was not uncommon, the dead bodies being left there for the vulture.

Lord Wellington's wound towards the end of the battle of Orthes saved the hostile army, and so they showed front again very soon at Aire. They always met us like lions; but in the end it was like hare-hunting. It may be that the French soldiers have a little more science in war than the soldiers of our country. The French look about them, and if they see their flanks being turned, or anything adverse to their forward movement, they consider it neces-sary to give way; while the ragged old red-coats always fought away right to their front, so long as they could see a Frenchman before them, leaving their officers to do the rest. This 'grand Welling-ton' of ours, as the Spaniards always talked of him, had a concep-tion for arrangement and promptness never surpassed, decision and immediate action in all his preparations. The best Generals often-times grope in the dark, but Wellington's head was never under a cloud. He was a born soldier, while others were educated for the trade. It is one thing to fight a battle without fruits, another thing to fight a battle with success!

We came up with the enemy again on the 2nd of March, General Hill in command of our division as usual. We fell on them at once. The action was sudden and severe, and was nearly lost to us at one moment when General Da Costa, a man of no ability, attacked with his corps of Portuguese in such a slovenly unsoldierlike way that he was repulsed and driven back in a charge by the French. As usual, we had to go to their aid. We had won the high grounds by this time, and spared two regiments, 34th and 39th to tinker up the damage. Our men got savage at the Portuguese for giving way, and I believe would have fired into them at the moment as heartily as into the French. With one vehement cheer, with one powerful charge, they went slap-dash into the enemy's columns, and drove them back on their reserves. But still they rallied, and renewed the battle with singular courage for fellows who had been whacked so often. But it was all in vain, the blood of the old bricks was up, and having now done so much, the whole division entered on the play, and with one great rush upon the poor French, General Harispe at their head, their ranks were broken, and we drove them into and right through the town of Aire. They crossed the Adour, broke down the bridge, and made their way into the clouds of night, leaving us their dead to cover up. About 100 prisoners and a vast number of conscripts threw down their arms, and went away to their respective homes. They got very much into this practice when the army of France passed their doors, and was not likely to return that way. They lost some valuable officers. Our General Barns was wounded, Colonel Hood killed, and some inferior officers, i.e. some Captains, Lieutenants, and Ensigns, small fry not worth talking of! It was not the fashion in those days to regard the death of a poor Subaltern more than that of a cavalry charger, yet many of the small fry lived to be great fishes. As to private soldiers, thousands upon thousands that joined the army from England were never heard of by their kindred or friends, dead or alive. They fought and they fell and were forgotten!

Before going into the town of Aire, I stepped into a house by the roadside to look for a drink of water, the day being very hot. The only tenant I could see was a very handsome young cavalry officer of ours, elegantly dressed, lying on his back and quite dead. He had been recently killed in an affair with French cavalry thereabouts by a shot from a rifleman. The fresh blood was oozing from a bullet-hole in his forehead, and, like so many of his brave comrades, he died facing the enemy. It was a charming day to spatter the early flowers of spring with human blood.

In sixteen days we had marched nearly one hundred miles, passed over five large rivers, forced the enemy before us, captured over 1,000 prisoners, six or seven guns, and magazines, and been everywhere victorious. Let us now have a little rest to patch up our duds. I got into a very respectable house, where the good dame had some knowledge of humanity, and must have seen a starvation-looking face every time she said to me 'Bon jour'. I had not a franc in my pocket, and was too proud to ask for anything to eat. I had my rations, which did keep me alive, and one day a ham was sent into my room for my acceptance, which I finished off for breakfast, even polishing the bone. But I may as well explain that it was a goose ham well cured, smoked and bronzed, the first I had ever seen; but they are common in that part of the south of France.

The English army became popular in time. All the supplies were paid for in gold by us, while their own army did not respect property. It was said at the time that Soult remarked, 'I may expect to find by-and-by that the inhabitants will take up arms against us.' I could see that the people rather liked the red-coats now, old prejudices were wearing out, our discipline was more perfect than the French, and everything was paid for. But there was no resting-place for the soles of our feet, and so we took leave of goose hams, and a quiet rest of a few days, to look after our fighting friends, and found them as usual well posted, and ready for action, at Vic Bigore, on the Adour.   General Paris was at their head, and he fought a vigorous little battle without any advantage. We soon slashed him out of his fine position at a loss on our side of 260 men and officers.   Colonel H. Sturgeon, a skilled and accomplished officer, was amongst the slain, a great loss to our service, and much regretted by all who knew his worth.

My comorado was out on picket tonight.   I went to see him in the evening at his country house, just for the purpose of knowing personally if we might eat his share of the ration dinner or send it to his post.   I found him in a comfortable château, with a jolly gentleman landlord, who was preparing to make him very snug for the night.   The cloth was laid for dinner, plate and wine on the table.   It was a beautiful sight and made me ravenous.   I required no second invitation to be seated and wait for what was coming. I supposed the good host considered me a reserve or support to this outlying picket, sent there for his protection, as he thought, and gave me a welcome.   My poor friend Mr. Simmons, the real officer on the responsible duty, went out every now and then to visit his sentries, being not very far from the enemy.   However, we had a real dinner and very good wine, so good that an extra bottle or two were discussed after the cloth was removed, and while the interesting subject of the war was talked over.

The landlord was all on our side, perhaps from policy; but it was all the same to us which battle he fought for this evening, because his cheer was good and we had no bill to pay.   We praised his wine.   This pleased him so that he begged us to take a magnum bottle of his best to our camp in the morning, which he brought up from his cellar at once, and planted on the mantelpiece in full view. He then showed us into a handsome bedroom, with everything complete for two, and bid us 'bonne nuit, messieurs'.   My chum could not indulge in the state-bed, of course, being on duty, so I volunteered to occupy it for him.   He slipped out and away to the barn to keep watch with his men, and I peeled and slipped into bed quite bewildered.   A grand French bed, damask drapery, fine polished furniture; a swing glass, six feet high; and such lots of nicknacks and china ornaments.   There was a toilet, also, that could only be arranged by the fingers and taste of a French lady, but yet we never got a glimpse of a petticoat.   I knew that I was safe, having an officer's guard over my slumbers, so I tumbled into such a bundle of feathers I was nearly suffocated.   I had not been in such a civilised apartment, or in a bed at all, for two years and more, i.e. such a thing as they call a bed in England!

I thought the night passed away in about ten minutes.   I was called at early dawn to have some coffee.   I sometimes allowed myself five minutes to dress, but just now I was in a hurry to be off, and might have taken three minutes and a half for washing and all, all the time having my eye on the magnum of wine which I had in charge. Someone now bawled, 'The French cavalry in the long avenue'. All the house astir and in as much commotion as if the whole army was upon them. I told them not to stir. My friend outside soon stopped their progress, and having emptied a few saddles from behind the barn wall, the cavalry took the hint. A few shots after them put them full speed, and they never again returned to the 'Château de la Reine'. There was some brisk firing near at hand.

I was rather out of place, so I buckled on my sword, jumped out of a back window in a violent hurry, and away to my regiment, which I found ready to move, having just given some French patrols notice to quit! In my hurry, alas! I forgot the magnum, a source of deep regret to us for many a day. I was well chaffed, and deserved to have my grog stopped, but consoled myself in the charming thought of having passed a night of luxury in a château where I had no right to be at all, and the remembrance of the finest omelet I ever tasted. I believe it is only in France they can make omelets and coffee.

We called in the picket *en passant*. The château and its people were respected and cared for, which was acknowledged by the kind landlord, and I have no doubt that he lived free and easy ever afterwards from such visitors, for neither party ever returned that way.

We had a respite now for a long time, i.e. from the smell of gunpowder, gradually feeling our way after our unsubdued friends. Some shins were cracked and heads broken here and there, little affairs of no importance, too small for the butcher's bill! The weather was fine; no place more charming than the south of France for a fight or a bivouac. On the 20th of March we came up once more with the *parlez-vous*, as our men continued to call them.

My regiment halted in the pretty town of Tarbes, piled arms in the street, and waited for orders. The cracking of rifles was heard pretty sharp outside in the vineyards; but here comes a cocked hat in a gallop, so we may as well 'fall in'. 'Colonel W——, your regiment is to halt here till further orders. The men may get under cover and be ready to turn out at a moment's warning on their alarm-post.' A gentle hurrah went through the ranks, every one happy but the Colonel, who wanted another fight and to be killed, and the most singular part of the play was that he never was killed, but died in his bed like his grandmother.

I was welcomed into a nice house in the street. We all divided, and were received with much civility, it being our first appearance on this stage.　A kind Frenchman brought me a large metal basin of water and a napkin to wash the dust out of my eyes.　I thought the introduction very agreeable, and a preliminary of something for the interior department, as I fancied I smelt an omelet.　The day was young, and the people here dined early.　I had my horse put up and saw him fed, and now for a peaceful and a pleasant day, as I rubbed my hands with delight, when that in——l bugle of ours, as all called it, joined in the naughty word, sounded the assemblée.　There was no appeal against this music.　There was a thundering cannonade going on not far distant, and so we were all out of the town in a crack, and killing each other in the usual way, *secundum artem*.

The French had been driven out of the town in the morning by the 95th Rifles, the most celebrated old fighting corps in the army, or perhaps in the world.　They retired to their position to receive battle once more and try their luck, and bad luck attended them as usual, as Mother Skiddy predicted.

The action really now began, about twelve o'clock.　Hill's artillery thundered away on the right, Clinton's on the left, Baron Alten attacked the centre.　The French General, Harispe, was posted very strong on a hill, but was assailed most gallantly by some rifle battalions.　The fight was brief and violent, a fiery combat, muzzle to muzzle.　Of course our men would not give way, so the French did.　Meantime we forced the passage of the river and sent Villatte and his troops away double quick.　The country was now covered with confused masses of prisoners.　Some tried to escape or hide themselves, others had thrown down their arms, crying out for quarter, while the wounded on both sides lay patient and still in all their agony.

This part of the country was flat, covered with vineyards, farmhouses, deep ditches, and inclosures, not at all suitable for cavalry. But our pursuit was stopped by General Clausell, who had four fresh divisions drawn up in our front right in our path, and all ready for battle.　He lost no time in opening upon us all his batteries.　However, it was now late, and night closed the scene upon all the combatants.　Fighting for this day ceased, and in the morning the stage was clear, and not a Frenchman to be seen.　We had lost a great many good soldiers, and a dozen valiant and most excellently brave officers.　When the prison of the soul was broken up, the poor shattered shell lay there without burial, with no kindred friend to close the late brilliant eye, or say the last leave-taking words—*Requiescat in pace*.

I lay down under a fig-tree very tired with the day's excursion (my horse, of course, being in the rear, as usual on all fighting days) and disappointed of enjoying the hospitality ready for me at Tarbes.

We pushed on the next day after our beloved friends over the green hills of la belle France. Soult, we understood, was making for Toulouse, losing his young soldiers by the way; for, as soon as a conscript passed his home, he deserted. However, every bit of ground was disputed on our line of advance. Fighting was our daily bread, and I believe that officers and men went at it *con amore*, as they would follow a pack of harriers.

When we came up with their cavalry yesterday, old Major Doghearty, of the 13th Dragoons, might be seen charging at the head of his regiment, supported on his right and left by his two sons. Was not this a glorious sight of war and chivalry? Deeds of daring and of victory, too, bequeathed as an inheritance to the future armies of England. A new race of younger men soon stepped into their saddles and their shoes because they had no friends; no reward for the many and great achievements of this war. That terror of all tyrants, the press, had not the power, nor the pen, nor the freedom, nor the courage to speak out for the army as they have in the present day. So all heroic deeds were forgotten and left in abeyance, and clouds of darkness over-shadowed the lives of hundreds of brave men who died in obscurity, many of them personally known to myself.

Our line of march was now directed on Toulouse, fighting our way and driving the rightful owners of the soil before us. A long wet day found myself and two messmates in a very comfortable and well-furnished château, of which we took possession for the night. The lawful owners having run away in alarm, the house now fell into the hands of three lads of different nations. We held a council of war how it was best to proceed with honour and justice. It was quite out of the question to starve in a cook-shop, or go without dinner in such fine quarters. A couple of old ser-vants had been left in charge, so we thought it best, like gentle visitors, to ask them politely to prepare some supper for three Generals! 'O mon Dieu!' they began both together, talking three-score to the dozen, keeping time with a jerking of the head, shoulders, arms and legs, in fact there was nothing in the house to eat or drink; but it was out of the question to take the word of an old French butler, so we began the evening's amusement in our way to forage. *General* Thomson and his servant took the outside of the dwelling, including the hen-roost; *General* Russell the interior; while *General* G. B. got up a good fire, collected feather-beds and blankets, and made a grand shake-down for three on the hearth of the library, where he lay in luxury awaiting the foraging

party. By-and-by the two *Generals* and their *staff* appeared
with a very good supply. The cook and butler got out of their
alarm, and busied themselves, like good allies, in helping to prepare
the evening meal. The library was a large room with a wide
fire-place, and good enough for all we required. A couple of
fowls were soon roasting before our fire, a flagon of wine on the
table, and sausages, with a yard of bread! They made bread by
the yard in this part of France, and sometimes in a ring as large
as a horse-collar.

We all lay down by the fire now, quite cosy, our wet clothes
hanging at the sides to dry, my little horse provided for. We were
all as happy as three kings, when that bird of ill omen, our Adjutant, raised the latch and walked in, opened his roster-book, and
warned me for outlying picket immediately! 'The men have fallen
in and are waiting, please look sharp, sir. I thought I would not
have found you out tonight.' 'Well, I'm very sorry you did find
me, but you are always in luck finding me when you want an officer
in a hurry for duty, besides, 'tis not my tour for picket tonight.'
'No, it is not,' he said, 'but Mr. W—— can't be found, and you are
next on the roster—you shall have an overslaw.' No use battling
with an old Adjutant like Peckett. Precise and correct in everything regarding his duty, he had been an excellent Sergeant-Major,
and always gave the time to a second. 'What time is it, Peckett?'
'Ten minutes and a half past one, sir.' He carried a load of a big
silver watch as large as a turnip, which regulated the whole
regiment!

Casting one glance at the fowls as they began to brown at the
fire, I turned out in the rain, and banged the door after me like
thunder. I suppose I was in a thundering bad humour, but away I
went in the dark about two miles with my good orderly men who
never complained; reconnoitred the country as well as I could see,
planted my sentries, and got the picket under cover in a brick-shed.
There was a village in front, occupied by our cavalry. If I had
been in my proper place, I ought to have been in advance of this
village, but that was no business of mine. 'Obey orders', was the
order of the day, and the night too.

I groped my way down to this cavalry quarter, called and requested to see General Long, in command of all the advanced posts
here. He and his staff had just done dinner. I touched at once
on the valour of his cavalry by saying, 'I am sent here, sir, to
support you. My men are close by, what are your orders?'

'I don't require your aid at all,' he said, 'you may go back if you
wish.' 'Very good, sir, I will return, for my men are wet and
weary after a long day's march.' 'But you had better have some

AIRE AND TARBES

dinner before you go, 'tis getting late.' I hesitated a moment, thought of home, and the pair of roast fowls and fireside! I declined the General's offer with all due thanks, made for my post, called in my sentries, and away we went quite jolly for our own quarters at a quick march.

All this took up as much time as would roast a sheep, but still I did not despond, but kept my eye on the mess dinner, in the luxurious hope of coming in for a bone. But, alas! when I got back, the *two generals* were asleep by the fireside where I left them, and the debris of the dinner on the table—some bones, a piece of bread, and the tail of a bottle of wine. I was horrified and called myself a stupid donkey, anything but an old soldier for not sitting down and eating my dinner at the table of a real General, when I had the blessed opportunity. I have not forgotten or forgiven myself yet, and thought—

> Who fights to the end may win, but doubly wise,
> Who knows the moment when to compromise,
> And for a bird in hand, forbear to push
> A doubtful search, for two inside the bush!

A ham and cold roast turkey just going from the General's table as I went in—dry bones, the tail of a sausage, a morsel of bread, and a driblet of wine was all I found on my return.

When dogs are hungry, they go to sleep—and so did G. B——!

Off again the next cock-crow, dodging our Gallic friends across the country. They roll people up in wet sheets in Germany, and put them to bed to make them warm. We are generally kept warm on the line of march, trudging along in our wet shirts, which dry on our bones when a blink of the sun favours us. We had got into a rainy week.

Our General now crossed the Ariège river. Of course we never did pass a river, or could walk peaceably over a green sod in France, without being insulted by a shower of musket-balls, cannon-shot, or a dragoon sabre, ready to cut off a fellow's nose. *Vide* poor Captain C—— of the Buffs, who lost his nose and an arm on the same day! Our dragoon sabres were sharp too, and left their mark behind them.

We were now approaching, at the beginning of April, the famous town of Toulouse, where Marshal Soult had pitched his tent, and hoisted his colours to make another stand, and another grand effort to beat Wellington. But six years of almost uninterrupted success had engrafted a seasoned, warlike strength and confidence into the very heart and muscles of our soldiers that made them invincible. They would willingly fall under their colours, and die in battle, but they would not be conquered at the eleventh hour, and so here was another pretty quarrel just going to begin.

My corps was distributed in some hamlets convenient to the river, where we kept watch, and kept ourselves warm for a few days, when the brilliant sun of France came forth to pay us a long visit, a most agreeable change which made us all very cheery. We had the big town before us; conjectures were innumerable; a thousand opinions issued every day from all ranks.

Our baggage was up; commissariat supplies enough to feed the troops. We had wine, rations, and everything but money; still kept six months in arrear of our pay. But we knew that England was a good paymaster, and it would all come in a heap some day, if one lived to see it.

The river Garonne, as everyone knows, runs through Toulouse. The position was a valuable one for the French Marshal. A town, not regularly fortified, but made very formidable by batteries, redoubts, intrenchments, loop-holed houses, an ancient wall, the river, and a canal. All these places were ornamented with cannon, ready to salute the British General on his first appearance before the city. The suburb St. Cyprian was protected by an old wall, very thick, with towers and intrenchments, loop-holed houses, and batteries in the streets, all very nicely arranged to stop the progress of Lord Hill and his division. This was our allotment in the part of the play which was to come off very soon, in the teeth of General Reille and two divisions of the French army. On the 27th of March our brigade was ordered up from Murat to get over a pontoon bridge at midnight. We found the river too wide for our number of boats, so gave that up. We tried it again on the 30th, when a new bridge was laid—crossed and recrossed, and yet that did not answer. I don't know why, I was not in the secret. It was a laborious work throwing over this bridge on a dark night. I was very tired! about two o'clock in the morning, the open door of a house which was close by invited me to look in; an old rickety straw bed, looking very *lively*, stood in the corner, upon which I lay down to have forty winks, positively no more, but was fast asleep in the crushing of a mosquito. Unlawful slumbers are never refreshing; I had no business to be there. One is always jumping up and saying where am I? What brought me here? I opened my other eye (soldiers sleep, or ought to sleep, with one eye open), by the glimpse of a rushlight, and found myself hemmed in against the wall by our Brigadier-General, the Honourable Sir Robert O'Callaghan, the biggest man in the whole division, snoring like a windmill. 'All right, little Bob (as he was sometimes called), if I have no business here, I'm sure you haven't, unless the pontoons

are gone down with the stream.   It is the first time I have had the
honour of sharing a bed with any of the Lismore family.   Bad luck
to the fleas and all backbiters!   Sleep on till I call you,' saying
which I cautiously crept over the giant, to put my wet boot upon
the face of another deserter, and to tumble over a third on the floor.
They both jumped up in alarm, and roused little Bob, who thought
the French had him pinned up in a corner.   I knocked over the
glimmer for safety, leaving the trio in the dark to explain, if they
wished, how they all got there while on duty!

I told this little anecdote to the dear old General long afterwards
at one of his dinner parties at Madras, when he was there as Commander-in-Chief, which made him laugh heartily, and introduced
many of the old stories and anecdotes of the Peninsula — not in an
old tent, but in a splendid palace.   He was a brave soldier, and a
powerful Irishman.   He carried a big sword, and used it at times
with great effect, slashing the heads of Frenchmen in the 'Donnybrook Fair' style.   He would cut them down right and left, and
upon one occasion, when his sword was shattered in his hand, he
got hold of a big shillelagh, and laid about him like a thresher with
a flail, and never afterward gave it up; it answered so well, he said.
But like the rest of the gallant band, he dropped into his narrow
cell, and was soon forgotten.

There were many ways of meeting the enemy in combat, but
who ever heard of an officer going into battle with a pocket full of
stones?   It was a sort of pastime with a Captain Irvine, of the old
'Slashers'.   He was a capital shot with a stone, and a very strong,
able, active man, left-handed, who delivered his shot with such force
and accuracy that he would knock a fellow into next week.   He
never minded meeting two or sometimes three Frenchmen, when
they were detached.   Pretty sure of knocking one down with a
stone, he sprang upon the other like a leopard, and knocked him
on the head with his own firelock, and with one great, thrilling
shout he paralyzed the third.   If he did not trip him up he
frightened him out of reach, pelting him with stones as he ran.
All this gymnastic play created at times roars of laughter amongst
the men, for it never was done in a corner, nor for bravado.   This
brave Irish gentleman and soldier survived the war, but never
reached any rank beyond a Captain.

CHAPTER 11

The Battle of Toulouse

OUR men began to fix their flints and examine their powder on the 9th as we approached the town, and took up our quarters in front of St. Cyprian. The weather was fine, everyone jolly, and the Patlanders in particular cracking their jokes. 'How the d—— are we to get over that big sthrame av a river to leather them vagabones out o' that?' says Paddy Muldoon, for he wasn't kilt yet. 'O, niver mind,' says another old cripple, who lost an eye on the Nive, 'that countryman av yours wid the long nose will show you the way when he's riddy.' 'O, be gar, then, we'll not wait very long, for I seen him over here this morn wid our Farmer Hill, spying them wid his long eye-glass, an' he won't keep us waiting. But there's oceans on 'em down there in the town pickin' holes in the wall, and fencen all the houses, so mind that other eye av yours!' They were ever laughing and cracking their Irish jokes at the worst of times.

The Duke crossed the river about fourteen miles below the town, on his pontoon bridge, with the Light Division; and early in the morning he formed his army. On Easter Sunday morning, the 10th of April 1814, I was very comfortably seated in the library of a château belonging to some stupid fellow who had run away in alarm, leaving his hall door open. We were preparing a breakfast of fresh eggs and bacon, which were quarrelling in the frying-pan outside in the sunshine, when bang! went the signal-gun, and Freeman, our trusty bugleman, sounded the assemblée at once. Whilst the men were getting on their packs and their arms ready, we gobbled up the contents of the frying-pan, left our traps in charge of servants, fell into our places, and marched down to join in the bloody fray of another Sabbath day's unholy work. It was very handy for us, not far to go, and all fresh as young colts. In twenty minutes we came to the scratch, and were hard at work fighting in the town, on the suburbs on the left bank of the river, where the enemy had two divisions under the command of Count Reille. It is always ugly, dangerous work fighting in a town; so many holes and corners, hiding-places and loop-holes, where one may be picked off by an unseen enemy. This was just our case, fighting from house to house and from street to street, our men having their bones cracked, and dropping off at every corner. As the enemy retired, or were driven back, they fired the houses they left, to arrest our progress, not sparing their own property. We found in many houses the furniture piled up in rooms, ready for the torch. The streets were barricaded, and cannon planted at every entrance, pounding away at the first blink of any red-coat. But our men dashed on through fire and smoke, and carried on the work surely and gradually, for we lost nothing that we gained. Our senior Captain Baker, had that morning got his majority, and was one of the first killed. He had come all the way from India to join our battalion. Other officers had been with the regiment in all its battles, and had never been hit five years—such is the fate of war!

There was a furious row going on across the river, a tremendous crash of great guns and small-arms. The two Marshals had met, with their two valiant armies, and quarrelled. They were always fighting and quarrelling. Saturday or Sunday was all the same to them, and here they were at it on an Easter Day, a festival of solemnity in all Christian lands, but not the least regarded on the banks of the Garonne. The battle went on with desperate fury, both sides determined to win the fight. It was a charming day, and worthy of better deeds than destroying life. We had the bravest, the best, the finest-disciplined and well-seasoned army in the world; fighting was their daily bread—it gave them an appetite. No other soldiers on earth had a chance against them in fair and open ground. The Duke knew it, and let them loose this morning.

There was pounding on both sides of the river in full force about noon, the French having all the advantage. Their two miles of position along Mont Rave were defended by intrenchments, breast-works, redoubts, and immense batteries bristling with cannon. Our side, too, looked as formidable. I never had, personally, any taste for fighting in the dark, or in the streets, although we used to practise the art of 'street-firing and retiring'. All fudge!

The advance towards the French position was very swampy and unfit for cavalry or the passage of guns. This alone would shake the nerves of any other man than Wellington, but, always confident, he relied on his own British soldiers.

General Freyve, a Spanish leader, asked permission to have the honour of leading his troops first into battle. Granted—and away they went, 9,000 strong, with a good reserve, very resolved to have all the victory to themselves. The French began to torment them, as they advanced, with a shower of lead. They wavered, and rushed for shelter into a deep hollow. The French, now taking the advantage of war, turned out of their breastworks and poured volley after volley into the poor Spaniards, the bullets hissing through their quivering flesh as hard as they could tear, the enemy at their heels, until too near our cavalry, mortifying to the Duke, but the only remark he made was—

'Well, I have seen some curious sights, but I never saw 10,000 men running a race before!'

Sir Thomas Picton failed in his attack at another point, entirely from disobeying his master's orders; turning a false attack into a real one, and losing thereby his chance of success, and 400 men and officers. Poor Sir Thomas never could bridle his ardour when he had a chance of a dash at the French. But dashing in war means courage without prudence.

We had now forced the first line of intrenchments and barricades on our side. The second we looked at, but it had such a very angry appearance that we slackened our fire to bide our time and listen to the music on the other side. The crisis was approaching with some good promise to the French, the Spaniards being utterly routed. General Picton had been repulsed, and our men, frightfully reduced in numbers, were making their way to the French position through a deep swamp tangled with many other obstacles, a heavy fire of great guns and musketry being poured into their teeth the whole way, they not returning a single shot. What other troops in the world would have faced such a storm of death? But they did advance, and met Taupin's whole force rushing down upon them. At this moment some rockets were discharged from our side, got amongst the Frenchmen's legs with an unheard-of hissing, curving, serpentining, biting, and kicking noise that they never saw or heard before. It staggered their courage and steadiness long enough to let General Lambert's brigade make a rush with a cheer amongst them, with such irresistible power that they went to the right-about and fled. Taupin was killed, and our people gained the platform.

Soult, seeing this danger, brought up all his artillery to make a clearance of this little force, aided by double numbers of infantry. But the domineering courage of British soldiers overcame this obstacle, and decided the first act of the play. The Scotch Brigade and the Portuguese, with Marshal Beresford's division, dashed on next, scrambling up the hill; all the breastworks and batteries in their front pouring a wasting fire into their face, did not stagger their courage. The French yielded here for a little, but rallied and returned with their reserves, and there was an awful struggle. General Harispe encouraged his men, and fought with them with great vigour. He surrounded the redoubts we had taken, and broke in upon the 42nd Highlanders. This gallant corps fought so bravely against such long odds that there were but few blue bonnets left in half an hour. The fighting was desperate here. Our men fell fast and were soon reduced to a 'thin red line' of old bricks. The French had the advantage from numbers and position, but the British, regardless of numbers at any time, go in to win. Harispe and another General had now fallen, fighting like game-cocks. Our 6th Division rushed on madly for a victory, and kept the ground until the French left the platform. Soult, seeing that the red-coats had won the day, abandoned the field, covered with slain, relinquished the whole of Mont Rave, further resistance being useless, and retired into Toulouse.

This was what I would call honest good fighting, face to face, hand to hand on the open field, the usual practice in the Peninsula. On the other side we had gained a good many streets, and kept them. Wherever a head appeared from under cover it was in danger of being cracked with a dozen bullets. I had myself some providential escapes. Passing into a long, narrow, shady street, very quiet, and no one visible, a cannon-shot came whistling past my head so close I felt the wind of the ball on my cheek, which whift me round. I darted into a house in a jiffy, when another came bang after me, passed through the room, and fell from the opposite wall. My Captain had just turned the same corner, when I warned him to look out, and only just in time to save his life, for which he blew me up, saying, 'You never keep your eyes open, or you might have seen that gunner at the top of the street just waiting to crack your wild head.' I peeped out at the door, and, sure enough, there he was, standing by his gun, ready to blow the match. I rolled his own shot out into the street, keeping my eye on him, but he fired no more. One of our men saw him, and 'made him lave that sure,' as he said, for 'I saw him fire on the Captain, and only waited to creep near enough to pitch him over!'

Curious to see how the battle was going on over the river, I invited our Colonel, Worsley, to accompany me for a belle-vue

K

quite at hand. 'Where are you going to take me?' he said, 'remember every house is full of sharpshooters, and if I follow you, it will surely be into their company.' 'Oh no, 'tis all safe. I have got a ladder here, we will top this house and see a bit of the fight on the other side. Did you ever hear a more terrific fire?' By this time we had clambered up to the top of a house, keeping a big brick chimney in our front, just high enough to look over to see some of the murder over the way, but had not long enjoyed the view when the brick-dust was knocked out of the chimney by a shower of bullets, we not having calculated that our heads were not only visible, but the very shell of humanity exposed to be cracked like an egg.

When the ostrich is pressed hard in the chase he runs his head into a bush or into the sand, and considers himself safe! I don't think we much exceeded the wisdom of this stupid bird upon this occasion of our curiosity. The next volley, which came fast, sent us away double quick rolling down, ladder and all, and nearly broke our necks. I got off cheap enough with a slight wound; Colonel Worsley had his epaulet spoiled with a shot, and a ventilator made in his shako.

We kept pounding away until night drew the curtain over a wide scene of painful misery. Multitudes of wounded lay scattered over miles of ground; the agony and torment and shrieks and helpless condition of thousands found no relief for a long time. Hundreds died in the night for want of care, for it was impossible for the medicos to attend to half the wounded. The living had a heavy day of fatigue and fighting with great excitement, but their hands and their hearts were up to their work, in spite of any reaction.

The programme of the Easter Sunday was now closed. The men lighted the camp-fires and sat round them cooking and chatting over the ration dinner and absent comrades.

Next day was a *dies non*, i.e. we had no fighting worth talking of. We kept all the town we gained, and the French kept the rest. We buried the dead in shallow graves. Both parties kept a sharp look-out on each other all day. I went on outlying picket at night with instructions to be wide awake, and feel my way at the dawn of day towards the bridge if I met with no opposition.

On the morning of the 12th, at grey dawn, I was feeling my way with the picket without opposition. Arriving at the fine stone bridge, I found it barricaded all the way over with hogsheads filled with earth and stones and gravel. Walking over these, I came to the ponderous iron gate, locked and fastened with heavy chains. When the people saw me advance with my party of red-coats, they came down with goodwill, with crowbars, and forced the gate open, and gave us a cheer and a welcome, so that I had the honour of being the first British officer that entered Toulouse. Here I halted until my own corps came up. We then marched in, colours flying, drums beating, all very jolly, and halted for an hour in the street waiting for orders. In the meantime most of the officers popped into a café to get some breakfast. The windows and balconies were soon crowded with ladies, waving their white kerchiefs, and throwing down amongst us bouquets of fresh flowers, as if they had sprung up spontaneously. The white cockade appeared as if by magic everywhere, although the French army had not been out of the town twelve hours.

We fancied that we were now to be left here in this garden of Eden amongst sweet flowers and pretty girls that were smiling down upon our tattered red coats—vain imagination! An atrocious cocked hat of an aide-de-camp came riding up with a smirk, saying, 'Colonel Worsley, you are to follow up the enemy on the Toulon road with your regiment as quickly as you can. You will receive subsequent orders'; and away he went, after destroying all our hopes and pleasant waking dreams. I believe our fighting Colonel was the only one who wished to advance in such a hurry, and not to retard our progress a moment, he paid the breakfast at the café and hurried us off.

The whole French army had taken to their heels in the night and filed through the town. As they passed on they broke down the bridges over the canal to impede our line of march. But we never came up with them again, nor smelt the perfume of tobacco and onions which tainted the air behind them. We halted at the little town of Villefranche, and there we heard by an express from Paris that Napoleon the Grand had abdicated, and that the Allies were in the capital of la belle France, and all the rest of it. This was all very serene, and I believe joyful news to most of us, for in reality we had enough fighting and marching and starving for a long time to come. At all events I thought so, and was quite content with the little share and small part I had in the campaign, having marched through Portugal, all over Spain, and well into France. I had been in thirteen engagements with the next best troops in the world, and escaped for three years out of the hands of the Philistines without any broken bones, a providential and rare occurrence in those days, when one considers the rough usages of war, and that we left in Spain and France the bones of nearly 100,000 men; most of them bleaching in the sun, after being picked bare by the vulture and the wolf.

We now considered the war at an end, and began to enjoy ourselves in a fashion, proud of our conquests and the glory of our arms, a stirring sound amongst all ranks. But war is never far away. From man to the very smallest insect, all are at strife.

After conquest one begins to count the cost. War is a great evil, and a very expensive trade. In this one England expended more than a hundred millions sterling money on her own operations, besides an immense expenditure on Spain and Portugal. Her land forces fought and won eighteen pitched battles, besides *affaires* and combats without number, took four great fortresses by siege, and sustained ten others. Two hundred thousand of the enemy were killed, wounded, and prisoners.

It was said the Duke of Wellington committed faults. Who ever heard or read of a great commander making war in all things faultless? He was a great general, with a patient foresight, a clear judgment, prompt and decisive, insuring the whole confidence of his army, and yet had to contend against the Governments of England, Spain, and Portugal; all retarding his progress and casting dust in his eyes. All those to whom he looked for support were jealous and vindictive, even the Cabinet Ministers of his own country. And they say he committed faults — what were they? England had no army until he made one. He landed in Portugal with 9,000 men, and beat back the armies of France to their own firesides. He had rare qualities as a commander. He overthrew the great conqueror Napoleon, the swell and dash of a mighty wave, before whom kingdoms fell. If you fight for England you should always win, and what English General was ever so victorious as Wellington?

In summing up accounts and returns for the last few days, it appeared that we had lost 4 Generals and 4,659 officers and men, killed and wounded. Total loss of the French, 5 Generals and 3,000 officers and men, ditto; a useless and lamentable sacrifice of life, Napoleon having abdicated before the battle. A Colonel Cook and a French Colonel, St. Simon, had been despatched from Paris to make known to the two armies that hostilities must now cease. These officers were detained on the road by the police, near Blois, where the Empress Louisa was holding a court. This officious detention cost the blood of 7,000 brave men, which flowed over Mont Rave and through the streets of Toulouse.

My regiment returned to the gay city of Toulouse, where we were quartered. The officers were billeted here and there through the town. 'Tis all a lottery; one may get into an hospitable house, another may find a vinegar-face of a landlady. I was not over lucky, but my room was clean, and I lived as best I could on my promissory note, the six months' pay due, the great sum of about

£55, deducting income tax, which was levied from the pay of the junior Ensign!

The Duke of Wellington established his headquarters in Toulouse. There was no end to gaiety. We were out at balls, concerts, and evening parties. We had the *entrée* into all the theatres to any part of the house for a franc. The people seemed happy and rejoiced over the new order of things. The town had not suffered in the least during the killing and slaying outside, excepting on our side of the river, which was plundered, fired, and demolished by the French troops as they were beaten back. The Duke did not suffer a shot or shell to be thrown into the city when held by the vanquished troops after their retreat from Mont Rave, and of course gained the respect and esteem of the citizens for his consideration and humanity.

The Duke d'Angoulême made his public *entrée* into the city escorted by Wellington and his staff, and all the dignitaries of the town and country. I went out with the rest of the cocked hats and feathers to meet him some distance off, being well mounted on a spunky horse, who would be in the front. He carried me, *nolens, volens*, alongside of the Royal Duke, when and where I was admonished by Sir E. P——, and ordered to fall back! I never had a very thin skin, and did not torment myself at this checkmate. But I have known an officer who was so hurt by receiving a rebuke at the head of his regiment that he went deranged, was placed in an asylum, and never recovered. He was a most excellent officer, and had his regiment in first-rate order, until he met this uncouth savage of an Inspecting-General.

The Duke's welcome home was echoed everywhere by old and young. Fresh and fair, aged men in heads of snow, all pressed forward to kiss his stirrup.

After six weeks of refreshing jollification, we got the route for Bordeaux. I was glad of the expected change of quarters; we had a few days' notice to quit, and lighten our baggage. I sold my three horses to raise the wind and pay my debts. I did not realise for the three so many dollars as one of them had cost me, the market being overstocked with horses, mules, and donkeys, all at a fearful discount, every officer selling off. I was not very well at this time. I suppose a regular kind of life and a feather-bed did not agree with my former manner of life on the green sod. Our doctor recommended me to go down the river with the invalids in an open boat. Barges were provided for the sick and wounded soldiers, small boats for small parties of officers. The weather being charming, we required neither sails nor oars, so away we went, smoothly gliding over the silver stream, one man steering (it was hard work for the poor horses pulling up those heavy barges against the stream).

We landed every evening at some village on the banks of the fine river to pass the night. The dames from the different auberges made a rapid descent upon us the moment we landed, with such a clatter and noisy invitation to go their respective houses—everything so nice, so good, superior, and such moderate terms. They were abusing each other all the time in the most *distingué* fashion.

We knew pretty well what was meant by moderate terms, all that they could screw out of famished pockets. After exhausting all their polite language, if it is possible to tire a Frenchwoman's tongue, we took a peep into their respective shells, selected our lodgings, and made our bargain. This was a necessary arrangement in France, and all over the Continent, to prevent disputes, overcharges, and imposition.

However, they bustled about with good humour, and made us all so very comfortable, that we would have remained there willingly for weeks if we could. The situation was so charming, so peaceful; no parades nor drills, nor a chance of one's bones being broken with shot or shell. How wonderful was the feeling of quiet; no trampling of horses, nor clashing of arms, nor tir-whit of a shell, or the whop of a cannon-ball, splashing the mud in one's face, or perhaps the brains of your camarado.

Three delightful days we passed on the Garonne, and then brought up in the beautiful town of Bordeaux, amongst fruit and flowers, choice wine, and nice friendly people. The first stage, homeward bound—it all appeared as a holy dream. Our last run down was a short one. On landing, four of us went to a café and ordered breakfast—a good one, and no mistake. We were hungry as hunters, and were well served. We cast lots who was to pay the bill. I was the Jonas, and it just cleared me out to a cent, and left me in every sense in light marching order. Not a penny at my command—let loose in a large city, full of luxury, frolic, and fun. I searched all my pockets in vain for a single franc to get a scrubby dinner, but it was no go; so I went in search of my billet. After roving about the city for some hours, I found No. 2 Rue St. Colomb —Monsieur Ducasse—knocked at the door and presented my ticket to the servant, who took it up for examination. After surveying me with wonder or admiration, never having seen a red-coat at No. 2 before, I was received kindly, and shown upstairs to a suitable room, for sitting and sleeping in combined, and left there to look out at the window, to turn over in my mind how or where I was to find my servant and my baggage, which was reduced into so small a compass that he could easily carry it on the top of his knapsack, along with firelock and the rest of his war tools, for I had discarded the frying-pan and all the other camp toggery. I made a start into the town, without money or credit—nothing but an alarming appetite. I knew I had my rations to fall back upon, but I could not find my servant, nor could he find me—we were both lost. I rambled about in search of him for hours, and did not find No. 2 till late, when I was presented with some light supper of salad or vegetable diet. A round of boiled beef would have been more in my way, but I never saw one in France.

The kind landlord now told me that I must never be out of the way at three o'clock—it was their dining hour. I must always breakfast and dine with the family, and be one of themselves while I remained, or he would be very angry, with an emphasis on the word and a smile on his honest face—a friendly offer which I accepted with thanks. Particularly lucky I thought myself, as there was nothing in my department but the rations and a thundering appetite. I had permission to draw my rations once a week in a heap, which was sent to the kitchen of my landlord. The next morning I made my *début* at the breakfast table, after waiting about three hours beyond my usual time. An early tasse of *café noir* keeps a Frenchman alive until the *déjeuner* at eleven o'clock. I was introduced to Madame and the fair Clementine, not out of her teens, and the son, an agreeable young fellow, who spoke English a leetle. We became great allies and correspondents for many years afterwards. I found my stray cook and butler, who was also a guest and lived in clover—nothing to do but clean my boots and study French in the *cuisine*. His name was Death, which may account for many escapes in battle, he being the destroyer never to be destroyed; but he was a stupid fellow at any foreign language!

The young lady played on the harp and piano, and was really an accomplished, pretty, bashful girl, who was sent to Mass very often with her maid, and to confess her sins to a crafty old priest who might have excused her innocence. The absolution was required within the box, not from the simple child on its knees outside.

They had little music parties of an evening. On one of those occasions a French officer came up to me and looked at my buttons, being, as he said, familiar with the No. 34, and asked me if there was an officer named Day in the regiment, and if I knew anything of him. 'Oh, yes! he was our Adjutant, but was unfortunately killed on the Pyrenees on the 25th of July last, when you paid us that most unfriendly visit.' 'Not so,' he said, 'but was mortally wounded. I found him on the battlefield after he had been plundered, and spoke to him. He gave me the sign and token of a brother of our craft, and, being a Freemason myself, I took him from that moment under my charge. I was sent to Bayonne with our wounded and many of your prisoners. Poor Day was my especial care—I got him so far, and made his wasting life as quiet to him as possible. He wanted for many things that I had not in my power to provide. I got him cash for a bill on England, which I may say was duly honoured, but he did survive over a couple of weeks or so, and was buried with Masonic honours.'

This was the finale of a good soldier. He fell into the kind hands of a brother Mason, and was not left, as we thought, on the field amongst the slain, to be devoured by the vultures. I resolved, after hearing this little chivalric story, to become a Freemason if I got safe home, and I kept my word. The Brethren are to be found amongst all nations; and if you can make yourself known, you may be sure of aid, friendship, and security. Although denounced by the Pope as heretics and out of the pale of the Church, I can assure his Holiness they are the most loyal of her Majesty's subjects, staunch supporters of her Crown and dignity, and of the Church of England as established by law, and on this subject the opinion of the Pope is worthless beyond the Vatican.

Our army was now encamped about seven miles from Bordeaux. As if we had not fighting enough, certain regiments were selected to embark for America, to begin a new war with people who could speak English. Our wise law-makers at home were too fond of settling disputes in those days with powder and lead. The expedition embarked for New Orleans under the command of Lieutenant-General Sir Edward Pakenham, brother-in-law to the Duke of Wellington, an able and gallant officer who passed through the Peninsular war to be killed by an American rifleman from behind a bale of cotton.

The rest of our army began to embark for England as ships arrived. In the meantime there was much unpleasant work and bad feeling between French and English officers. Both were so habituated to fighting it seemed quite out of their power to give it up—like two game-cocks who meet on the same path, they must have a kick at each other! There was a feeling of deep jealousy against us; we received much attention, and the ladies favoured the British officers with smiles, which made things worse. There were many quarrels, and the *Duello* came into practice. The theatres were crowded, and some of our officers were insulted one night by their antagonists. To insult one red-coat then was an insult to all, and so there was a general row, the French officers being driven out of the house. The next night there was a great muster of both parties, I believe for the purpose of renewing the war or opening a new campaign at Bordeaux. The Frenchmen had their swords, the English officers none. The Irish gentlemen carried shillelaghs, as they do at Ballymacrack, in Tipperary. Somehow a nice little quarrel was soon got up about some ladies who were receiving attention from the boys of Kilkenny, every one of them nearly six feet high. Indeed, the sweet girls of Kilkenny, although not so tall, are very fine specimens of Divine art—so fair and so fresh—

> Their cheeks are like roses,
> Their lips just the same,
> Or like a dish of ripe strawberries
> Smothered in cream.

The French ladies not appearing to countenance any but those big Irishmen, sharp words were spoken against all red-coats, a great many frowns. Swords were half unsheathed and dashed back into the metal scabbard with a sort of clang of defiance—the blood of St. Patrick was roused. Those gentle creatures, whose trade was killing and slaying, did not require much fuel to get up their steam. One of the Fitzgerald's 'Light Division', a battering-ram of himself, drew his stick half-way up through his left hand, and sent in down again with a bang on the floor, looking pistols and daggers. There were some sarcastic words, then a shove and a scuffle, which soon increased to something like an Irish row at Donnybrook Fair, when the Frenchmen were banged out of the theatre wholesale. All this play began in the lobby between the acts, and, as the last of the blue-coats went rolling down the stairs, some one above cried out, 'Exeunt omnes!' and all was quiet. Next morning was fixed for the *Duello*, the general finale of such sports. Blood was spilt on both sides very freely, and one or two gentlemen were qualified for a wake. Preparations were being made for a great fighting field-day on the following morning, but the whole of last night's campaign being reported to our Commander-in-Chief, hostilities were suspended by a general order. All officers were prohibited going again to this theatre, under certain pains and penalties.

The French officers were ordered by their chiefs to retire across the Garonne to their own quarters.

In defiance of the general order, some of our officers had the imprudence to return to the same theatre, but found a sergeant there with a book to insert the name of any who insisted on going in. With one exception they all retired, and that exception was the senior Captain of my own regiment, an old officer who ought to have shown a better example. When the book was sent next morning to the Adjutant-General, Captain B—— was placed in arrest, and had his choice to stand a court-martial or quit the service. He chose the latter, and gave a step in the corps, a most unfortunate finale and deeply regretted by all his friends. But the first duty of the British soldier is to obey orders!

My regiment lay in camp some miles from the city. I was too comfortable myself with my kind friends at No. 2 to mix in any of these broils. Their hours were early, and the family quiet and happy, nor was it my part to be out late, so I stayed at home. The good landlord used to say to me every day at dinner, 'No ros-beff, Monsieur George', and the kind lady always gave me Benjamin's portion at breakfast *a la fourchette!*

My corps had nothing to do, so they did not want me, nor was I at all anxious to leave my town residence.

I went out one day to pay them a visit, and to see Sir Lowry Cole on a little private affair. General Cole was a neighbour of ours when at home, and always ready to do me a service, but we seldom met. He commanded the 4th Division of the army. On this occasion he got me leave of absence to precede my regiment going home. My turn for leave was far distant, so I came the old soldier over my seniors. But they forgave me after much chaffing, such as 'We suppose that General Cole is going to take you on his personal staff, and, of course, you must go home for your cocked hat and feather.' 'O, no doubt, old fellow, lucky enough for the man who has a home to go to. I will be happy to see you all at my château when your time comes to be quartered in our country town.' And the time did come in reality, and the officers, one and all, were welcome guests at Belle-vue when I was far away, frying in the East Indies, in another campaign, and in another regiment.

But here I am, still passing a day at the camp near Bordeaux hearing all the news, seeing all my old comrades, the men of my company, and everyone, as if I had been absent a year, everybody jolly, oceans of money, and no end to good living for man and horse! An issue of six months' back pay in gold opened the eyes, and the mouths, and the hands, and the hearts of a whole army. The matter was how to spend it. Soldiers like sailors win their money like horses, and spend it like asses. There was no lack of wine-houses and restaurants, dominoes, pitch and toss: Head, I win!—tail, you lose!—anything to catch the penny. So their thirty or forty dollars did not last long.

'What about our old friend, Mrs. Commissary-General Skiddy?' I asked one of my sergeants. 'O, be gad, sir, she's all right and fresh as a chamrog. There she is, sir, crossing the green, would you like to speak to her?' 'Yes, I will hail her myself. Hiloo, mother Skiddy, come over here till I look at you, and see if it's

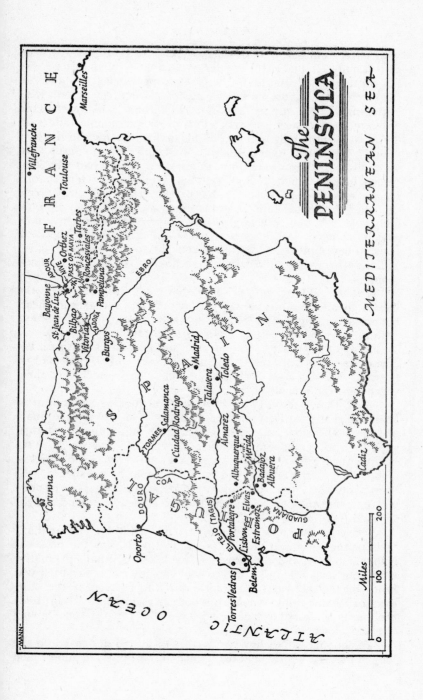

The PENINSULA

MEDITERRANEAN SEA

FRANCE

Villefranche
Toulouse
Marseilles

ADOUR
Bayonne
St Jean de Luz
NIVE Orthez
PASS OF MAYA
Roncesvales
Pampeluna
Bilbao
Vitoria
ADOUR
EBRO
Burgos

SPAIN

Madrid
Talavera
Toledo
Salamanca
Ciudad Rodrigo
Almarez
Albuquerque
Merida
Badajoz
Albuera
TORMES
COA
DOURO
TEJO (TAGUS)
GUADIANA

Coruña

Oporto

PORTUGAL
Portalegre
Lisbon
Elvas
Estramoz
Belem

Torres Vedras

ATLANTIC OCEAN

Cadiz

Miles
100   200

yourself or your ghost?' 'Oh then, Musha, God bless you my dear, sure it's myself that's glad to see your honour alive, after being kilt on the top of a house in the great battle when I was away in the care of Dan. Sure they reported down where I was, you were kilt entirely. But, my fegs, it's right well you're looking, the Lord Presarve ye, and sure Dan was so sorry for yer honour, and said, "how many's the mile you carried his firelock for him on the long march", for he was sometimes bent, tired, and ready to dhrop. An ye know, sir, when I found him smashed up in that battle at Saint Peter's, he says to me, "Biddy," says he, "I'll never march any more, for my leg's bruck in two heves, by that pagan that kilt me." Well, sir, when the doctor cum to set his leg, it wasn't bruck at all, only a big hole in it, but 'twas mighty sore; an sure I have him here now as good as new. All the men as was wounded, barrin' the killed, cum up here t'other day. Would you like to see Dan, sir?'

'Surely I must see him before I go home — I'm going to Ireland soon.'

'Is it to ould Ireland, sir? sure that's me own counthry, the blessin' av all the saints be wid yer honour, sure it makes me heart bounce when I think av being there agin.' And wiping her eye with a corner of her very white apron, she ran away for Dan.

He was a very wiry piece of stuff, not over five feet three, but able to do more work than two lanky fellows all backbone and no muscle. He was always at his post, and a great enemy to them vagabones, the French!

'Well, Dan Skiddy, I'm glad to see you looking so fresh after being killed at Saint Pierre in that big fight. You will soon be qualified for the pension, and we hope you'll get the shilling.' 'O, then good luck to yer honour, and sure it's yourself that would make it fifteen pence if ye cud, for I marched a power in Spain, and kilt a good dale av the French, bad scram to them the vagabones.' 'O Dan, avourneen, don't be cursin' the frinch now that we're done wid 'em; sure they couldn't help it, the crathers, bein' paid to fight for ould Bony himself.'

'Well, you know how they murdered my leg, Biddy.' 'Sure that's their naither, dear, to murder every one av us, but the pace has made them quiet and civil now. O, me back!' 'What's the matter with your back, Biddy?' 'O, yer honour knows how my back was bruck on the rethreat from Madrid down to Portugal in the short days of winter rains, when everybody was lost. But Dan made promise niver to tell any one, and there he is forenenst me,' giving him a sly look for permission to tell her story.

'Yer honour minds how we were all kilt and destroyed on the long march last winter, and the French at our heels, an' all our men droppin' and dyin' on the roadside, waitin' to be killed over agin by them vagabones comin' after us. Well, I don't know if you seed him, sir, but down drops poor Dan, to be murdered like all the rest. Says he, "Biddy dear, I can't go on furder one yard to save me life." "O, Dan jewel," sis I, "I'll help you on a bit; tak' a hould av me, an' throw away your knapsack." "I'll niver part wid my knapsack," says he, "nor my firelock, while I'm a soger." "Dogs then," sis I, "you 'ont live long, for the French are comin' up quick upon us." Thinkin', ye see, sir, to give him sperret to move, but the poor crather hadn't power to stir a lim'. Now I heerd the firin' behind, and saw them killin' Dan, as if it was! So I draws him up on the bank and coaxed him to get on me back, for, sis I, "the French will have ye in half an hour, an' me too, the pagans." In truth I was just thinkin' they had hould av us both, when I draws him up on me back, knapsack an' all. "Throw away your gun," sis I. "I won't," says he. "Biddy, I'll shoot the first vaga-bone lays hould av your tail," says he. He was always a conthrary crather when any one invaded his firelock.

'Well, sir, I went away wid him on me back, knapsack, firelock, and all, as strong as Sampson, for the fear I was in. An' fegs, I carried him half a league after the regiment into the bivwack. Me back was bruck entirely from that time to this, an' it'll never get strait till I go to the Holy Well in Ireland, and have Father McShane's blessin', an' his hand laid over me! An' that's all the thruth, yer honour, I've told ye.'

'Well, Mrs. Skiddy, you are a wonderful little woman. You saved a good soldier for yourself and the service. All the regiment knows how well you acted on the march, where we lost so many of our gallant comrades. You have been always a most useful person, well respected, and I wish you safe home to the Green Isle, and a safe meeting with your friends and Father McShane! But where was your donkey all this time?' 'Och then, yer honour knows when that murderin' villain shot our poor donkeys. I helped on the back of my wee fellow all that he could carry, to save what I could for the poor women whose dead beasts were left on the roadside. So I was left to walk myself, and carry poor Dan a bit. The curse av the crows be on his fire-finger that shot the donkeys.'

I bid this wonderful structure of humanity a friendly farewell, after squaring a long account with her for about a year's washing and darning. She was reluctant to take anything, saying, 'O, sir, sure you always belonged to me own company, an' you're welcome to the bit av washing.'

I hope Dan got the shilling, i.e. a shilling a day pension for life.

But the Government of the day that wasted with unsparing hand England's gold in millions, passed off with a sixpenny pension the old soldier, bearing many scars, and very often with sixpence or ninepence a day for nine, twelve, eighteen, or twenty-four months, when it ceased and he became a pauper. The sinecures held in those days by the aristocracy and their friends and relations for doing nothing would have pensioned for life thousands of brave men who fought nobly for their country and their king. But the war was now over, and as the historian, the great and gallant good Napier, said in his conclusion, 'Thus the war terminated, and with it all remembrance of its veterans' services'.

NOTE

LIEUTENANT GEORGE BELL returned home to Ireland from his service in the Peninsula towards the end of the summer of 1814. One suspects that for the next twelve years he felt rather like a fish out of water. He had tasted glory and had taken no small part in the battles that are emblazoned forever on the colours of a score of regiments. If, in after life, he felt a trifle bitter at the way in which the army authorities treated him at this period, he can hardly be blamed. For months he was 'at a loose end', being neither on regimental duty nor on half-pay. After a time, he was given command of a 'recruiting area' a few miles from his home. The post was almost a sinecure and irked him, in spite of the fact that it added about 37s. 6d. a week to his pay! Then Napoleon escaped from Elba, and George Bell's hopes ran high of seeing another spell of active service. His regiment reformed, most of the old Peninsula men flockng back to have 'another crack at ould Boney'. The 34th, a regiment of seasoned campaigners, stood-to in Ireland, waiting and praying and begging to go to Belgium. They never moved out of the town in which they reformed. Raw, untrained troops were sent to Wellington. Waterloo was fought and won without the 34th Foot! When Napoleon was safely on St. Helena, the army was virtually disbanded. George Bell was granted a retiring half-pay, at the age of twenty-two, of 4s. a day for the rest of his life. For over eight years he pestered the Horse Guards for re-employment, only to be snubbed for his pains. In 1825, he had an opportunity to speak to H.R.H. the Duke of York, the Commander-in-Chief, and he made the most of it. Within a month he was gazetted as Lieutenant to the 45th Foot. Within another month, complete with a young wife and a newly acquired baby daughter, he was on his way to Ceylon to join his new regiment. The days of boredom were over!

Danger and adventure, which followed him all his life there-after, started immediately. Shortly after leaving Gibraltar, the crew were all ready to mutiny and turn pirate. The bo'sun, a hairy, brutal giant, supported by two-thirds of the crew, decided to batten down all troops between decks, murder all the officers, both ship's and military, strip and ravish all the younger women on board immediately, after which the more attractive would be kept for the men's use and the remainder fed to the sharks. This plot might well have succeeded as it was so unexpected that the ship's Captain refused to believe it. It was only because a soldier's wife accidentally heard the bo'sun plotting the final details that it became known at all.

The voyage to Ceylon took four months from Gravesend. On arrival, George Bell found that his regiment had moved to Madras. Within a month of arriving in Madras, he had had three very narrow escapes from cobras and was embarked with his regiment for active operations in Burma, then unknown and unexplored. He describes the now proud city of Rangoon as 'a wretched village of bamboo huts, built on platforms . . . stinking on a warm day'. There may not have been a great deal of fighting in the Burmese War but George Bell certainly took part in all that there was. The privations and sufferings of the troops in the campaign are horri-fying. They had no rest, day or night. The climate was the worst that any British soldier had ever been called on to face—the best in Burma was far, far worse than the worst in India at that time. Cholera, typhoid and malaria were rampant, and officers and men alike died like flies. When the survivors of disease were not being attacked by the enemy, they were plagued by packs of tigers, which would stroll nonchalantly around the lines seizing ponies and occa-sionally some unfortunate soldier, leap silently away and devour its prey almost in sight of the camp. Other constant and nightly horrors were myriads of venomous snakes, revolting and poisonous centipedes, and whole armies of vicious, man-eating rats!

When the campaign was over, the troops were such a collection of physical wrecks that the army gave orders for the survivors to be transferred to hill-stations in India within three months—all except the 45th, who were to remain on garrison and police duties. More or less by accident, Bell met a Lieutenant of the 1st Foot (Royal Regiment) who *liked* Burma and who had reasons for wish-ing to stay there. George Bell most emphatically did NOT. He wanted to see his wife and child. The two officers arranged an 'exchange' then and there, on the spot. George Bell returned to Madras a very junior Subaltern in the 2nd Bn. Royal Regiment (now the Royal Scots). He remained with the regiment until,

on promotion to Major-General, he left them in the trenches at
Sebastopol, thirty years later.

Bell spent the next seven years in various garrisons of South
India, with one spell in Calcutta.   He seems to have spent every
available moment travelling on foot, on horseback and by gig 'off
the beaten track'.   He learned a certain amount of Tamil, Hindu-
stani, and other languages, and he saw as much of the villages as
possible.   His powers of observation were acute and, by the time
the Royal Regiment sailed for home in 1833, Brevet-Captain George
Bell was about one hundred years ahead of his generation in his
views on India.

When the Royals disembarked in England, they marched into
quarters outside Chatham.   As quarters, Captain George Bell did
not think much of them.   He says:

CHAPTER 12

Great Britain and America

I WAS dreadfully disgusted at my new quarters. I had two wretched little rooms not fit for a dog-kennel, fitted up and furnished with four ricketty old chairs that paid barrack damages enough in their day to furnish a drawing-room; two small deal tables patched and impaired, very black from old age, and a smoky chimney; three rusty fire-irons of great antiquity, an old bellows and an iron candlestick completed the dwelling of a Captain in the British army. I wished myself back in India a hundred times over.

The Adjutant-General from the Horse Guards, a very cranky old North Briton, came down without any notice to inspect the R.R. The men were in tatters, their accoutrements worn out by nearly twenty years' service instead of ten, when they ought to have been renewed. The breast-plates were polished bare and bright, no mark of the regiment left about them. This was all the better for the Colonel of the corps; his off-reckonings or income from this source was nearly doubled. The old soldiers were seasoned old bricks and well bronzed, fit for anything but to appear before the Adjutant-General of the British army. He found fault with everything. We were not the rosy-cheeked, well-dressed royal people he expected to see just so lately from the great empire of India, where pagodas grew on the trees, and everything was so rich and rare. We were found to be a ragged pack of red-coats not fit to live in England, and so an order came down in the night to be off in the morning to Edinburgh, two of her Majesty's ships of war being

L

ready to take us away. Well, we had nothing for it but to obey orders, jump out of bed, and begin to pack up our traps hurry-scurry. I had some nice things I brought home with me, but they were nearly all smashed in this hasty, useless move. Ladies were left to shift for themselves and take the land route. We were all clear away from Chatham without our breakfast, baggage and all pitched into boats, and we going down the river to the ships on one of those charming, foggy mornings of November so very salubrious to the health, comfort, and convenience of soldiers, who are supposed to have nine lives and no feeling. The *Galatea* and the *Stag* took us on board and kept us there three days before the fog cleared off to let them see their way. In the meantime the captain of our ship, a jolly good fellow, offered me his cabin if I would go back and bring down my little family. I jumped at the offer. I groped my way back just in time to catch them before they left Chatham. I have generally found that everything comes right in the end, and so it was here in spite of the many blessings poured out on Sir J. McD——it G——l.

It was a long voyage and the men were nearly perished with cold, being so very unprepared for a sea trip at this season. Admiral Napier commanded the *Galatea*. We had some very calm weather. He had a mechanical fancy, got up paddles to his ship, turned by a windlass, and kept his crew and our men warm enough at this work!

If we left Chatham tattered and torn, we were in no better condition when we marched up to Edinburgh Castle to be inspected next morning by General Patrick Stewart. We appeared decidedly out of the dress circle, and got a hint that we might go further north. But there was another voice against any further ascent towards the North Pole, and so we passed an agreeable winter in modern Athens. The good people were hospitable and kind, and took a more favourable view of the Royal Scots, their oldest corps, and did not forget that they had done something at Culloden in the olden time. They did not forget that in later days we had only to unfurl our standard at any time, and let them see there was not a more brilliant spectacle of British valour emblazoned on any colours ever presented by a crowned head to any regiment; and we were proud of them. Old musty general officers who had never seen service could not understand this. All they cared about was the book of regulation, and counting one's buttons, and even measuring the distance with a pocket-rule from button to button with great gravity. I do not know if this put men in good training for the battlefield, but I know it made them very jocose and merry after the ordeal was over! Sir Patrick patronised a play one evening, which was intimated to the garrison; none of us went. As far as red-coats were concerned, there were empty boxes, which was considered personal. I believe it was nothing of the kind. However, we soon got notice to quit, and changed our quarters to a tumble-down place of antiquity called Fort George, planted on a moor far away north in Scotland, thirteen miles from Inverness, the nearest town in those parts. The Duke of Gordon was now our Colonel, and a right jolly good Duke he was. He came over from Gordon Castle to pay us a visit, saw his regiment in the field, and was so much pleased with the general appearance of the men, their efficiency, good conduct, and sobriety, that he addressed them himself in a complimentary speech, and ordered them several barrels of ale to refresh them after a long field-day. He took the head of the table at our mess, made us all very happy, sung a good song, and invited most of us to Gordon Castle, with our wives and families, on whom he personally called to pay his respects. I need hardly say how deservedly popular he was with us all to the end of his valuable life.

We had nothing to do here but to eat, drink, and be merry, nothing more of drill than was needful. Our Colonel G. A. Wetherell, knew very well how unnecessary it was to drill men to death, as was too often the custom when one had the chance of a broad carpet to tramp over! We got our salmon fresh out of the nets at 6d. a pound; if other people paid 2s. 6d., such was the regulation here, and, I believe, was never revised. We had picnics to Cawder Castle, the Fall of Foyers, and other old-fashioned places. Just as we began to like our country quarters, we were required in Glasgow. We found our way up the Caledonian Canal to that commercial city, very famed for smoking chimneys and mountain dew. Our barracks, of course, were planted as usual in the most blackguard part of the town, hardly fit for wild beasts. Before we left this unhealthy, wretched, goodenough place for soldiers, we were all smoke-dried and baked brown. Our next move was back to Edinburgh Castle, a gentlemanlike quarter, and classic ground, high enough to look down the chimneys all about us. Of course we were now perfection, being under the eye of the Duke of Gordon of late! But still 'Auld Reekie' was not to be our dwelling-place. We were transported to Manchester, where the volumes of smoke that were wafted into our rooms spoiled and tarnished our richly-embroidered uniforms. We tried a place called Bury, where we remained just long enough to unpack our luggage, get all snug, pack up again, and be off out of the kingdom. I never could understand why we were always sent to sea in winter, unless the Q.M.G. at the H.G. thought it necessary to have every man's stomach cleared out once a year of all superfluous bile; and he succeeded.

We were as nearly lost as possible in a gale of wind at this time crossing to Ireland. It was a terrible night. The steamers were crowded and the wind was blowing like fury. The horses got loose; one very valuable one, belonging to Captain Raymond, was killed (no compensation—he was not a Field Officer); others were injured. After a long struggle in a pitch-dark winter night, the skipper got the steamer round into shelter under the hills of Scotland where we lay a day and a night until the gale got lighter. If we had been crossing over to fight the French, or do battle for one's country, nobody would say a word about it, but this most unmerciful practice for no purpose was to be condemned.

Newry held us in its watery embrace for the rest of the winter, when we moved to Dublin, and on to Cork, whence we embarked for Canada in July 1836. The regiment was embarked on board an old transport swarmed with vermin, called in France *Punaise*. The men had not standing-room upon the deck when assembled for divine service on the sabbath-day. We were packed like red herrings in a barrel; to sleep at night was impossible, from the multitude of B—— flats that had entire possession of the ship. Some ladies had never gone to bed after the first night during the seven weeks' voyage of persecution. They sat patiently in an armchair by night, and got a snooze as they could catch it. The soldiers' children resembled small humanity just rising out of small-pox, they were so dreadfully bitten; and provisions ran short. We messed in a hole below, where the officers had uneasy berths. No thanks to the authorities at home if we arrived safe in the colony, for they surely took all means to destroy not only the comfort but the safety of her Majesty's Royal Regiment. We had been due at Quebec for three weeks past, and when we did land at the wharf in presence of Sir John Colborne and the *élite* of the city, the people expressed great pleasure and amazement to see a whole regiment turn out of a transport as clean and as nice as if they had emerged from a barrack for a field-day. The first impression was favourable and never wore off afterwards. Cape Diamond barracks, the Gibraltar of America, took us in for the winter—a jolly cold winter for those who liked it. But it froze up my eyes and no mistake, and when the wind blew from the east with the thermometer at 34° below freezing, your eyes begin to water as you go your night rounds, the eye-water immediately congeals, and you are frozen up. You may be frost-bitten too and not know it until someone makes a sudden attack upon your nose with a handful of snow, and begins salting you like beef. The first rush that was made upon my visage was when crossing the Hog's back one evening as I was going round my sentries. I was very much inclined to give my unknown friend a kick on the shins when he bawled out, 'You are frost-bitten, sir.' 'No, I am not,' I said. 'Yes you are, though.' And he went on scrubbing my face with handfuls of snow. The part affected becomes as white as paper. You do not see it, but your neighbours can. There is no present feeling, no discovery by one's self, so that all concerned near at hand consider it a duty to make a dash at every frost-bite they see. 'We cannot see ourselves as others see us!'

I had four rooms and a stove for cooking. My furniture arrived in Quebec before me. I had one of Wurnum's pianos—a first-rate instrument—and got settled down in three days. Our windows looked down upon and over the grand St. Lawrence into the island of Orleans, and commanded a fine view of the Falls of Montmorencey. This was all glorious at the start, and, while the sun was bright and warm, our field-days on the plains of Abraham were a pleasure; and there lay a big stone marking the spot where General Wolfe fell at the head of his gallant and victorious army. There was no stone to mark the spot where Montcalm dropped at the same time and place, but, nevertheless, one of our governors, Lord Dalhousie, erected a monument to both the warriors, equalising their merits.

While the summer lasted I was in love with the country, and often thought of closing accounts with the War Office, and becoming a settler. I was very much urged to it by all the young fellows I met on a little excursion I made into the eastern township—a beautiful fertile country, and no mistake. I went so far as to buy a felling-axe to begin, and inquired the price of farms ready made and not made. What a fine thing it would be to have a landed estate, woods and forests, horses, dogs, pigs, and poultry, and no parades nor drills! I went into the forest with my axe, and had a little exercise trying to fell a big tree, which I thought would be so easy and pleasant. I worked away for two hours and made but small impression; my back was nearly broken and I gave it up. The professional woodman never bends his back. He cuts three feet from the ground, and leaves the stumps there for ten or fifteen years, burns the timber, digs lightly between the stumps, scatters his grain, covers it up with a thorn-bush, and has a succession of fine crops for a dozen of years without any manure. The yield of potatoes is abundant and good. I went away far up into the west country beyond Niagara, where I met an old brother officer, who asked me to go out with him and stay a few days at his farm and see life in the forest. He came into Blandford and took me away in a donkey-waggon—a curious piece of ingenuity upon wheels. There was no road; we got over some miles of ground through the

stumps, our bones nearly out of joint. The last stage was a cordoroy over a swamp. A cordoroy means trees felled and laid close
together to keep one from floundering in the deep spring and mud
swamps. We came to a little log-hut at last. 'That's my house,
and you're welcome. We must hunt about for some dinner,' and
he loaded his gun. 'Have you much game', I said, 'hereabouts?'
'Oh yes, wild turkeys, hares, deer, fine large partridges that perch on
the trees, and on the moors, all in their season.' And he let fly at
a hen and knocked her over. 'That's for our dinner,' he said, 'they
get so wild I have to shoot them.' He took it into the hut and
came back to me with a spade in hand to dig some potatoes, and
a finer crop I never saw. The hen was boiled with a bit of salt
pork he took out of a barrel, and with vegetables we had a right
hearty dinner. One glass and a teacup sat upon the table with a
bottle of the country whisky which had a peculiar flavour, but not
bad while we stuck to a single ration. We had no supper, but went
to roost early. He proposed his only bed for me, which I declined
to occupy on any terms. Rolled up in my cloak, I slept on a bundle
of straw. There was plenty of fresh air all about us, and our sleep
was never disturbed but one night when a wild Indian got into our
house, for what purpose we could not say, unless to scrape an
acquaintance with the barrel of pork, or, what they liked better, a
bottle of whisky. My friend had his gun loaded, and had a shot
after him as he glided amongst the trees in such a hurry as to leave
one of his mocassins behind him. There was a little tribe of American Indians not far off — quiet Aborigines who lived by hunting in
the winter. We went over to pay them a visit, and asked the chief
to come and pass the evening with us, i.e. as was understood by
Takayongwakie, to drink whisky, to which they were all too much
addicted when they could catch it. This old fellow with the long
name was up to time, and came armed with his tomahawk and
feathers in his head to smoke the pipe of peace and drink his rations.
After swallowing about half a pint of whisky, we asked him to give
us the war dance. 'A little more fire-water', he said, and the teacup was filled. When this went down he jumped up and, under
great excitement, he went through the dance, yelling and flourishing
about his tomahawk within an inch of my head. He grew quite
wild and furious, frothing at the mouth, and displayed something
of the aboriginal too near to be safe or agreeable. He now lay
down and fell asleep, and when morning dawned he was gone.[1]

I enjoyed this wild life in the woods for a week, and began to
think it would not agree with us in the long run, however pleasant

[1] How proud the old Indian felt when pointing out to my friend J. B——n
the scalp nailed to his door, and telling how and where he took it.

it might be to ramble about solus in the sunshine. So I returned home cured of my wild dream of burying myself and family in the woods of Canada, and stuck to my own trade a while longer.

Lord Gosford was governor. He was a very kind, hospitable gentleman without any pride or state about him except on state occasions. We dined with him very often, and he had balls and parties and big suppers for the Canadians, which they enjoyed, taking home little souvenirs from the table for the children! 'Where are you going?' he said one day to me. 'I am going the rounds, my lord.' 'Very well, then you must come and dine with me, and you will be half way for your night work.' I had to pass his château about eleven or twelve o'clock every night that I was on duty. He was always doing kind things in this way.

I was ordered to Montreal as a member of a general court-martial in the middle of winter, and was accommodated with a seat in a sleigh for 180 miles over the most atrocious snow-road. Every few yards it was bump into a hole and jerk out again until my whole body and bones were bruised most painfully. In ten days the trial was over, and I had to undergo the same torture. Everybody in Canada knows what *cahrots*, or, in English, car-holes, are in snow-driving. The leather-headed French Canadians—a retrograde people—ran the same sleighs their great-grandfathers used on the low runners, spoiling the roads. Nothing but an Act of the Provincial Parliament compelled them to become civilised and adopt the high runners, which they ever afterwards used with pleasure and profit. We had a Tandem Sleigh Club, which met once a week, the president always leading; wherever he went, the rest were obliged to follow. If a good whip, he led through the most difficult paths, down hills, amongst the stumps, etc. Every now and then there was an upset or a smash, the ladies going down head foremost into the deep snow. Every gentleman took a lady or two in his sleigh. The horses were very good, and enjoyed the tinkling of their own bells. The harness was beautiful, and the sleighs perfection in their way.

The bachelors of the R.R. rejoiced the hearts of all the girls in Quebec, and out of it, by a fancy ball given in our barracks, the following account of which appeared in the *Quebec Mercury*:

'Last night the bachelor officers of this distinguished corps gave a splendid entertainment to a numerous and fashionable party in their quarters at the citadel, for which invitations had been issued some time past, with an intimation that the company were expected to appear in "full or fancy dresses". Such entertainments are not of frequent recurrence here, and, when they do occur, create an additional excitement from the preparations required for those who choose to appear in fancy dresses, and in which even those whose age exempts them from assuming a masquerading disguise to a certain degree participate. At the ball of last evening fancy costumes were more generally worn than has been customary at similar entertainments in Quebec, and the variety and splendour of the dresses, amongst which might be found the garb of almost every nation, from the graceful and flowing garments of the East to the tawdry finery of the North American Indian, mixed with a variety of uniforms, naval and military, British and foreign, together with the splendid dresses of the ladies, formed altogether a scene of uncommon brilliancy. The company entered the officers' house by the centre entrance, but as the entire lower floor was made available for the entertainment, the passages extending the whole length of the building, 280 feet (the mess-rooms excepted), were tastefully lighted with Chinese lanthorns, and at intervals with variegated lamps, being in arches of evergreen boughs. The ornamenting of the dancing room was simple and military in character; stars of bayonets, surrounded with wreaths of evergreen, were on the walls; but at the end of the room was the proudest decoration a soldier would desire to display—the colours of the regiment—rich in the bearing of many a hard contested and glorious field, hung as proud records of the honourable service this old and gallant corps has rendered to the country. The floor was tastefully chalked with appropriate devices. At the upper end was the flower commonly known as the "bachelor's button", in a medallion surrounded by a garter, with the motto, *Sic fata volunt*; in the centre, in a larger medallion, was the Sphinx, and the word "Egypt"; at the lower end, the National Thistle, with the motto, *Nemo me impune lacessit*; whilst on scrolls, between and around the medallions, were inscribed the several victories borne on the colours. The company began to assemble about nine o'clock, at which time his Excellency Lord Gosford arrived, and was received by Lieutenant-Colonel Wetherell, dressed as a private of the corps in the uniform of 1745 (not so smart as that of the present day, but still a very soldier-like habiliment), who conducted the noble guest to the dancing room, where Mrs. Wetherell, as lady patroness, received the company. Sir George and Lady Gipps were present, and a part, at least, or almost all the principal families of the place, with the officers and ladies of the garrison. Among the dresses some were splendid, many very appropriate, and in a few the characters represented were admirably supported by the wearers. Amongst them we must especially notice an inhabitant of the Celestial Empire [1] who, throughout the night, except at supper, kept up the character

[1] Lieutenant-Colonel C. B.

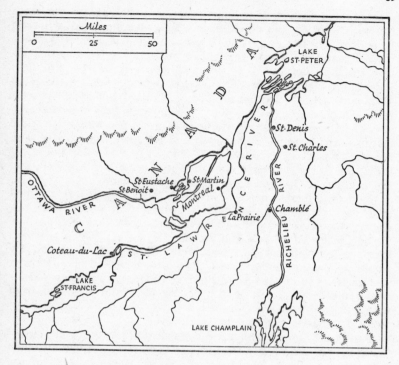

of a Chinaman; an American free negro was an admirable imitation of a sable dandy, and acted his part with spirit, as did a Yorkshire lad, who, however, retired early, not having yet accustomed himself to city hours. Of the gentlemen's dresses, three possessed particular interest, as being connected with the history of the regiment, the oldest corps in Europe. These were an imitation of the dress of the corps at a very early period, with gorge armour, and the Red Cross both on the breast and back; a second was the dress to a later day, when the regiment was the Scotch Guard of Louis IX; and the third was the uniform in which the Colonel appeared, and of which we have above spoken. They are all taken from a series of drawings in the possession of Colonel Wetherell, which are esteemed to be faithful representations of the uniforms of the regiment at different epochs of its existence. The dance was kept up with spirit till one o'clock, when supper was announced, consisting of every luxury, and wines of the finest quality. A large draught had been made on the hours of this 17th day of January before the party began to grow thin; and when prudence, rather than satiety,

warned them it was time to depart, they retired highly gratified with
the hospitality of their chivalrous hosts, whose fancy ball will long
be pre-eminent in the annals of the fashionable gaieties of Quebec.'

We found the 32nd Regiment at Montreal, a corps as remarkable for their hospitality as for their gallantry in the field. We
joined their mess for a few days until we got up our sign. Captain
Markham, a great sportsman, kept his mess well supplied with
game. Moose-deer, wild fowl, venison of different kinds were
always falling to his gun. He would be out for weeks at a time
in the snow, with his Indian hunters, following moose-deer, and
bivouacking at night in the snow with only a blanket, but a big
fire at his feet. He was a man of wire, but he was not iron, and .
broke down at the last in an East Indian climate.

I never bothered my head about politics, nor do I ever intend
to do so. The French Canadians about this time seemed very discontented, and were led on by one Papineau, the Dan O'Connell of
Canada, to break the law, and became very formidable in mischief,
threatening to kill and destroy all loyal people, particularly the few
troops we had in the country. They formed their headquarters at
St. Charles, a pretty town on the river Richelieu, and prepared for
attack and defence. Sir John Colborne planned a little campaign
with the handful of men we had, and sent the Royal Regiment to
attack St. Charles, and disperse the rebels.

November 17th. This day opened the campaign in Lower
Canada. The rebels fired the first shot, and rescued some prisoners
taken up for high treason by the Montreal cavalry. Two of the
cavalry officers wounded, one trooper ditto, three horses killed.

18th. Four companies of the Royals and two six-pounders,
under the command of Colonel Wetherell, marched early from
Montreal, crossed the St. Lawrence, and went in search of the
rebels. They fell in with them on the road to Chamblé, where
they took to the woods, which Captain Bell scoured with his
company, taking some prisoners.

19th. Captain Bell was sent to Montreal with despatches, and,
on his return the following day, had to ride for his life to escape
the enemy, being called upon to halt, which he declined. The
darkness of the night and a good horse were his best friends upon
this occasion.

22nd. Four companies of the Royals, one ditto of 66th, and
two guns under Captain G——, the whole commanded by Lieutenant-Colonel Wetherell, marched from Chamblé, at seven o'clock at
night, with orders to attack St. Charles next morning. The night
was dark and rainy, and the roads almost knee deep in mud. Fires
were lighted at different points the moment we marched to give the

enemy notice of our departure. Crossed the ferry in scows, which took four hours. A terrible night, making only about a mile an hour. At daylight the men presented a frightful spectacle. Arrived at the house of Colonel Rouville the following morning at eleven o'clock, where men and officers were most hospitably entertained. He opened his house and his cellars to the officers, and his barns and outhouses to the soldiers, with a liberal allowance of spirits to every man. Here we remained until the morning of the 25th, when our men were pretty well refreshed, with their arms and appointments in good trim. Our grenadier company joined us the day previous, and we marched off in gay style, mustering a small force of 280 men, two six-pounders, and a few of the Montreal Volunteer Cavalry. The town of St. Charles is prettily situated on the right bank of the river Richelieu, in a fertile champaign country. After receiving a few shots from some houses on the roadside, which we returned double quick, and fired the houses into the bargain, we advanced towards the town, the rebels keeping up a straggling fire from the opposite side of the river. At two o'clock we came in front of the town, where it was fortified by a breastwork. We halted in column, a short distance on the right of the road, out of the direction of their guns, and summoned the rebels to surrender. The reply was a volley of small-arms and a cheer. Then we opened a fire of round shot shrapnel amongst them; but they were well under cover, having the houses and barns loopholed. We deployed into line, and advanced, the light company being divided and extended on both flanks in skirmishing order. The enemy now opened a brisk fire from their works, which was returned with effect. About 300 men left the town cheering, and moved into a corner of the wood on our right to turn our flank. The grenadier company moved up, and beat them back. The centre companies of the Royals and a company of the 66th, and a few of the Montreal Volunteers, were ordered to storm the barns in our front, making a little detour to avoid the fire from the thickest part of the stockade. Those companies were advancing too far, and still under a heavy fire, when I was ordered with all speed to bring them into action, while my own company charged in front. The ground was difficult to cross, being lately ploughed, and the frost very hard. The men, too, were dropping by the enemy's shot pretty fast. When I got up we brought our right shoulders forward, and with three cheers bore down upon the barns and breastworks, which were still lined with the rebels. In this advance Colonel Wetherell had an escape, his horse being mortally wounded. The Adjutant, MacNicol, was also unhorsed. Twenty-one of our men fell, of whom one sergeant and four privates were killed, the rest wounded, some very severely, two of my best men mortally. On entering the town there was little quarter. Almost every man was put to death, in fact, they fought too long before thinking of flight. Many were burned alive in the barns and houses, which were fired, as they would not surrender. Gun-barrels, and powder-flasks were exploded all night in the burning houses, and the picture that presented itself the following morning to my eyes was terrible. A number of swine got loose, and were eating the roasted bodies of the enemy who were burned in the barns and killed in the streets: those brutes were afterwards shot. The loss of the rebels was great. Their position was strong, and they defended it with desperation, but they were totally routed, and received a lesson that they are not likely ever to forget. We took twenty-eight prisoners, destroyed a great quantity of arms and ammunition, spiked their two guns, and sunk them in the river. We burned every house from whence a shot was fired, turned the priest's house into an hospital, and the church into a barrack. I found a journal in the house of the priest, the Rev Mr. B——, which gave a daily account of all our movements from our leaving Montreal on the 17th of November. So accurate was this information that it mentioned our having marched from St. Hilaire on the evening of the 24th of November, at eight o'clock. So far this was quite correct, for Colonel Wetherell marched our little force out of the town at the hour mentioned merely as a ruse to deceive the enemy. We returned to our quarters in about two hours after night, thus leaving our friends to defend a position on our route all night, which they did to their great chagrin.

On Sunday the 26th some few people came into the town, and asked permission to look out their friends amongst the dead. We encouraged the unfortunate creatures to return to their deserted homes, but few came in while we remained at St. Charles. Two genteel, nice-looking young women came to me and asked if I would accompany them to look for their father amongst the slain. I went along with them, and, alas! he was indeed found with his head shattered to pieces, and a most dreadful corpse, frozen like a log, with his limbs extended in the manner in which he fell, and the blood and brain congealed and forming a part of the horrid mass. These poor girls, with some assistance, had him placed upon a sleigh, and covered up. One of them never shed a tear, the other was in agony. I could fancy their inward feelings, and I pitied them from my heart, poor souls! It is such scenes as these that make war so awful, and, above all, civil war amongst a naturally quiet, domestic people like the Canadians, led on by a few ambitious, democratical agitators, who have nothing to lose and everything to gain. The inhabitants are a quiet, homely, contented people, very ignorant about state affairs or forms of government, but easily roused by their clergy, and not so easily tranquilised once they are led to believe that the British Government is trampling upon their rights and privileges. The truth is, no people on earth enjoy so many privileges or have so little to complain of as the humble Canadian. He eats his pork, smokes his tobacco, and sits by his hot stove in the winter. In summer he attends his farm, and jogs on in the same manner in which his great grandsire did before him without attempting the least improvement. He has no wants, and if told he was living under the best form of government in the world, he would believe it, and be happy. If told there must be a change, he would think so too.

I had no great fault to find with my quarters in St. Charles during my short stay, only that all the doors and windows of the houses were smashed to pieces, and it was very cold. I never changed my dress from the day I left home until my return. Perhaps the best reason was that I was in light marching order, and had nothing with me but what was on my back. The house I occupied belonged to Mr. D——, formerly a decided Radical, but then a Government man, and one of the Executive Council. Having deserted his former principles, the rebels took possession of his property, and kept him a prisoner until he escaped in the middle of the night, shortly before we marched for St. Charles. His house was neat and commodious, handsomely furnished, with every comfort inside and out. His barns were well stored, he had four carriages in his coach-house, with some good horses. The young ladies had their garden, enriched with all the choicest plants and flowers, but all were nearly consumed and destroyed by fire and sword. There was a handsome piano in the drawing-room, which had lost a leg in the action by one of our stray cannon-shot. Two of my men propped it up with a log, and commenced playing a duet in the evening after supper. All the fine trees had been cut down to barricade and form breastworks. The cattle were killed, and put into store for winter rations. The cellars were open to all who chose to regale themselves. An extensive library of books was scattered about like chaff; the young ladies' letters, dresses, bonnets, and all their pictures, paintings, etc., were in the rough embraces of unprincipled rebels, semi-barbarians, before we got into the town. Thus it was when I took up my quarters on the evening after the action. There were plenty of feather-beds, blankets, Brussel carpets, and some furniture untouched, with abundance of provision, wine, spirits, etc., and my men were cooking and feasting all the night. As for myself, I did not attempt to lie down, but I patrolled about the town all the night in case of any attack

from a secret foe. Every time I went out of this wretched house,
the dead bodies presented themselves at my feet, the night being
light as day from the flames of the burning barns. I sat amongst
my men in the once happy and comfortable dining-parlour of a
family that never could pass another night there, listening to the
rude jest, and the different tales of the past day. 'Well,' said old
Charley Plumb, 'them fellers fought well. I worked amongst them
till my bayonet was bent on a tough back-bone, yet I only killed
three on 'em!' This was said in the coolest manner, with his pipe
in his mouth, and without the least idea of boasting. 'What a head
that fellow had,' said Bulger, 'who was just going to shoot the Captain, there, till I sent him to the other world.' This I was witness
to. I saw the bayonet plunge into his ear, and through his head,
and then Bulger stood on the body to pull out the deadly weapon
—oh, horrible!—Such a scene I hoped never to witness again, but
three weeks did not pass until I saw others quite as terrible. Such
is war!

Sunday, the 26th, was passed getting our men into a proper state
for future operations, attending to the wounded, and carting the
dead to the churchyard, where they were thrown in one mass, to
be interred in one grave. We buried our own dead in as decent a
manner as circumstances would permit, then sent for the priest of
St. Denis to witness the havoc made at St. Charles. He came, and
I took his reverence round the works, and showed him all before a
corpse was disposed of. It made him sick. He was then ordered
back to report to his people what he had seen, and to tell them if
they did not return to their allegiance and to their peaceful homes,
St. Denis would not exist in twenty-four hours. This had a wonderful effect. He did go home, and prevailed upon his people to
act according to our wishes, after which they never fired a shot
from that rebellious town. I may now say a few words about this
little town of St. Denis. It also lies on the right bank of the Richelieu, seven miles below St. Charles. When we were ordered to
attack St. Charles, another force, under a staff officer, embarked in
steamboats at Montreal, sailed down to Sorel (or Wiliam-Henry),
there disembarked, and marched for St. Charles, to attack that place
upon the same day that we intended doing so. The weather was
dreadful, the men fagged and quite unfit for action. On approaching St. Denis, they found themselves unexpectedly and strongly
opposed by a large force there posted in stone houses, which
opened a heavy fire. Captain Markham, 32nd, was severely
wounded, with several of his men, and a few killed. In fact, they
were repulsed, and obliged to retreat, leaving a howitzer in the
mud, and their wounded in the hands of the enemy. It was upon

the morning of this unhappy day that Lieutenant Weir, of the 32nd Regiment, was taken prisoner, and most barbarously murdered in the street of St. Denis. His body was afterwards found in the river, most shockingly mutilated. This repulse gave the enemy courage, and made them fight well at St. Charles.

On the day of our return to Montreal, 30th November, Colonel —— was embarking with a larger force and two guns, to retrace his steps to St. Denis, to kill and slay all before him; but his march was not intercepted. He found his howitzer, burned the property of the rebel Nelson, marched to St. Hyacinth and St. Charles, but saw no enemy.

Never was such a joyful welcome as we had on our return to Montreal. The inhabitants had been kept in a state of the greatest excitement and alarm during our absence, a rebel force being on the west side of the town, threatening fire and destruction. They were only waiting to hear that we had been defeated at St. Charles, when the whole country would have been in a blaze from Quebec to Toronto.

The red-coats went up now a hundred per cent.—nothing but feasting and fixing of flints for the next ten days. The gentry presented Colonel Wetherell with a very handsome and valuable piece of plate, and her Majesty sent him the honourable distinction of C.B., an honour conferred only for distinguished service in the field.

On the 13th of December, the force under Sir John Colborne, consisting of the Royals, 32nd, and 83rd Regiments, five guns and some rockets, the Montreal Cavalry and Rifles, with some Volunteers, marched from Montreal in two brigades, to attack the town of St. Eustache, and drive the rebels from this part of the country. We halted the first night at St. Martin, and on the following morning proceeded to the point of attack, making a long detour to avoid the usual road, which led to the ferry opposite which the church of St. Eustache was situated on the bank of the Ottawa, and which was strongly fortified and garrisoned by the enemy. We crossed on the ice about three miles below the town, which, fortunately, was strong enough to carry the force over in safety, although it gave way a little, and we lost one of the tumbrils with ammunition. I mounted a paling, and first saw, glittering in the sun, the double spires of that church which was doomed to ruin, and to entomb many of its then unfortunate and fated inmates. On our near approach, the guns opened a brisk fire upon the stone houses adjoining the church, while the infantry surrounded the town, in order to cut off the retreat of the rebels, the greatest part of whom had, however, retired on the first fire, leaving about 400 to defend the church. From the priest's house they kept up a brisk fire upon our men. The guns came up to a corner of the main street, and riddled the church door. The Royals then were ordered to storm it, which they did in most gallant style, firing the adjoining house, which burned out the rebels there. Under the great column of smoke that issued from this building, many of the enemy escaped from the church, and crossed the river on the ice. But they met the Volunteers who were waiting for them in the wood, and were slaughtered. The flames soon communicated to the church. There was but one choice left—to bolt out and be shot, or burned alive. There was no escape, and they died as they fought, regardless of life. Chenier, the only chief who stood by them to the last, was killed in the churchyard, a ball having passed through his body, entering his left side under the ribs. This shot saved the Government £500, being the reward offered for his apprehension. He was a genteel-looking young man, about twenty-four years old, and had a wife and family. I took the stock from his neck, which was made of the common cloth of the country, it being a system amongst those unfortunates not to wear anything of British manufacture. This was one of Papineau's schemes to injure our manufactures.

The wounded were most severely riddled. Many of them bled to death for want of surgical aid. I found one poor fellow with his arm shattered above the elbow with a grape shot. Some soldiers were just going to dispatch him, when I came up. He was crying for mercy, and the blood was pouring from the wound most rapidly. I took off one of my mocassin strings, and bound his arm tight, which stopped the effusion of blood. It was amputated the same night, and I believe he recovered. I had some difficulty in saving a few other prisoners from the soldiers, who were much excited. I walked about the most part of the night, not being in a sufficiently composed state to lie down. The town was in flames. The cries of the wounded were piercing, many of them being roasted alive. The heat of the fire melted the snow, and the street was in a puddle. The soldiers were cutting down houses, to prevent the fire reaching the hospital, and altogether the scene was too terrible to permit me, fagged as I was, to retire to my humble billet.

The fire reached the church clock just at twenty minutes past two p.m., and the roof fell in about six, burying in its ruins many an unfortunate misguided wretch. I saw their ruins next morning, some only partially burned, others almost entirely consumed. We marched on to St. Benoit, alias Grand Brulé, next day in pursuit of the rebels, but found none. They deserted the town, and dispersed all over the country. This being one of the chief seats of their disloyalty for years back, we burned the whole town, church and all, and then retraced our steps to Montreal, bringing home 108 prisoners, many of them wealthy men, and leaders of the blind. G——, the general-in-chief, was so hotly pursued for some days, he blew out his brains while in the act of being made prisoner. I saw him brought into Montreal on a train immediately after his death. He was considered a reckless ruffian, and proved himself a coward.

On the 3rd of January 1838, I was appointed Commandant of the fort and garrison of Coteau-du-Lac, a place of some importance, situated on the edge of the St. Lawrence, and by the side of the main road leading to the Upper Province. The rebels having threatened to march upon this place and secure the guns, previous to the attack at St. Eustache, it was deemed prudent to have all the cannon sunk in the river, as there were no troops in the country that could be spared to defend it. The guns were accordingly disposed of in this way, after which Colonel S—— of the militia took possession of the fort in the Queen's name, collected some volunteers, and placed himself in command, with full pay and rations. However, this did not long continue. When I superseded him in the command, I found everything in the greatest disorder, irregularity, confusion, and a total want of system. The fort was in the most defenceless state, the men without the shadow of discipline, eating up Government provisions, and just doing as they pleased. I commenced to work immediately, and to reform abuses. I got a drill sergeant, whom I promoted to the rank of sergeant-major. We had regular parades and drills, when all officers were present, and drilled in the ranks amongst the men. The guards were regularly mounted, and sentries posted and relieved according to the rule of the service. I formed the men into messes, and instead of cooking at all hours during the day, appointed stated hours for breakfast and dinner and provided them with knives, forks, plates, bowls, etc., and soon got order and regularity established. Superintended the workmen employed by the engineer department in putting the fort into a state of defence, and in the course of a month had a very respectable, orderly garrison, officers and men well acquainted with their duties. I now thought it possible to get a gun or two out of the river. Having first found out the place where they were deposited, I cut away the ice to the brink where they lay, and the water being clear, I distinctly observed four twenty-four pounders at the bottom. By the help of about twenty men whom I employed, I got ropes and chains passed under the guns, had long poles cut in the woods, laid them sloping from the ice down to the guns, and by main force hauled them out of the water.

M

Each of these long guns weighed two tons and a half. They were all spiked, and, most unfortunately, with patent spikes. Having applied to headquarters to have my guns now examined by an artillery officer, Captain Stanway was sent up to see them and report; but his report being unfavourable, the matter dropped at headquarters. I got two clever fellows who promised to take out the spikes for a consideration. I agreed to give them two dollars a gun if they succeeded, if not—no pay. They drilled them all out in three weeks, very nicely, and without injuring the vents. As this operation was reported to Sir John Colborne as impracticable, I took some credit to myself for perseverance. I mounted two of those guns, having made platforms for the carriages of the strongest material. I recovered, by dint of perseverance, upwards of four thousand cannon-shot from the river, and I now commanded the country all about for the space of a mile. Within that distance I could have destroyed every house from my batteries. Captain S—— was again sent up to examine and report upon my works. He returned perfectly satisfied, and reported my platforms unexceptionable, guns well mounted, and skilfully unspiked. I fired several shots from these guns up and down the river to try the effect and strength of the platforms, and to calculate the distance at which I could knock down a house. I also wanted the good people about to know that I was well prepared in the event of any future disturbance.

I received the thanks of the Lieutenant-General, who now sent me a *carte blanche* to do as I liked, and ask for what I wanted. I recovered twelve more twenty-four pounders in the middle of the winter, erected a sawpit in the forest, cut down my timber, finished more platforms, erected four batteries and a drawbridge, and made myself secure against any enemy. This was a place of great importance, the rapids being in front, and all boats going up the St. Lawrence having to pass through the canal locks in this fortress. I had a weary winter of it; but it suited my taste, and gave me a brevet majority. I won my spurs, and it made me joyful.

May 22nd 1838. Major Henry John Warde, Royal Regiment, died this morning, deeply regretted, aged thirty years.

August 10th 1838. Went with despatches to Lord D—— and Sir John C——; the former, at Quebec, being now the Governor. I dined with his lordship, and returned to Sorel, the summer-house of Sir John C——. I got his despatches and went off with them to New York to meet the Great Western steamer.

13th. Left Montreal at nine a.m., crossed the St. Lawrence to La Prairie, nine miles; took the railroad per steamer to St. John's, eighteen miles, dined there—excellent dinner—and embarked on the Burlington steamer, the handsomest and best conducted boat perhaps in America. Every part of her was as thoroughly clean as Buckingham Palace, with an excellent table. Sailed, two p.m., for Whitehall, 150 miles; touched at Plattsburgh, Burlington, and other places on both sides of Lake Champlain, making the distance 175 miles. Arrived at five a.m. next morning. Scenery down the lake and river very fine; thousands of wild ducks rising from the rushes within shot on both flanks. The river, approaching Whitehall, which is situated in the mountains, becomes so narrow that a steamer cannot turn, and the many windings make it difficult to navigate.

14th. Had breakfast, and started at six a.m. by the canal to Fort Edward, twenty miles, through a rich and fertile valley. Took the stage to Saratoga, twenty-four miles, over a very fine country. The stage-coaches take nine passengers inside, which is by no means very agreeable in such hot weather. I never had the good fortune at any time to travel by stage with one passenger less than the full number. In Great Britain people are frequently disappointed in travelling. 'Coach is full, sir.' Not so in America. There are always plenty of coaches ready, and if any to spare, they are sent back to the yard. They are well horsed, and easy to ride in, with both sides open in fine weather, having no glass windows. No old dowagers to sing out, 'Please to shut up that window on the right, sir, I'm catching cold.' Arrived at Saratoga at four p.m., jumped out, and into a rail car, which started directly for Troy, thirty miles, over a beautiful country. Pulled up for a few moments at Ballston, famous for its mineral springs; a pretty little village, and likely to become a flourishing place; it is intersected by a canal. Crossed the North River over a covered wooden bridge, nearly half a mile long, and stopped at seven p.m. at a very fine hotel. Troy is a very beautiful flourishing town; population 19,500. It has handsome houses, fine wide streets, well paved, with rows of shady trees on both sides of many streets, which is a great luxury. There are fine public buildings and excellent shops, where may be had everything that England can produce. In front of the hotel, a beautiful fountain showered forth its crystal waters, which sparkled and refreshed the bright green grass all around it. The town is well lighted with gas.

15th. Left at five o'clock; delightful morning. Took a small steamer to Albany, six miles, a very fine, handsome flourishing town on the right bank of the river. Transferred myself to a large steamboat here, and set off for New York, down the beautiful Hudson, 150 miles. This is considered one of the finest rivers in North America for its beauty of scenery, quite an English-looking country on both banks, diversified at every point with hill and dale, beautiful villas, handsome towns and villages, gardens, orchards of apples and peaches, extensive fields of Indian corn, meadow, and all sorts of grain, mountains of pine, and rocky hills covered with plants and shrubs not known in Europe. At West Point there is a battery commanding the river, with a barrack and some handsome buildings on the brow of the hill. Higher up, on the Catskill mountains, 3,000 feet above the river, you see a splendid hotel peeping through the forest, where many an invalid enjoys the purest air that blows, and is glad to visit in the hot summer months away from the bustle of New York. Passed the town of Hudson, still reeking from the effects of a disastrous fire, which too commonly occurs in America. Arrived at New York at eight in the evening, put up at the Astor House, the finest, largest, and perhaps the best conducted hotel in the world. Everything is carried on with the greatest carefulness, propriety, and attention. Breakfast, dinner, tea, and supper on the table to the moment. Everything is of the very best, and the cooking excellent. Two dollars and a half per diem is the charge for board and lodging, wines and liquors not included, of which there is abundance of the best in the house, but very expensive. There is a separate table for families; but in America all boarders at hotel dine together. Seldom or never such a thing as a separate dining order, if so, it is generally a separate charge. People never sit long at their meals. They take their wine at dinner, and get through the whole ceremony in less than an hour.

There are many other fine hotels in New York, and always crowded. It is a city of enterprising merchants, a beautiful city, and worth seeing even at a great expense. The best and most numerous servants are the blacks; they are cheerful and attentive, honest, and always in good humour. The American ladies are far inferior (generally speaking) in figures, manners, and personal appearance to the English. And the men are too much engaged in business, smoking, and spitting, to study the politeness and etiquette of English gentlemen. They are unpolished; their whole conversation was about dollars, trade, real estate, stock, etc., *calculating* and *guessing*.

16th. Went on board the Great Western steamship and deposited my despatches with Captain Hoskin.

17th. Met some old friends, dined with one of them, and passed an agreeable evening.

18th. Up at five, and took the route to Philadelphia, ninety miles—first, per steamer, up the river, twenty miles. Style of houses along the banks for some distance, particularly at New Brighton and Bristol, very handsome; fine rich country, but very

flat. Took the railroad to Boardenton, thirty-five miles. The little
boys and girls jumped in with their baskets of apples and peaches
at every halt, for sale. A refreshment car accompanied the train,
where you might call for anything you wished. Joseph Bonaparte's house and property stands upon the Delaware, at the end of
this railway, where we took again to a steamer, and went up this
fine river to the city. Beautiful châteaux, villages, and fine farms
attract the attention all the way up. Landed at two p.m., in light
marching order, i.e. without any luggage. What a comfort, sometimes, just to take all you require in your pocket! Stopped at the
United States Hotel as Major B——, R.R., British Army, and received every attention. What a luxury are such lovely trees as
ornament many of the streets of Philadelphia. I observed one
very fine weeping-willow, of great size, at Bonaparte's door, double
the size of that over Napoleon's grave. Philadelphia is one of the
most regularly built towns, perhaps, in the world, laid out like a
chess-board. The streets are very long and very wide, and are
called after trees, Chestnut, Walnut, Cedar, etc., or 1st, 2nd, 3rd
street, and so on. The squares are all shady and green, grass well
and cleanly kept. The market is entirely covered in, and extends
up the middle of the street for nearly a mile. Yet this street is so
wide that a double railway passes through it, and there is more than
enough room for two carriages to pass on each side. The market is
well supplied with everything the country affords. I saw a fine
statue of Penn in front of the hospital.

The public buildings are handsome, many of them entirely built
of white marble. The basement and steps of some of the houses
are also of marble.

The new museum is a very handsome building, and boasts the
longest and loftiest room I ever saw. The only object which particularly attracted my curiosity was the skeleton of the mammoth;
the tusks were very perfect and of enormous size—perhaps three
times as long and as thick as those of any elephant that I ever saw.

19th. I made my acquaintance with an American officer on
his way to join his regiment in Florida, who gave me some information about his service. I find both officers and men are better paid
in their service than in ours, and that they inflict corporal punishment on bad characters, when not quartered in large towns.

Crossed over to Brooklyn, a pretty large town, which would be
included as part of New York were there a bridge. As it is, steam-
ferries ply every five minutes and take you over for four cents.
This island lies so much higher than New York, that many people
lodge there during the summer, coming over to their business in the
great city every morning. I embarked on the *Swallow* at five p.m.

for Albany, 150 miles. This is the fastest vessel on the Hudson, or, perhaps, in America. We arrived at the end of our voyage at half-past three o'clock in the morning, including stoppages at different parts, in ten and a half hours. She was crowded with passengers and can make up 300 beds. This is all very well for the owners, but a great nuisance for other people, there is so much bustle, such eating and cooking, and spitting amongst the Yankees, and smoking and chewing tobacco. They never miss a meal. I believe, if it was the fashion to have three dinners a day, they would join them all. Yet every meal is a separate charge. There is, however, no noise about the navigation of the vessel; everything in that department is perfect; not a word is ever spoken; all is managed by the tinkle of a bell. Had breakfast in Troy, where I remained three hours, walked to the top of a hill and took a good look at this beautiful country. The rail steamer took me up at the hotel door, and I bade farewell to *Priam* and his city.

21st. Arrived at Saratoga at ten a.m., and put up at Congress Hall, a very fine hotel and of great extent, being large enough to accommodate from 300 to 400 people. The verandah in front measured 222 feet long by 18 feet wide. There was a similar one in the rear, looking into the garden. I went down to the spring at once and had some of the water so famed in America. It is by no means disagreeable to drink, and rises from a neat sunk well under a colonnade. The spring must be very productive, as a man is constantly employed bottling the water for exportation, besides what is daily drank and carried away. There are several other springs in different parts of this little town or village, as it is called, and a great number of very fine hotels. Indeed the whole place consists of hotels and boarding-houses, and they are always full. We dined at two o'clock; all sat together, as usual (in America) at the *table d'hôte*. Two old warriors sat opposite to me—one called General, the other Major. The latter, as is often the case in our service, was the older. They talked of the revolutionary wars, and so forth—of rank and titles which they never wished to see in their land; no aristocracy, no hereditary titles or honours except what was gained by merit. There were many ladies at dinner; some eat their pudding with a knife, and others picked their teeth at table. There were many of them young and handsome, well and fashionably dressed, but this Yankee fashion spoiled all. A band, consisting of five or six black fellows, performed during dinner. It was mighty enchanting, perhaps, to some of the company. The gentlemen were chiefly of the first class, and there was little spitting. It appeared to me that it was indispensable for everyone here and at New York to wear a brooch in the bosom of his shirt.

Diamond pins carried the day, although they would have cut a more brilliant appearance by night. The company arose from dinner with one accord as soon as they had finished eating. The ladies retired to the drawing-room to chat, and the men to idle about, drink gin-sling, cocktail, sherry-cobbler, smoke, and spit over the balconies, a very intellectual amusement. I believe those said American ladies are very idle. I never saw one of them with a needle or at any sort of work. I am told they do not make very domestic wives. They danced, and played, and sang in the evening, quadrilled and waltzed. They were very lively, but not graceful. The music was of ancient date and jig-time, with the exception of that played by one plain-looking girl, who sang very well, but whose attitude at the piano was very awkward.

Saratoga is the Cheltenham of America. People visit the springs from all parts. The town is improving and will, no doubt, be a place of great note. The main street is very wide, with rows of shady trees on both sides, making a pleasant and refreshing walk in the heat of the day. There are yet few amusements beyond billiard-tables and a circular railway, where two may start in a kind of chair and propel themselves round at the rate of twenty miles an hour, so long as their steam lasts. About three times round is a mile. The ladies sometimes ride on horseback, or drive out to different parts of the country. The morning is occupied drinking at the wells.

22nd. Up at three (horrible), and off towards home, with all anxiety to get back; forty miles of as bad a road as any in the world, and nine inside passengers. The coaches only carry one outside. Had breakfast at Sandy Hill.

Brother Jonathan, in showing off his dexterity as a whip, cutting round a corner with his six fine horses, upset the coach and pitched us all on top of each other. All the band-boxes were broken and he rolled down the hill, but was up in a jiffey, pulling some ladies out of the upper window, saying to one burly dame, 'I guess you too round to come out of this hole.' He took the whole matter as a joke, or something that he was accustomed to in this hill country.

Took steamer to St. John's, and arrived there at seven o'clock on the morning of the 23rd August.

Arrived at home at eleven o'clock last day of the races. It was too hot to attend, but I went to a picnic dinner with my family, and dined in an orchard on the top of the mountain commanding one of the most extensive views in Canada.

While stationed in Toronto, I got my promotion—Major, 1st Battalion, Royal Regiment, quartered in Gibraltar. And to Gibraltar I was obliged to go—a long and expensive journey, chiefly

by sea. I had not been there five months when I was promoted to
be Lieutenant-Colonel, by purchase, in my old battalion, and had to
retrace my steps all the way back to Canada, where I arrived in the
spring of 1844, and found my old friends at Quebec, who gave me a
joyous welcome. Soon after this we were ordered to Halifax.
Before my arrival, the whole regiment had embarked in two ships
for the West Indies. One vessel cleared the river St. Lawrence, and
got away safely. The right wing was wrecked off Cape Chat in
a snowstorm, but all hands were saved and picked up by the very
last steamer of the season. They were carried back to Quebec,
where I found them. On this occasion, Lieutenant Lysons, a most
intelligent, active young officer, made his way to Quebec, across
the country some hundred miles, partly in snow-shoes, and just
arrived in time to catch the last steamer of the season. Why were
they sent away in winter, in the snow winter when the river
was closed? Wooden heads somewhere, incapable of any safe
calculation and indifferent to life or property, manage these little
matters, at times!

I called at the Horse Guards when I arrived from Gibraltar, and
asked for orders. 'Go to Canada,' they said, 'and take command of
your regiment.' They knew that my regiment had sailed from
Canada, yet this red tape department insisted on my going to
Quebec for the purpose of following in the wake of my battalion to
the West Indies. As it happened, I did meet one-half of my people,
but that was an unexpected hit.

I asked the Adjutant-General to allow me to proceed direct from
England to the West Indies, and join my regiment there.

'No,' he said, 'go to Canada.'

'The St. Lawrence is closed, sir, with the ice. I can't get that
way.'

'You have got your orders,' he said. And I was bowed out.
My business was now to obey orders, and so I did, however in-
wardly reluctant.

I next applied for a passage out. This was no go either, and as
unjust as the other was provoking. I was told to provide my own
passage, and make all haste. I need not tell what I was inclined to
say or do in this emergency, but I believe I acted wisely for once!
I went away with my constant companion same night to Liverpool.
Went on board a sailing ship for New York, and arrived there after
a long, boisterous, dark, cold, and rainy voyage. The skipper was
a Yankee, wore top boots, and a very long great-coat, but always
kept his weather eye open. 'What sort of weather is it above,
Captain?' 'Thick as mush,[1] and can't blow any harder, I guess.'

[1] Mush—a porridge of Indian corn meal.

We passed the summer in Halifax, where fishing was our chief amusement. I had my men on St. George's Island, and I believe every one of them had a fishing-rod. We caught lots of good sea fish, and speared lobsters by torchlight. We serenaded the fleet in harbour with our band and choir by moonlight, and had such nice picnics by daylight! When the snow came on we embarked for Barbadoes in the *Pique* frigate, Captain Stopford. Mrs. G. B. and self messed with the Captain, and, according to regulation, she was charged 14s. a day! I paid in proportion. The ship rolled dreadfully, and sickened my poor horses almost to death. When we anchored off Barbadoes I had them hoisted up and dropped into the sea, when, joyfully snorting, they swam away to shore. Barbadoes is quite a sugar island, bare enough of trees, and considered very healthy when there is no sickness! It is an island of white coral. The roads are white, wearying one's eyes when the sun shines, and that is always by daylight. Every spot is cultivated and bears sugar-cane or vegetables, or black children who grow like Topsy! The people are idle, fond of pleasure, and live for lazy enjoyments such as they are, and do not much scruple at little thefts, and do as little work for their wages as they can. Fuel is scarce and dear, and only required for cooking: mine often disappeared before the time. I watched my Master of the Horse going home one evening with a long walking stick as thick as his leg, part of my fuel, helping himself along, quite lame, of course! In his old hat on top of his woolly head was a lump of English coal; of course he could not tell how it came there! I had a nice bungalow and abundance of Guinea grass for my horses, and plenty of Guinea fowl, which roosted in a beautiful tulip-tree in front of our door. Noisy birds they were, but laid plenty of eggs when I could find them; so cautious and cunning, I have watched them for hours creeping to their nests. We had plenty of poultry and lots of eggs, Humming-birds were always fluttering about the windows, losing their way and getting into the house. The humming noise is made by the rapid action of the wings: pretty little darlings, and of all colours, sizes, and shape, we loved their society.

NOTE

IT is difficult to tell from Lieutenant-Colonel George Bell's memoirs exactly how long he served in the West Indies. It is, however, much less difficult to deduce that he was not particularly happy there. His writings telescope a period of from five to seven years to read like a few months, at the most. It was during this period that his really remarkable character began to show itself unmistakably, and his actions and reactions to prove that he was one hundred years ahead of his military generation.

He was now a Lieutenant-Colonel, and in 1844 a Lieutenant-Colonel commanding the garrison in a group of West Indian islands was a person of considerable importance. This was the age when Commanding Officers thought it no shame to amass a small fortune out of 'Army Contractors' — pocketing the proceeds of 'cut-price' messing for the troops: second-rate or irregular clothing and accoutrement supplies, *et cetera*. A Line battalion was considered as good as £600-£800 a year in a C.O.'s pocket: a Cavalry regiment brought in £1,000-£1,200: a regiment of Foot Guards or the Household Cavalry, anything up to £1,750. Most of it came from — to put it bluntly — *baksheesh* from the regimental contractor. It came, too, from the stomachs of the N.C.O.s and men, and from totally illegal 'stoppages of pay for kit replacements'. There were no *A.F.P.1954* in those days. (D. L. Murray's novel of the Crimean War, *Trumpeter, Sound!* gives a magnificent and accurate account of the effect of these abuses.) In those days, most officers regarded their men as of less importance than their gun-dogs. To George Bell, this attitude and mentality was like a red rag to a bull. He knew every man in his regiment by sight and by name, and he knew the family histories of most of them. Their ignorance of things spiritual and temporal appalled him. He started a Bible Class, took drastic precautions to see that 'suckers-up' (his own descriptive phrase) were excluded, and taught it himself. He ran lectures on Politics and World Affairs, and appears to have instituted some form of 1st, 2nd, and 3rd Class Certificates of Education years before the Army Council ever thought of it. He was absolutely ruthless with the indolent, languid, Piccadilly-Johnny type of officer of that day. They did not last long in the 2nd Batt. Royal Regiment and were soon replaced by men of his own calibre. At a time when soldiers were flogged unmercifully for even trifling crimes, George Bell said, 'Never, in any circumstances, whilst I command!' In all the years that he commanded, first a detachment, and then a full battalion, he never once permitted, or authorised, a flogging. In this, he was almost unquestionably unique in the British Army.

On arrival in Barbadoes, the first thing to arouse his ire was the fact that the military graveyard was right underneath the barrack-room windows. This caused much despondency among the men and the island had a bad record for suicides as the result. George Bell could not shift the cemetery, but he could — and did — shift the barracks (a disgraceful erection of timber and sheet-iron, in which men died of heat-stroke by the dozen) without asking permission, and presenting the authorities with a *fait accompli*. He had far too much sense to clamp down on the multitudinous brothels and wine-shops, both of which type of establishment had done a roaring trade since the day of the Buccaneers. He weaned his men away from such delights by instituting regimental cricket and football teams, organising sports and—again something unique in 1844-45 —building a recreation-room and starting a library with books and periodicals for which he paid out of his own pocket.

In 1847, Colonel Bell, with half of his regiment, was despatched in a hurry to help a West Indian battalion quell a minor rising amongst the *peons* on the sugar plantations in British Guiana. His only comment on this episode is that the whole area was 'creeping and slithering' with swarms of vicious, aggressive, and deadly snakes. He did NOT like Guiana. Then the trouble amongst the sugar workers spread to Trinidad and Granada, and Colonel Bell found himself Military Governor of the three islands and Guiana, on the mainland. The trouble fizzled out in due course, and the Royal Regiment returned to Barbadoes.

One feels, on the whole, that George Bell found the life of an O.C. Garrison, in the West Indies, singularly boring after soldiering in the Peninsula, India, Burma, and Canada. He could hardly contain his joy when the transport arrived to take the regiment home.

CHAPTER 13

The Peninsula Medal

I DID not like the lazy life of Barbadoes and it was a joyful day that brought a big ship into the offing to carry us all to England. I got on board at once to see our house, and to ask the Captain a hundred questions, when he would be ready for sea, and so on. He said, 'I'm not come for you at all, I am to take home the 89th Regiment.' 'They are all detached,' I said, 'and scattered over the islands, and cannot be got together for an age.' 'I don't care,' he said, 'I will be paid demurrage for every day I am detained.' This struck upon my ear like music. I galloped off to the General and asked him to embark my regiment. 'Ready to go on board, sir, tomorrow. You will save the public a large sum. The next ship can take up the 89th.' A word for the public and one for myself just in time. It prevailed against a mighty opposition from the Adjutant and Quartermaster-General's department. We got away, and very thankful to my gallant old friend, who was as obstinate as a crooked stick, if anyone dictated to him. I loved him, because he was a brave *Talavera* man! One dark stormy night we were struck by a gust of a hurricane and a water-spout at the same time. The ropes were torn out of the blocks, the sails flapped about tattered to ribbons, nothing on deck was visible. It was a moment of terror, when, as we thought, the ship was going down, after one of those quivering motions that has so often preceded such calamities. It was a little time of breathless anxiety, the ship righted, the ferocity of the tempest blew over, and we were saved by the Power who rules the trackless deep.

178

Twenty-eight days brought us to the Cove of Cork, but nobody in authority would acknowledge us. We were not the correct regiment at all; this they miraculously discovered after we had orders to disembark, although I had sent ashore my returns. We were kept on board for several days, until official applications went to Dublin Castle, and then to the Horse Guards, to know how we were to be disposed of. 'Send them round to Scotland.' Now, taking the direct course up St. George's Channel, three days would have finished our voyage. But the wooden heads sent us down the English Channel through the Straits of Dover, and all round the east coast of England to Scotland, in terrible weather, blowing and snowing, for twenty-five days longer clothed in West-India dress. And in white trousers the men were employed clearing the decks of snow when famishing with cold, and short of rations. So much for the beautiful arrangement of one of our military departments at this time.

We were passed on to Glasgow direct, and as the next winter set in with the usual gales, we were embarked for Belfast in something like a hurricane.

I was detached with my company to Castlewellan for the rest of the winter, where we enjoyed the hunting season, and a good share of Irish hospitality, particularly with the Murland family, and at Mount Panther. But we were always sure to get the hookum to march when we got into snug quarters.

After a short stay at Parsonstown, where we partook of the hospitality of Lord Rosse, and had many a peep through his wonderful telescope, our next move was to Dublin. Plenty of duty, field-days in the Phoenix, parades and drills, great mess dinners, public and private parties, and plenty of fun for your money. Poor Paddy does say and do such droll things in his own peculiar naïve manner, everyone laughs but himself. Look at that notice on the door over the way: 'Asses' milk every morning fresh from the cow!' A wild-looking fellow from the country came into the barracks one day, and said he wanted to 'list. 'Why do you want to 'list, Pat?' 'O faith, I left me father's house this mornin', bekays I found he was only my uncle, an' I'd stay no longer.' The Queen paid us a visit, and received the warm reception she deserved from all her Irish subjects, who went crazy for a week. I claimed the honour of receiving her Majesty with a guard of honour, and the standard of my regiment: being Commanding Officer of the Royals, the oldest regiment in her Majesty's service, and that of which her father had been Colonel. There was much competition for this honour, but my claim was irresistible. Her Majesty paid a visit to the Duke of Leinster, where I was invited. It was a great day at Carton. Our

band, and other bands, went down, and there was music and
dancing and feasting all day, and a jolly come home at night. The
Queen rode on an outside car, which carries the wheels inside, as
the inside car carries her wheels outside. Everybody was pleased,
and nine-tenths of the people were d———. No, just merry—every
night, for the joyful opportunity of getting screwed. Then's the
time when Paddy's best feelings possess him—out comes everything, good, bad, or indifferent. The levee at the castle was a scene
of the most admired disorder. Everything was so arranged, or so
disarranged, that everybody pressed on together in one wide scene
of helpless confusion. The rear ranks closed up so tight that
dresses were torn, officers' spurs rolled up in lace flounces, and
dowagers' wigs driven from their right position. Feathers were
flying, and some ladies were presented to the Queen minus parts of
dresses which cost so much anxiety in arrangement. My wife had
a grand dress for the occasion, which was tattered and torn, but it
was a great day for Ireland.

Outside, there was a flare up amongst the police and the carriages. Coachmen all wanting to be first at the door, got out of
place, a knot was tied not to be unravelled; the dragoon escort even
failed. I saw one of those swordsmen cutting at the reins holding
in a pair of fine spanking horses. Every cut that he made was fruitless, the coachman letting the ribbons drop slack at every blow.
He baffled him in this way, and kept his place.

The Peninsula medal was tardily bestowed. Some few dozen
of the old coves, amongst whom was the gallant Sir Charles Napier,
assembled in Dublin on the anniversary of the battle of Toulouse,
10th of April, 1814, to celebrate the day and display the medals.
We had a joyful dinner-party, the band of my regiment was in good
voice and fine feather, and sang a song which I pencilled off for the
occasion in the morning. It was encored, and the chorus might
have been heard far and wide. The fourth verse alludes to the
brave, the noble, and persevering Duke of Richmond; but for whom
every old warrior at the table might have gone to his grave without
a bit of ribbon.

On another occasion, while quartered in the city of the Limerick
lasses, Lord Gough was entertained, in his native town, at a public
dinner. The old song was once more sung by our Royal band, the
last verse being added by me in honour of so great and gallant a
soldier.

I had enough of Dublin joys, like others, and was not sorry when
we got the route to Cephalonia, one of the Greek islands in the
Mediterranean. In the second month of the year 1853, I formed
my gallant old regiment in the square of the Cork barracks for em-

barkation. Every man was steady, sober, remarkably clean, and fit for anything. The band was tuning up for the old song, 'The Girl I left behind me', when the postman came up with the letters. One was addressed to me from the Secretary of State, desiring that I might remain behind, repair to London, and be ready to give evidence before a committee in the House of Commons on the important affair of an Irish election. An Irish election always involves one or both parties in trouble. In one hour afterwards I embarked my old comrades as they were loudly cheered by the multitude, who were lavish with hurrahs and kind wishes for the Royals. Many were the weeping eyes of wives and sweethearts whose white kerchiefs fluttered in the breeze, until the steamers were well away down the beautiful 'lee' to meet the transport at the Cove. The General-Commanding had a peculiar way of doing things, not for the comfort or convenience of a certain class of officers encumbered with extra family baggage. I had two carriages on shore, ready packed to go on board, but my friend, the General-Commanding, passed the day on board to see everything in its proper place, and ordered not a pound of extra baggage to enter the ship. My friend, Admiral Purvis, commanded the ships, if our General ruled the troops, and he sent all my traps with his compliments to the Captain, to be not landed, except in Cephalonia. There, I found all safe on my arrival.

We passed a week with our esteemed and hospitable friends, Mr. and Mrs. Leycester, at Bella Vista, Queenstown, then crossed the Channel, leaving Bristol on the morning of February 24th in a first-class express train for London. The day was bright, cold and frosty. After passing the Ealing station, five or six miles from London, tearing away at a frightful pace, the train ran off the rail up a bank fifteen feet high and toppled over, down upon the rails, wheels up, and G. B. & Co. down!

We were in the midst of the débris, covered up by the wreck in darkness and terror; in fact, buried alive, unable to move hand or foot, until the carriage was broken up in search of the killed and wounded. We were then discovered amongst the latter, and laid out upon the bank to breathe more freely. I began to examine our bones, and tried my legs. All right, not even a fracture, although otherwise severely injured, it being two years before I recovered the use of my bridle hand. Mrs. B. was very much shaken, but less injured, part of the wreck having formed a sort of arch over her body. It was the hand of God saved us, and to His Name be all the praise. One of our passengers, a Director (Mr. Gibb), was killed, and several badly wounded. Still the accident must have been worse, had not the locomotive broken away, kept the rail, and

stopped the down train from running into us. This would have
smashed up the whole concern, for it only pulled up twenty yards
from our wreck. I was detained a long time in London with this
election affair, where there was a great amount of swearing *pro*
and *con*. When some Paddies take the book into the swearing position, if not watched, they may by accident kiss a thumb, or push a
nose against the Bible, and give a smack as if it was done well; and
if there happens to be no Cross, lies don't count.

Being released from many a long walk in the lobby of the House,
and left to myself to go in search of my regiment, we made up a
nice little family party and started from London on the 21st of May
1852 for the Greek Islands.

NOTE

THE British Army appears to have had some strange assignments
in the early 1850s. The Royal Scots, some artillery, and a few
specialist officers, were on garrison duty in the Greek Islands from
1852-54. Why? Colonel Bell does not explain. Except for a
very terrifying experience in an earthquake, Colonel Bell and his
regiment led a most halcyon existence. Forty per cent. of his
regiment seems to have spent its time on leave and he took a considerable entourage of officers, N.C.O.s and men, on a series of
'escorted tours', enlivened by lectures on the Classics and Greek
Mythology! When he *was* with his regiment, he restarted his Bible
classes, taught in his regimental school for soldiers' children and
adult illiterates, and studied archaeology.

In October 1853 he scented an air of battle and, fearing that he
might be left in Greece, he applied for leave to go home and find
himself a job in the Army that was even then preparing for war in
the Crimea. He was unlucky and, after being kept hanging about
at the Horse Guards for two months, he received orders to return
to his regiment. On 30th March 1854 he was at Marseilles, very
disgruntled, and preparing to embark for Athens. Then his fortune
changed. He met the Duke of Wellington (son of the 'Iron Duke'),
who offered to 'use his influence' and to go back to London with
him after conducting some secret diplomatic business with the
British Ambassador in Paris. As the result, Colonel Bell found himself transferred from the 2nd Royal Scots to the 1st Battalion, under
orders for Turkey. History repeated itself and he found himself
in exactly the same position as he had been at Halifax, N.S., ten
years previously. Owing to a mistake by the Admiralty, his regiment sailed a few hours before he reached them! As his diary
records, this happened *again* at Malta, a few weeks later.

CHAPTER
14

'Help for Turkey'

To my delight, one of our fellow passengers was the Duke of Wellington, son of my old master in the Peninsula. The Duke mentioned that he and the Duchess had left the Paddington station one morning in February, when they observed a locomotive passing by rather in an unusual way. They remarked, 'There is an accident', which proved to have been the case, for they pulled up just in time to avoid a collision, and saw a dead man and several wounded lying on the bank.

'Well,' I said, 'I was amongst the latter, as well as my wife, and how we escaped was miraculous, for the débris of the carriages lay over us until we were dug out, and if the guard had not gone on to stop your advance, we might have been all destroyed.'

We hurried on to Paris, as I became anxious about my future destination. A great, big, lumbering diligence was then the quickest conveyance for most part of the road. When we got to the railway, or *chemin-de-fer*, we met the Duke again, going our way. The 7th of April found us in London, and on the 8th I presented myself at the Horse Guards to report my arrival and ask for a command. The Commander-in-Chief (Lord Hardinge) offered me the 1st Battalion Royal Regiment, under orders for Turkey, nothing else then being at his disposal. I accepted, and was next day in General Order, to take the command, and embark with them at Plymouth on the 21st. I had twelve days to look about me, and get ready for the campaign in prospect. According to the General

Order of the army, forty-eight hours are allowed for troops to settle down and get snug on board before sailing. I was well up to my time arriving at Plymouth, and having a lawful twenty-four hours to spare. But things don't always run so smoothly as one calculates. The regiment had been embarked the day before, and sent to sea at once, against all precedent! Here I was in a fix — the ship was out of sight, and I stood on the beach, not very well pleased with myself or the official who hurried away my corps. I was back in London same day, by express, reported the following morning at the Horse Guards, and was permitted to find my own way out, at my own expense. All this from a hurry-scurry blunder of the officer commanding at sea, the consequence of which was, the ship caught fire, everything was in confusion on board, and thanks to Providence all were not lost. Another leave-taking, and away to Paris on the 25th, down by rail to Châlons, to Lyons by steamer on the Saône, and on to Marseilles, where I passed an agreeable day with Monsieur and Madame R.

May 1st. Embarked in the French steamer *Osiris* for Malta: fare 239 francs. We were crowded with troops and horses, officers, and priests going out as chaplains to their army. Major-General Rose and Major Claremont, of my own regiment, were passengers going out on the staff of Marshal St. Arnaud. Sir Stephen Lakeman, too (who came home with us), going out to take a command in the Turkish army. An agreeable party, but rather crowded. Cloudy weather and light breeze.

4th. At ten a.m. arrived at Malta; the steamer with my regiment had just left! Called on Admiral Sir H. Stewart and General Ferguson, and asked for a passage to the Ionian Islands. No communication there. Lunched with our 68th Regiment, and dined with the Governor, Sir William Reid, an old Peninsula officer. Sir Stephen L. took up his quarters with me for the night at my old apartments — hotels all crowded.

5th. A frightful accident occurred this morning at one of the batteries while the gunners were at practice with red-hot shot. I was on my way to the battery when I met the staff-surgeon, an old friend, who drew me off to see the general hospital. A thirty-two-pounder gun burst; the fore part bounded over the parapet wall into the ditch below, the after part exploded into small pieces, flying about. One gunner had his head knocked to bits, his blood spattered against the wall. Another one had his leg blown away; another an arm; others wounded. The next gun in battery, a thirty-two, was blown quite out of its bed, and the carriage smashed to bits. A thirty-two on the left had its carriage much damaged and torn. A third gun-carriage, at a distance of 240 feet, was smashed by a heavy portion of the metal, which afterwards rebounded, and broke one of the large stones in the battlement, whilst the ground was torn up in many places by the flying fragments. One of the sufferers was carried into the hospital to have his leg amputated. He bore the knife and the saw courageously, was silent when the flesh-needle and thread gathered the tough skin over the stump; but the pale, bloodless face, rolling eye, and tight dovetailed fingers showed me his sufferings. Continued my voyage on the *Osiris*, thankful that I did not leave my bones at Malta.

8th. Syra early this morning; went ashore and walked up to the chapel on the conical hill; a long pull and very hot.

9th. Here I embarked again in another steamer, for Kallimaki; sailed at six p.m.; voyage four hours and a half; crossed the Isthmus of Corinth in seventy minutes, and embarked once more in the steamer *Messina* in the Gulf of Corinth, for Cephalonia. Look after your baggage amongst these wild sons of Greece. An English amateur just found out that none of his traps were in the van. 'Did you see them put in?' I asked. 'No, I expected all was right.' 'Well,' I said, 'all goes wrong in Greece unless one is wide awake. We don't sail till seven. Don't lose a moment, be off to the start-ing-point or you will never see so much as your night-cap. The Greeks have a weakness for red-hot woollen night-caps, to keep their heads cool.' Exit ——, returned in the evening. 'Got your traps?' 'No, nothing. Leather bag, patent-leather trunk with fine locks, all missing; can't be opened.' 'Excuse me,' I said, 'a lock upon leather, and a knife in one's pocket. Look out for a new kit; the old one is somewhere in Mount Parnassus, being inspected by some of these Greek bandits; baggage never looks after itself.'

Met some four score Greeks armed to the teeth, and bearing a standard, marching towards Athens. They are flocking back from all parts of Turkey, having got notice to quit; stupid fellows, attempting a struggle against the Sultan, backed up as he is by England and France. They had better go home to the vineyards than swagger about the country playing at soldiers without leaders, money, or arms. Better revolt against their own vile government than attempt to aid Russia with a feeble arm.

11th. Anchored at Argostoli at four a.m. Some of my officers were on board to meet me before I was up. A welcome home by the whole regiment and an invitation to be their guest as long as I remained on the island; a banquet in the evening, and free quarters provided for me. My old servants came back to their old master, and volunteered to share my fortune in the campaign. I accepted their services, and they fell into their old places once more, joyous and happy. Visited all my old friends the next day.

The barracks, the men, the school, and everyone were all delighted
to see me back.   Many were the expressions of deep regret that I
was now but on a short visit.   I called a holiday for the school, and
the bugles sounded 'no parade' for the regiment.   All seemed weary
of their island home, tired of such monotony, and anxious for any
change.   The prospect of war gives hope of being emancipated, and
all are desirous to see that one vacant space in our colours filled by
another victory, or more.

My regiment, 1st (the Royal) Regiment, the oldest in our service,
or perhaps in the world, has just now emblazoned on its standard
the following record of distinguished honours won on the battlefield:

The royal cypher within the collar of St. Andrew, and
the crown over it.

ST. LUCIE	EGMONT-OP-ZEE
THE SPHINX	EGYPT
CORUNNA	BUSACO
SALAMANCA	VITTORIA
ST. SEBASTIAN	NIVE
PENINSULA	NIAGARA
WATERLOO	NAGPORE
MAHEIDPORE	AVA

Was it not a glory to command such a distinguished corps?
Up to the 20th all feasting, and fun in moderation.

The freemasons of the regiment, officers and non-commissioned
officers, opened their lodge to have one last opportunity of meeting
their old commanding officer.   I had the invitation of true men.
We were all bound in one mystic tie, but entirely apart from any
system of equality in duty, obedience, or discipline.   After the lodge
was closed, the supper-room, handsomely decorated for the occasion, was thrown open.   'Welcome!' in olive-branches bearing the
fruit, and many appropriate devices decorating the walls.   'Go
where glory waits thee!'   'G. B., our much esteemed commanding
officer', in a wreath of flowers and olive-leaves, etc.   A most excellent supper being over, and the toast of the evening proposed by
the Sergeant-Major Whinton, the old barracks rang with one great
cheer, inside and out, for the whole of the men had assembled outside waiting for the signal.   I was quite taken aback by this demon-
stration of united kind feeling, and so nicely arranged.   I was proud
and gratified to think I stood so well with men I had commanded
for ten years in honour and satisfaction to us all.   A finer body of
zealous, intelligent, high-minded, respectful non-commissioned
officers I knew there was not in the service, and they knew that I
respected them as they deserved.   These few notes are but a little

record to keep in remembrance a pleasing incident in the life of a soldier, and cannot be interesting to anyone else; we like to fight our battles over again in the evening of life, and when memory's path is choked up with the old laurel leaves, one can look into his record.

The Sergeant-Major said: 'Brother non-commissioned officers, the toast I am going to propose you must all anticipate. We have drank to our Queen, and now we have amongst us once more our honoured guest, who so kindly answered our invitation this evening. One under whom we have served cheerfully and most happily for many years — our friend, our adviser, our advocate, our highly esteemed and distinguished Commanding Officer. One who has never swerved from his duty in defending our rights and advancing our interest in the service, and to whom we are indebted for the many privileges we enjoy. We are all grieved at his departure from amongst us, but he is going where glory awaits the true soldier. Our kindest wishes attend him, and may he safely return with additional honours to his family and friends. I give you the health of Colonel Bell, our late much respected and honoured chief.'

The rest, indeed, was a long and loud nine times nine and one cheer more. The response came from a heart touched with a spark of military feeling known only to soldiers in the meridian of glory. All this little attention brings out the true character of a commanding officer, and is more valuable than fine gold. The band was brilliant in their selection; some fine songs and glees were sung, and as I rose to depart, 'Auld Lang Syne' was smothered with the cheers of my old comrades of all ranks in the mess-room and from the barrack outside, waiting to cheer me to my quarters. There may be an appearance of egotism here, but no, 'tis a simple narrative.

Lieutenant Turner, my Adjutant, volunteered to share my fortune; in fact, he would not stay behind. He resigned his appointment; I had him transferred to my new battalion, and if volunteering had been the order of the day, I might have had half the regiment. I had been waiting for a Constantinople steamer up to this time. We left Cephalonia in the night of the 21st and arrived at Zante next morning at seven o'clock. I put up with the resident, Colonel Staunton, 31st Regiment, and dined at their mess. I got my horse ashore and purchased two fine mules for 115 Spanish dollars to carry my baggage, and paid their freight, £20 17s. 7d. From this point I got a free passage to join my new corps, having paid enough out of my own pocket for the blundering mistakes of official red-tape in sending troops to sea before they had time to shake into place. There is no safe place for embarking horses at Zante. The primitive way is to shove them off the jetty into the flat, at the risk of breaking their legs, as they never volunteer to jump down five or six feet into a boat. I had to accomplish this with a nervous feeling, and as the big steamer bowled in at two in the morning, dark as you please, and dropped her anchor far out at sea, we pushed off in the sanitary boat and got on board. But here was another fix; the bear of a Captain at once declined to take my mules on board. I insisted; he was resolute. I showed him bill and receipt of lading: 'he didn't care'. I began to think they would be turned adrift, when the port captain, who put us on board, stepped forward and told this skipper if he did not take my animals on board he would detain the steamer and keep his papers. This threat brought the Austrian savage to his bearings. When he gave the word, 'hoist them in,' up they came all safe.

25th. At Syra until four p.m. *Egitta*, from Constantinople, came slowly in. Some amateur officers on board said my regiment was at Gallipoli. This was just what I wished. I had lost nothing. Went ashore, and had a dip in the blue sea.

26th. At ten a.m. anchored off Smyrna. Went ashore to see some horses that I expected, rough and ready little ones; very hardy, but too small. Called on the Consul for news, who said that the three chiefs had met at Varna to arrange for the campaign. I thought as three of a trade never agree, and no one was chief of the combined army, it was just possible there might be a split in the camp. Three chiefs never can command an army; *nous verrons*.

Many Turkish women came on board as passengers, all huddling together in what I called the dove-cot, in a part of the poop distinct from the crockery part of their creation. They wore the yashmac, the nose and eyes only visible, and very brilliant eyes some of them had. They seemed so patient and content, but evidently were under some restraint that they would willingly cast off, and will some day. As night came on they wrapped themselves up in their cloaks and shawls, bundled together in their Zante quilts, and went to sleep. This sort of passengers, men and women, always live and lie on deck, and feed on their own stores. Bread and cheese, curds, pickles, a small piece of meat with sweeties, and water, make their repast. Coffee is indispensable—such wretched stuff as it is!

27th. Gallipoli. Anchored at half-past five p.m. Harbour full of steamers, English and French ships of war, and transports. John Bull's English gold beginning here to fly like chaff. Here I can see is the beginning of troubles—of many sorrows. Who will live to count the cost? Who will see the end?

Here is a lively scene. The tented field of 40,000 men of France, flanked by 6,000 British troops, the advanced guard of a war picture. Millions of gold won't do it. We landed all safely. My horse was saddled; baggage packed on the mules; turned out ready for the field. Poor Turner by my side was joyful. Away we went, inquiring for our Royal residence. It was quite dark before we found the camp. We pitched our tent by starlight, whistled the old tune, 'My lodging is on the cold ground', and soon went to sleep.

Up in the morning early. Took over the command of the 1st Battalion Royal Regiment. All hands ready to fix me up in a new home. It is little the soldier requires in the field; having an ingenious turn, he may always be snug in his tent. A very light stretcher, with some blankets, makes one's bed, a couch, and a seat. A pot and a frying-pan and a table if you can. Knife, fork and spoon is in possession of every loon; a kettle to boil your tea, just as we used to make it at sea,[1] a tin mug, and a water jug, a piece of soap, and always a coil of rope, a good horse to ride, and a baggage-mule besides, and at every peep of day let your motto be, *Toujours prêt*.

28th, Sunday. Divine service at six a.m. and a vast deal of drunkenness at six p.m. A fine country. Hill and dale, rich and fertile. A healthy position for the camp. Plenty of water. About six miles from Gallipoli. The usual cry at home and abroad is 'Help for Turkey!'

29th. Brigade field-day. 'Help for Turkey!' Manoeuvring in the cornfields.

30th. Rode away to see the French camp and the beautiful and fertile valleys on towards the town. How rich the soil, and how pretty the lanes, so like many I have seen in England, deep in the country. The hawthorn, wild rose, and jessamine, embracing the fragrant honeysuckle. Thanks to kind Providence for health and strength to enjoy the blessings of nature, speaking so eloquently all around us, the weather too so charming.

31st. A grand review of all our army by the French Marshal, St. Arnaud, who came to the ground like a Marshal of France with an escort and staff of 200 warriors, finely mounted and equipped in splendid uniform. Prince Napoleon and General Canrobert accompanied him. We assembled some miles from our camp for good ground. As the old Marshal passed down our long red line —(my regiment always takes the right of the line)—and I presented arms, he said, 'How you do, Colonel Bell?' I dropped my sword, with a *Vive l'Empereur!*

'More help for Turkey!' We manoeuvred in the standing corn, some four feet high, and destroyed the green crops to perfection. After five and a half hours in heavy marching order, we got home to

[1] Throw your tea into a kettle and boil it well.

prepare some breakfast. Men nearly suffocated with those hard leather stocks choking them under a broiling sun, so very injurious to the health and pliability of our soldiers. It is difficult to persuade the old red-tape authorities to relinquish their antiquated customs. I remember my regiment being inspected once by an old general officer who measured the distance between the buttons on the soldiers' coatees![1] I have seen the men fight best with their necks bare and their coats open: never mind the buttons.

Turner dined with me today. We had a capital ration dinner. First course, mutton and broth, pot taken off the fire and placed between us on the sod, tin soup plates, filled with a teacup. No want of appetite. Finished the broth and ate up the mutton. Second course, two slices of fat bacon and eggs fried, plenty of brown bread, someone had sent me a bottle of wine. Nothing more wanted. We laughed and enjoyed it more than a club dinner. The wild dogs make a great row at night, but their barking don't disturb my slumbers. The horses and mules sometimes break from their picket posts, and get entangled in the cords of your tent, when down it goes on the top of your head, a regular nightmare flourish, and no dream.

June 1st. Camp near Gallipoli. Brigade field-day at five a.m. Royals, 38th, and 50th Regiments. A blazing hot day. Next brigade neighbours, 4th, 28th, and 44th Regiments. We dine at mid-day, and at six p.m. We ride away to the blue sea of Marmora, for a dash into its refreshing waters. Strip, mount our horses, and swim them out to sea, which they enjoy, snorting all the while. Ride quietly home and go to roost.

4th, Sunday. Divine service at six a.m. and a most excellent sermon by our chaplain, the Rev. Mr. Mockler.

5th. Dined with Sir John Campbell, our Brigadier, at Gallipoli. Dangerous to ride over the broken streets of that wretched tumble-down place. It might have been paved a hundred years ago. There is not a square yard of even ground at present within its walls. The French are trying to make some improvements in naming the streets, and numbering the houses, etc., if they deserve the name of houses. One crooked old narrow street they have named 'Rue de Rivoli'. Another the 'Corso', and so on, in derision, while the indolent Turk looks up in amazement and exclaims, 'Allah kerim!' and takes another pull at his long pipe.

6th, 7th, 8th. Sirocco winds and heavy gales, filling our tents, our beds, our hair, and eyes with refined hot sand. Glad to ride off to the sea, and get under water.

Bought another horse for £8 10s. from a Turk. Not very big,

[1] He had a small rule in his pocket for this admirable practice.

but good of its kind. He may have been looted, but no use in asking such a question.

Up at four to change our ground. At half-past four tents struck, packed up, and we were all away. Encamped near the Sea of Marmora; happy change and fine position, the sea below covered with steamers, ships of war, etc., all bound with troops, munitions of war, and stores up to Varna and Constantinople. My tent is being pitched under the shade of a large walnut-tree. While I write my notes, the inside is like a fiery furnace. Thermometer 160°, with a rattling breeze coming over the sea. Water scarce. Gave orders to place sentries over the springs, and also round the camp, to prevent the men entering the vineyards, or cutting the fruit-trees, or damaging private property, and to keep the horses out of the cornfields. All soldiers have the organ of destructiveness, and nothing will grow where they plant their feet. 'Let the sentries keep a sharp look out.' 'Yes, sir,' and away went my good lad, Turner, to perform his duty, for he was again Adjutant, the appointment having become vacant, and being in my gift.

11th. A visitor, young Edwin Freshfield, walked from Gallipoli, under a scorching sun, to see me. He was fresh from Jerusalem, and on his way to Constantinople. I gave him a ration dinner, the best I could get up, and sent him back on horseback, joyful and astonished at our manner of life.

12th. Up at four. 'Help for Turkey!' Five thousand men manoeuvring across the country and in the cornfields, the sun, playing on the patent-leather shakos, warmed their heads. No sort of headgear could be better for the sun's attraction, and, of course, many men fell under the *coup de soleil*. I tried the experiment of frying a slice of bacon on top of my shako, exposed to a vertical sun. I had our doctor present, and made him eat part of the cooking, to show him the effect on the brains of humanity. We have wonderfully wise men at the head of our war department!

While sitting in my tent, in the heat of the day, I heard a noise like the whiz of an angry rocket rushing in between my legs, and lo! a snake was coiled up under my baggage. I called to the sentry outside to send in a group of officers standing a little way off. I pointed out the game—he was driven out, and hunted down the hill, without a chance of escape. They brought him to show me; 'A great beauty, five feet long, well made', etc. I don't wish to see any more such beautiful visitors. The last was a great centipede, and earwigs are too numerous.

'Tis a calm evening, so pure and bright, the air so dry. I hear the bands playing in their camp four miles off, and how well their canvas town looks in the distance! More transports going up with troops, and we don't move, though all ready and willing and anxious for a change.

14th. A brigade field-day, and great help for Turkey. Trampled down some fine fields of corn which will never rise again. I don't see much use in my protecting the crops. I never see a peasant, a farmer, or anyone to claim property. Swimming our horses in the sea this evening.

I built a cook-house, and had a leg of mutton roast, to the wonder of passers-by. Nothing on such a grand scale in the *cuisine* department has ever been seen on the Marmora heights before today. My Adjutant dined with me. The mutton was served in a hot tin dish, and a bottle of wine made the banquet quite a treat. O, for the life of a soldier!

15th. Rode about twenty miles today in search of new ground to encamp, our water failing; found a beautiful spring, on the side of a hill, bubbling up like a fountain. How very refreshing in a thirsty land, reminding one of the wells so often a contention of strife in ancient times! We came on a valley rich in corn and vines, fruitful as land could be, and a river running through it, but nearly dry. At the foot of a woody hill, an old farm-house peeped through the foliage, the storks stood on the top corners like statuary, while the hen-birds sat upon their great basket nests, hatching their eggs, with their long beaks wide open, gasping with heat. They are harmless domestic creatures, and are held in veneration by the inhabitants. In the outer court a fine fountain was gushing forth sweet water, of which we partook with our horses. I blew my whistle at the hall-door, when the inmates looked out and beheld for the first time in life some mounted soldiers at their threshold. The alarm was given, causing a great rustling inside. Two black slave girls lost no time in barring the doors and shutting the lattice windows, then all was silence. I gave a thundering knock, but there was no response, so we left them in peace to tell a long story afterwards, how they had been attacked by red banditti, who were repulsed by their brave jet damsels, etc., etc. They are specially fond of telling long, marvellous stories in the calm evenings. Approaching the camp homewards, we came upon the line of rifle practice, and although half a mile off, the Minié bullets made us gallop out of their way. Home at ten minutes past ten p.m.; a ration-dinner as tough as leather, but good soup and a glass of grog, cheered by the report that we go to Varna next week.

17th. Extremely hot; thermometer over 100°. Lost my keys on my way home from bathing; this was quite a calamity. I had little to lose, but could not afford to lose that little for want of lock and key. The flies are a torment, they set our horses wild with their venom.

18th. Made it known in camp that I had lost a bunch of keys on my way home, and should be glad if any of my men would go over the ground, as nearly as I could explain, in search of them. I thought it a forlorn hope, but they were brought to me the same afternoon, found in a vineyard three miles from camp, by one of my soldiers, who was so glad that he was lucky he would not take any reward. Dined with Sir R. England in Gallipoli, and got home at night by the light of my watchman's lamp over frightful roads.

19th. Up at four. Division field-day and extremely hot. Destroyed some twenty acres of standing corn, nearly ripe, in our manoeuvres. O, you farmers of England, what do you say to all this? No one here visible to look after the most splendid crops, left to the tender mercies of an army of men and horses. Keep in mind that it will be just your lot, if ever you permit foreign troops to land upon your shores.

20th. I marched my regiment down to Gallipoli to exchange our percussions arms for the Minié rifle. We met a division of French troops going to embark; they were crossing our path, but halted to let us pass, their band playing 'God save the Queen' — a nice, soldierlike feeling. We gave them a true British cheer in return, with a *Vive l'Empereur!*

21st. Vittoria day; no parade or drill. The men knew very well that the seven clasps on my Peninsula medal meant seven holidays when the days came round, and this was one of them. I believe every officer and soldier in the battalion highly approved of this old custom of mine. The officers invited me to a dinner on the occasion, for which they had been preparing. A green bower was built, all cooks of celebrity in camp employed, every good thing to be had in Gallipoli was sought for, few as they were. The banquet to be held on the sod at six p.m., in camp fashion, i.e. each person to bring his servant, with knife, fork, spoon and plate. In fact, there were great preparations and great expectations, but at twelve o'clock an aide-de-camp came riding up to my tent. 'What news do you bring?' I asked. 'You embark today for Varna, at four o'clock; get ready, no time to be lost; you know the rest!' and he galloped away. 'Bugler, sound the officers' call.' They were soon at my tent door. 'Gentlemen, we embark at four o'clock this day. Get ready, I will march away in two hours.' The next bugle sound was to strike the tents, and down they went with a cheer; then to pack them up, and away to collect the baggage animals out at grass. All hands busy and at work, *con amore.* 'Dash it!' says one, 'the dinner is quite floored. Let's have something grilled, and a go-in at the beer before we go.' 'Oh, hang the dinner, I can't find my mule!' 'Where's my pony, Mick?' 'Gone to Gallip, sir, to be shod. Bad luck to them Turks, sure they take a week to hammer an iron plate on his fut.' 'What shall I do?' 'O, bedad, sir, the quartermaster may give your baggage a lift down to the ship. I'll run and be first at him.' Tats, undrilled, kicking and flinging off their loads, and away over the hills, the men after them like a pack of hounds—tally ho!—until they were caught, brought back, and whacked into submission. All was hurry-scurry to be up to time, but many hands, they say, and all our hands were right willing. Everyone was only too anxious to assist in forwarding our advance. I looked at my watch: 'Sound the assembly!' and in a few minutes my gallant regiment was formed in column, and away we went cheerily down the hills, singing the old song:

> Merrily, merrily march away,
>   Soldier's glory lives in story.
> Our laurels are green, if our locks are grey,
>   And it's heigh for martial glory.

At four o'clock our first boat pushed off from the place of embarkation to the ship, but it was long after night before we all got on board. The steamer took seventy horses besides baggage, stores, my regiment, and the staff. Every man was present, and not a look back of regret at the lofty hills above Gallipoli. We soon fell into our respective places to rest our weary bones after a long day of warm excitement. We sailed at 9.30 next morning, hot as you please; plenty to eat, and tough as leather; worse cooking than we had ashore, but rolled on quietly. What a noble country this would be in the hands of England: great fertility of soil, and the crops on both sides looking well under bad farmers. Anchored off Scutari in twenty-two hours.

23rd. In the *Golden Horn*; went ashore to see the great Turkish barrack at Scutari. Met some officers coming out very busy sweeping the fleas from their clothes, so I declined entering this lively building. It is capable of accommodating some thousand troops, and has an imposing effect in the distance. But, like the great city of mosques and minarets, so fairy-like, better not approach too near, or the pleasing dream will turn out a delusion, and give you heaps of dirt, mangy dogs, break-neck streets, brawling boatmen, and the air perfumed with tobacco-smoke. Called on the Commissary-General, 'by order' for some stores to take on to Varna. Everyone seemed to be doing nothing. I tried the Admiral. All red tape here too. 'Make your application through so and so.' I gave it up. Most of the officers went ashore. I missed five of them at

dinner hour. We got under way and left them behind. They just
saved their distance by hiring a six-oared caïque, and cutting along
the shore of the Bosphorus at a rapid pace, getting ahead of the
steamer, and shooting out in to the stream, all very much amused
with their adventure, when they scrambled into the right place.
At this time, when two great armies were on the move to save
Turkey, spending millions of gold to keep her out of the claws of
the Russian bear, the Sultan was amusing himself with his annual
wedding, squandering money like chaff, while his soldiers were in
arrear of their wretched pay and being cheated by all their war
department. The 'sick man', however, takes a fresh young wife
every year according to custom, adding another treasure to the
harem!

25th, Sunday. Remained on board.

26th. Up at half-past three to disembark my regiment, got to
our ground two miles west by ten a.m. and everything on shore by
twelve. Took up my position on the right, and front line of the
army, according to the rank of my corps, and it happened to be on
the battleground where so many thousand Russians left their bones
in 1829, fighting for Varna. On my way up, I met Lieutenant-
General Sir De Lacy Evans, sitting at his tent-door with his aide-de-
camp, Captain Alix, one of my own officers. Invited to stop and
breakfast. We never refuse such kind offers in a campaign. 'Twas
a welcome invitation, and at the right time, for I had given up any
hope of a morning break-my-fast. A right good one we had, and
tearing sea-appetite to play with it.[1]

An hour or two establishes one in camp if he is an old soldier.
The mules unladen, the tents pitched, baggage arranged inside, dig
a little trench all round, leaving a sloping cut for the water to run
away. Kindle a fire: put three stones together in a shallow pit,
rough and ready, a few bits of dry wood, and you have a blaze to
boil your kettle. But unless the kettle boiling B, filling the tea-pot
spoils the T. Put up your bed, and make the little household
arrangements, then away to bathe in the lake. I have just done all
this, and now to visit my men and see all snug with them, and make
ourselves at home till the next move. General Pennefather called,
and asked me to dine with him in his green bower, so I was fixed
up for my first day in camp on the Devna Lake.

[1] Sir De Lacy Evans was one of the gallant and brave old Peninsula
heroes, who had seen great service, and held out the right hand of fellow-
ship to an old *camarada* whenever he met one.

CHAPTER
15

Varna and the Crimea

THE view from my tent-door is extremely grand. It comprises at sight the bay of Varna and its multitude of ships and steamers; the encampment of the British, French, and Turkish armies. This forest of canvas-dwellings contains as yet only 60,000 men, all ready to move at an hour's notice, and the sooner we move from this the better, for I can see that the troops are on sickly ground. Up to ten o'clock a.m. all is clear and bright and beautiful; for six hours after that the camp is almost in obscurity from the hurricane of white dust. This daily west gale fills our eyes, our hair, our tents, with white limestone powder. A perfect plague; give me hail, snow, thunder, lightning, rain—anything but dust.

All the Generals are in camp, except Lord Raglan and Sir George Brown. Called on Prince George, and the Adjutant-General Eastcourt.

29th. Nothing new; nothing to do but eat up the rations and speculate on the future.

30th. Rode up the hills some miles to see the French camp on the tableland overlooking the Black Sea. It is well laid out and very extensive. Their tents are not so good as ours, but their huts and bowers are extremely neat, built of green branches to exclude the sun. Bands playing, and the soldiers amusing themselves at different games, as contented like as if they were all in la belle France. A little box fastened on a pole in a shady recess was marked 'Boîte-à-poste Zouave', the Zouave post-office. I was told that a Zouave soldier was shot this morning for stabbing a comrade in his anger. They are fine-looking, intelligent, active, hardy fellows, but hasty in temper. The country up here is not unlike some of England's finest and extensive parks; it only wants an old mansion here and there peeping out of cover. The fine old trees on the ground of a hundred years' growth, dotted over a thousand acres, here and there waiting a Christian tenant. Oh, what a home it might be made for a little colony of friends—Quakers if you like!

Descending homewards another way by a zigzag path, shaded by drooping trees and shrubs, with a break now and then for a sea view, I was struck with the beauty of the scene; pine-trees, vine-yards and crystal springs, wild flowers perfuming the path, of which I gathered a grand bouquet for my white house on the plain, where I arrived in the evening to my ration dinner of mutton broth and the bone that made it. The usual thundering of artillery goes on daily. There seems to be no lack of powder. A salute is being now fired in honour of the birth of a child in the palace of the Sultan, as if that were any novelty, seeing he has as many wives as Solomon.

The *savants* seem to be in a fix about any move. It is time we were going from this, and doing something for our rations; eating up all the beef and mutton in the land, and burying the dead, is our chief employ. Who will pay the bill if we win? Somehow, we always win, and never get paid. An additional tax on John Bull, and some more millions to the national debt.

July 1st. Blowing a hurricane of hot wind and sand over the camp. Tents sometimes invisible; many of the men gone to hos-pital almost blind. These land gales are frightful and destructive, but there is still a remedy if commonsense could see it. I have no patience with wooden heads. Change the ground; can't you see the white, dusty road running through your camp?

2nd. Divine service in the fields at six a.m.

3rd. 2nd Division marched away this morning at four. Omer Pacha arrived at Varna to confer with the allied chiefs. A wet night and a boisterous, cold morning. How pleasant, being awoke in the night by the rain spattering through your canvas bedroom, and putting on your damp clothes before sunrise! Invited to an evening party held in the hospital tent, there being no sick. It was a symposium on promotion. A plank was nailed on two hedge-stakes fastened in the ground, which did the duty of a table. Four candles in empty bottles (our usual candlesticks) gave us light. A bayonet is a better substitute when one sits on the sod; give it a dig into the turf here or there, or anywhere, and it sticks firm.

Brandy, lemons, sugar, water, and cigars, were *ad libitum* on the

table.   In the middle of the floor a washing-tub was placed, flowing
with cold rum punch, an A, D, L, L as Walter Scott's Gaberlunzie
would call it, was swimming on the top for baling out the liquor.
Tin tots were put in and filled by the President.   The company sat
round in a ring in the fashion of tailors, and the song went merrily
round, nobody excused.   Two French officers were of the party.
We all drank the health of the Emperor.   One of them returned
thanks, and gave as a toast the 'Queen of England' in return; then
the health of Colonel G. B., and a hearty welcome, nine times nine;
a compliment always the most acceptable to a commanding officer,
showing the barometer of the corps.   All went cheerful, merry,
and joyous until the lights burned into the bottle, when the lads
dispersed, all in harmony.   Such is one of the features of camp life
on service.

5th.   Mounted my gallant grey, and away early, to see a grand
review of 40,000 French troops on the heights facing the Black Sea.
Looking down upon its unrippled surface, the sun was bright and
melting, glistening on the arms and steel-clad cuirasses of the
cavalry.   The troops were formed in quarter-distance columns.
Now we hear the war trumpet, and a cavalcade of chosen horsemen
emerge from the green woods, followed by a troop of Lancers
winding up the steep ascent.   Then Marshal St. Arnaud, with Omer
Pacha by his side, dressed in embroidered gold finery, with the usual
head-dress of the Turkish soldiers—the fez.   Lord Raglan and Prince
George of Cambridge came next, other Generals and their staffs,
Admiral of the Fleet Dundas, and many naval and military officers
in the train.   The rear was brought up by a troop of most extraordinary wild-looking Arabs, not unlike old women or witches on
horseback, from their peculiar dress—a white night-cap (such as
sometimes worn by old country crones in bye-places in the land o'
cakes) bound round the head by a dingy black kerchief.   They
wore a flowing red cloak over a loose white robe, wide white
trousers and spurs, or spikes fastened to the heel of a sort of boot,
the foot resting in a rusty iron shovel stirrup.   A long firelock was
slung over the back, a sharp sword girded round the waist, and
pistols in the holsters.   They were bronzed, weather-beaten fellows,
from a life of warfare in Africa, and had the Moorish cast of
features.   They managed their Barbs with dexterity, and swept
across the country like the wind; rode short, and spurred their
horses on the flank.

This review being got up for his Highness, he was conducted
along the line of a noble body of disciplined troops by the Marshal
of France, and expressed himself much pleased, as he might well do,
seeing the contrast between the French and the *Turkeys*.   The

troops wheeled to the right, marched past in review, and away to their respective camps, where some of them did not arrive until six o'clock p.m.

I doubt if we will ever become what I call field soldiers, or if our present chiefs will allow us to be comfortable in the possession of what nature has blessed us with — the full swing of our legs, arms, joints, and muscles. Some officers were called on today to send their reasons in writing why they appeared on the review-ground in undress, i.e. not buttoned up to the chin in full uniform, just as they would appear at the Queen's levee at St. James's Palace; they were observed looking on in the distance under a broiling sun, and were called to account for such a deep transgression, and got reprimanded. Many a stout man has been lost to the service, and will be lost in the very hour of need, from the red-tape system of choking the soldier with a stiff leather collar about his neck, and as much leather harness on his back and round his carcass as would tire a donkey. Give the soldier freedom on the line of march and the battlefield, let his lungs play and his arms swing easy in the grasp of his firelock. Pitch that leather stock to the ——, and you will always see him in his place before the enemy, instead of floundering in the rear when the battle has begun. But there is no rooting out old hereditary prejudices in our ranks, nor will there be, until we have a brush with those Russian heroes, who seem to frighten the world, and until we number our absentees, who have dropped behind, not from want of pluck, but for want of the breath of life to keep them moving on. Our officers high in rank are but young and inexperienced soldiers, brought up in the school of pipeclay. Not ten in this fine army ever saw a shot fired in anger, pushed on, as they have been, by interest and money, they top the old warrior, and, in the event of a war, will rob us of our inheritance.

6th. The *London Gazette* just come into camp. I see I am there Colonel G. B. Well, always glad to get a step forward, but still 'tis not agreeable to see in the same list fifty officers of my own rank, long junior to me in the service — men who never saw a battlefield — put over my head, so as to reap all the advantages for the time to come. This is gall and vinegar to me and a few more of Wellington's old soldiers, but there is no redress.

Omer Pacha returned to his headquarters today at Shumla. On the way some Turks were in the act of robbing one of our people. They made off into the bush when observed. One of them was taken, when Omer ordered him to be hanged upon a tree at once, and he was hanged accordingly.

7th. Marched out in brigade for exercise: very hot. A great

o

many of the men fell out exhausted. The weight kills them in ten miles, choked with leather as well. Had a refreshing bath in the Black Sea. The brown beetle swarms, constantly on the wing, annoy one badly; they dash at your face, get into your hair, and won't be warned off. They appear about five p.m., and retire at dark. I hear, at sundown, the Turk soldiers sound a sort of bugle, and give three wild cheers as they keep guard on the walls of Varna.

8th. The bashi-bazouks are coming in, forming a camp, in vast numbers, to be organised under their chief, General Yussuff. Every one has his own horse, small, but active and hardy. I like riding through their camp: they are a wildlike sort of mounted banditti, and will play Old Harry if let loose in an enemy's country, or in any country. I'm sure they will not be of any use to us, nor will they ever be under proper discipline. They have no regular dress, one fellow had seven bits of looking-glass arranged in his cap, and six or seven fox brushes in tail behind. I put this dragoon down as huntsman or whipper-in of this pack of wild devils on horseback. They get pay and rations to keep them from plundering, but John Bull's gold pays for all.

Captain Peel, R.N., and Major Hunter, 71st Regiment, came to see me. I asked them to stay to dinner, but fortunately they were engaged. I had nothing in the pot but the ration of beef and soup.

No getting one's horse shod, although native farriers on pay are attached to the brigade on 3s. 6d. a month per horse. I went myself to be sure of getting my horse shod. I found the party sitting idle under a bush, without a nail in their box, and none nearer than Constantinople. Here is a simple illustration of John Bull's gold being cast to the winds—a fine military arrangement!

The Turks shoe their horses in old style. They hammer a round iron plate on the foot with nails as big as a hazel nut. There is a hole in the centre of the iron plate to let in the mud and gravel, to keep there until this rough piece of work falls off. And so such things go on without any improvement in this country from generation to generation. I got a hammer and a few nails, tacked on a shoe myself, resolving never to be without spare shoes and nails again whenever I got the chance of a supply. A soldier on service should know how to put his hand to everything.

The lake looks feverish, a damp haze arising always at night; death is approaching our camp.

9th. Divine service at six a.m.—half an hour! The rest of the day unobserved as a Christian Sabbath. There is a vast harvest here, but few labourers in the vineyard. A strong body of Turkish lancers has just come into camp and taken up their ground. Our forces are rapidly increasing, and there will be work for all. There will be ample employment for us. I give 550 men for duty today.

10th. Four a.m. I hear the clarion band of some cavalry in the distance; up and away at the sound to meet them. Here they come; close to my hall-door. What a line! two miles in extent. They are French; fine horses, fine men, beautifully equipped, all looking so fresh and well after a seventeen days' march across the Balkan from Gallipoli, halting a week at Adrianople. Look at that regiment, with their polished steel and brass helmets glittering in the sun, breast and backplates as brilliant still, sparkling like diamonds in the distance, as they wind through the underwood, a noble sight. To breakfast now. 'What's that passing, George?' 'Some Highlanders, sir, carrying a Frenchman home on a stretcher: they found him dead in the bush.'

12th. A thunderstorm, lightning and rain. Found some goat-herds back of a ditch, watering their milk for the camp! Soon got into the London fashion of doubling their profits. Bought one of the goats at once, and am now all right in the dairy department. I have been roasting my green ration coffee in the frying-pan, grinding it on a stone with a mallet, and making the best of a hard bargain which after all is a mockery, and may breed discontent in the ranks. A soldier of the 28th drowned in the lake.

14th. Blowing a gale, hot sirocco wind. My whole establishment blown over; left on the sod without a house or home! It soon rose again. A few of my merry men built a green bower for me, large enough to pitch my tent inside, while I was taking my daily ride along the breast of vine-clad hills overlooking seventeen encampments below.

Had a visit from Doctor McGregor, of the 6th Inniskillen Dragoons, to give me a detail of the loss of their ship by fire coming out. The *Europa* had half the regiment and horses on board. My old friend Colonel Moore was lost, but nearly all the men and officers saved. The Colonel remained to the last, and then was not equal to the exertion of saving himself.

20th. Cholera in the French camp; thirteen deaths last night. The lake and damp weather begin to tell on the troops, who have no choice, but must obey orders.

Rumours of a move, rolled up in mystery. Everyone speculates it must be by sea—no land transport to take the field, even as far as the Danube. There will be of course a great sacrifice of life wherever we go, and it is wise to be prepared.

21st. Called on Colonel Mallet, French infantry. Tells me they have lost many men and officers, two Generals, one of them the Duke d'Esslingen, second son of the celebrated Marshal Ney.

General Canrobert's division marched away this morning along the
seacoast towards the Danube. One or two divisions follow—a
reconnaissance, I dare say, in favour of Omer Pacha. Preparations
for a general move. Orders and counter-orders. The real chief of
our army is the Cabinet at home.

Eleven thousand horses on forage today, according to the Com-
missioner-General's return.

22nd. Up at five and away for a long ride by the lake to Alla-
dyne, to see the 1st Division camp. Arrived at nine to breakfast
with A.C. General Strictland. Called to see Sir Colin Campbell,
found him in his shirt sleeves, in a greenwood bower, taking his rest
after an early drill. I had a long chat about olden times, then met
Captain McCall, 79th, the brother of a dear lady friend of mine.
Wherever British officers form a camp, you are sure to see a race
meeting and other manly sports got up, as much to cheer the men
as to amuse themselves and break the monotony of a field life.
Here we had gentlemen riders on small *tats* and baggage animals,
shirt sleeves, and few saddles, the thermometer 100° in the sun; no
better fun at the Derby, and all for love and pale ale! Took an
observation from a rising ground of my home route, and made as
direct as I could guess across the country for Varna; arrived at six
p.m. tired and headachy.

Diarrhoea and cholera have fixed their deadly venom amongst
the troops in all the camps. Many officers are now laid up. We
must change our ground or die—no mistake about it. I should have
done so long ago had I the power. I never knew a cure for cholera
in the field but an immediate change of ground.

Tormented with the plague of flies. No rest nor peace in my
tent. They swarm in tens of thousands, stick to one's face, hands,
and eyes. I blow them up with gunpowder, close my tent, light a
fire, and suffocate them with smoke. But no go, they are as
numerous as ever the next hour; so I leave the house to them most
of the day. Dined with the good and amiable General Eastcourt.

23rd. Up at five, church parade at six, breakfast at eight,
orderly room duty at ten, and my own little tent service at eleven.
'Where two or three are gathered together', there is a promised
blessing. Large working parties are employed in the bush making
gabions and fascines for the siege of some place. French troops
are moving away, and great preparations are being made for some
grand mysterious coup. Resigned my tent today to the army of
flies and black bettles, with permission to return at bedtime, when
I will pay them off in their slumbers. Bashi-bazouks away to the
front. I will back them for plunder more than I would for fighting,
wherever they go.

24th. Cholera making great strides towards us, and Varna so filthy inside and out. I fear the plague will gain upon us if the wise men will persist on our retaining the infectious ground—it really looks like Pharaoh contending against the Lord.

Some kind friend sent me a present of a goose last week, but his domestic habits have preserved his life so far. He walks into the tent with such confidence, asking in his own gabble for his rations and water, talks to me as well as he can, and I assure him I will never pick his bones were he as fat as the Durham ox.

25th. Up at three-thirty to change our ground at last. In one hour every tent was struck, baggage packed, and all clear away from the fog banks of Devna Lake to the heights of Gallata, on the south-side of Varna Bay. I pitched my tent by the side of a very large and old pear-tree, full of unripe fruit, arranging for the afternoon shade, the morning sun being more acceptable. The next thing was to build a bower all round outside the tent cords, high and thick, to keep off all intruders and make my dwelling private. The colours of my regiment were piled outside, with a sentry over them, who also kept watch on my premises. My servants were within call—a fireplace was set up, my cattle picketed. The goat had the length of his tether to feed amongst the bush, and so I was quite snug in a few hours. The dear old goose was sitting by the door waiting for his breakfast, happy at being tumbled out of a bag.

The view from my hall-door was commanding and cheerful. The Black Sea was in front, dotted with ships and steamers, the fleet in Kivarna Bay, the country far and wide well wooded. Mount Olympus is seen in the distance, capped with snow. A great city of canvas is all around, alive with red-coated warriors, with all the arrangements of a great, of a noble army, preparing for war—the whole scene grand and exciting.

26th. The cholera has got loose indeed amongst the troops, and when or where will it end?—stopped too long on the Devna Lake. Hear firing in the distance.

29th. Cholera increasing, and men dying fast. Every case taken in at the General Hospital in Varna has gone to the grave; fifteen dead last two nights. The old pensioners sent out with the ambulance waggons are dropping off fast. I expect they will all be buried at Varna. Worn out before coming here, they get drunk when they can, and die like dogs.

Sir George Brown returned from a reconnaissance of Sepastopol. Edward W—— called and told me that he saw the great mighty fortress; they were fired on, their steamer being hit twice. It is decided that we are to cross the sea, and be let loose at this Russian stronghold very soon, the sooner the better; better to die in the battlefield than in a cholera hospital. I hope the people of England will not expect too much—Sebastopol is not made of ginger-bread, nor will it fall like a pack of cards. At all events 'tis time to be making up our accounts—no man ought to delay. The danger is great, and the time draweth nigh; may the promise of God to Joshua be ours, and all will be well (Josh. i. 9). A stormy night, thunder, lightning, and rain, camp looking desolate, seventeen cholera funerals this evening. Our poor chaplain was wet to the skin after his melancholy duty. The dead are sewed up in their blankets, and planted anywhere under a bush, or in some quiet corner, no matter where—'tis but a narrow, cold, ill-furnished house.

30th. Very rainy, no Divine service for the troops; had a little family worship in my tent for the servants.

31st. The good chaplain dined with me today, and went off afterwards on his daily duty to bury the dead; private Thomas Brady drowned in the sea.

August 4th. Nothing to note but death by the score. Poor Colonel Maule, brother of Lord Panmure, has fallen, greatly esteemed and regretted; three of my men, and sixty-seven of the French: they suffer most. Turkish fleet in Varna, and preparations being made for our embarkation, but everything goes on at a snail's pace.

7th. 1,250 French soldiers have died already near this camp; 700 of them in Varna hospital. It is generally believed that no man comes out alive who is carried into that plague-house. The very fear of going in there has caused our men to conceal their illness until too late for medical treatment. A soldier of the 50th Regiment shot himself this morning—worst of all deaths.

8th. Paymaster of the Rifles, and Colonel Ewart, 79th, died last night of cholera. Toothache and rheumatism disturb the few comforts of my camp life at times, but I ought to be thankful for the many blessings that I do enjoy, when I see myself surrounded by the dying and the dead. 150 of the French have died in one night in the hospital; it is almost incredible, but an o'er-true tale, and I fear it is growing worse. Major E. Wetherall came over to dine with me, one of the most promising officers in the British army. I had an excellent dinner for him, got up in good style, a roast leg of mutton (4 lb. weight) and a bottle of cool wine. I only wonder how poor George Haws could roast a joint under a bright sun, and with his apparatus, when also in deplorable health. If I send him to hospital he is sure to die, so he may as well die in peace beside me. His brother is my groom, and if he is curable, we will save him, poor fellow.

10th. Great preparations and great expectations. All sorts of mechanics called for; not an idle man in my regiment out of 845. I can hardly get enough to cook the ration dinners, and very bad rations we get, worst of bad beef and bad bread, yet there is not a murmur in camp — discipline!

I dined today with Sir Richard England, our General of Division. After dinner our attention was called to two objects from opposite doors of his marquee. One was a moonlight scene on the Black Sea, with a sentry in the distance, standing on the cliff in bold relief, the moonbeams dancing on the unrippled deep dark waters. It was one of those fairy scenes which make a lasting impression. We all looked at it with silent admiration, until our attention was diverted to the opposite door of the tent — Varna on fire! in a frightful blaze, and close to the powder magazine. How it does flare up, throwing a glare of golden light all around for miles. Here comes an aide-de-camp, and orderlies, and staff officers, to report and ask for orders. The most decided order, I would say — put it out. The French had 60,000 lb. of gunpowder in the magazine, and the walls were getting hot. The British soldiers, regardless of fear, mounted up, and heaped wet blankets over the building, laying the hose of a fire-engine (sent ashore from a ship of war). Rugs and blankets were saturated and handed up, and water passed in buckets with order and regularity, all efforts being directed to save the magazine. The main street was burning furiously, every shop and store yielded to the flames, all burned to the ground. The English and French commissariat stores to the amount of £30,000 totally destroyed. Barrels of wine, rum, and brandy had been hauled out into the streets, the consequence being no end to drunkenness, but still plenty of steady, sober working men, who saved the powder. Flour, biscuit, and valuable stores to an immense amount were destroyed just at a time when we wanted everything. Nobody set the town on fire, of course, but suspicion fell on the Greeks, who were all on the side of Russia.

Much sickness. The doctors are alarmed. Cholera has got into the ships; officers who can are going home. Sir John Campbell, *hors de combat*; Colonel G. B. in orders to command the Brigade; two field-officers, 79th, reported dead at Allandyne; new-made graves everywhere. The soldiers are now laid under the sod without funeral parties or firing. The dead are carted out of the General Hospital at night in heaps and thrown into pits prepared for them. All this is very bad, and leaves a sadness in the minds of men who seldom think much of anything serious.

14th. Fine sea breeze, beautiful weather, charming scenery, but all this does not seem to rally the late buoyant spirit in the camp while we are losing twenty-five men a day. The division is being kept well employed at different works preparing for the embarkation which is much looked for. Loss of stores, etc., by the fire at Varna is estimated at £50,000.

Edwin Freshfield, whom I first met in Greece, found me out here once more, and always rejoices in a ration dinner. He is seeing much service as an amateur at sea. He is a polished scholar, a perfect gentleman, with a joyous, cheerful, and intelligent countenance; so full of life and energy, that I often used to say, 'I wish you were a soldier, that I might have the opportunity of making you my aide-de-camp.'

19th. Experimental embarkation of artillery and infantry, superintended by Lord Raglan, Sir George Brown, and Admiral Lyons.

20th. Dined on board the *Melbourne*, with Champion.

21st. Another rehearsal of embarking and disembarking artillery. Colonels Thesiger and Cardwell of the Guards, and Major McCaskill, 55th, reported dead in the other camp at Allandyne. What a world of grief and sadness, and sudden death, careless tranquillity, apathy and slothful feeling for sacred things! From appearance, God is not glorified in our camp, nor sought after till the eleventh hour. In fact, the world is one great dissolving view —the moment we begin to live, we begin to die.

22nd. A plague of locusts came across the Black Sea today with an east wind. Thousands of millions darkened the air before they alighted down on our camp. They were so very tired, the soldiers captured them easily. Next day they were very lively on the wing, and eating up every green thing, so densely thick were they, and flying so low I charged through their columns on horseback, sword in hand, slaying them in myriads. But millions would not be missed out of such a host. They disappeared as quickly as they came. The Highland Brigade marched into camp and took up ground to our right. Called upon Sir Colin Campbell, in command; a brave old warrior, with great experience.

27th. Sunday. Divine service. Afterwards, the Sacrament was administered to upwards of fifty officers in the General's tent.

29th. Ten regiments embarked today. What a scene of life and activity about the harbour! All so anxious to clear away from this region of death.

30th. My regiment ordered and countermanded for embarking three times today.

31st. Up at four a.m., after a very stormy night of discomfort from the worry of yesterday, which has left me a headache, and otherwise unwell. Struck tents, and in two hours we were all on board the transport *Alfred the Great*, 1,300 tons. I left my second tent standing, with my sick servant, and my groom in charge of my mules, for commanding officers were only allowed to embark one horse each. The goat and the goose bid me goodbye. Of course I never expected to see them any more. The poor goose became a general favourite with all the soldiers. He was so very intelligent, and so fond of the men, he would walk up and down with the sentry at his post all the day. When he ordered his arms to stand at ease, the goose would sit down beside him, and when relieved, he would meet the next sentry coming with a welcome gabble. At night he sat outside my tent. Early in the morning he came nibbling at the door-cords to call me up or try to get in. As soon as I appeared, he bid me good-day most distinctly in his own way, and than sat down to await his breakfast of barley thrown into a dish of water. When he finished, he joined the sentry outside, and paced up and down on his post as usual. 'Stupid goose!' No, indeed. This soldier goose of mine was a very clever military goose in his way, and I was sorry to leave him where he was sure to fall into the hands of the enemy.

My mules were so singularly attached to my horse, I feared they would go wild without him. They did not require to be picketed like other beasts; they went loose all day, and would never leave him. Going to water, they always followed, kicking and flinging up their heels, galloping about wild-like, but never lost sight of him, coming back to their own ground. When I went out riding, they astonished the natives by prancing alongside of me wherever I went. But this I found inconvenient, and I had them tied up when I went my rounds.

We were now on board, and bound for Russia; but for what part we could not tell. Sebastopol was in every eye, in every mouth, in all conversation, but where the landing was to be, no one could discover.

Our freight consisted of our General, Sir Richard England, and his staff; Major Wood, Assistant-Adjutant-General; Brevet-Major Colborne, Assistant-Quartermaster-General; Lieutenant the Honourable Arthur Keith, son of my old hunting friend, Lord Kintore, and Lieutenant England, two aides-de-camp. Also my regiment, 803 souls, all hands included, and the regulated number of horses.

September 1st, 2nd, and 3rd. Embarkation of horse, foot, and artillery, going on as briskly as the first day, and not yet ready. We want cavalry, cavalry, cavalry! No use going to war without cavalry. We know that Russia has been always strong in her Cossack cavalry, and in that arm we are weak, and leaving too many behind.

The Captain of the *Emperor* steamer was quite well yesterday, and at his duty. He was buried this morning. Such is life amongst cholera!

Eight pages of printed regulations are published for instruction. First rendezvous—anchoring off the enemy's territory, and disembarking the army and material, under the orders of Sir Edmond Lyons, G.C.B. Signed, Dundas, Vice-Admiral and Commander in-Chief. It is a long programme, and, to landsmen, complicated; but we soldiers have only to obey orders. I hope no link in the chain will be broken. The final signals are: for the boats to assemble round ships, to disembark infantry and artillery, one black ball at fore of the *Agamemnon*; two black balls, to form line abreast, three black balls, advance in line; four black balls, to land. Lord Raglan to be on board the *Caradoc* steamer. Every division has its distinguishing flag, viz. first division, blue, triangular blue; second division, white, triangular white; third division, red, triangular red; fourth division, red, with white fly triangular; fifth division, cavalry blue, with red fly triangular; light division, checked flag. All boats carrying infantry to have in their bows a red flag, eighteen inches square. Paddle-boats of *Spitfire*, *Triton*, *Cyclops*, and *Firebrand*, to land regimental staff officers. To proceed to sea by signal to-morrow. It appears that 308 boats, of different sorts and sizes, will dash off at once with troops, to land in front of the enemy, and against all opposition.

11th. Still lying calmly in the deep Black Sea, steam up and ready for anything, but the game is all a blank to us; we know nothing. I have to thank God for preserving my life today. While sitting in my cabin a pistol-bullet came smash through the panel, quite close to me; —— came in directly, very pale and nervous, but got bright when he saw me all right. His revolver accidently went off in his hand, when only about ten feet from me.

12th. A somnambulist, last night, going about like a ghost, in his shirt. I heard my door open in the middle of the night, when I saw this white spectre glide in, and gently feeling its way round the cabin. I called out, 'Who are you, Mr. Ghost?' but got no answer. It went off to disturb someone else. After some flighty intrusions it was laid hold of, and locked up in its own crib. Nothing would persuade our Quartermaster next morning that he was the ghost who haunted the ship.

Fleet anchored in the Bay of Eupatoria, six or seven miles from land, which looks black and cold.

13th. Anchors up at nine a.m. Signal, 'Close up and prepare the troops to land'. Ran down close to the town and anchored, all the fleet closing up by seven p.m. Country looking better; corn, hay, and cattle appear to be abundant. Proclamation sent into the town, intimating friendly relations with the peaceful inhabitants, etc. At night the bay is illuminated, lights innumerable flickering over the deep darkness. What must those on shore think of the multitude of ships coming here as if by some magic arrangement—a grand but terrific apprehension of danger is near.

The Alma

SEPTEMBER 14th. Memorable day. Early up. Fleet got under weigh, and ran down the coast some forty miles. Down with the anchors and up with the signal, 'Land the troops'. With the exception of a few Cossack videttes, no enemy in view.

It was now a race of boats between England and France who should first plant their standard on hostile ground. The French had the inside of the course, and had the advantage, and even if they had not the first landing, they would have claimed it. The landing was accomplished most admirably and with great success, thanks to the great Russian army who declined to be inhospitable to England's first visit to their soil. Had they marched down in hostility, there must have been a frightful smashing of our boats coming ashore, from their guns and mortars, however well we may have been covered by our own ships of war. But so it is in war, the invading or attacking army have the advantage of selecting their own time and place for action, and here we took the enemy by surprise. The sea was calm, the sandy beach favoured our approach, and every boat landed its cargo in safety. The different divisions quickly formed and marched onward a mile or two to bivouac. It was dusk when I got all my regiment ashore and ready to move off. The men left their knapsacks on board by order, taking three days' cooked provisions in their haversacks; a blanket, greatcoat, shirt, pair of shoes and socks, all strapped up in the greatcoat. The officers had nothing but what they carried on their backs, little or much, as they pleased. We were all in full dress uniform! Mounted officers were better off, as they could take what their horses could conveniently carry. As an old campaigner, I laid up a good store, filling my holster-pipes with a little tea, sugar, chocolate, and brandy. A greatcoat, Scotch plaid, socks, shirt, comb, razor, and soap I had well strapped up and fastened to my saddle-bow. A very little tiny valise, containing a few little things for the field, was fastened to my saddle behind. Two haversacks full of ration prog, tied together and thrown across the saddle, completed all my arrangements for an indefinite period, all our baggage being left in the ship to the mercy of honest comrades, who never slept on the sod. I left it to my groom to see my horse landed at the proper time. I marched off my regiment about dusk, and got on to some higher ground. The General walked on along with us. It became dark and cloudy and we were ordered to halt, pile arms, and make ourselves comfortable for the night. It was now pitch dark. It began to rain a little, and gradually increased to a tropical torrent, until the flat ground beneath our feet became a broad sheet of mud and water. The men had their greatcoats and blankets— some protection for a few hours—but nothing could keep them dry. I kept walking about all the night, at times standing for half an hour with my back to the storm, half asleep and soaked like a wet sponge. How I did long for the morning! It came, and with it such a scene of misery and wretchedness, we did not know each other. No one was inclined to speak, the mud-paste sticking to our trousers above the ankles, everyone looking as if just fished out of the sea, and so far as we could see over the extensive plain there was not a particle of fuel, not a twig, and it was the wildest plain I had ever seen. The poor chaplain looked half-drowned and shivering in his wet clothes, more dead than alive.

I gave my fellows a cheer and ordered them to disperse in search of something to make a fire. I knew that if such a thing was within miles they would hunt it out, and away they ran and in the right direction to the beach. Six or eight of them came back with an immense log of wood on their shoulders, part of a wreck. It was now tally-ho! away they rattled off in scores, and brought up lots of fuel. Great fires soon blazed, and we began to get dry and warm as the sun came to brighten our hopes.

15th. We pressed the first sod in the Crimea yesterday, and a soft sod it was. When daylight appeared this morning we had the pleasure of seeing the French army under cover—they brought with them their *tentes-abri*, or tiny tents, carried by the three men they shelter; here they beat us at the start. I wore, last night, a gold-embroidered scarlet coatee, with epaulettes that cost me twenty guineas, rather an expensive and uncomfortable nightdress, and much the worse of the wear this morning.

The sun came dashing out about ten o'clock, and dried us all up very soon, ground and all. Tired and weary I sat down to rest, and fell asleep in spite of all my efforts. My cap fell off, and I only awoke from the hot sun beating on my bare head. Oh, such a headache, and anguish, and fever-feeling; knocked down, prostrate, unfit for anything and had nothing. I looked out anxiously for my horse and trappings, to get a little tea, or anything. 'The horses are coming, sir,' said my orderly. I was thankful, and staggered off to meet my gallant grey. There he was, sure enough, with a wet blanket on his back, the sole remnant of all my valuable kit. I was almost speechless. I had met with a terrible loss. At any other time or place I could have passed it by without much notice; here there was no hope of anything being replaced, and I really sat down in sorrow. Nothing went right after the troops left the ship. There was delay in getting out the horses when they were lowered into boats alongside, which were kept knocking against the side of the vessel till ten o'clock at night, and were then swamped. Some horses swam out to sea; mine made the shore, but the groom was drowned, and next day the missing horses were cast ashore, dead. Not so the poor groom: he was never seen again, and all my traps disappeared with him. I crawled down to the beach, with the hope of getting out to our ship, but the surf ran so high, no boat would venture to cross it. Here I met Lord Raglan and told him my sorrows. He was looking at the swell casting the wreck of boats and dead horses ashore, and perhaps thinking how very providential it was that he had been directed to land his army yesterday. Today it could not be done, and the enemy, only one march distant, might have come down upon us full swoop.

Returning to the bivouac, I passed the night under the remnant of my camp equipage, very unwell. A damp blanket was my bed, and the sod my pillow.

16th. Some naval officers had come ashore to look at our bivouac. Someone had told them of my misfortune, and they asked me to go out to their ship for the night. 'No,' I said, with kind thanks, 'but if you will put me on board our transport where we left our baggage, I will be much obliged.' Always kind and generous, as sailors are, they carried me off. I had indeed to rouse myself up and get on my legs, for I was nearly prostrate with that sort of listless, feeble, feverish feeling that leaves one helpless. It was dark when we got to their boat, and after four or five miles of a pull through a forest of masts, I got on board. I got some tea, and went to bed on a pile of blankets, very tired. Slept soundly all the night, and got up quite well in the morning, rejoicing and thankful to the great Physician who healed me.

Captain Dacre, of my regiment, who was left sick on board and not able to land, assisted me with some necessary articles I required—a saddle for one thing. I loaded myself with as many articles from my baggage as I could carry, and got ashore to find that tents had been landed and pitched for the army, and all things wearing a cheerful appearance. A review of our division had been ordered, and I was just in time to ride past the General, at the head of my regiment, on a blanket, my saddle not having yet reached the camp. I could see my own men smiling as one of them lifted my leg to mount my charger, but it was a pleasing smile, for I knew they valued their Commanding Officer ten times more so on this parade than if he had been on a prancing steed and caparisoned like a Knight Templar. I soon got fixed up in a sort of a military style. I had my little Canada axe—a first-rate tool for a campaign—which I fastened to my saddle-bow. Captain Dacre's 'navy' sent me a new blanket, and so I had two under my saddle—the way blankets are always carried in the field. But I miss my good Scotch plaid, blue frock coat, and clasp-knife.

Water scarce, and we send four miles for it daily, with an escort of 100 armed men. As far as the eye can see across this plain, there is no rising ground—one of the steppes of the Crimea. All the army under arms every morning half an hour before daylight. What a grand military spectacle meets one's eyes as the dark shades of the morning disappear: 70,000 fighting men all ready for action.

A hare got into our camp by some unfortunate mistake on her part. A general hue and cry arose, followed by a thousand red coats. She doubled amongst the tents and through the lines with great dexterity and skill, considering it was her first appearance in a British camp. But poor puss got bewildered, and was knocked down by a 'Royal' huntsman and presented to me. 'To make hare soup: first catch your hare'—but I had neither pot nor pan, pepper nor salt, cook or fire, so a milestone might have been to me as acceptable. I was content with a biscuit and a bit of cold beef.

17th. During Divine service this morning an immense flock of sheep came galloping into our camp from across the steppe, having, unfortunately for their individual safety, mistaken their way. The men not engaged at church parade thought all this a providential meeting with fresh rations, and, without leave or licence, made a rush amongst the flock, killing and slaying them off-hand in a very coarse and uncouth manner. The General gave me a nod and a look of displeasure, meaning to say, 'Look at those vagabonds how they are plundering.' He did not move until the service ended. Then the order was—'Stop that disgraceful scene, and confine every man caught in the act', but the culprits vanished amidst the forest of tents, leaving lots of fat sheep with very fat wags on the ground, some dead, some half-dead, some skinned, others cut up in a new fashion, so that very fine, fat Russian mutton lay on the grass for the picking up. The General was very angry, so was G. B., but in some way or other a joint got into my tent. I suppose the fairies put it there, and I could not offend the good people by rejecting the gift. A French officer sent his servant over from his camp with a polite note to me requesting a bit of mutton, if there was any to spare (I suppose he had been riding by or looking on at the time of the slaughter). At the moment a fine sheep lay on the sod at my feet. I said, 'Take that bit of mutton to your master with my compliments.' Away it went, on the back of his nimble rifleman, double quick, a valuable prize, for I had such a bundle of thanks the next day. The rest of the slain were collected, handed over to the Commissary, who purchased the remainder of the flock, paying cash to the shepherd, who went away rejoicing.

We captured a large convoy of flour, going to Sebastopol, with oxen and camels. The only one of the escort I saw wounded was a poor lad who was shot in the foot, a painful hurt, and he was crying bitterly. He stayed by his oxen and looked so bewildered I examined the wound, and requested our doctor to look after him. The flour, we much needed, was heaped in piles, sentries placed over it, not a pound was issued to the troops, and there it was left when we marched away. Two p.m. Ordered to strike tents, which our men carried on their backs down to the beach for the night with orders to be in readiness to march away at four o'clock in the morning.

19th. The whole army was formed on the plain before the dawn. When daylight removed the cloud, a grand spectacle was presented to all eyes—the three united armies on the march towards Sebastopol, and anxious to measure swords with the Russians, wherever they might be found. The day was bright and warm, too hot for the pace we marched. By one o'clock the field for miles back was dotted with red-coats. Our men dropped like stones, over-weight, want of water, and the chokers of stiff leather girding the throat. All this outstripped all their valour and desire to keep up; the bands ceased to play, there was a grave quiet. All toiled on, few spoke, the pain of weariness had begun, until about two o'clock we halted at the Bulgenac, a small rivulet running across our path. Its water resembled pea-soup, but still it was very sweet. Being a little refreshed, an exciting word was passed through the ranks from the chief—'Artillery to the front'. They limbered up, and went off at full gallop up the inclined plain, for we were now over the broad flat. At three o'clock the first gun was fired in anger at a Russian enemy. The return shot smashed the leg of a British gunner and driver. Now there is a cannonade, and we march up to the crest of the rising ground, and form in line of battle. 'Here they are, at last!' was the passing word amongst the men. A long line of Cossack cavalry presented themselves on the plain below, with their patrols in advance, in circular motion. A large column advanced from their rear, opened out and unmasked a battery of artillery, which gave us a grand salute, killing four of our artillery horses, and wounding two men. This harmless play went on until the shades of night shut out the panorama. When we bivouacked it was dark, but I rambled about until I found a bundle of dry weeds. Then I made my way back to where my horse was picketed, boiled our kettle, and got our breakfast at eight o'clock p.m. On these occasions, where two or three mess together, one seeks for water, another for fuel, and a third keeps watch and makes little arrangements for the *cuisine*. Dr. Hearn, my Adjutant Turner, and self chummed together the best way we could. Three pounds of fresh meat always makes better soup than one pound, and we also had three chances against one of falling in with something or other. Tea was the most refreshing of all things—our greatest luxury.

Too tired to eat a bit of cold meat, we lay down on the sod to rest our weary bones and dream of the morrow—a last night of rest to so many in this world. But it is wise and benevolent that man knoweth not the 'day nor the hour'. The dew of the night was like rain, and there was much illness on the field. My men who had fallen out on the march had all come up in the night, and still retained their blankets, greatcoats, and camp kettles, while others had divested themselves of everything that impeded their progress, so anxious were they to keep up.

20th. Before daybreak the whole of the British army was under arms, the watch-fires were smouldering out, the men had shaken the dew from their blankets, regiments and brigades were formed in order of march. The spare ammunition was loaded on arabas, camels, and tats, yet it was eight o'clock before we got fairly away from our last night's lodging. We had a beautiful little army of as fine men as ever I had seen, in rude health and vigour, highly disciplined, and ready for any encounter, although not one of them had ever fired a shot in anger, nor were there beyond eight or ten officers amongst us all who had seen any active service.

The French advanced on our right. Seven thousand Turkish infantry, under Suleiman Pasha, moved along by the seaside. On their left, the divisions of Generals Bosquet, Canrobert, Forey, and Prince Napoleon. The whole right of the allied army was

P

supported by the fleet which moved along our flank in beautiful
order, commanding the land for some two miles from the shore.
Our order of march on the French left was:

8th, 11th, and 17th Cavalry

Light Division   Artillery   2nd Division
1st Division   Artillery   3rd Division
Cavalry   Commissariat Train
4th Division   4th Division
Rear Guard

It was now about nine o'clock, and we all got clear over the
brow of the hill which had sheltered us from the view of our formidable enemy on the previous day.   The morning was fine, with a
refreshing breeze from the sea; the sod under foot was as green
and smooth as a racecourse; the descent to the Alma river, a gentle
incline, and right before us on a range of hills stood the Russian
army in battle array.   They were measuring our advance, counting our numbers, and preparing to meet us with 40,000 chosen
troops and 100 guns.   The breast of their position was intrenched
and full of sharpshooters and gun-batteries.   Their outposts lined
the left bank of the serpentine river running through the vineyards,
which gave good cover, while a long chain of skirmishers were
lying *perdu* on our side of the stream.   The Turks did nothing.
The first fire was given from our fleet, throwing up shells at random
upon the Russian left.   The French tirailleurs opened the ball by
driving in the enemy's skirmishers, and following them up across
the river, which was fordable here and there.   The French columns
now followed up, and attacked the hill with admirable courage,
driving the enemy from their breastworks, but falling at every step
of the rugged and steep ascent.   Having gained so much ground, it
was now our time to advance upon the right and centre of the
Russian host.   As we lay upon the grass out of the range of their
shot, looking on at the gallant attack and defence going forward,
and seeing every shot falling, I believe our soldiers were eager and
burning to be let loose.   I could see no other desire, whatever may
have been their real feeling, but no one may tell me that he goes
into the battlefield unmoved.   I could not give credit to the soldier
who has ever said so, although I know there is a desire to get into
action, and a hopeful desire to get out of it in safety.   Once engaged, there is little time for reflection.   The whole matter is to
commit yourself into the hands of the Almighty and do your duty.
   As we advanced now in close columns, the enemy fired a little
village in our front.   Under cover of the smoke and flames they
opened their batteries upon our men, and their shot went bowling

over the plain, after making many a bloody plunge through man and horse. Our artillery replied with shot, shell, and rockets, while our gallant foot-soldiers advanced through a storm of bullets, and rushed on towards the enemy. There was a wooden bridge in their front, crossing the stream, partly destroyed. A causeway led to this point wide enough to allow a column to march down, and here our people were met with a storm of leaden hail. Some crossed the bridge, others passed through the shallow water, and formed on the other side as well as they could, under a murderous fire of grape and musketry. The river was now crossed at other points, and a general rush made at the batteries and breastworks on the hillside, which were severely contested. The battle now became general along the line, bloody and obstinate. The greater power of their artillery told against us, but our Minié-rifle practice balanced the account. Both sides fought with determined fury. All our steam was up, the British lion renewed his strength and courage, the men saw their bravest officers falling at their feet, the carnage was frightful, but the cry was still 'Forward, and Victory'. The flag of England floated over the heads of the brave in every regiment. Those flags were riddled with shot, but after three hours of hard contest amongst the dying and the dead, the British colours were planted triumphantly on the heights of the Russian position with such cheers as can only be heard on a battlefield by a victorious British army. The day was ours, the battle won by the best and bravest blood of England, for the bravest blood of England often runs in the veins of the sons of labourers and mechanics, who have devoted themselves to a military profession. They perform their duty in defence of their country, without the hope or expectation of being distinguished by the rewards which only reach those over them.

This, our first battle on Russian ground, was well fought and nobly won, all the odds being against us. The face of nature, with its lovely plants and flowers, was saturated with human blood. The scene was now changed, the dying and the dead of five nations lay scattered over the field. The groans of the wounded, and their cries for aid, for help, for water, were unattended to, for the battle was not yet quite over.

Horses, gunners, and drivers, waggons, artillery, and soldiers, with all sorts of water material, lay heaped up together as we passed over this ground of suffering in pursuit. Our wounded lying thick, and faintly crying, 'Oh, take care, for God's sake, and don't ride over us; we are all disabled, sir.' We pushed on after the fugitive army, who were now in active retreat; our guns pounding into their ranks. They were strong in cavalry, and that arm

made a show on the plain, which I fear prevented our Cavalry
Generals from measuring swords with the Cossacks.   It was my
opinion, and ever will be, that had our cavalry gone at the Cossacks,
supported by some of our guns, they would have soon smashed
through them, and captured the Russian artillery, which was all
carried off excepting two guns taken in the battle.   The 4th Division, too, were in reserve on our left flank all the day, quite fresh,
and ready to support our cavalry.   But the opportunity was lost,
and it is futile to speculate on what the consequences might have
been.   Some felt ashamed and disappointed.   Others no doubt
admired the singular caution and prudence that was displayed.
We achieved a great victory, but it would have been still more
complete had we captured the enemy's guns.   Lord Raglan was
very cool and collected.   Being much exposed during the battle,
one of his staff said to him, that he was too far in advance, and
exposing himself too much.   His answer was, 'Do not speak to me
now; I am busy.'   Our loss was more severe in this action, because
the brave and gallant 7th, 23rd, and 33rd Regiments were not able
to re-form before charging up the hill, but were fighting in a heap.
Marshal St. Arnaud had changed the order of battle, fearful of being
driven back in his attack on the left of the Russian position, requesting Lord Raglan to advance without further delay.   Regardless
of the overwhelming masses of artillery in our front, and no longer
adhering to the original plan, our chief gave the order to move
forward—to death or victory—it was to both.

On every battlefield there are mistakes.   He is, I think, the best
General who brings most men out of action after a victory, but
to make an omelette, you must break the eggs.

I heard it often asked why we did not follow up our victory
after the battle: this depended on the two allied chiefs.   I suppose
the Turks were not consulted.   They had nothing to do and did
nothing.   If they had been brought into action, most likely they
would have spoiled the beauty of the contest by running away;
therefore they were more properly kept in reserve.

Two great cavalry lords were on the ground, and no doubt all
ready for battle, waiting for the Hookum.[1]

On the plain covering the retreating army, the Cossack cavalry
hovered about, and kept in dense columns on the defensive, their
courage evaporating seeing the double quick march of their whole
army in retreat.   I thought this was just the time to be at them.
All our cavalry, as well as the French, were fresh, rough and ready.
Our guns were at liberty, and the gallant Cathcart at the head of
his division, which had not been engaged, stood there looking on,

---

[1] Hookum, word of command.

while his men were nervously anxious, and grinding their teeth with excitement to do something. This force alone, I thought sufficient to clear the plain, and insure a double victory by capturing the whole of the Russian guns, which were within our grasp. The enemy lost head and heart, rushed off in a quick pell-mell over the Katchka, leaving all their artillery on our side, where it reposed undisturbed all night. In these matters there is always a difference of opinion, and always will be. But I confess I was much disappointed, seeing our friends being let off so quietly, which they did not expect, and such a turf for cavalry! There they stood looking at each other like—

> Lord Chatham with his sword drawn,
>   Stood waiting for Sir Richard Strahan;
> Sir Richard longing to be at him,
>   Stood waiting for the Earl of Chatham.

But war is a series of difficulties and blunders.

We now bivouacked on the crest of the hill, so long and so lately occupied by our adversaries. It was rather impure ground —not in the condition of our English encampments. There was a general rush at some hay and picketing sticks left by the Cossacks. I got my share—the fuel to boil our kettle, and the hay for my horse and my bed. When the battle was going on, I met Sir George Brown, commanding the Light Division, on his legs, his horse being killed. I gave him a remount, and passed on at the head of my corps, stepping lightly over the wounded, the dead were quiet, lying in heaps and scores, and hundreds.

'Who is that you have on your back?' I said to an old sergeant. 'Colonel Chester, sir, my commanding officer.' He had been nearly cut in two by a cannon-shot. 'Can you lend us a stretcher, sir?' said another old soldier. 'Who for?' 'Lord Chewton, sir. He is lying there mortally wounded.' I sent him away off the bloody field.

We had no ambulance waggons, not one. The bandsmen of each regiment had eight stretchers for carrying off the wounded; a piece of canvas between two poles. They were all well saturated with human blood, from carrying the helpless down to the shambles where the doctors were assembled. For twenty-four hours men lay there on the sod, before their wounds were dressed, for the lack of surgeons; although those we had were indefatigable in the exercise of their calling. It was after dark when we lay down to rest for the night, being sixteen hours on our legs. Some of us were tired, but still the men were jolly, and cracking their jokes like schoolboys. They had to go back to the 'Alma' for muddy and bloody water to cook their rations in the dark. Not that there was any tinge or red tint on the stream, but it was trodden over by 50,000 men, and many a bloody and ghastly wound was washed in its stream this day!

I was very ill in the night. The cholera broke out all at once. The doctor was up with me four times before morning, and some of our men had died already. It was very alarming, but morning came, bright and cheery, and I was on my legs after a fast of thirty-six hours. Near to me and unobserved lay a Russian soldier, awfully wounded. A cannon-shot had taken off one of his arms, and laid his bowels open, which were lying beside him. Yet this poor suffering creature was alive: nothing could be done for him. He managed to take a drop of water and died — such is war.

21st September. The roll is called. Where are the absentees? I hope they live, to die no more.

General orders: 'The army will halt today.'

Got something like a breakfast, mounted my horse, and rode off to see the left of the enemy's position of yesterday. It rested on a perpendicular cliff, washed by the Black Sea. On the ridge, but a very short distance from the cliff, there was a round tower of some kind, with a deep dry well inside. This was now being filled up with the dead who fell about here — some from the explosion of shells thrown up by our ships. It made a good cemetery for a certain number of the slain, who were pitched into it by the French sans cérémonie.

We had a thousand men employed for two days collecting the wounded and burying the dead. Every regiment gave a fatigue party. A trench was dug a certain length and six feet wide. The bodies were collected and laid in a row beside this long grave, when fifty or sixty of them were dragged by the heels into this pit, packed side by side in their bloody uniform, and covered up.

As I rode along the position, I was astonished how we ever got possession of the heights. Nothing but the valour of such an army could do it with all their steam up. It was from the tower above-mentioned the ladies of Sebastopol assembled to witness the battle and the allied army turned back. And from this place, it was said, Menschikoff wrote to his imperial master that 80,000 troops could not disturb his position. We took it in four hours, and the ladies took to their heels. It was, however, a grand sight for the Russian chief, and all his staff and fair friends, to see three armies moving down upon him all abreast, in separate columns, glittering in the sun. They could count almost our every man, as we advanced along and down the gentle slope. They quaintly said they did expect to meet British soldiers, but not red devils.

Having buried our own dead by themselves, the wounded were carried on stretchers and hammocks by the sailors down to the beach, and conveyed out in boats to the shipping. Many died by the way down, and hundreds that were placed on board were very soon committed to the deep for want of medical aid, and for want of everything. I was told, with very great indignation, that some Russian soldiers who lay wounded had fired upon some of our men who had been kind in giving them water, and had killed one of them; and this after the battle! If true, they must have been in a state of frenzy with the raki they had got to keep their courage up. As I rode amongst them they were all supplicants. I got off my horse to give one poor sufferer a little rum and water. He was terribly wounded. I have not forgotten his imploring look as he grasped and kissed my hand fervently, and again raised his eyes to the blue sky in anguish. His hour had come.

22nd. Very unwell all last night. Can't eat anything. Very little to eat, but no appetite. At twelve o'clock ordered my horse and took a long ride, visiting all the positions. Again wondered how we mastered such ground. The Russian loss was 7,000 killed, 4,000 wounded, and 700 prisoners. Amongst the wounded were a fine old Russian General, and his son, his aide-de-camp, a handsome youth about seventeen, looking quite cheery. His wound was slight. They were sent to the ships together, prisoners of war.

I stopped at the 'Alma', tied my horse to a tree, stripped and had a good wash. Seeing that my shirt required the same, I gave it also as good a scrubbing as I could without soap, tied it wet to my saddle and made for home.

23rd. Up at four, and found eleven cases of cholera; three deaths. Poor Edwards, my orderly-room clerk, one of them—a fine, healthy, strong young fellow the previous night.

We formed in order of march. Lord Raglan's address was read to the troops. Flattering, complimentary, well received, and well deserved. And so we passed away from this pestilential ground, expecting to meet the Russian army again on the Katchka river, quite as formidable a position as the Alma. But they had had enough pounding from the 'red devils' of late, and declined any further incivilities in the meantime. This was really a grand military position, and had the enemy rested, with their guns on the left bank, they might have pounded us in return. Our side was extremely rugged and rocky, the descent very rough, and exposed to the opposite side, which was well wooded and covered from our fire. The bridge had not been destroyed, and this passage between two steep hills was a sort of Thermopylae. Just as lucky for us, it was abandoned.

The valley of the Katchka is very pretty, fertile, and abounding in orchards, vineyards, and vegetable gardens. Everything was ripe, grapes excellent, apples very fine, vegetables abundant, and all so inviting to an army on their hungry march. In spite of all precaution, there was little left the following morning. The French are skilled plunderers. As soon as they get on the scent, they go it wholesale. Their gleanings make a clean field. We bivouacked for the night on the left bank of the river, which gave our men the chance of an evening ramble amongst the orchards and hen-roosts. The poor people all took fright, and fled with their army, hearing such tales of the 'red devils'. Had they stayed at home, their property would have been respected.

Some handsome country houses belonging to the gentry in Sebastopol stood in this valley. As I rode past, I looked into one of them, which was occupied by soldiers of many regiments. A couple of Grenadiers were playing a military duet upon a grand piano; others were usefully employed breaking up a large pier glass for portable use! Ladies' bonnets and gloves had been abstracted from wardrobes, and found useless. There was a great run after the ducks and the poultry in the farmyard, and the wine cellar commanded peculiar attention. If one desires to have a house thoroughly cleared out of everything valuable, just let a regiment of soldiers have their fling for half an hour or so, and you may open a new score with all your tradesmen next day.

I met Captain Neville,[1] of the Guards, then aide-de-camp to Sir R. England, riding off like fun with a big cabbage under his arm. I called out to him to pull up. 'What is it?' he said. 'I will thank you to lend me that cabbage. You are sure of some sort of dinner, and it would fit so well into my camp kettle with a ration of pork.' He laughed, and galloped away, but I suppose his conscience checked his course, for he pulled up, came back, and handed me the prize like a thoughtful soldier which, with our piece of pork, made us a good, substantial sweet dinner.

24th. Hill country. Crossed the 'Belbek' river. Here was a position again equal to the Alma or the Katchka, but no opposition, and we had the mortification of being told that if we had followed up our victory after the Alma, we would have captured the Russian artillery at the Katchka, as they lay there all the night.

Here, again, is a beautiful valley, fertile in vineyards, orchards, and vegetables. Abundance of fine grapes, quite ripe, but the locusts have left none for the next day. Marched on, and bivouacked in

[1] Colonel N. dined with me seven years afterwards, when we had a good laugh about the cabbage dinner on the Katchka.

an oak jungle. I carried my little axe at my saddle-bow, cut down a bundle of young branches to sleep on, and some old ones to make a bower to cover my head. Nothing to eat but a hard, brown biscuit, and a bit of cold pork. Poor Colonel Tyndal, R.E., died. What an affliction awaits his beloved wife! How happy they were at Corfu! One of our doctors died this evening, and my poor friend the chaplain was so very ill that he was carried along all the march today on a stretcher. We have a savage appearance; no change of dress since we landed, and living like wild beasts. I am almost afraid of myself when I look into that fragment of the big mirror which I picked up in our camp. I wish I had never washed this horrid shirt of mine; it will never dry. A great gun was fired in the middle of the night. The whole army up and under arms in a twinkle. Some false alarm; all quiet, and so we turned in, on our respective oak beds, covered with dew.

We have lost sight of the fleet, and have hard work to press through the thick jungle. My clothes, such as they are, have been torn off my bones, worming my horse through the very thick cover. But the weather is fine, which cheers on the army, and makes us laugh at our condition.

I found Staff-Surgeon Forest very snug under an oak this morning, with his kettle boiling, and some slices of ham in the frying-pan, so very savoury, it increased an appetite too big for my scanty ration. 'Good morning, doctor, the fairies have been kind to you; I would like to make their acquaintance.' 'Better make yourself acquainted with that frizzle on the fire, and a pot of tea before we move; the assembly has gone.' 'True,' I said, 'it has just sounded, and I have no time to boil my kettle. I will accept of a mouthful before I mount.' I think I astonished him before I got up from the sod, having cleared out the frying-pan and three pints of tea. But he had an araba to draw his tools and the drugs, and a sick man or two, and, of course, his own little private stores, which seemed to be of the right sort. Poor Mockler was now stretched on top of this araba, or very rough, uncouth bullock-car, quite unable to move, patient, full of hope, and resigned. I saw that his days were numbered, and I never beheld him again.

On our way, at M'Kenzie's farm, as it was called, our van fell in with the rear of the Russian army, put them to flight, taking some valuable spoil, including Menschikoff's carriage and camp baggage. In fact, the two armies were in ignorance of each other's movements. When the Russians were thrashed at the Alma, they fled to the south side of Sebastopol, where they took courage, and looked about them. Naturally supposing that we would push on to the north side, and attack the Star fort and the town from that quarter, the Prince Menschikoff made a counter-march to get into our rear, and was on this move when the two armies nearly clashed together at 'M'Kenzie's farm'. They took the road to Baktchi Serai, distance from Sebastopol twenty-two miles. We got orders to halt here for the night. I was principal officer on duty, and took the command, placed my outposts, planted a cannon on the road, made all snug, lighted our fires, the doctor foraged and got a bottle of good port wine which we *did* enjoy, and now the night was closing. Instead of a farmhouse there was a large barrack here. Not being in use, it was full of fleas, so that no one had the courage to look at it as a dormitory. But it contained sacks full of hazel-nuts, which kept the men cracking their jokes for some days. A few little innocent pigs and some poultry were found wandering about, and were kidnapped, of course. One of my men left me a large cloth cloak, lately the property of a Russian officer of the 34th Regiment. I was just going to dream under this prize, when we got orders to 'march directly', and away went the whole British army, making a flank march in the darkness of black night down the steep hills. High and craggy rocks were on our right, and deep and dangerous precipices on our left, quite unprotected. We crossed the Tchernaya, or black river, at Traktir Bridge, about four o'clock in the morning, and halted. I lay down, tied my horse to a bush, and fell asleep on the roadside. It was broad day when I awoke. I had no power to move, nor could I stir until two of my men lifted me on my legs. When the sun came out, warm and cheery, I got the use of my limbs, but had to be assisted on my horse, when we marched on and bivouacked in the valley of Bala-clava—fine cavalry ground. The valley was a great arena, between high and wooded hills to the south, and a range of high ground to the north, shutting out any view of the sea on either side. The sod was green, firm, and dry, a bonnie spot to encamp, so peaceful-like, under a bright sun. This was the 25th. The old castle above Balaclava made a feeble effort of defence, and immediately the harbour was occupied by our ships of war. The entrance is very narrow, lying between mountains of rocks; it serpentines about a mile, and is so deep that the *Agamemnon* lay alongside the bank.

Mounted my gallant grey, and away to forage for man and horse. The cottages were all deserted, and, as a matter of certainty, they would soon be plundered. I carried off some hay and veget-ables, with a hen or two, handed to me by a 'red devil' who was first in the field. The cottages were comfortably furnished—pro-ductive gardens, lots of hay. The great misfortune was that the simple people all fled and left their property to the winds.

27th. Poor Colonel Cox of the Guards died last night of cholera, very deeply regretted by all who had the pleasure of his acquaintance. I rode over the hills today and saw many nice comfortable farmhouses, vineyards, and cornyards, all deserted, and left to the tender mercy of a great hungry army, worse than locusts, and without compassion.

CHAPTER
17

In Camp before Sebastopol

THE power of war is now unchained, and, alas for the poor, happy, industrious country people of this district, ruin is just upon their thresholds, and I do grieve for their coming misfortune. Rode on two miles farther, to the brow of the hill, and looked down, for the first time, on Sebastopol, the renowned fortress, the handsome capital of the Crimea, so long and so earnestly talked of, the doomed city, which will yet cost so much blood and treasure; there it lies in its security, the bells ringing, the bands playing, and the ladies walking in the gardens, their fleet at anchor in the harbour and outside, keeping watch. The cavalry pickets are in front covering the town, the artillerymen at their guns, all ready for a grand flare-up; fine houses, buildings, churches, squares, and public gardens, everything looking so bright and gay.

28th. Ordered to march at eight a.m.; a scramble for breakfast; counter-ordered; an hour getting into our old place. 'Stand to your arms!'—up and ready again. 'Pile arms and wait orders.' We did get away at last, and bivouacked on the crest of the hill looking into the city—rather a mistake. We had hardly appeared when a battery opened on the Royal Regiment, which kept our eyes open, the cannon-shot whizzing close to our heads and our heels as they got the range. We changed ground three times, by order, and then settled down for the night. But there was a want of head here in this brigade command which vexed me exceedingly. The men are cooking their dinners; when half done, an order to march immediately comes, kettles are all upset, half-cooked rations tumbled into haversacks, and we hardly away when ordered back to the same sod to make all snug for the night. This worry and want of decision almost made one swear. I placed my pickets, the men pulled down a house, in the distance, for firewood, to cook their parboiled pork in the dark, then went to roost on the dry sod. It was as cold a night as one would wish to sleep out of doors. The north-east wind was so cutting I gave my poor, shivering horse one of my blankets to keep his heart warm, for he had nothing to eat.

29th. I slept like a top. All up an hour before daylight—our usual custom before an enemy. And now the Sebastopol guns opened upon us with gusto: shot and shell—the quarrel had begun.

My poor friend, the reverend chaplain, took possession of his narrow, dark, cold, ill-furnished house; the house appointed to all living (1st Peter, v. 4). Death is written on all things.

Changed our front to the left, some miles, and took up a new position facing the town, and got cannonaded, by the way, without harm. Bivouacked on the edge of a fine vineyard full of ripe grapes. When the men had piled arms there was a rush at them, and a run of 1,500 red devils into this grapery, as they called it, which they cleared out in no time. Changed our ground again, as the kettles began to boil, and fell back half a mile, carrying our half-cooked rations along with us. Enough to make a dog swear. Bivouacked, and down went the pots again, for people can't live upon grapes. Fuel was wanting, but a supply was found in a farm-house not far away. Nice tables, mahogany chests of drawers, chairs, and other furniture, well seasoned, served to cook the ration-pork. I was really grieved to see this wholesale destruction of property. If the proprietors had but remained at home, all would have been safe, so far as the British soldier was concerned.

30th. A bright sunny morning. An alarm roused us all up at twelve last night. One of our steamers closed in and threw some broadsides into a shore battery that was annoying us, and retired to the fleet before receiving a shot.

October 1st. Forgot the day of the week; told it was Sunday and went out on the hilside to read a chapter or two in my little Testament, which was a pocket companion of mine. Our days I knew were all numbered, but we did not number the days, nor did we keep holy the Sabbath day. A cannon-shot sloping up from the town warned me to be off. It came plop into mother earth and lay quiet beside me. I took the hint, took off my cap, and retired.

2nd. Shot and shell from the batteries below annoying us. A

fragment took off one man's knapsack and another's pouch. Close shaving.

3rd. Passed a quiet, cold night. The dew from heaven kept our heads cool enough, but nine tents were sent up today from Balaclava for the officers of my regiment and the sick men, so that we will get under cover at last. We had up to this date lain on the sod, but thankful the weather was dry. In former times I had lain on the cold ground for six or eight months at a time. In the Peninsula the climate was mild and dry in summer, but we were often exposed to the rainy season, which was overwhelming; no tents, continued privations and exposure, marching and fighting. Hungry and thirsty, day after day, we often lay on ploughed land by night, soaking wet, and without any cover. Thousands fell into an early grave, but many survived to see the last shot fired in anger at Toulouse. I was one of the fortunate number, and I'm thankful.

A round shot came flying up from the town just now about two miles distant, so heavy I could hardly lift it. There it lies at my tent door for inspection—a specimen of cricket balls à la Russe. They are busy as ants in their batteries and defences, while we are idle for want of siege guns and everything. Sat at my tent door darning my old pair of black socks with some yellow wool, while my servant boiled my only shirt. The shot and shell are flying up and exploding much too near. They make one wink, the fragments are so vicious. Things begin to look very serious. There is a limestone quarry on the brow of the hill in front of my tent. An immense quantity of prepared stone for building is lying about, the workmen decamped, leaving their tools, as we came up. From this ground we have a fine view of the city and all the works. The slope down for a mile is covered with oak brush, three and four feet high. In this brush the Rifles are bivouacked and not very comfortable. For the moment a curl of smoke ascends from a fire, the enemy open a battery and drive them about like rabbits. Lord Raglan rides up here of an evening to look about, and it is a sort of rendezvous for the officers of our division, *pour conversazione*. It is a safe retreat too. As the shot come flying up, we have to duck behind a stone barrier until they pass over our heads or bury themselves deep right or left. We see the flash from the guns and calculate the time of arrival; then the whiz of a round shot is something more than alarming when close to one's head.

Our Staff Surgeon and forty-six men died last night at Balaclava. They will persist in huddling the sick into a pestilential hospital, as they did at Varna!

We have got up our tents for the men at last. How long will they last on these bleak hills? They are but rags that have not improved lying in store for forty years! Some regiments have pitched right in view of the enemy, and will attract their attention and give them a good range, if I don't mistake.

5th. Some rain last night and a thundering cannonade from our neighbours below, which awoke me from a comfortable bed of hay, a great prize I got yesterday. Nothing to be had now but the rations. When a ship arrives at Balaclava everything is bought up by people on the spot at any price. I got a loaf of black rye bread a few days ago, but so hard and crusty no teeth but those of an elephant could make an impression on it. There goes a shell into a tent of the 68th. It explodes; the house is on fire. 'Run up, Charley, and see what damage.' 'Two men killed, sir, and three wounded; the tent's in rags, sir, and one poor fellow's brains all scattered about, sir.'

Young campaigners don't know their trade when they pitch in sight of the enemy. Now they strike and retire behind the crest of the hill when the damage is done. This is called Cathcart's Hill, of celebrity. One thousand sick reported at Scutari, and pits are being dug to bury our dead from the hospital at Balaclava.

A thousand sailors and fifty guns landed from our ships of war. There they go, jolly dogs, dragging them up hill, one fellow riding on the foremost gun playing a fife, while the rest pull together and keep the step. Everything begins to look lively and serious, but still we are very tardy. The enemy's batteries increase in strength daily before our eyes, and we can't stop them.

7th. A sixty-eight pounder going up, drawn by eighteen English horses—a simple mark of a difficult beginning. They are pounding at us from below, like fury, today. Rode about, and over much ground to look at them, and to observe the multitude of their batteries, which are increasing and being made shot-proof. Cannon-shot will knock down stone walls, but only penetrate earthworks, to lie there *perdu*. There is but one stone tower in all their defensive works, with a large traversing gun on the top, which has a vicious inclination to do us some grievous bodily harm. Their fleet lies in the harbour, some at the top and some at the bottom. The topmasts of the latter mark where they lie right across, saying 'There is no admittance'. Woe be to the ships that attempt an entrance here, or to contend with the shore batteries on either side! Their destruction would be a certainty. 568 guns will meet them.

8th. Divine service at two p.m. Poor Mockler was singing praises where the weary find a rest. *Requiescat in pace*, in the rest that knows no troubling. Be thine also the peace that passeth all understanding, which the world could not give thee here, nor take away from thee now.

9th.   A very cold night and a colder morning. No fuel but the green brushwood. Slow in our progress to capture this place, which some inexperienced people think will be done at the very first assault. I quite disagree with them. We have not yet one battery established on the line of our extended position. Was awoke in the middle of last night by a heavy cannonade, and while I write these few notes at eight a.m. shot and shell are flying into our camp. Three shells have just exploded amongst our tents, while everyone is calling, 'Look out', 'take care', etc. See that horse, how he snaps his tether, and gallops away with his tail curled over his back, as a shell goes whop into the ground beside him. Sensible fellow! the shell explodes, but he is safe. One of the fragments kills a soldier who was less cautious. What boys those soldiers are! They run to pick up the round shot, and as often find a shell, which may explode long after it falls.

The sun breaks forth warm and brilliant. How very welcome! I pitch my tent afresh, and change the door from north to south. Build a mud wall all round, against a coming storm.

My groom, George Hawes, all right again. Arrives from Varna with one of my mules, sent over by authority, as a charger! Wonderful people! A bitter cold evening, and our cattle suffering for want of forage.

10th.   Some round shot and shell roused us all up early today, as they came ploughing into our lines, and too close for our safety. A tent of the 44th Regiment close by was just struck by one, which exploded in the very door. Walked over to see the result; the tent was in tatters, several stand of arms broken, and one shako, leaving nine men harmless who were lying down at the time. One of them, Private John Dudgeon, of Captain Fenwick's company, said that he got a 'dinge on the back wid a lump av the shell, but nothin' more'. A most providential escape.

A General Order for a working party of 700 men to parade this evening under the command of Colonel Bell, of the Royals, Captain Chapman, R.E., to conduct the work. I advanced in the dark with caution and silence for about two miles, with the whole of my regiment. Captain Chapman laid out with his white tape the first line of the trenches. I divided the men some six feet apart. Each man being provided with a pickaxe and shovel, laid down his firelock and went to work. Thus we broke the first ground for the 3rd Division batteries—'Chapman's', or the 'Greenhill battery'. By four in the morning we had worked under cover, although the ground was rocky, which gave us double trouble in carrying earth from the rear to fill up the embankments.   We stole away back to the camp undiscovered before dawn, being relieved by another corps.   And so I had the honour of breaking the first ground before Sebastopol.[1]   I had supper about twelve at night on the ground and in the dark—a bit of black bread, an onion, some rum-and-water, and a headache.

11th.   Had a small sleep after last night's work; then boiled my shirt again.   We had no soap, and took to boiling our shirts. I had worn mine twenty-eight days, having never undressed since I landed in the Crimea.

I feel much shaken today, and not well prepared for a winter on the sod.   The weather is still fine—thank God for it!—but who feels equal to the coming storm?   A tremendous cannonade opened on one of our merchant ships, which drifted on towards Sebastopol. We watched her with excited interest.   The shot from many batteries splashed about her like hail, some crashing through her hull, but still the British flag floated in the gentle breeze.   One of our war steamers put off, took her in tow, and carried her off triumphantly, amidst a shower of cannon-shot from the north batteries. In their disappointment, the enemy resolved to be avenged, and opened a fearful cannonade on our camp.   Sent many shot and shell into our tents, by which one of my men was killed.   The only wonder was that two oo were not added to the one.

12th.   I was roused up at two this morning by a sharp fire of great guns and musketry along our front—an effort of the enemy to destroy the works we had thrown up during the last two nights. Blue lights, with shot and shell, were thrown up amongst our people.   The bugles sounded the alarm and assembly; the camps were roused up, and all went to their respective posts directly, everyone under arms.   A thousand men marched down to support our working parties, and cover their front, when the enemy retired, and we returned to finish off a broken night's rest.   This is what we call the harassing work of a siege, it being the interest of one party to keep the other in continual alarm, and destroy their rest.

am quite crippled with rheumatism, but otherwise pretty well, with a very good appetite, and nothing to eat but the everlasting salt pork.   My mess chum, Doctor H——, takes care of me, but all hospital comforts are wanting, with nothing at the disposal of regimental surgeons but their carving-knives.   The whole department shamefully and cruelly neglected.   However well that 'Memorandum for the information of Medical Officers' may read in English newspapers, signed John H——, M.D., Inspector-General of

[1] Before the fall of Sebastopol the trenches of the allied army extended sixty miles!

Q

Hospitals, 'tis all bosh. He begins with spring waggons and medical comforts, which he well knows were left on the other side of the Black Sea, and ends by a return of killed and wounded to be sent to him after an action.

—— Perhaps, Mr. J. H., M.D.,
'Tis lucky that I'm not Commander-in-C.

13th. They keep pounding away like fun. 'Tis all music to our ears now. I don't know that we could sleep so well after any cessation of those bellowing guns. I have just been forty-eight hours in the trenches instead of twelve — one of the usual blunders of a brigade major (not ours, who is a first-rate fellow), but very inconvenient to keep one's eyes open so long, and depending on a wretched ration of pork and biscuit, doled out by night — the only time our Quartermaster dare show his rosy face for fear of being knocked over.

Colonel Waddy, 50th, hit on the head by the fragment of a shell, which bothered his brains for some time. But he recovered, and said that he would be a C.B. or a dead man. The gallant Waddy got the C.B. and lives to wear it. I had some narrow escapes myself from those flying fragments of destruction that clear away all before them. It requires a sharp lookout and a quick eye to guard one's head.

14th. A month today in the Crimea. One of very great excitement and military execution; yet we have hardly begun our work. Such a fire as opened this morning on the French batteries; so quick and so sharp, we soon lost sight of the belligerents in the clouds of gunpowder smoke. Both sides keep pounding away until noon, when the 'Rooskies' (as our men call them) go to dinner, and the fire slackens. Sir Colin Campbell going down to command, and defend Balaclava. And he is sure to do it well. A large Russian force beginning to show themselves, commanded by General Austin Sacken, who will probably get a good 'whacking'. Two thousand men gone down to the trenches this evening. What an everlasting rattle of artillery in one's ears, but now so familiar 'tis hardly noticed. I take my evening stroll to some distant point, sit down upon a rock, and with my glass watch the progress of the siege. The multitude of working parties; the never-ceasing roll of cannon belching out fire and death; the stretchers carrying home the wounded; continual movements of troops; the vast encampments on the north side of the harbour; their steamers crossing and recrossing constantly, the steam up night and day; both parties watching each other like cats, rifle in hand, to have a pot shot.

16th.   At 9 a.m. a red flag was hoisted from one of the batteries in the town.   The whole city seemed to pour out; every point for a grand view was occupied.   I went up to the quarry hill to see the fun; not what we expected.   By signal, the whole of the guns in the great fortress opened upon our works with shot and shell.   Such a fire, perhaps, never was seen or heard before; it was the most terrific, the most frightful exhibition of intended destruction that can possibly be imagined.   All their guns were brought to bear upon our works, as well as those of the French.   No one dare show his head above the trenches, and the covering parties lay down flat until this hurricane of iron passed away.   It was their intention to have totally swept away all our works by this tremendous fire, but after all they did not do us much injury, and our casualties were few.   We will repair damages tonight, and be ready to return their incivilities tomorrow.

17th October 1854.   Our opening day!   The day fixed for the allied armies to open the siege of Sebastopol, about the strongest fortress in the world.   Whose pen shall describe the scene, and who will return to the camp after the first day's work is over?

I was up at three o'clock in the morning, and away with my whole regiment to the trenches long before daylight.   I arranged my men in their proper places; my right resting on the drop into the Worronzoff road, which curved through the craggy vale down to the city.   My left was on the right of Chapman's Battery, where I cut the first sod on the night of the 10th.   The Russian batteries were firing lazily all night at random — as much as to say, we are wide awake.   6.30 a.m. was the time appointed for us to open the ball.   Everyone was on the *qui vive* waiting the signal-gun; all had been in silence on our side during the night.   Exactly at half-past six our signal-gun bid them good morning.   The time had arrived to return them all civility for nineteen days of incessant cannonade.   With right goodwill, and an anxious desire to pay off old debts, a scene opened, such as never had been witnessed since the invention of gunpowder.   It was a battle of artillery — some 2,000 great guns opened their mouths of thunder, and iron hail was showered from each side with the most determined and vindictive desire to destroy life.   The distance was 1,300 yards or thereabouts between us.   All our batteries opened at once.   We saw the enemy at their guns; we saw every fiery flash, and felt their metal.   Both parties soon got the range, and such pounding and hissing of shot and shell, cutting through the air with that velocity that bewilders one in his endeavour to protect his head when the shot has really past!   Flop, they come into the very bank you are leaning against, and lodge there.   A cross fire now pours in upon us, ploughing along our

intrenchments.   We are enveloped in powder smoke; a breeze from
the sea clears all away.   Both antagonists in view of each other
laying their guns to the mark; shot coming and going like hail, and
shells cracking death and destruction wherever they explode.   No
delay beyond laying the guns and loading.   The sand-bags fly out of
their solid beds.   The dust rises in clouds at every volley, and breastworks topple over amongst the infantry.   With glass to eye at
every favourable moment, I can't resist looking over at our friends,
who are working their guns like skilful soldiers, replacing those
that are disabled, so quickly and fearlessly.   Look out—a shot
coming; see the flash.   The word is hardly spoken, when it is buried
in the bank, or takes the crest of the cover above your head, or
meets a big stone, which turns its course.   But they come so quick,
'tis dangerous to move.   Look out again—down, men; a shell, it
falls in the midst of us and explodes.   Oh! horrible; seven of my
poor fellows; three killed and four wounded.

Hark, there goes one of their magazines in the Redan up in the
air.   The smoke overshadows in darkness this very formidable
field-work upon which we make no impression.   Their guns are
silenced for the moment, but, alas! there goes one of our tumbrils
into the air, horse and all.   Now they make double exertion at all
their batteries, and the elements are alive with the tur-whit of the
shell, and the whiz of shot.   Who is that down beside us? 'Doctor
O'Leary, sir.'   'Is he hurt?'   'Killed, sir.'

When we were looking over the breastwork, glass in hand, a
heavy shot toppled the bank between Captain Wells and myself.
It landed about a foot from our heads, knocking the stones and
gravel in our face and eyes, bounding on, up the hill a hundred yards
at every stretch, and thus this race goes on all the day.   The French
batteries all shut up and knocked to faggots by the well-directed
fire of the Russian guns, and so they open a double fire upon us by
way of closing our book for the day; but 'tis no go.   Six hours have
we been pounding at that Malakoff Tower—that only piece of
stonework in all their defences.   And there sinks the last gun
through the top platform.   A very large traversing gun it was, that
gave our side much annoyance.   But farewell to the Malakoff; stone
walls won't stand against artillery.

See that officer on top of the Redan, where the magazine exploded, giving his orders in defiance of all danger.   He gets up more
guns, and they blaze away as fresh as formerly.   Shot and shell
come bounding up to us from new quarters, tearing all before them.
The ship guns are now let loose, and new batteries open that we
cannot see.

In all this tumult of death and excitement, I see some of my men asleep and snoring! so habituated are soldiers to danger. It is one thing being actively employed, firelock in hand, and another thing to lie waiting in a ditch to resist an enemy.

The evening closes over a day on which some peaceful citizen would say that hell had broken loose with all the destructive powers of darkness. Night comes at last. I shut up my notebook. All is quiet but the groans and the moans of the wounded, who are now sent up to camp; the dead are covered up. The Quartermaster comes down in the darkness with his little barrels of ration rum, a welcome visitor. Pickets are posted, haversacks opened, breakfast, dinner, and supper, on a bit of pork and onion, and a biscuit, washed down with a little rum and muddy water; lie down in the ditch, and asleep in five minutes. Reliefs come down at three o'clock in the morning, all up and away to camp, tumble into our respective tents to finish our slumbers, and up again early to see the opening of another day like the last.

18th. I thank God for our lives yesterday. Many were called and many more will be added to the daily list of our casualties; 'tis a scene of grave-digging all day long. If I am spared, I suppose I shall have nothing else to note but fighting, contention and strife, battle, murder, and sudden death. The grave itself is but a covered way, leading from light to light through a brief darkness.

Our fleet got a terrible pounding yesterday, as they attacked the harbour-forts, by way of a diversion in our favour. It was madness to run so many fine ships against stone walls and the heaviest metal. Star fort, guns, number not known: the Wasp battery, 8 guns; Fort Constantine, 104 guns; Battery, 80 guns, 30 and 34 guns. South side: Fort Paul, 30 guns; Fort Nicolas, 192 guns; Artillery Bay, 50 guns; Fort Alexander, 64 guns; Quarantine Bay, 50 guns; besides many others that I don't remember. Enough guns to sink all our ships, and which would have happened had they not hauled off in time.

A repetition of yesterday: pounding away with a fury and determination on both sides. But the truth is, that our guns are not heavy enough for the work, and it is said the town is being spared. I say, fire the town and the birds will fly. To save it will be a great sacrifice of life, for they will never yield an inch of ground without a fight for it. And if they do fail in their defence, they will blow up all, retire across the harbour, take up the North position, and be as strong as ever. *Nous verrons!* What a thundering noise that sixty-eight pounder of ours does make, as the shot from it passed over us yesterday, *en route* to the Malakoff. I thought, more than once, my head was off. The terrible whiz, as it cut through the air a little above one's head, created a nervous sensation which all felt and none of us wished to feel. We now call it the express train going down to Sebastopol.

Two p.m. Clouds of smoke. Nothing to be seen but the crimson flash from the cannon's mouth. Home to my dinner: man must live.

19th. An interrupted cannonade on both sides. What the *Rooskies* lose by day they build up at night. We do the same and make no impression. Got up five more guns last night; the French batteries in the meantime being disabled is a great damper, and the enemy throw all their attentions over to us in consequence. Hurrah! the French batteries are open again, and our shot, shell, and rockets are pouring into the Russian lines with effect.

Colonel Hood, of the Guards, just killed. Evening closes with a hurricane of shot, shell, and rockets going into the town, and the express train going down the road. A liberal allowance of eighteen bottles of wine issued today for the sick and wounded of six regiments.

20th. Day dawns on hundreds of guns, belching forth fire and destruction. There goes the French magazine into the air, a pillar of a cloud that reminds one of that which preceded, by command of Jehovah, the Israelites in the wilderness. It is a column of dense black smoke, amazing in its girth, with a white curling top, gracefully turning over like an ostrich-plume. The French are importunate, they claim everything, and when Sebastopol falls, they will be unwilling to divide the honour with their neighbours. There is a good smashing of barracks in the town from our batteries, but we must batter the whole city to dust before we get possession of such a stronghold as it is, and it gets stronger every day. Wherever you look, a battery stares you in the face, and you had better look out. Went over to see the practice of a Lancaster gun at the Malakoff, which is no longer stone, but an earthen battery increasing in strength and size every day. This gun throws a sixty-eight pound conical ball and made such an uproar I was nearly deaf; they had but four shot left to continue the siege. The practice was good, but the shot lodged in the solid, deep, earthen works, and of course there is no harm done, unless a gun is disabled or a few men killed.

21st. Great guns and small-arms did not disturb my slumbers last night. Day dawns with the red flashing of batteries at every corner; three officers, 44th, wounded; Captain Brown lost his right arm. A sailor in the Naval Brigade Battery, whilst in the act of taking up a round shot with both hands, to load his gun, was struck by a cannon-ball from the Redan, and terribly wounded. Colonel Alexander, R.E., in command of that service here, died last night.

A magazine in the enemy's lines blew up, so did one of our tumbrils. The Rooskies made a sortie, and spiked five French guns. The whole of my regiment are for the trenches tonight.

22nd. Divine service in the midst of a tornado of fire and fury. A forty-two pound shot lodged in one of my tents without harm. I dug him out, and there he is, in front of my door, quiet and easy. It had come about two miles, and buried itself out of sight.

23rd. Up at three in the morning, and away to those everlasting trenches. Before daylight the fiery ordeal began on both sides, shot and shell as hard as they could fly. Wishing to see the whole of our batteries in action, I took my chance and went from right to left. The round shot were flying about galore, and kicking up such a dust, picking off some poor fellow every round. One topped a breastwork, as I passed, with a crashing velocity, and next moment I had to dodge a big fragment of a shell that I saw coming, a regular triangular ripper, large enough to kill a horse. Stayed by Captain Childers, of the Artillery, watching his practice for a while. Glass in hand, he had followed the line of his own shot to see the effect and range, when a return shot from the Redan took off his head—I thought he exposed himself too much. Those things don't make much impression now on the blunted feelings of men too careless of life. A little farther on, three gunners were killed and seven wounded, five guns disabled, and one exploded, from red-hot shot.

Captain Brown, of my regiment, had a good escape, being struck with a fragment of shell on the head, which took off a scalp without cracking his skull, which someone said was very thick.

Part of the town on fire and burns brightly. Our guns did their work well today, and deserve praise. My humble breakfast, back of a ditch—an onion, piece of pork, biscuit, and some grog. I feel weary and broken with this hard nightwork, but I may not say so: hope on, hope ever.

24th. The resources of the enemy boundless. The French are approaching the town by the trench-work, in spite of a continual and destructive fire.

A frightful storm of rain at eight p.m.; every man for duty marched away for the night, as wet as if he had been soaked in the sea. Thank goodness, it is not our turn.

CHAPTER 18

Balaclava and Inkerman

OCTOBER 25th. Memorable day! The story of this day will be told by a thousand tongues and in many languages. I can only relate what I saw. There was heavy firing in the night. Very early in the morning the Russians advanced a strong corps of cavalry, supported by infantry and artillery, into the valley of Balaclava. On their right, as they advanced, they could see the French line of our defence along the ridge of hills, but they halted a little out of range of our guns, a large hill keeping them well concealed. Another range of high hills well wooded and overhanging the sea covered their left. In the plain nearer to Balaclava our cavalry were picketed. About a mile in front of them three redoubts extended across the valley on three separate rising grounds, occupied by the Turks; one of these redoubts had nine guns, the others were unarmed.

The Cossack cavalry advanced at a rapid pace, captured all the guns, and dispersed the Turks before they fired above a few shots. The enemy's horse further advanced upon our cavalry, who had merely time to boot and saddle, when they were up on our lines, ay, to the tent-doors, for there lay the slain. Our heavy dragoons now went at these celebrated, long talked-of cavalry, and left their mark on every man in their way. Wherever our broadswords fell, it was death or a disabled soldier. The crest of our position was crowded with spectators looking down into the arena upon this grand tournament in reality. There was some fatal misunderstanding about an order sent by Lord Raglan as to the recapture of our

238

guns. Captain Nolan, a dashing young cavalry officer, was the bearer of this order to Lord Lucan, who commanded our cavalry. He at once ordered Lord Cardigan to advance his brigade, charge the enemy, and take or recapture our guns. Here there was a discussion and remonstrance. It was said Captain N. was excited and determined for a charge, and as there is no evading a General Order on a battlefield, he volunteered to lead the way. The brigade went madly forward, and poor Nolan was the first to fall, being struck by a round shot or shell. Our cavalry dashed on to the charge, led by Lord Cardigan, got amongst the Cossacks, and cut them down right and left. But we had gone too far, for now the Russian artillery opened a destructive fire of round shot and shell upon our people just as they swept round the elbow of the hill. Still our men galloped on and cut down the Russian gunners under a shower of musketry that emptied many of our saddles.

It was a terrible slaughter of man and horse without any result other than to prove the metal of British cavalry. Here the Russians felt the weight of an English sabre for the first time. Our dragoons clave their heads almost in two, and cut them down like thistle-tops.

Now let us go down and ride over this battlefield. You see the ground divided, pickets and patrols out on both sides keeping watch, in the broad space between. The dead are lying thick beside their horses, many of which are badly wounded; some unable to rise are biting at the short grass within their reach. Poor things, they must die of their wounds and starvation at last; 381 of ours lie dead. See the effect of our broadswords, such ghastly dead, such terrible wounds. That stout fellow how quiet he lies upon his back with his eyes open; an English sabre let out his life-blood under the left arm; his long, dull grey-coat does not look very 'militaire' just now, it is drenched in gore — a shocking spectacle! That next body is more hideous to look on, his head nearly cleft in twain as if by an axe, his long beard matted with blood. He sleeps soundly. This fellow wears an embroidered hussar jacket. His bridle arm is cut in two, but it was that deep thrust between the ribs which sent his soul away, I hope, to a more peaceful land. That one is a young, fair-headed, youthful soldier. His light-blue eyes are open wide, his two hands are clenched tight, as if he grasped at something in agony before his soul took flight; he lies in a bloody bath. This one here was of another regiment. A sky-blue cloth shako, high and broad in the crown, lies beside him uninjured; it fell from his head, no doubt, in his fruitless combat with some Enniskillen dragoon, whose Lough Erne arm and skill dyed with life-blood the cold green sod on which the young warrior sleeps. Many tears of sorrow may be shed for this poor youth, but who will ever know his fate?

Only one red-coat lies here. I hear his death-cheer for Old England, as the prison of his soul was broken up, as the spirit left its shattered cell. But there are too many red-coats on the ground out of my reach. Not a month has passed since I was in bivouac on this very ground, all peaceful and joyous, now covered with the brave in death, their life-blood staining the plants of autumn.

The poor horses, too, I do feel for those noble fellows, snorting so lately in their pride of war. As their masters left the saddles empty, they scorned to run away, but galloped in the charge side by side of their own old comrades. Look to your front and see what a havoc the Russian guns have made there amongst our cavalry. The plain is dotted with the gallant Scots Greys, mingled with the Blacks and Bays. Look through my glass and you will see our dead lying amongst the good steeds who bravely carried them into the charge, but could not bring them back. All this was very brave, but was only a murderous onset that might have been avoided. The French were looking down upon this combat with great interest and excitement when General Canrobert remarked, 'C'est magnifique; mais ce n'est pas la guerre'.

Our loss was, 13 officers killed, 27 wounded; 150 men killed, 154 wounded; 381 horses killed. Russian loss, 26 officers killed and wounded; 524 men ditto.

See, the Cossacks are in motion, and ride hard; let us be off also. There is something else brewing, and away we went to Balaclava, fell in with our old ship-captain, who asked me to go on board and partake of his early dinner, or rather a tea-supper. I did not refuse the invitation. On leaving the ship he gave me two loaves of white bread, which I joyfully carried home to my tent six miles off, and astonished my doctor and Adjutant next morning at breakfast; 'actually loaf-bread,' they exclaimed, 'Where—did—you—get—this?'

No tragedy more tragic, no comedy more comic, no romance more romantic than that of real life.

26th. All goes on as usual, pounding away from both sides. Took a look at the Rooskies late in the evening. Quiet and comfortless in their bivouac. Pickets of horse and foot out in all directions.

27th, 28th. Wholesale expenditure of powder and shot, with little impression on the works of the enemy. Their barracks are crumbling down, and some stone houses outside the town. I don't see that we have gained anything.

29th. Went to my straw bed very unwell. The ringing boom

of the cannon and exploding of shells don't improve a headache. A cold piercing north wind, and nothing to keep one warm inside or out; a gloomy Sabbath day. We had our little service in my tent for the very few of our household.

30th. Cold and cloudy. At noon the sun peeped out and cheered us. Conversation or a voice from the next tent: 'Barnacle' (servant to poor Turner). — 'Sir.' 'Did you boil my shirt?' — 'Yes sir.' 'Is it dry?' — 'Not quite, sir; I'm going to get some sticks to mend the fire.' Half an hour passes. 'Barnacle, is my shirt dry?' 'Faith, it's dry enough what's of it.' 'What do you mean?' — 'O, be gad, sir, it fell in the bit of fire when I was down there grabbing some bits of the bush.' 'Is it much burned?' 'Well, there is a sleeve and the tail left, sir, and devil an inch more.' Poor T. gave a cheer and a laugh, and asked to see the finale of his last and only shirt, when it was reported that our baggage was coming into camp. And here it comes, sure enough, after forty-six days' absence, during which time we had no change of dress. We were in rags, and not very clean rags. For forty-six days and nights I never undressed, but to wash myself, and as for the old shirt it fell to pieces.

The poor men were all in filthy rags. Russian knapsacks were cut up and bound round their legs, their feet were swollen, and many were without shoes. They converted old Russ coats into sandals, and wore them day and night, wet or dry. But all this was the beginning of sorrows. I don't know how many voyages our ship took after our landing up to this time, but I got my baggage safe, while others were plundered, particularly of their guns, and the soldiers' knapsacks were pillaged; for such grievances there was no redress.

31st. Last night was so calm and quiet I heard the clock in the great church strike the hours, and the sentries challenge in the town together with the whop, whop of the round shot as they struck their object. It is said in camp today that we are to make the grand assault on Sebastopol on the 7th of November. If so, I pray that the God of Israel will give us a victory, and preserve us from all those dangers to which we must be exposed.

I made a prize on the battle-day, securing a fine horse, whose master, perhaps, was slain. On minute examination, I found the brand of the 11th Hussars on his hoof, so I handed him over to the first man of that corps whom I met.

November 1st to 4th. French approaching near the town. We got up another battery of fifteen guns last night. At three o'clock this morning the most terrible fire was opened on the French approaches, so quick and so heavy, it alarmed our encampment. We aided our allies by a cross fire upon the town, that let them see

that we were wide awake. I reconnoitred the whole of the
Russians in our rear, some 30,000 men posted chiefly in the vale of
Balaclava, threatening our defences. Sir Colin Campbell, with the
Highland Brigade, is there ready for any emergency, and has fortified his position from Kadukoi to the very top of the cliffs overhanging the sea. We are all safe there. The allied army now
stands *dos-à-dos*, an interval of about a mile between us. The
French along their intrenched heights watching the Russian army
in the valley, while we are carrying on the siege in front of the
town. In fact, we are all hemmed up in a corner, besieging and
besieged.

The weather is cold and variable: a Russian winter in a tent will
not agree with British soldiers. A heavy cannonade from the city
since four a.m. Between the roaring of the guns and the whop of
the shot, we distinctly hear the fine, mellow, deep tone of the
church bells, as if tolling for the dead.

Took a walk down the valley of death. It leads into the Worronzoff Road, which winds between rocky hills into the town. This
deep valley is full of cannon-balls, all of which were fired at our
batteries.

Doctor H.T. and myself tried to count them in a space of
twenty or thirty square yards, but could not. We crept along to
get a nearer view of the town and some batteries that were annoying us, when a shell exploded at our heels, and sent the fragments
whistling about our ears. A cannon-shot then came plop on our
very path, and made us run for it. We crept alongside the rocks,
and got into some caves for shelter; one was large enough to hold
100 men. We stole away again to a three-gun battery got up last
night to keep down the fire of a ship in one of the creeks that
annoyed our people. After a few shots from our side, she sheered
off round a corner.

Two of their batteries new began to pound at our three guns
very playfully. We watched their practice, and ducked when the
shot got the range. We saw the men at their guns, saw them apply
the match, saw the flash, and then down behind a rock, till the
shot went plop into the side of the hill just behind us, which will
be found in 100 years hence a wonderful iron mine. Here we
had a fine view of the town and harbour, etc. The vast piles of
shot and shell stacked in the arsenal yards were prodigious. Our
practice from a mortar battery was very bad. I watched the course
of some shells of large dimensions, which generally fell short, or
burst in the air. I asked the officer the cause, and he said, instead
of a supply of the best war material, they sent us out all the old
fusty shells from Malta, that lay there forty years, and the fuse is

not serviceable!   When one of those big shells did pop into a house,
it blew up the whole concern from the garret to the cellar.   Here
we were close on the right of the French works, their riflemen 100
yards in advance of the parallels; what a bedlam is here.   An unlucky shot came now bounding over from the Rooskies, and killed
one of our gunners.   So we bolted, made a rush out of the line of
their guns, and got home safe to a fine dinner of Irish stew, and
rum punch.   No duty tonight, a good sleep and look-out for the
morrow.

Sunday, 5th November 1854.   We little know what a day may
bring forth.   Before the dawn I was awoke by a heavy cannonade,
which did not disturb me in the least; but on the heels of this
tumult came a pattering of musketry, a sure indication of an attack.
I jumped up and looked out to listen.   It was a raw, ugly, drizzling
peep o' day to cool our courage and damp our powder.   I heard
the frenzied yell of the Russian bloodhounds coming on with a
quick and thickening fire, buckled on my sword, and ordered the
assembly to sound.   What do we muster?   '374, rank and file, sir;
all the rest are in the trenches.'   I marched off to the right by order,
and took up position on the 4th Division ground, Sir George
Cathcart having gone forward to the right with his troops to share in
the battle.   We advanced across a ravine to the next hill, where we
had a sixty-eight pounder battery; it had been taken by the enemy,
and retaken.   It was here that the brave Captain Sir Thomas
Troubridge lost both his feet by a cannon-shot, and there he lay in
patient anguish.   The Russians made another effort to gain this
battery, and advanced on both flanks, and right up the breast of the
hill.   Dividing my force, I rushed down to the battery, and sent
two companies into the two ravines, one on each flank, to keep the
enemy in check.

Our position here was of the greatest importance.   The enemy
made great efforts to get possession of our ground by turning our
left.   But to lose our grasp would have been fatal, so we held on like
grim death.   It is no easy matter beating the red devils on any
ground, but to try it up-hill was a forlorn hope; with all their
powerful artillery, we crushed their every effort.   The Russians
charged our troops with incredible fury and determination.   Ninety
guns on the field were pouring death and destruction into our
ranks, firing our tents, and killing our horses; shells exploding fast
and furious.   Fresh Russian columns were now advancing, before
whom our slender line gave way, rallied, charged, retired, and
returned to the charge against long odds.   The rolling of the musketry continued to the right, centre, and left, as the enemy gained
ground.   They drove their bayonets through our helpless wounded,

who lay at their mercy, like dastard ruffians, and beat in the heads of our officers while yet alive. One in particular was frightfully abused. He was found on the field after the battle, and lived on till next day in pain and sorrow. That was the gallant Colonel Carpenter, who commanded the 41st Regiment. Our men got savage at this cruel warfare; but yet, although they fell in scores at every volley, they seemed to multiply. It became a hand-to-hand, sanguinary struggle, marked by daring deeds and desperate assaults.[1] In glens and valleys, in brushwood glades, in remote dells, the battle went on. At every corner fresh foes met our exhausted troops, and renewed the struggle, until at length the battalions of the Czar gave way before the men of England. It was a great and glorious victory—as much as any victory can be glorious!

A hundred pens might write the deeds of a battle-day. All might differ, yet all be right, for no one can witness the spread of a battlefield. Terrible as were the incidents, and prodigious the acts of valour, it does not furnish much of the art of war. It was a succession of battles; each regiment had its hosts of Russians to repel.

The Guards were on the right, and met the enemy's advance there in mortal conflict. Here regiments mixed together from time to time, for support against the crushing numbers thrown upon them from the steadily advancing Russian columns. A two-gun battery stood here, to our extreme right. The Russians had a desire to possess it, and, after a mighty struggle, it was all their own, but it never had been armed. The Guards mustered all their strength, and made such a rush, and a cheer and a charge, they drove the enemy from it with great slaughter. But they could not hold it long. In fact, it was taken and retaken so often that a 1,000 men were slain upon this spot. Every hollow and ravine, nook and cranny, witnessed some sanguinary conflict, leaving piles of wounded men to look upon the dead, their only neighbours. So close were the combatants that, after firing, there was no time to reload; the bayonet did the rest, and the bayonet goes through a man like pasteboard. In one glen, five of our Generals fell, of whom three lay dead on the field. Poor Strangways, commanding artillery was ripped up by a shell, and in this torn, bleeding, frightful torture, he mildly said, 'Will anyone kindly assist me off my horse?' He died more easily on the sod.

Lord Raglan estimated the Russian force at 60,000 against whom

---

[1] Here a Royal Prince, commanding his Division, led on his men, who were proud of being commanded by a General so nearly connected to our Queen—an example to royalty in future to enter the battlefield, and share the dangers of war. Prince George was in the thick of this battle, and I only wonder how he escaped out of such a shower of leaden hail.

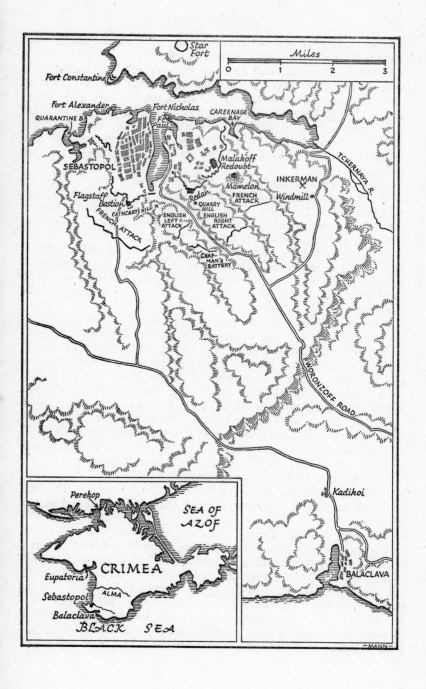

Star Fort

Fort Constantine

Miles
0   1   2   3

Fort Alexander   Fort Nicholas   CAREENAGE BAY
QUARANTINE B.   Ft.
                            Paul   TCHERNAYA R.

SEBASTOPOL   Malakoff
                                    Redoubt
                                         Mamelon   INKERMAN
                                                   ×
Flagstaff   Redan   FRENCH   Windmill
    Bastion   QUARRY   ATTACK
FRENCH   CATHCARTS HILL ×   HILL
    ATTACK   ENGLISH   ENGLISH
                            LEFT   RIGHT
                            ATTACK   ATTACK

                                    CHAP-
                                    MAN'S
                                    BATTERY

                                                       WORONZOFF ROAD

                                              Kadikoi

Perekop
                    SEA OF
                    AZOF

         CRIMEA

Eupatoria
              ALMA
Sebastopol   BALACLAVA
Balaclava
     BLACK   SEA

— MANN

we held our ground from dawn of day with 8,000 British until eleven o'clock, when 4,000 French came to our aid. The battle was prolonged until about half-past two o'clock, at which time it was no longer doubtful. The English and French cheered together, and gave the Rooskies a last charge, when, retiring across the valley and bridge of Inkerman, at three o'clock I was glad to see their ugly backs turned in the right direction. When evening closed, and they called the roll, they would be surprised to find they had left behind them in killed, wounded, and prisoners, 2,000 more than our entire force!

Inkerman was a surprise. A surprise is lawful in war. It may, or it may not, be successful. The Russians planned a victory, and gained a defeat. They had all the advantages: a grand army—a powerful artillery—the choice of ground— time to attack, and open their fire upon an unprepared foe.

We purchased our victory with the blood of a hundred officers and a third of our force. It was a great triumph, but dearly won, and will cause tears of sorrow at many a home fireside soon. The Lord Jehovah fought on our side, and to Him be all the honour and glory.

We now retired to our tents for the night, to eat our ration dinner, and talk over the events of this memorable day. We had a joyful young fellow in our camp last night. I heard his laugh, the last and loudest. He was a general favourite in the regiment, and had been with me on foreign service in former times. Being early killed, I sent a party in search of his mangled body. He was found among the slain, and brought to my tent. He slept tonight under the colours of his old regiment. Poor fellow! he was nearly cut in two by a cannon-shot. Next day we buried him with military honours close to our camp. A bit of stick marked his grave, with his name and rank—'Captain Alix, Royal Regiment'.

The next painful duty was a letter to his parents.

6th. A battle-day is one of terror and excitement. The day after the battle is one of reflection, of thankfulness, of sympathy, of sorrow.

At four p.m. Sir George Cathcart, Generals Strangways and Goldie, with eleven other officers, were to be buried on Cathcart's Hill, Lord Raglan attending. Fourteen of the brave and gallant officers of the Guards were interred together near the Windmill. All others were buried here and there, in some snug corner near to where they fell. The Windmill and Cathcart's Hill became two remarkable places in this war—one as a cemetery, the other as a look-out post. There was an old underground vault, which Sir John Campbell dived into as a winter quarter. The Windmill stood about a mile to the right, now converted into a powder magazine. An old garden enclosure of some extent was selected as a sort of pen for the gathering of the Russian wounded. Here they were ranged round the walls, as thick as they could lie, for the convenience of the army surgeons to use their carving-knives, who were amputating for three days. The unfortunate disabled were day and night exposed to the cold without any covering, nothing to lie on but the wet sod, groaning, yelling, agonised, and dying. The dead being removed, fresh patients were brought in and filled their places. The whole side of the country was covered with wounded. Fatigue parties from every corps were out all day collecting them. They accumulated at different points until brought forward to the great slaughter-house yard at the Windmill. They had lain out in the cold and rain for two nights perishing, and when raised from the ground their wounds opened afresh, and many groaned away their tortured lives from the shattered shell before they reached the surgeon's knife. I never witnessed in all my days such a frightful scene of human misery. It made one's heart bleed. The strife was over; those men but did their duty, and who could blame them? It was by their ambitious master, who commanded time and place, had brave troops and fresh, led by his sons and by Generals of high degree, and well versed in war—who possessed all that could make a mighty host brave and formidable, and sure of conquest, that these men were sent up these hills, and were sent back to say, 'It can't be done'.

It crossed my mind, in the midst of the great conflict, that our people at home were assembled in the House of God, and might be repeating and praying that beautiful prayer, 'From battle, murder, and sudden death, Good Lord deliver us', at the moment when the Czar of Russia pushed on his troops in defiance of the Christian Sabbath, saying, 'I care not for the Lord of Hosts', and sent 10,000 souls from earth—where to?

7th. I went out early to have another ramble over the battleground, and to form some opinion of the general position—how it was we were not all knocked to bits and driven into the sea, according to order. There were many of the wounded still scattered about in the bush. I found odd ones here and there, some glad, others careless and looking stern, first at broken limbs and then at me, as much as to say, 'Why am I left here to die, after three nights' suffering?'

Amongst all the dead where Cathcart fell, I found but two living soldiers. Both had lain there, disabled, on the road since the battle. They lay in their blood, parched with thirst, two rainy nights, and would not die. Those two men were hardy old Russian soldiers,

R

and did not lie together. I got off my horse, and filled my tin pot with good rum-and-water, and let them drink. Poor fellows: how they did enjoy it! It brought back life and hope. One of them grasped and kissed my hand, looking up to the skies, and speaking in his own, to me unknown, tongue. I gave them some biscuit too, and now came down their deadly foes to bury their dead. There was an immense empty limekiln here, which the Turks hit upon at once to dispose of their share of the labour. They went lazy and disgusted to work, dragging the dead by the heels, and pitching them into this huge pit, until a hundred of the human race were lying on top of each other, in all the distorted, frightful positions in which they fell. I gazed down upon this hideous spectacle of mangled humanity, and shocked my own nerves with the sight. A man kept count (as they were cast in) for the official returns. I was told the pit contained, when full, 100 bodies. As for my two living friends, I had them moved away out of the tender mercies of those Turkish fanatics, and I hope they live. Before our own men were buried, I wandered amongst them. What ghastly wounds! What varied positions! That man was in the act of loading his firelock. His left hand grasps the barrel, his right hand raised to ram down the charge. He fled from life so quickly that his muscles never relaxed; he holds his firelock fast. That one lies on his back, white and livid, all his blood beside him in a pool. Here a ball passed through the eye. I can see no other mark. This body is riddled with shot; both hands shattered here. And here, again, both legs are broken. This man's jaw-bone is carried away; his comrade's knee-cap is shot off, and four balls went through his body. There is a multitude of dead here, many of whom passed away in agony; others look as if peacefully asleep. This young officer lies at his tent-door partly dressed. He had just got out of bed, when a ball passed through his head, and he was gone. Such scenes of woe picture what the human heart is subjected to endure, and the human frame to suffer. Hear those piercing cries. Men don't often cry, but now they rend the air with life's last shriek of agony. They are being carried away on mules, their legs and arms, and mutilated bodies, only hanging together.

Here I met the kind Sir John Pennefeather. 'Did you ever hear anything so terrible as the screams of those poor fellows?' he said. 'I am going away to get out of hearing such misery. They are all about my tent there, lying day and night on the wet ground, starving and dying, and screeching in agony.'

I might write on for days, and not finish the small part of the tragedy that came under my own eyes.

The Russians committed two great blunders on the battle-day

which relieved our anxiety extremely.   One was this: Early in the
morning Prince Gortschakoff entered the valley of Balaclava, with
a corps of cavalry, artillery, and infantry.   He did not advance far
until he opened a fire of great guns, and made a grand show of his
force.   That his object was a feint was soon discovered, but did not
stop Bosquet, with a few thousand men, coming to our aid at the
nick of time.   From below the Prince could not see this movement
of French troops.   They came along the slope of the hill at a quick
pace, Zouaves leading, at the moment when our men were giving
way for want of ammunition.   The Zouaves now saw their prey
and were let go—they went at them like tigers, fresh, active, and
willing, their very quaint-like dress throwing a chill over the
Rooskies, who formed squares, a most convenient movement for
those light troops, who rattled amongst them volleys of musketry,
and then went at them with the bayonet.   The Russian guns still
did great execution, but the *esprit fort* of the army was on the
wane, and one united rush of French and English troops finished off
this grand field-day.

The second mistake in our favour was the loss of a whole division of the enemy, which might have changed the fortune of the
day.   They had orders to make the centre attack on our position, by
forcing their way up a deep, craggy ravine, very steep, and one of
the strongest and most easily defended places I ever saw.   In the
darkness and drizzling rain our friends took a wrong turn coming
up the glen, and got into a *cul-de-sac*, where they stuck too long to
be useful.   Had they been discovered and had we troops to spare,
they might all have been destroyed or made prisoners.   War is a
series of difficulties and errors.

Gortschakoff waited in the valley to cut off our retreat to Balaclava, expecting, as a matter of surety, that the whole allied army
would have been entirely defeated, and the war decided by a *coup
de main*, our shipping destroyed, and no means left for a single
man to escape!   We certainly were placed in as difficult and dangerous position as any army was ever jammed into, and nothing
but the hand of God directed us to hold out and fight hard to keep
our ground.   If Prince G. had advanced two miles farther into the
valley, and threatened Balaclava, the French could not have come
to our aid in the battle.   If the Russian column had not been lost
in the *cul-de-sac*, the centre of our *cordon militaire* would have
been cut, and the effect disastrous.

With all our success, there was a panic and a division of opinion
amongst our Generals—an uneasy feeling.   Another such victory
would have ruined us.   Admiral Lyons insisted on our holding
Balaclava, after the ships had been ordered to clear out; and lucky

that the English Lyon prevailed. Somehow, we struggled on, and the Rooskies lost the great prize. From prisoners we heard that 'our forces were very small, we made a great show in tents, we were all very rich, there was no end to the wealth in the camps, and before sundown all the plunder was to be at their disposal'.

It was late in the forenoon when Lord R. determined to get up two eighteen-pounders. With great exertion they were got to the crest of our position, and went to work like good ones. They were discovered, and pegged into from two Russian batteries, which were doing us much damage, and now they got our range, killed the Commander and some of the gunners. New men sprang forward, got their range to a nicety, and demolished both batteries. I went down afterwards to see the damage at one battery, sixteen horses in harness, with the gunners and drivers all lying in one great pool of blood. The other was in the very same condition, with seventeen horses killed. A round shot from one of those very eighteen-pounders of ours took the head clean off a driver, but he held his whip so tight in his hand I could not release it from his grasp. The gun-carriages were all smashed, but they cleverly carried away their guns. They left behind them intrenching tools, with which they intended to fortify themselves on our position the same night!

The Inkerman heights were considered the safest part of our position, and the least likely to invite attack. Owing to the distance, the Guards were excused from trench work, and were living at comparative ease until this gunpowder plot exploded! After the battle, the heights were fortified and put in a state of defence, a good look-out established, and no chance of our friends paying us such another visit.

48,000 Russians had just come down from Perekop to aid in this battle, accompanied by the Grand Dukes Michael and Nicholas, who, I believe, carried back the despatches to their Papa, which must have torn his ambitious heart.

9th. The hammering siege goes on. Every hole and corner inside and outside of the town is being made stronger daily.

A sale of the officers' effects killed in action is held daily in the different camps: Sir George Cathcart's, Colonel Seymour's, and Captain Butler's today.

10th. Anniversary of the Battle of the Nivelle between England and France. I hope we will have no more quarrels. General Order: 'Colonel Bell, Royal Regiment, to command the 1st Brigade, 3rd Division.' (He commanded a company at the 'Nivelle'.)

11th. No end to the rains. Country one ocean of mud. Everyone wretched; trenches full of water. It is wonderful how the men survive the excessive fatigue, privation, and want of everything.

People say, 'Sebastopol will fall soon'. A young engineer says, 'We will be in there in six days'. I said, not for six months. This shut him up; he only looked as if I knew nothing about it.

12th. Cleared up. Divine service in camp. Took a walk to warm myself, and look at the graves of the brave, not far from my hall-door. Sir George Cathcart lies here, my old friend Goldie sleeps on his right, Strangways on his left, and Seymour at his feet, and many others keep them company.

Soon after dark this evening a tremendous fire opened from the town upon the advance of the French position, wind off land, no sound from the guns reached us, the crimson flash told the tale. I ran up to the quarry hill to see the contest. Unfortunately for my own comfort, peace, and tranquillity, I never could keep my nose out of anything! It was a brilliant sight, but rather dangerous to those engaged. After an hour's fighting in the dark, and a few cartloads of men killed and wounded, the gamecocks retired to their respective posts till next time.

A Pole deserter came into our camp today. He says, 'The Royal Dukes are in Sebastopol, the Emperor is coming, and another grand attack upon us is talked of. They are told, if they desert, the French and English cut off their ears. Their daily ration is three pounds of black bread, and one-third of a pound of meat—nothing else, except when going to fight, they get a little rakee, a spirit which sets them wild. The officers and non-commissioned officers beat the soldiers. They have 20,000 men in the city, 30,000 in our rear, and 50,000 on our right in camp on the north side.'

13th. It poured rain all night. Nothing can be more wretched than the camp and its furniture.

Men in the trenches twenty-four hours at a time, soaked to the skin. No change when they come up to their miserable tents, hardly a twig now to be got to boil their bit of salt pork. Short of rations, too, for want of transport. Everything cheerless, the sick lie down to die in peace in the miry clay, they have no energy left. Thousands might have been saved, but for the red tape! How many more are yet to suffer?

CHAPTER
19

Red Tape, Neglect and Misery

14TH. Last night the wind increased to a hurricane; the tents are all down or blown to rags. It pours in torrents; the poles shoot through the old decayed canvas tops, and down they come by the run, Anything and everything exposed is blown away out of sight; barrels or casks, full or empty, once set in motion away they go never to return—clothes, hats, caps, blankets, rugs, buffalo robes. It was a terrible night, and lucky was the soldier or sailor who kept his house standing over his head till morning. I had hard work to weather the gale myself, but my external mud wall, and my servants hammering down the pegs every now and then, while I held the pole inside, kept all up upright.

The top of a wet, raw, cold November morning is not an agreeable look-out in any country, and with all the accumulated misery collected on those barren hills, I could not resist a laugh when I looked out of my den upon the very ludicrous scene around. The first curious thing I observed was a head with a red nightcap on it, whose owner lay under the weight of a wet tent. After shouting in vain for a while, with the rain pattering on his face, the red nightcap disappeared under cover. This was poor Captain N——e; he left a bonnie little wife an early widow! Under the next tent some living things were rolling about nearly smothered—four officers who had all gone to roost in the usual way since they had got beds and blankets, were now in their shirts, and not able to reach any covering. At length there was a sally, and out they crept, determined to raise the prostrate house of wet canvas. Every effort only made matters worse; the cords cut their legs, the old tent split like a ship's sail in a gale of wind, and flapped about their naked bodies, when they all took to their heels and disappeared amidst roars of laughter. I lay *perdu*. Had I opened my door for the reception of strangers, one gush of such a hurricane might have whirled my tent into the air. I still held the pole tight, to keep it steady, fearing every moment it would shoot through the top, and descend upon me like a wet blanket. The whole town was now down, church and all, the General, Sir Richard England, under the ruins of the last edifice (a marquee). He scrambled out with a blanket about him, and made for an old wall, where he lay for shelter. The hospital tent lay upon the dead! Horses were blown from their picket-posts. Weakly men were whirled off their legs, or could not resist the violence of the wind until they were far away down from their lines. This was all wretched, but still we were on dry ground, as commonly expressed, while ships and sailors were battling with the deep, and going down, down, down, one after another. No coast could be more fatal in a storm. There rode our ships, under craggy and perpendicular cliffs, to be battered to staves, without remedy, within a few lengths of the harbour, where they were refused admittance the day before. The red-tape system, it was said, caused the loss of eight fine ships and their unhappy crews. The *Prince*, screw steamer, a noble ship, laden with clothing for the famishing army, provisions, powder, shot, shell, and stores, was all in pieces, scattered along the coast next morning, the bodies of the poor crew being battered against the rocks. I heard that the captain of this ship made several applications to be admitted into Balaclava Harbour the day previous, being apprehensive of a storm, but was refused a berth—I won't say upon what grounds. The loss was most deplorable, but those things are kept close. A ship was driven ashore to the north side of Sebastopol, the sailors took to the rigging, and the Cossacks came down and shot them out of their last death-grip—like cowardly savages!

All now very cheerless; our camp-ground for twenty miles boundless in desolation, gloom, and deep mire. Officers and men sat looking at each other in a sort of despair, shivering in wet rags. I see no help, but hope on, hold fast, cling to life, and am thankful we are not at sea. In the midst of all this pleasing attitude of affairs, a ration of green, raw coffee berry was served out to the men and officers! A mockery in the midst of all their misery. Nothing to roast coffee, nothing to grind it, no fire, no sugar; and unless it was meant that we eat it as horses do barley, I don't see what use the men could make of it, except what they have just

done, pitched it into the mud! How patient those men of mine;
how admirably they behave. In silence they bear with all privations; away they go to their daily bread, ankle deep in mud, and
wet to the skin, down to the trenches. Thus is the British soldier
most to be admired. This is discipline; here he is in all his glory.

17th. Everyone building mud walls around their tents, and
fortifying against another storm, dry, and cold. Siege drags on, and
powder getting scarce. I foresee it will be a winter struggle.

18th. Changed my ground, and pitched my tent on a slope
facing the Redan, at the entrance to the valley of death, so called,
as I remarked formerly, from the men of our division going down
by this way to the trenches, and so many of them never returning.
I now began to build a dry stone wall all round my tent outside the
ropes, a laborious work, but it gave me a good space inside my walls,
which were four feet high. My entrance gateway was of hewn
stone; there was plenty of it up at the quarry, a quarter-mile off. I
had willing men to aid me. I had the stones rolled all the way;
they fitted well. I built my gate posts, went to Balaclava, picked
up some bits of wreck, made a door, plenty of dead men's buff belts
lying about, which made good hinges, and I slung my gate. Being
now secure from wild dogs by night, and stragglers by day, my
friend, Doctor H., and my Adjutant, Turner, pitched beside me.
We messed together on anything we could catch, settled down for
the winter—determined to brave all, and no surrender.

No time to note anecdotes, or one might fill a volume. Collecting the dead for interment on the day after the late battle, two
Irish soldiers were carrying a Russian to the pit. Colonel W.
passing by, cast his eye on the body, and thought he saw it move.
'Where are you going?' he said. 'To bury this Rooshin, yer honour.'
'Why, you rascals, he's alive.' 'Oh, yes, yer honour, but we had a
consultation 'pon him; 'tis a mighty bad case, and ye see, he can't
live long!' The funeral was postponed.

Many a man, I fear, was buried alive, supposed to be dead from
cholera; all hurry-scurry to get them under ground.

When the Russian army began to retreat, they were followed up
sharp by our riflemen, who dropped off one by one as the enemy
neared the town. One gallant fellow alone continued the chase.
We watched him with great interest as he crept along the hillside,
loading and firing from behind the rocks, and making sure of his
game. He could not see his danger, nor could we give him warning that a whole column was crossing his path on the crest of the
hill, and his days were numbered. He crept on to the top, and all
at once found himself alongside an army. He acted promptly and
with great decision, fired his rifle into the middle of the flock, right

about face, and down hill as hard as he could tear, and got clear off, when we expected to have seen him riddled with shot. When out of danger, he halted to load, and went leisurely back to join his company. Perhaps he never mentioned the adventure to anyone except in joke. A characteristic type of a brave British rifleman.

When I remonstrated with one Barney Quin, a broth of an Irishman for fighting, 'did you not hear the bugle to retire? You seem to pay no attention to orders?' 'Och, sure, an it's murder to go back, when the bush is full of them vagabones,' raising his fire-lock, and taking another crack into the thicket. The Inkerman battle was fought chiefly in the oak bush from three to four feet high.

20th. Raw, cold, and rainy; 200 riflemen just gone down to drive some Russians away from our front, where they have established themselves in what we call the ovens—caves in the rocks. Hark, I hear them at it. I'm off to the quarry hill. How dark, and cold, and dreary, nothing to be seen but the spark of the rifle, and the crimson flash from the never-ceasing cannon.

21st. Our rifles succeeded last night after a sharp contest in taking the ovens. Lieutenant Tryon, a gallant young officer, was killed with eight of his men, and fifteen wounded. The Russians made a desperate attack today to regain this post, but failed.

23rd. What a fearful storm; the rains have swelled into torrents, streaming down the valleys like highland floods, country inundated, roads, or rather mud tracks, impassable. Men are worked to death in reality, rations curtailed. Men from the trenches this morning going down again tonight in this dreadful weather, wet to the skin. Don't see how they can survive.

24th. Rains continue. All is dreary and desolate; the stretchers passing with the wounded as usual. Lieutenant Martin, R.E., just brought up very badly wounded by a rifle-ball in the groin. The doctors can't extract the ball; he suffers much.

27th. Continued heavy rains, constant alarms, rations falling short, no rum today, a terrible damper to the poor men. They consider this the greatest privation. They go down to the trenches wet, come back wet, go into the hospital tents wet, die the same night, and are buried in their wet blankets next morning! Nine of my good men lay stretched and dead this morning outside one tent, rolled up in their blankets waiting to be carried home! We have given up the old funeral firing parties long ago; hardly time now to bury the dead. I asked our surgeon if there was anything that could be done to save the sick. He said, 'no, nothing; they are too far gone when they come to the hospital tents. I have got no medical restoratives, and they snuff out.' So it is, they die from overwork, privation, and neglect. The regimental surgeons do all they can; make continual demands on the chief of the medical department, but get nothing. Staff-Surgeon Pine reported to the General the other day, 'It is just a mathematical calculation. The strength of your division is 3,000 men, so many die daily from overwork, want of food and clothing, short living, bad food, and no medical comforts. I calculate on the utter annihilation of the 23rd Division of your army before spring, unless something is done to preserve life.' Pine told me the same. He spoke out truths very unpalatable, and was removed from the division to die in Balaclava shortly afterwards! He saw that we were beginning the winter with a perishing army in want of everything, but it was next to treason to divulge anything that might reach the public. The P.M.O. here issued very fine orders to his medical officers, recommending all sorts of hospital comforts for the sick, when he must know, or ought to have known, that a ration of salt pork and some green raw coffee berry, is the sum total of their dying comforts!

Look into this tent and observe the household. You see it is in rags all about the skirting, and the floor is a thick paste baked nearly dry by the heat of the fevered patients. That bundle of a dirty, wet blanket rolled up contains a living creature, once a comely useful soldier's wife, now waiting for death to release her from such misery. This nice-looking youth is one of my band; hear how well and cheery he talks of Christ and his sure recovery, and home, and friends who will take such care of him. Poor lad, death has him already in his grip, and will never let him rise from that damp sod. Those other men lying about, who are able to pay attention, and glad to hear a kind word, hear a Bible warning, or an encouraging paragraph, and seem thankful. That young woman, once perhaps the belle of her village, now in rags, but in good health, is eating her dinner, the broth of a bit of salt fat pork, with broken brown biscuit pounded into it; a tin plate and iron spoon is all her fortune. I had ten or twelve women who stuck to the regiment throughout the winter. 'What is that down the hill there?' 'O, sir, that is poor Mrs. H——, sitting on her husband's grave; she is always there shivering in the cold.'

Visited all the outposts with Sir John P——. The bridge over the Tchernaya is now cut and commanded by our batteries. We got a full view of all their works before being discovered. When they did see us, bang went their guns from the upper lighthouse battery, ploughing up the ground about our horse's feet, which made us scamper out of range. I rather like those little adventures. If one does not venture his nose here and there, he might as well be at Ealing with some of my friends who are satisfied to read *The Times*, and go to bed after an oyster supper.

28th. Road to Balaclava impassable. No ration of rum for two days. I but note a repetition of daily events, one day so much like another, it wearies myself.

29th. A most frightful day of rain and storm. All the elements of destruction seem to be gathering against us. It is dragging on a miserable existence in miry clay. No fuel, no clothing, no rum, short rations, no communication with Balaclava, wheels cannot move, cattle starving, so weak and exhausted that they have not power to move under a load. Forty-five men of our division died last night.

30th. This is a bright day. Lord Raglan paid me a visit at my tent door, admired my fortress, as he called it. It was now ornamented with cannon-shot from Sebastopol, my gate pillars bearing two very large shells. His lordship always had a kind word with me about the Peninsula where we served together. I asked him to confirm my appointment as Brigadier. He said that was done at the Horse Guards. I applied to the Horse Guards. The reply was 'they had nothing to do with it'. Very encouraging. But the Horse Guards had everything to do with all military appointments. As for Lord Raglan there never was a kinder heart nor a more brave, cool, decided, gallant soldier. He could not say an unkind word to anyone.

1st December 1854. Rain, pouring rain, raw and damp, but it does not extinguish the fire of the guns. Hardest fire in the night, and at early dawn, to let us know they are wide awake. Can't get up a gun to replace those disabled from the heavy mud roads.

2nd. A dry day. Got my house put in order. Everything damp, mouldy, and mildewed. All dry and snug before night. About half-past four o'clock this morning a Russian yell woke us up, a sure sign of an attack somewhere. The minié rifle and great guns went at it pell-mell. They attacked our front parallel, got into our trenches with the bayonet to tease our people. The British lion was up, and with one cheer and a charge drove the whole swarm of Rooskies (as our men called them) head over heels on their main body, and far from our lines. We got off with a loss of eight killed and six wounded. Of the latter, one man had seven bayonet wounds, and such is the constant annoyance we are subject to.

3rd. Very wet morning. No church parade. Had a little service in my tent for the servants. Damp, raw, cold, and dreary.

4th. An awful storm of rain last night. The flood-gates of heaven seemed to open upon the camp; the hailstones pattered on the tents like rifle-balls. 10,000 men on duty were paralyzed, dead

to everything, soaked to the skin before they marched off, and lay
in the trenches all night as much dead as alive, but death came
afterwards. Average loss now is sixty-five men a day. I hope it
will not soon be double.

5th. Another terrible night of wind and rain. Rode over to
the farmhouse to see Lord Raglan; the mud was knee deep all the
way up to his door. Saw the Duke of Newcastle's despatch about
the cavalry charge at Balaclava. Great praise from the Queen to
all concerned. Always gracious, most generous and thoughtful,
but it was only a useless destruction of life and loss of our cavalry
to give battle against such odds. Our men longed to measure
swords with Russian horsemen, who will long remember the
weight of a British sabre and the strong arm of an Enniskillen
Dragoon.

The enemy opened a terrible fire last night against our works.
Shot, shell, and rifle-bullets fluttered about to the great danger of
her Majesty's troops. The elements were illuminated with the
flashing of great guns, and the shell fuze rolled overhead like meteor
stars. It turned out a feint to harass our people, so we returned
to our cold, damp dwelling to finish another sleepless night.

6th. Found a wretched little covering in the celebrated Balaclava, where I sent my cattle to save their lives. My groom prowled
about all day collecting bits of timber, and brought up a load to the
camp now and then; the six miles cost him twelve hours' work
going and coming.

7th. Visited our advanced works and reported to the General.
The whole line of our defence I found in a tumble-down condition,
with all the _débris_ of broken carriages, guns, and the material of a
siege, ponds of water in the trenches, and mud ankle-deep. We fire
a shot at their works now and then, which they do not mind, but
go on working like ants at the Redan and Malakoff, which are now
tenfold stronger than they were fifty-three days ago when we began
the siege.

8th. Frost last night, very cold, and no fires; not a twig to be
seen now as thick as one's finger; all cut away and burned up.
Staff-Surgeon Boyle just died in the next tent—a few weeks in camp
finished his young life.

10th. Another detachment of young lads arrive to fill up gaps
in my regiment. They are fine, healthy, blooming boys; a rush to
look at them and their red cheeks! Where will they be in a month?
Forty of the last batch died in three weeks. I will keep them out
of the trenches for a week to acclimatise them in a small way.

12th. Last night about twelve o'clock I was roused up by a
more than usual roar of Russian artillery. 'To arms!' an attack on

our front—up and away to the alarm-post in a jiffy. Got my brigade under arms in the dark. All that we could see was the direction of attack from the crimson-flashing of the cannon, the rolling of shells through the air, and a carcass pitched here and there to discover our position. A carcass is a large shell, with five holes, filled with combustible, which throws out, and all around it a brilliant light. It does not explode, but burns out where it falls, and discovers the troops, when the guns open upon them. This was a grand flare-up; about 500 killed and wounded in this nocturnal amusement. The attack was made just at the place I reported insecure the other day; the damage is done, and now it will be attended to.

I heard a great deal of grumbling and discontent today amongst officers, about the everlasting salt pork and hard biscuit. The people at home were deceived regarding our position, some being congratulated by their nearest of kin at their present comforts in camp, and no wants, etc., etc. This induced me to write a letter to *The Times*, which was entirely successful. A Mr. Cook in Bath, a gentleman I had never seen or heard of, sent me a note saying he had read my letter in *The Times*, and took the liberty of sending to me for my disposal twenty-one cases of such things as he thought would find acceptance, all paid for as well as the freight. He also said that anything more that I required would be also willingly sent as a free gift. This was generous indeed, and most acceptable. It came at the right time too, and gave us a feasting, the sick men having the first choice. One of the cases contained twenty-one hams! After this, many presents were sent out by anonymous friends, and good things began from that time to flow into the camp! The letter which had such a salutary effect was as follows:

To the Editor of *The Times*

'Sir, As the eyes of the world are all turned this way, and the hearts of the generous people of England are with their army, I take the liberty to suggest that our country might do us some little service at no cost, while we are endeavouring to perform our duties, under very trying circumstances, on the bleak and barren hills of the Crimea, before the great city.

'I would propose that the Home Government, or some patriotic company should send out a ship to Balaclava, laden with stores of provisions for the officers of this army—such as flour, butter, onions, oatmeal, tea and sugar, rice, pepper, curry-powder, "Moore and Buckley's Concentrated Preserved Milk", hams, and pickles; we don't ask for any luxuries; the above would be all luxury to us, but, above all, flour and butter. We are all cooks and labourers now, and scarcely an officer who cannot make his flour scone or a dough pudding, as well as handle his spade and pick to aid in the building of his mud hut underground; with a barrel of flour and a small kit of butter in every little mess, we should be independent for a long winter coming on us. Short commons and cold fingers are never very agreeable, coming home from the trenches and outpost duties, when there is nothing in the *larder*! I would wish it understood that if anyone undertook this speculation a remunerating price for the good things named would render it satisfactory, and every article should have its fixed price. As it is, there are speculators who do bring things to Balaclava, and sell them at a profit of 400 or 500 per cent. I ought to have included candles, and oil and lamp-wick, for our nights are long and dreary, and few in camp that are not roused up every night for duty of one sort or other; indeed, our hardest and most dangerous work is performed in the dark. A return ship might have plenty of ballast, in the shape of cannon-shot, to any amount for the picking up; they lie on the hillsides and valleys in thousands and tens of thousands—all lately the property of the Emperor Nicholas, but now at the disposal of anyone on this side of Sebastopol! Our men are cheerful under privation and hard work such as the English army never before encountered; we are a savage-looking people; very hard up for fuel, not a twig now to be seen for many miles in the distance; the men grub up the roots of the late brushwood to cook their little rations, and I am not ashamed to say that I cut and carried home on my back, a distance of two miles, a bundle of sticks for my own fire, to cook my ration of salt pork. Being rather an old soldier, I cared but little who saw me at this work of necessity. Little do people know what it is to campaign in the mud and mire on the bare hills of the Crimea, but hope is always alive in the hearts of her Majesty's army here, and we all say "No surrender". We only look for *The Times* to see that our country is satisfied. We have a kind, generous, and considerate chief, and if some are still doomed at the evening of life to go round like the horse in the mill without promotion, better die in harness than that war should ever approach the firesides of dear old England.

I am, Sir, your obedient servant,

GEORGE BELL, Colonel, Royal Regiment,

Commanding 1st Brigade, 3rd Division.

Camp near Sebastopol, Dec. 12, 1854.'

13th December 1854. Received a copy of the 'Inkerman' despatch. One is always gratified in seeing their names honourably mentioned in a public despatch from the seat of war; besides, it brings its reward. Her Majesty was pleased to confer on me the distinguished honour of a 'Companion of the Bath', which is only given for some good service in the field before the enemy, the name being first submitted and recommended by the General commanding the army.

14th. We are getting up guns and mortars today to the artillery park. It required thirty-eight horses to drag up one mortar through the mud from Balaclava. The Russians say that their three best Generals will soon be in the field to shut us up, viz. Generals Frost, Snow and Rain. Very facetious of them to say so. *Nous verrons*, who will best weather the storm? Whoever pounds longest will win.

15th. Rain in torrents all day; all swamp, ankle deep in miry clay. Almost too much for humanity to contend with. No rains ever extinguish the fire of the Russian guns that bellow away day and night like thunder.

16th. Rained all last night, and snow this morning; the deep misery and wretched condition of the troops cannot be described.

17th. The snow has melted away, and left the whole country in one ocean of mud and slush. From the camp to Balaclava, horses and mules lie dead and dying all the way marking the original path. Poor things! it makes one's heart sore to look at their agonies. Worn down by hard work and starvation, they drop in the miry clay never to rise again.

18th. Saint Nicholas day, the patron saint of Russia. Got notice to prepare to resist an attack tonight upon our trenches. I suppose much will be left to the decision of the saint. There are plenty of them, but all non-combatants.

19th. I was roused up in the middle of the night to take command of the troops in advance, an attack being expected at daylight. Groped my way in the dark down to the trenches, and posted 1,500 men on the defensive. Waited till dawn, and then went forward to reconnoitre. Stole up to within 600 yards of their advance battery, but all was quiet. They were working like bees, digging a ditch twelve feet wide by twelve feet deep, leading down from the Redan, with rifle-pits in front. Some of my stupid men showed themselves now, when a brisk fire was opened at every head visible. Two men were killed and three wounded. I had to run the gauntlet over the brow of the hill back to my post, the balls whistling over my head and turning up the sods at my feet. I never kept in one direction, but went on tacking about, the safest way to keep out of a direct line of fire. Since my former report on this part of the position, it has been well watched; and being

myself the cause of all the trouble, I suppose it was all right
sending me to look after it.

20th.   Fine day, and sunshine delightful.   It works up one's
martial feelings to see a clear sky, even for a day.   A good omen
for the 17th and 89th Regiments, just arrived from England, the
latter added to my brigade.   I asked Major Egerton to take pot-luck
with us, by the way of breaking him in.   He was rather surprised
when he was asked to sit down upon the sod and begin.   Four of
us sat round a pot of Irish stew, with our tin plates and iron spoons,
a piece of cold pork on the sideboard, and the kettle boiling outside,
to make a jorum of rum punch.   We were not to be sneezed at
this day; the first to entertain a field officer just come from a
London club.   I believe the gallant major dined on his rations the
next day, and many a day afterwards.   I know that we did.   After
riding over much ground, and showing my friend a hundred thousand ugly customers, called Rooskies, I told him to be always on
the look-out, and sleep with one eye open.   Then I bid him adieu,
and went home to my work.   I laid my tent with flat stones, to
keep off the damp, and raised my little sleeping cot, stretched a
long plank before it eighteen inches high, put a curtain across, and
secured one half the tent as my private apartment and dormitory.
Here nobody intruded; the other half or north side of the pole, was
our banqueting hall and reception room.   No one was admitted
until a certain number of pounds of mud was scraped off his boots
with an iron hoop by my man Tub, who sat at the gate.   Fortunately one day I fell in with a little round table, I won't say how,
which apparently belonged to a Turkey, from its short legs, about a
foot long, as they squat low when feeding.   I cut a hole in the
centre and cut off its legs, raised my tent-pole three inches, slipped
in my table, raised it to the proper height.   Then I drove three
stakes into the ground, made the whole level, and nailed all tight.
Some one looted three old chairs, and next day we all sat at table
like Christians.   I also bored a hole through my tent-pole, and
passed a ramrod through it for slinging my sword-sash, etc.   Who
says an old soldier cannot make himself snug in fine weather?

There goes a salute from the Royal Albert flagship, for the departure of Admiral Dundas, succeeded by Sir Edmund Lyons.
Sixty-fourth day of the siege, and the guns blazing away as fresh
as ever; their batteries increasing daily.

21st.   At one o'clock this morning, the Rooskies made a sortie
on our position, right and left.   The darkness became visible, from
the flashing of guns, exploding of shells, firelights, and all sorts of
flare-up combustible for the destruction of life.   It was a bright, but
dangerous scene.   The loss in my brigade was one field-officer,

Major Moller, dangerously wounded; Captain Frampton and Lieutenant Clerk missing, 14 killed, and 17 wounded. The Russians attacked with 10,000 men, but signally failed in every attempt to surprise our troops. This night fighting is very dangerous work; 'tis part of their game, and an ugly game to play in the dark.

22nd. Pouring rain all day. The men gone to the trenches wet to the skin. All again is gloomy, raw, and cold.

23rd. No such rains since we occupied these barren hills. It poured in torrents all the past night, and continues. Two men died in the trenches. Major M—— died of his wounds, and was buried near his own tent door. All the way to Balaclava one ocean of mud, the starved oxen dotting the miry course, and the Turks cutting them up for food, as the Zouaves cut a steak from a dead camel *en passant*.

Got the shell of an old tin stove, and some charcoal dust from B——, and made something approaching to a fire in my tent. Endured the smoke for two hours; found it unbearable any longer; pitched out the whole concern after being nearly suffocated. The sick are dying by the score. Everything coming, but nothing appears until the men are dead. Two doctors reprimanded in General Order by Lord Raglan for want of attention and care of the sick and wounded (297) on board the *Avon*, ordered from Balaclava to Scutari.[1]

24th. Rain, sleet, and snow. 1,200 men going down on duty, wet to the skin. 89th Regiment one week in camp and have buried fifteen men. The young lads cannot endure the fatigue; they lie down wet on the wet sod, helpless, unattended and shiver away their young lives in silent sorrow.

25th. Christmas Day. Hard frost, clear and cold. No rations for my men, while everyone is making an exertion for a Christmas dinner. I kicked up a dust about this neglect. Commissary said the cattle were stolen or strayed away in the night. At the close of the day he did serve out a small portion of fresh meat. Too late! no fires, or means of cooking. There was no feeling of discontent amongst these orderly soldiers; they bore everything with most wonderful patience.

Dr. H—— would have a plum-pudding for our dinner, and he made it himself, but it was a failure. The salt pork fat, instead of suet, would not amalgamate, and I believe there were other ingredients wanting. It was what the boys call stick-jaw, and I don't think I will ever eat plum-pudding again, at home or abroad.

29th. Poor Major Daly, 89th, died last night. Nine days in the Crimea finished his career.

[1] A reprimand in the camp, and a K.C.B. at home. Wonderful people.

S

The French are aiding us in getting up shot and shell; they say that we have no system. In every department all seems confusion, starving in the midst of plenty, for Balaclava is crammed with all sorts of good things; but there is no transport over this six miles' sea of mud. Then there is so much red-tape, one gets tired being pitchforked from one office to another, and goes home in disgust. These red-tapists, however, never lose a night's rest nor a day's rations. Few get behind the scenes in the French camp. Their system may be better than ours, but they have not so much work on hand. They have no 'special correspondent' to report on all they do, so that people at home are not in their secrets. They have plenty of men, and they sacrifice them by thousands to gain any advantage, and so often fail. Their losses are not reported, while everything we do is booked and sent home by Mr. Russell for the press, and I think he astonished all England with his 'o'er true tales'.

30th. Hard firing all night. Men exhausted and dying. 2,900 of 3rd Division sick today. The sick and non-effective in our small army amount to 10,000 men; biting cold.

31st. Snow on ground, Divine service. Took a long walk to warm myself, and looked into the devoted city, a good deal demolished. Brigade sick today, 896. Poor Turner came back to us from Constantinople with his hands full for our little mess, so we had a capital dinner to finish off the old year. Soup, ham, and potatoes, with a kettle of rum-punch to drink the health of all at home, and shut out old '54, the most memorable year of my life; a year of travel and excitement, of battle and bloodshed, and the thousand other horrors of war. It is to the Lord Jehovah I am indebted for the continuance of my life and preservation, and to Him be all the honour and glory. May peace be established in righteousness! I have seen much this year and former years of the horrors of war, and in it may be included every cruelty and every crime.

1st January 1855. Cold, raw, and rainy. Another twelve months will pass away, and there will be more widows and fatherless children, and weeping and lamentation.

What a jolly, cheerful account of the British army was given in a Parliamentary speech on the 12th December 1854, in order to blind the public. How men can stand up and make such statements when they know very well that our men were dying like dogs from over-work, cold, and starvation, and in want of everything at the very moment when *they* were preparing their speeches over wine and walnuts! The Government of the day knew themselves to be responsible for all our trials, difficulties, and dangers, but were too anxious to keep straight with the public and the press.

O for the simple truth. I wrote my letter to *The Times* on 12th December, which differed so much from the fine speech above referred to that either must have been wrong, and I was condemned, not publicly—they dare not do that—but privately, with a vindictive spirit and every desire to do me wrong. I complained to Lord Raglan, and by him I was supported. He did not disapprove of my letter; on the contrary, he writes to me on 5th of February, before Sebastopol.
Extract:

> Before Sebastopol,
> 5th Feb., 1855.
> My Dear Colonel: I received today your letter of the 3rd. I think it due to you to say that I do not discover anything objectionable in your letter to *The Times*, and you may assure the General Officer to whom you refer that nobody has attempted to create a prejudice against you in any way.
> Yours faithfully,
> (Signed)   Raglan.

His lordship could not do anything but what was becoming the character of a noble and gallant soldier, nor could he say an unkind word to anyone; a better heart never breathed. But a noble lord at home in power did endeavour to injure my prospects. He is gone to his account.

Up to the 6th rain in torrents, soldiers looking miserable in their clay-cold death beds; no fuel, extremely cold, nothing joyful. People at home are led to suppose we are all living in huts, i.e. little wooden houses. We are existing in ragged tents full of slimy mud, the men in the same tatters that stuck to them since the landing, their sole covering, and often a bed of drifting snow by night. Four logs of fuel served out yesterday to my brigade, 3,000 strong. A green tree, branches lopped off, was triumphantly carried into camp by the Turks who are on working pay. Each regiment got about one pound per man to keep himself dry, cook his rations, roast his green coffee, and, as the G.O. said upon this great occasion, 'Be careful that the fires are put out at night!!!' The snow is deep and drifting, my pipkin of water and cruse of oil frozen last night. But what of that when one looks out on their famishing comrades taking their patient but painful departure from all their miseries.

8th. Hard frost and snow; men frost-bitten and found dead in their tents of a morning. Two doctors died last night. A captain of artillery found dead in his tent, suffocated by charcoal. All in a frightful state of confusion for want of system. I have no time to keep a lengthened diary to relate scenes the most painful.

9th. Inspected the Brigade. Found the men all in tatters, but their powder dry. Their old clothes were tied about their half-naked frames, and old knapsacks bound about their legs!

Some pickaxes served out to grub up roots for fuel from under the snow. One Johnny Raw was looking about in despair, when I pointed out to him in a poetic way how to go at it—

> When you see a twig above the snow,
> Dig, and you'll find a root below.

They persevered and laboured until there was not a root left within their reach.

Someone has laid a simple headstone by the grave of poor Strangways. I scraped off the snow, and found the following recorded on one side, and a Russian inscription on the other:

SACRED

TO THE MEMORY OF

BRIGADIER-GENERAL FOX STRANGWAYS,

Killed in Action,

November 5, 1854

Nothing as yet to mark the cold grave of Sir George Cathcart, Goldie, Seymour, Tryon, and others, who lie side by side till the last assembly. What does it matter? 'He is faithful that promised' (John xiv. 3). The death of the body is the life of the soul.

Nearly 15,000 sick, 5,000 killed and wounded, and about 10,000 dead since we landed!

My three servants *hors-de-combat* from fever, frostbite, and diarrhoea. One had both feet frostbitten, became quite helpless, went to hospital, and died—a hale, stout young man!

Scurvy is now prevailing in our ranks. The gums get soft and spongy and sore, the teeth loosen. The men, unable to eat their biscuit, try to soak it in water, which has all along been very scarce. A want of vegetables and lemon juice, together with salt meat, creates this disease. The unhappy P.M.O. was not aware that there were oceans of lemon or lime juice in store at Balaclava, until this horrid disease had gained a victory!

Officers who have favour and influence at home are sent out here at this late hour, to pitch their fortune, and rob us of our inheritance, who have borne the heat and the cold, pestilence and privation, the battle and the siege—we are to be set aside for the elect.

A Colonel of the Guards has just arrived to see what he can get. (All Captains in that favoured corps rank as Lieutenant-Colonels in the Line, and may exchange into the Line and command a regiment at once!) There is nothing vacant, but a Guardsman, even without any service, without ever having smelt powder, must be provided for. So he was posted to command the Brigade, and Colonel G. B——, his senior by fifteen years, was sent back to command his regiment. No comment is necessary. The act is condemned by the voice of the whole camp. He belonged to the dress circle at St. James's. Such favouritism only excites one's pity and contempt. A piece of churchyard fits everybody, and he, poor fellow, has since got his six-feet-by-three. He was an excellent, gentlemanlike, good officer, and no blame to him for working his way up in his profession.

It was intimated to me privately from home that I would get nothing, having written a letter in *The Times*. And so I supposed this to be my first punishment.

10th. Snow gone again, all slush and paste. See those poor horses how long they struggle with death, stretched in the mixture of snow and mud, their heads moulded in the adhesive clay, every now and then making an effort to rise, but too feeble. How the frame quivers in the cold! Witness that agony, and say that the poor brute creation in silent suffering is not less to be felt for than humanity. 'Tis a piteous scene.

Those nine artillery horses, lying in a heap, all died last night in the storm. Look about, and you may see them in scores dead and dying. And see the graves of our poor men, how near they approach our own tent-doors! There lie three officers not twenty yards off, killed in action — 'tis well that they should sleep near their own comrades!

The 46th Regiment, just two months in camp, have buried 189 men! The sick of my own regiment today 356; Brigade ditto, 1,220; the Army, 14,800!

Soldiers are sent from the Balaclava Hospital in shiploads, to die at Scutari. Hundreds are thrown into the Black Sea. They arrive without clothing; a wet blanket covered with vermin, a ragged coat and trousers, with an old forage cap, is the extent of their kit. 1,473 were buried from the hospital in January 1855. Their graves were close to the general hospital. Dead dogs, horses, and vermin lay all about to increase disease. The floors of the hospital were wet, and would not dry. The whole plain was undrained, and the men were poisoned with animal matter. From June '54 to June '55, the hospitals in the Bosphorus received 43,228 sick and wounded soldiers, of whom 5,432 died. Fire and sword contributed but 4,161 admissions, and 395 deaths. In November, December, and January, the admissions into hospitals were 11,000, and amongst this multitude there were but twenty-two shirts! Miss Nightingale issued from her private stores 16,000 shirts.

The men were overcrowded in the hospitals, a murderous process which sent them quickly to the grave. In the open field they might have lived, but they were packed together in wards and corridors, where the stench was intolerable. Diarrhoea, gangrene, cholera rapidly filled the burial-ground, but the vacant places were being continually filled up from the Crimea; 4,000 were admitted in seventeen days in December. But all this is but a brief account of the misery and wretchedness of our army, which was little known to the English public, it being kept as secret as possible.

See a book called *England and her Soldiers* by Miss Harriet Martineau, who explains with wonderful judgment and truth all this wretchedness and misery. She deserves the Legion of Honour.

14th. Up to this date the weather has been worse and worse each day, a succession of snowstorms, intensely cold, and no getting at a root now, the pickaxes are broken, and some of the men are without shoes, their feet tied up in old pieces of knapsack. Nothing coming to camp; all is obscurity; heads of most departments 'froze up'. No end to red tape, and the poor soldier left to die in the mud.

We seldom see any of the red-tapists in our camp. I don't know how they amuse themselves, and wonder if one of them has ever had the curiosity to look into the trenches. I proposed, when there was some snow on the ground, to put runners on the arabas in sleigh-fashion, and get up provisions from Balaclava, a simple matter, and easily accomplished. Oh no! It did not emanate from the proper quarter, and was pooh-poohed. I was a meddler, and so on. In three days the camp might have been amply supplied with abundance of stores from that wretched Balaclava, a place every day presenting a scene of great interest, particularly to a stranger. Varna, when full of the usual variety of rabble, shopkeepers, and allied troops, crowds of natives, and all sorts of vagabonds, could not hold a candle to Balaclava just now. There was the harbour, the mountains, the old Genoese fort, the straggling village, our steamships of war, moored broadside on or across the harbour, to sweep the country, if necessary, crowds of transports and small craft lying in rows closely packed stern to the wharf. Here are six or seven transport with their numbers painted on the quarter, 'laid on for sick', next a Maltese craft full of bottled ale, cheese, and hams, then a monster steamer or two, emptying out bales of hay or troops recently arrived, their bright scarlet coatees and white belts provoking a smile from the ragged, shabby, dirt-bedraggled old stager, with his legs bound up in an old *Rooshan* greatcoat or knapsack. Balaclava is approached from the country through half a mile of liquid mud, from the camp of the 3rd Division through six miles of tenacious clay. One day, to the surprise and satisfaction of all travellers, were found two regiments of French infantry employed in making a road through this Slough of Despond, with intelligence and alacrity, and under the guidance of their officers: at any work of this kind they beat our fellows to sticks. A tape marked the boundary of the road on both sides, a line of men was extended the whole length, who passed stones from hand to hand. Nor were their labours stopped by constant interruptions, throngs of travellers, artillery dragging up guns, twenty horses or more yoked to one carriage, long strings of dragoon horses carrying our forage to camp. Occasionally a sack of barley bursts and the whole contents fall into the mud. The trooper ignores it—no remedy, no use in stopping, better reach the camp with what's left. Now comes a *cortège* of commissariat mules and carts, with biscuit and rum, and next a flock of lean sheep just landed, with their picturesque shepherds, having bearskin caps, crooks, and antique firelocks. Here comes a packhorse with an officer's kit, trunks and bed, valise, looking so clean and new. How different they will look in a week hence. Here you have a dozen or two 'Bono Johnnies', in pairs, each of them carrying out a dead comrade in haste, to put him in a very shallow grave. Mixed up with all these are soldiers, English, French and Turks, on all sorts of errands, eating, drinking, smoking, swearing, thrashing refractory mules, and driving weary ponies that will never reach the camp. Some soldiers' wives are, of course, to be seen straggling through the mud, much in everyone's way, and here comes a smart Cantinière on her horse, suitably clothed, no longer in scarlet pantaloons and boots, but in warm woollen stockings and sabots. The wharf and main street are the chief thoroughfares; in both the mud is knee-deep. The ruts are unfathomable by horses' legs. To add to the dangers of the wharf, the hawsers and chain-cables of the ships are stretched across it, at from six inches to two feet from the ground. Yet here are the Ordnance and Commissariat stores, the military chest, and all the public offices. Here comes everyone to pay or receive money to fetch a truss of hay, a bale of blankets, a great gun, or a tent-pole. Here the ambulance waggons draw up with their wretched and helpless inmates and here lie the boats into which they are transferred for embarkation to the hospital ships.

In the main street almost every house is now a shop or store. A morsel of board a foot long announces that some Jew, Greek, or Maltese rascal supplies spirits, groceries, beer, etc. An unbroken string of carts, waggons, arabas, with dromedaries and pack-ponies, fills the centre of the street, while under the projecting eaves of the shops is a crowd of officers and men, mingled with saddle-horses.

The men are drinking ale and porter at 2s. a bottle, a thick biscuit with a lump of butter or cheese in every man's fist. Officers bawl for tea, hams, or jams, pickles, candles, brandy, American chairs, tobacco, butter, herrings, or anything they can catch, at 500 per cent. above the value. They cram all into holsters and saddle-bags, or secure them in any way for transit to camp. In the midst of the mud, clamour, and confusion, scattered here and there, are the newly arrived mounted staff corps (Irish policemen) in fanciful helmet, red tunic braided with black cord, and mounted on a pie-bald Spanish horse, looking very much as if they had escaped from Astley's, or were the advanced guard of some equestrian troop coming to open a circus in the village. These 'nice young men' prance about in the mire, or stand sentry with drawn sword at a ruined house near the entrance to the town, in the vain hope of preserving some order among the multitude of travellers. An un-happy attempt at imitating an index finger in mud or charcoal, on a white wall, pointing down a very narrow, filthy lane, serves as a guide to the post office, that haven of hope and centre of interest for every man who has a heart and a home. Whether it be mailday or not, no one thinks of leaving Balaclava without a call at the post office, for there is always the chance of a letter or a paper being overlooked. The evening begins to close, and away goes a legion of wild-looking half-naked soldiers, ploughing up to the knees in mud towards their respective encampments, and others to be killed tonight in the trenches, and others having bidden an eternal fare-well to Balaclava. This is Russell's description of this celebrated seaport town, and I endorse it to the very letter.

"'What had you for dinner on Christmas Day?' said a noble young aide-de-camp to one of my men. Answer: 'A bit of char-coal!' 'Have you got your clothes yet?' said he to another old weather-beaten royal. Throwing aside his tattered greatcoat, and lifting one leg bound round with a piece of an old knapsack, 'cloth-ing? No, I'm just as I landed that terrible night in September, and, barrin' a strip of a Rooshan's coat on this t'other leg, I've got no clows at all.' The sleek aide-de-camp, with his polished boots, rode on and asked no more questions."

15th. The snow, which fell heavily last night, was dug out of my tent this morning; everything looking dismal, men shivering to death. See that little party, trying to light a fire. What do you think they have got? Some old shoes, to boil their ration dinner. 'Well, my lads,' I said, 'that is a sort of fuel I never saw tried before.'

'Oh, indeed, sir, they burn very well, if we had more of 'em an' they were a bit dryer.'

Set out on foot to take a turn over to the next division to see Sir Colin Campbell, but floundered about so in the deep snow, I returned home very unwell, doubled up, and nearly frozen without gaining half the distance. My men had a present of a pair of shoes each from the public, but as they were made and supplied by contract they soon went to pieces. Some flannel bandages were issued to men in hospital. They, too, were supplied by contract to the Board of Ordnance, poor, wretched, threadbare things stitched together loosely; the buttons dropped off, no man had a needle and thread, and so they became useless, and this is the way that soldiers are cared for here.

A little visitor comes to see me every night, cuts my biscuit bag, carries the contents into my bed while asleep, then cuts a hole in my blanket and deposits the wool and the biscuit in store against a rough winter. This throws a slight upon the neglect and want of foresight as regards the gathering storm around our army. Wisdom may be gathered from the preparations of a Russian field-mouse, for such was my companion.

16th. The last night was another snowstorm, and I was dug out of my dwelling, i.e. the drift snow had fallen so thick within my walls, I was a frozen up prisoner until released. Stood away to see the result of the past night. Met the 17th Lancers, each with a led-horse, all covered with snow. They kept their brass helmets turned to one side against a sharp, biting north wind and snowdrift. 'Where are you going?' I said. 'To the 4th Division, sir, for the 63rd Regiment. Where will we find them?' 'Their tents are up there on the hill, but the men are nearly all dead.' 'We want to carry the sick down to Balaclava, sir.' 'Rather a rough day,' I said, 'for moving sick who are unable to sit upon a horse.' But it was one of those very considerate arrangements so frequently made. There were only twenty-nine men of the whole regiment fit for duty. I turned into one of my own tents and found five of my poor men dead and frozen. In the hospital tent I asked, 'What rations do the sick get here?' (knowing very well all about it). 'Salt pork and green coffee berry, sir.' Returned to my tent, wrote out an official report of all this frightful scene and barbarous mockery, put the report into the hands of the General to be forwarded to headquarters. Still the men were left to die, and no help for it now. Too late, everything was too late.

17th. Deep snow and hard frost, north-east biting wind. The troops are in a deplorable condition; 365 of my own men in hospital. What is an hospital? Any old tent where sick and disabled are huddled together unfit for duty and under the care of a medical officer.

Up to this time we are accountable for 54,000 British soldiers sent to the Crimea. We have today 14,000 effective men. Where are the 40,000? How artfully it is endeavoured to conceal the gradual decay of the army, and how venomously any officer is marked who dares to use his pen in defence of his perishing comrades, but yet the lamentable accounts appear daily in the English papers in spite of all efforts to suppress the news so unwelcome to some. The press has already told truths that makes one's hair stand on end, and if anything is to save a remnant of the army, it will be *The Times* newspaper, and their special correspondent, Mr. Russell.

The third plague of Egypt (Exodus viii. 17) is now in all its disgusting horror, spreading through all the encampments, particularly amongst the sick. There seems to be no remedy. One man infects another until their very old rags are seen moving on their bones.

9th Regiment have only 150 men for duty. Hands and feet frostbitten, and always wet and weary.

20th. One ocean of melting snow and mud. Men are out grubbing up roots, and the Russians waste their powder and ball trying to drive them off, but people only laugh at them and work on; so much for habit and indifference to danger.

Away to explore to the most advanced part of the Inkerman heights, and close to the mouth of the Tchernaya. Plenty of wild fowl, and very good shooting, if a body had 'licence'. Their great ship, *Twelve Apostles*, and many others lying in peaceful tranquillity, but all doomed for destruction. Look out, they have found us out. Here comes a shell, with its flick-flick-flick, cutting a tunnel through the damp thick atmosphere—whop, it falls, sudden and heavy. I was behind a rock in a moment. It explodes; bang; tearing all about, the fragments spinning and whistling in all directions. A clumsy lump of the metal fell close to me all haggled, so as to torture man or horse and tear their limbs to tatters. In the bush I fell in with nine or ten dead bodies just as they fell at Inkerman strife, and many dead horses. The men were not decomposed, head and hands quite black. They were Russian soldiers and lay in their uniform. The bush was full of them, with firelocks, belts, and all the *débris* of a battle-day. Got home safe to a fine dinner of cow's head soup and cabbage.

21st. No Divine service for a long time past; had a little congregation in my own tent to keep in remembrance the Sabbathday. A mild day; took a stroll with Sir Richard England, to see the effect of some Rus-batteries firing upon us. Dined with him in the evening. Walked ankle deep in mud all the way to his tent. My dinner dress was an old bearskin coat, mud boots, and a thick, red, woollen necktie. Sir Richard was always kind to me from first to last; we had many a ride and a stroll together. He was always at his post, and never made a difficulty; like most old soldiers, he saw that what could not be cured must be endured.

22nd. Made a reconnaissance towards the fortress, and took my physician perforce, to trot him out a bit to see *tout le monde*. We lost our way, and came too close to some Russian rifle-pits where the enemy were lying *perdu*; fit-fit-fit, came the rifle-balls about our ears. The doctor thought the safest way of escape was to cover his face, so down he went, flat as a flounder. I thought he had been hit, but finding it only a feint, I gave him a poke on the side with my stick, with a decided 'Up and follow me, for your life.' So we went off at a gallop, tacking along the breast of the hill under some sharp rifle practice, but got safely into the advanced trenches to see fresh blood. 'What means this?' I said. 'Only some man just killed sir.' The Turks were employed here in our works, on pay. A small boy with a spoon would have been a match for any of them. They represented a wretched spectacle of misery. One might as well use a spade in a tar-barrel, the soil being so adhesive. They could not be encouraged to exert themselves to get under cover. Their general reply was 'Allah kerim', God is great and merciful. I hope He was merciful to those poor fellows, for they were dying by scores every day, and put into such shallow graves, the first heavy rain washed them out again. We got well to the front after all, and had a good view into the city of desolation where they were working like bees; 260 guns pointed our way ready for a salvo. Our pickets now within pistol-shot of each other. Both quite alive to their dangers, but the Patlander soldier will pop up his head to see the Rooskins, and he gets popped on the head. Mild weather up to the 26th. Bright sun at times. Snow nearly gone again. Nights cold and frosty, and the country one ocean of mud. Early in the morning, when the frost is still, our spare guns are run down from the artillery park under the brow of a hill by our men, kept there until night, when they are quietly moved on to the batteries to replace disabled guns or form fresh batteries.

Many of my men sadly frostbitten, hands, fingers, and feet dropping off from mortification, a sad, painful, sickly sight.

The death reports are sent in every morning, as the ravens swoop over the camp with their ominous croak-croak.

63rd Regiment reduced to twenty men! So they are sent away altogether. Our army is now so much reduced by sickness and death, that we have given up the right of our position to the French, no longer able to hold it and do the duty.

I might say with St. Paul, as recorded in 2 Corinthians ii. 27, but not in so good a cause, we pass our weary days.

About nine o'clock each night the French on our left throw their evening bouquet into Sebastopol, which is gracefully returned, i.e. with a grand salvo of live shells, a pretty sort of official fire-works. These iron orbs play in the elements passing each other in their flight of darkness, the lighted fuze sparkling like the fire-fly, travel on until they drop into the arms of some sleeping party, who are blown into the next world, or get their bones cracked.

Mr. Sparling, a little midshipman in the Naval Brigade, lost his head by a cannon-shot at his battery. There will be weeping for him at home, poor fellow. Twenty-two of our guns in the Green Hill Battery have been disabled by the enemy. We are getting them replaced as fast as the ocean of mud will allow wheels to revolve. Our ammunition is short, and we don't fire much at present.

Had a long ride with Sir Richard. Pointed out the pass and the cul-de-sac where the corps of Russians were lost in the morning of Inkerman; and most fortunate for us they got into such a trap. The heaps of dead horses tainted the air, and many dead bodies lay all quiet in the brush, but were not offensive. What sharp fellows those Russians are. We were soon discovered, and had a salute of shot and shell from the Careening Harbour, which gave us warning to quit.

28th. Divine service in the mud near to my tent door. No sermon. The guns were roaring all the time, and now and then a shot would come whop! into the breast of the hill beside us, without attracting the least attention. It is an effort to drag one's body along, from the heaps of adhesive, slimy clay that gather round the boots, and stick on like glue. This kills the poor horses, striving in their weakness under heavy loads.

We got a present of a goose from a ship in harbour, the first of those jolly old birds we had seen in this country. It was given in charge to one of the servants to be fed and cared for in the most affectionate way. Next morning it was reported, to our horror, that the goose had died in the night of apoplexy. We had a court of inquiry and lamentation. It proved that the goose was taken into the arms of the barbarian to keep him warm, and he overlaid it. However, it was decided that the goose should go through the cere-mony of being killed in the usual way, and hung up for some days to make him tender. At the end of a week we got up a nice fire, had him roasted for dinner, when we all agreed that a better goose never was cooked!

Last night, when the guard marched off to the trenches, Private Michael Broderick, 50th Regiment, tired of life, fell out of the ranks, loaded his firelock, took off one of his boots, put his toe to the trigger, and sent his soul to an endless eternity! Twenty men of my Brigade in the death report this morning.

Reported that only thirty-five horses of the 11th Hussars exist up to this date.

31st. Away with the General to reconnoitre all the passes, glens, dales, and valleys in front of Inkerman battleground. One I named the Pass of Thermopylae; in that steep, narrow, rugged defile, 100 men might keep 10,000 in check. Looked well into the town. No end to their works in and about the Malakoff and Redan. Thousands of men, as busy as ants, raising new batteries, and strengthening their works in every convenient and command-ing spot. Here we fell in again amongst the dead, lying in uniform just as they fell three months ago, the hands black and parched and dry; no decomposition. The sides of the hill covered with dead horses, cannon-shot, the fragments of shells, and rifle-bullets knocked into all shapes against the rocks, after having dismissed the immortal part of humanity.

A couple of round shot warned us off the premises. So, taking the hint, we rode away.

'I want to call at this camp,' said the General, 'to see an officer whose mother has written to me about him in a state of great apprehension and anxiety. Can I see Captain B——?' said the General, to the first officer we met. 'No, sir, I'm sorry to say he's dead and buried.' Some secret feeling, perhaps, which tongue cannot describe, informed the poor mother that her son was in danger when she wrote this imploring letter.

'How gets on your regiment, Colonel L—— (23rd)?' 'We have buried ninety-eight men in camp this last month, sir!' and so it goes on everywhere. The early cry is 'Bring out your dead!'—something like the London Plague in 1666. The 3rd Division of nine regi-ments—1st Royals, 4th, 9th, 18th, 28th, 38th, 44th, 50th, and 89th—lately 7,000 strong, can muster this day but 2,500 effective men. So, according to this progress in killed, wounded, sickness, and death, it is a plain, mathematical calculation what we may soon expect if we are not let loose at this great fortress, to capture it while we can or die in the attempt.

February 1st. The Russians made a grand sortie last night on the French. The fight was kept up till morning. The night thick, foggy, dreary, and cold, with a sprinkling of snow. I kept awake, listening to the row, till 5 a.m., when the fire slackened, and I went to sleep. The French lost some 300 men and a few officers; the Rooskies as many, and no advantage gained on either side. This night fighting is a most odious, unsatisfactory, barbarous mode of warfare.

Up to the 6th, raw and rainy; hard frosts and piercing north-east winds. Men become living icicles in the trenches, and are daily put under the sod. 1,437 of 3rd Division sick in camp. One wood hut has really been got up to camp, to accommodate twenty of the worst sick cases.

7th. A wet night and a hard gale, which reminded us of the 14th November. What a very changeable climate! Today it is fine and mild. French soldiers selling brown bread in our camp to the men, at fifteen pence a pound!

Carrying down shot to the batteries, each man slings one in a bag over his shoulder, and away they go. If it is a sixty-eight pounder, it takes two men, the shot in a bag slung on a pole. Weary work for half-starved, half-naked, famishing soldiers, but the work must be done. The crocus begins to spring up amongst the graves, and under my bed. Everywhere they put up their pretty tulip heads; they are larger and better marked than those in England, and so welcome.

11th. Up to this date very variable, rain and snow alternately. A frightful snowstorm today, with a cold north-east wind that cuts one in two, everything looking so desolate and cheerless here. We are enveloped in a Siberian winter once more, and our men worked like horses. 150 went to Balaclava yesterday to carry up deal boards for flooring their tents. Fancy a man carrying one or two long, thin boards over his shoulder on a windy day, flapping about his ears and the glutinous mud above his ankles at every stretch holding him fast. Some of the men went into hospital when they got down there, and others got back by great exertion the same night or next morning without shoes!

14th, Valentine's Day. A pleasant day in old England! I mustered up all my courage to make a cruise to Balaclava, a place I always hated and avoided. The six miles' ocean of mud I thought worse than the 3,000 miles across the Atlantic, which I have passed six times when on duty. If some wise heads had finished off a road from the camp when we sat down before Sebastopol, it would have saved thousands of lives and ten thousands of gold. A sure mode of transport once secured, all this calamity would have been prevented. This was a plain duty, but there was no one competent to perform it. At that time staff appointments were given to friends and favourites generally, and if the press, particularly *The Times*, found fault with any who failed or broke down in work they knew nothing about, these lucky gentlemen were sure to be rewarded; their being censured aided their preferment. In my own case, as I have already mentioned, I was made a convenience of to provide for an excellent gentleman who never saw any service and who was my junior in the army by fifteen years. By way of explanation I was informed through a friend that, as I had written a letter in *The Times*, I would get nothing! I could only reply by saying, 'Another time, perhaps, I may unfold some tales that may astonish the public!' And so the matter dropped. Who did not write in *The Times*? Very many letters were afterwards laid to my charge which I knew nothing about. I don't approve of this kind of correspondence generally.

All the ground from my tent door to the village is one sea of mud and glutinous mire. The world never presented such a sight as the little town and harbour: the way to it marked all along by dead animals. As you descend into the plain your horses sink up to their girths. On what was once a pretty green sward you see nothing but soldiers of all corps ploughing through it, laden with different articles chiefly for field hospitals, the little half-starved bat ponies reeling under their loads with extreme patience, pulling up one leg out of the deep before the other is let down into the gulf. Look here! Good gracious, we are in a burying-ground. See how the horses sink into the graves; nothing to mark the sacred spot but some rough stone placed at the head and feet of comrades slain in battle on Balaclava's plains. Here, again, as you near the village, are acres of dead, and the helpless Turks are giving a hasty covering to their comrades. They lie together as thick as turnips in a home field. Graves here and there and everywhere; all the world seems to have come here to be buried; this is the place where human harvests grow!

See the confusion in the little town. Thousands of bales of goods for the army are lying in all directions; nobody to deliver them, no one to take them away, no transport, all confusion, and total want of everything in the shape of working system. Ships as thick as reeds in a marsh, and no getting at them although not twenty yards from shore. Made a desperate attempt to get into a store to buy something, but was signally defeated. The dismal hole was crowded to suffocation inside and out, all waiting a chance of getting something for the camp. It was a deadlock; I gave it up in despair, and went to see an hospital on Miss Nightingale's system. Some of her nurses were attending the sick; a happy change for the patients who got in here. All was comfortable under this management, but 'twas a small place. What an inestimable woman is this Miss Nightingale! How thoroughly she understands the good work she has taken in hand; a ministering angel everywhere, and so loved and respected by the soldiers.

A hundred sick are embarked here every day for Scutari! Navvies at work on the railroad. Sawmills erected. Everything in this department going on in a business way, being all planned beforehand and brought out from England by Messrs. Peto, Brassey

& Co., to begin and finish their work. They brought out their horses, and their stable and forage. Their horses were not disembarked until their stable was built and their hay in the rack!

A handsome yacht lies here, where a noble lord shelters himself. Horses are eating their tails off and dying in the mud. This is no travellers' story; starving horses stand together and keep nibbling at each other's manes and tails, until they are all demolished and scraped bare.

Got back to camp about dusk and found I was told off for the trenches. Got my hasty ration dinner, and went down to my post. Went my rounds about eleven o'clock, visiting all the outposts in advance. We were now within about forty yards of the enemy, too close to be agreeable with loaded rifles. The night was very boisterous and very dark; difficult to hear the crack of a rifle even at a short distance. There was some firing. One of my men was killed, and I might have been served out also, but kind Providence never lost sight of G.B. I was often spared when better men were sent to their account with an ounce of lead. I got off cheap, and am thankful. Copy of Lord Raglan's despatch:

I enclose a return of casualties up to the 16th inst. . . . I have great pleasure in stating that Colonel Bell, of the Royals, who received a slight wound in the side from a musket-ball, when commanding in the trenches on the night of the 14th inst., experiences little inconvenience from it, and has felt well enough to continue to discharge his duty with his accustomed zeal.

(Signed)   Raglan.

His Grace the Duke of Newcastle,
    Minister of War, London.

CHAPTER
20

Invalided Home

February 15th. Fine morning; got home tired and jaded. Went to roost for awhile to rest my very weary bones, and got plastered up. Lord Raglan came to see me during the day, and was glad (he said) that he might yet say, 'I was still as sound as a Bell', shook hands, and passed on to his old ground to look out, the Rooskies blazing away as usual, bad luck to them.

17th. I had a present of a big loaf, which won't last three hungry fellows over one day. But we have got some flour and preserved tatties, a capital standby. My cook Tub, our factotum, makes a potato cake for breakfast every morning, when we can provide a fire. As for the ration pork, none of us can look at it now, yet it is very good. I have had three hens and a cock for a month past, in reserve against a famine! They have behaved so well, and got so domestic I cannot permit them to die. The poor things go about the tents all day, feed with the horses, and of an evening come into my tent to roost, not molested or disturbed by anything. Their tips are getting red, a sure sign of the egg season.

19th. Fine and dry; one may walk out in slippers. What a climate! — so cheery. The grass is springing up under my bed. Tomorrow the French General Bosquet intends to attack the Russians in the valley of the Tchernaya, a division of English to aid him; to march at two o'clock in the morning, and make a *coup de main*, if possible. All our troops to be in readiness to turn out; no man to leave the camp. Seven of my men released from misery.

T

All are sewed up in their blankets, lying at the tent door, while the unfurnished house is being got ready.

20th. The wind shifted last night to the north, and such a storm of rain, snow, and sleet followed. We have had nothing so bad. Thermometer 4° below freezing; snow drifted into every crevice. The sentries like pillars of ice, move about in a jog-trot, to keep alive. 'Halloo! there, outside!' I called several times. 'I say, sentry?'—'Yes, sir.' ''Tis a bad night out there; are you cold?' 'Freezing to my firelock, sir.' 'Come over to my tent door.' 'Af I can find the way, Colonel.' 'This way; do you hear me?' 'I'm near you now, sir, I think, but the snow's in my eyes.' 'Come up close to the tent door. I have a totfull of rum for you in my hand. Take care now; order your arms, and put out your hand.' 'Be dad, I've got it, sir. God bless you, an' your health. O! it'll save my life, sir.' And lucky it was that on many a night like this, I had a spare bottle of rum in my tent for such purposes. At what an easy rate you may win the affection and respect of your men in the army. They never forget a kindness, and any officer may be popular if he has commonsense and the feeling of a Christian.

The attack upon Leprandi was postponed *sine die*—after the different troops had been wandering about half the night blinded with the snowdrift.

21st. A terrible night has passed away. My thermometer went down 14° below freezing! A cutting wind and drift snow today, with frost and sunshine. It cost me two hours to clear away the drift snow out of my tent and make snug, as the sailors say against another gale. The whole country once more under the 'tablecloth', I hope sincerely for the last time. But such a treacherous climate I have never seen. I coughed all the night, and never warmed. Feel very unwell, but brighter days may come; and some of us may yet live to see home. Never say die.

22nd. We found it no sinecure in the trenches last night; it was intensely cold. Lieutenant Garnie, 38th, shot through the leg. How the poor men cling on to life in the midst of an incessant rattle of musketry in the dark, and in the day, and a universal whirling of shells from both sides, eclipsing the stars with their iron orbs, curving and tearing the air asunder with their musical 'tir-whit', as they describe their angry flight in the sky. Now a sortie and a death-struggle in the dark, now a repulse. Another infernal fire of cannon, and a lull—lie down and fall asleep for a few moments; up again, roused by the explosion of a shell. Collect the wounded, bury the dead where they fell, and back to camp before the dawn.

23rd. Cold, raw, dull, and hazy; frost, snow, and a north wind; bad ingredients for the speedy cure of a cough and a cold. About

10 p.m. I popped my head out to see some rockets going to pass the evening in Sebastopol, from the French camp. It was too cold for anything; popped in again, closed my door, and stole under the blankets. I had no light, nor was I bothered with sheets for my bed. A quarrel was up on our right, between the French and the Rooskies, which became alarming, and sleep of course was postponed. The Russian batteries opened all along with a tremendous crash, the glaring blaze illuminating the elements. The pattering of the rifle, too, was quick, sharp, and in battle style; smart and lively as at Inkerman, and on the same ground, or nearly so. The roaring of cannon, the increase of independent firing, the cheers of the French, the yells of the Russians, kept us wide awake, expecting every moment to hear our own bugles sound the assembly. At 3.30 in the morning the firing ceased, and I fell asleep. What was all this midnight battle about? The Russians got up a strong fieldwork and battery in front of the French lines to command their advance. The French were determined to drive them out of it, and failed after a loss of 1 General, 16 officers, and 100 men killed and wounded! So much for the night's amusement. I don't like fighting in the dark. There is always confusion, and friends kill each other too often.

24th. First voice I heard this morning was the croak-croak of the ravens, as they glided over the camp, scenting out the dead. Next, was that of the bells in the town, chiming for the victory of the last night. Then the French bands, playing some martial airs in the cold breeze. I do not think that Sebastopol will ever be taken by assault; it must be pounded to dust and ashes.

25th, Sunday. Four men bowled over in the trenches—one cut in two by a round shot, two shot through the head, and the other with a rifle-ball in his abdomen. It is wonderful the variety of ways that death calls for its victims. No man's life here is worth a day's purchase, nor do the men seem to care about it. I am now *hors-de-combat*, and quite unequal to hard work; cold and cough, general debility, weak in vision. Ague and fever has grasped me, too, and has left me no energy. The doctors advise me to go to sea. No! I will hold on and live in hope of a bright recovery.

27th. Fine, bright, warm day. The beautiful crocus springs up afresh and decks the silent grave. The men look weary and overworked, sick and exhausted, but are avoiding the hospital tents as long as they can hold out. Very correct accounts appear in *The Times* of the misery and suffering out here. Everybody writes to *The Times*, everybody writes a different account, but everyone writes the truth without name or signature, and so the authorities in their wisdom at home will have a difficult task to contradict all

those statements. Better for them to confess that all the evils
originate at home—not out here.

The doctors still advise me to go home. They say a change is
imperative, that I can't live here. To abandon the field and all my
old comrades at such a time is not at all my wish. Dr. H—— says,
'Of all men you are the last I would like to see leave the camp, but
I won't be responsible for your life if you stay on'. Hope says
hold on a bit and see if you won't rally. You have a brave regiment that will follow you to the death, and there is no man, they
say, more popular. Goodness knows I have no desire to blow my
own trumpet. Everyone must do his duty without the expectation
of fee or reward. In the days of Wellington is was 'Blessed is the
man who expecteth nothing, for he will not be disappointed!' Few
men were disappointed there; they never got anything but broken
bones from the enemy!

28th. Those men passing down there are sailors and soldiers,
very unlike either from their tattered, ragged dress. They are
carrying down shot and shell to the trenches, always employed.
If they are not fighting, they are collecting material for smashing
other people's limbs.

Strength of brigade today, 4090; sick, absent and in camp,
2,506; effectives, 1,585; deaths the last five days, 53 men.

Five of my men are being now sown up in their blankets.

March 1st. Snowstorm, and cold enough to freeze the liver
of a Laplander. Very unwell, and my sight failing; general debility,
and unable to work—in fact, fairly broken down. A medical board
assembled, examined, and pronounced me unfit for duty, and ordered
me home. Singular enough, I just then had a letter from an old
friend, high in office at home, offering me a staff appointment in
England. 'I can't keep it open,' he said, 'say yes or no, by return
of post.' I said yes, and began to prepare, although my heart lay
in the camp, and with Regiment No. 1, and my comrades. It was
an effort to tear myself away from a home of twenty-nine years.
I made over my house and my hens to my friend Doctor H——,
and began to arrange for a retreat as fast as the R.T. would allow.

2nd. The last night was fearful in the trenches. Ink and oil
frozen in our tents. Dragged myself out for a short walk over to
the hospital tent. Here was a sad scene. One poor fellow had
been so severely frostbitten both his feet were dropping off from
above the ankles in mortification—yes, just dropping off. He was
suffering greatly, and his days were numbered—too far gone to bear
amputation! Three more were raving in a fever, besides many
other bad cases, and no hospital comfort, no restoratives! Passed
on to what was a very fine vineyard in October last, now a

graveyard. Soldiers of different corps at their occupations. Three packages of dead men were lying ready. 'What regiment, lads?' '44th, sir. We're dying fast.' 'That's a big grave you're digging.' 'Yes, sir. There's three on 'em; we usually put 'em in two's, but there's an odd one just now come down, so we'll put 'em together. The weather gets warm, and soon we won't have so many.' It just happened to be spitting snow at the time. The grave digging kept him so warm he thought it a change of climate, little thinking, perhaps, that soon some brother of the trade would do for him what he had done for hundreds!

4th, Sunday. A little tent service for the last time in camp. My name appears in G.O. for England. I ordered an auction of sale of my cattle and my few traps. Farewell to all my friends, many of whom were still to be killed before the fall of this mighty fortress, which will hold out for many a long day, and be the death of thousands before it falls; but it must fall.

7th. Left the camp. The ride to Balaclava tired me out. I got into a wretched hovel with my paymaster, who made room for me until I could get on board. Applied to Admiral Boxer for a passage. No ship ready; bide my time.

8th. Fine day and warm. Balaclava begins to smell very strong! All the shops and storekeepers cleared out of the town by G.O., Turks, Croats, Jews, Greeks, Maltese, French, Armenians, Russians, Tartars, Poles, Italians, and all sorts of camp-followers. All are in for plunder, robbery, and imposition, anything to catch the soldier's penny. All are now settled down in temporary sheds, tents, and booths, half a mile outside the village, carrying on a brisk trade — everything a ransom: two guineas for a little ham, and 3s. a bottle for porter to wash down a slice for dinner. Everything else in proportion, extravagant. The French manage things better than we do. They put on a tariff, allowing the sutlers a fair profit. If they are not content with this, they may cut off to some other quarter.

The Croats are employed covering over with baskets of earth those sons of the Prophet who were washed out of their graves by the last rains. There are acres of them about here. The Russian priests are proclaiming far and wide that Providence gave the allied army a victory at the Alma to lead them on to be sacrificed before Sebastopol, where their armies now lie buried and manure the soil. This is not quite true, but the multitudes in Russia believe it. Able to ride out a little.

Called to see Sir Colin Campbell and to examine his defences, extending three and a half miles from Kadikoi to the summit of the hills, dipping into the sea, where, rolling about in the surge and

dashing against the perpendicular rocks, float pieces of the wrecks
of the 14th November 1854. The Balaclava is well covered and
quite safe under the gallant and able chief who, from his age, great
service, long experience, and meritorious conduct as a soldier, ought
to be commanding an army instead of a brigade. We were at the
Battle of Vittoria together.

Sir Colin Campbell was considered very ill-used, the oldest and
most experienced soldier in the camp. Few in the British army
had seen such good service. A man of great experience and courage, but he had not been considered high enough in the dress circle,
and so he was passed over.

> The rank is but the guinea stamp,
> The man's the goud for a' that.

He may be wanted by-and-by.

Russell, *The Times* correspondent, comes in from a stable-loft,
where he dwells, to our den of an evening to have a chat, a glass of
brandy pawney and a cigar. He tells some droll stories, sings a
good song, and is a very jolly good fellow.

16th March. *Jour de ma vie.* Embarked on the *Emperor* for
Malta, unable to help myself. I took one of my servants with me,
and provided for the others; heard the last cannonade as we
stretched out into the Black Sea.

Lieutenant Smith, 68th, died today of fever on board. His
father also died of his wounds received at Inkerman.

After I left the camp, amongst others, Captain Muller of my old
corps was killed, a fine young fellow in his youthful prime, greatly
regretted. He was a grandson of Lieutenant-General Sir Theophilus
Pritzler, our old Chief in India, was born in the regiment, and died
where a soldier ought to die, under his colours in the battlefield.

When I arrived at Constantinople my ship was sent on a cruise
to look for cattle somewhere on the coast of Dalmatia, so I had to
cut and run ashore to look for another. After some red-tape delay
at many places and melting under a hot sun on the Bosphorus in
search of a steamer, I did at last get a passage on board the
Adelaide screw, bound for England, with a cargo of sick and
wounded officers and men. Some very bad cases amongst them.
One young officer was carried about like a child all the voyage from
the sad state of his feet from frostbite. Some did not live out the
voyage, which was long and very boisterous. For a couple of days
the pumps were going constantly to keep the leak from blinding the
fires and getting into the engine room. We put into the Island of
Sardinia for repairs. Glad to get ashore on any terms. Had a stroll
amongst the orange-groves; the perfume was so charming, and the

gardens so rich with vegetables and fruits, I would have wished to bivouac here for a week. The people seemed very poor and under great subjection to priests and Popery.

We had a cargo of sick and wounded men and no fresh meat. The Captain used every exertion to buy an ox, which he selected from a herd of cattle. The owner very willing to sell, but it was a feast-day, and the holy priest would not permit it!

The Captain of our steamer told me some strange but true stories about Crimean wisdom and jobbery. He said a dozen steamers often lay at Balaclava, while they might have been gathering thousands of sheep about Eupatoria and other places for the army. They lost their chance, for the Russians came down and drove them all away for their own use. As for winter stabling for the cavalry horses he said there were sails enough and to spare to cover every horse in the camp, if they had been demanded from the ships lying idle there on full pay! He had taken out ground coffee, sugar, and rice to Balaclava for the army, but no one would receive those necessaries, although our troops were in the greatest want. He then went away to Smyrna, and ultimately delivered this part of his cargo at Constantinople three months afterwards!

29th. Anchored at Malta. Here it was all summer; fruit and vegetables, green peas and fresh salad. Inquired after the gunner who lost his arm when I had last been here, by the fatal explosion, while firing red-hot shot. He had recovered the amputation. Enjoyed myself ashore until next evening, when we sailed for Gibraltar. We had terrible weather, and some nights of terror during our passage, but arrived safe at Gibraltar the 7th April. Went ashore and slept at the Turf Hotel. A great luxury it was to get into a real bed again. Passed the next day with Sir Robert and Lady Gardiner and slept at Government House. We had a nice dinner party. Subject of conversation hung upon the Crimea, everyone anxious to hear the latest news. Gold and iron are the two great hinges of war, and both in full play when I left. The English gold was flying like chaff, the other not in demand anywhere but in the batteries. Lady G—— gave me a grand bouquet to take on board, and was extremely hospitable and kind. Visited my old quarters and some military friends before I sailed. Weather very hot, but cheery. Nothing remarkable until the 19th of April, when we arrived at Portsmouth. Home, sweet home! How few of my people will ever reach those shores of their home! Three hundred of my poor fellows fell before I left the graveyard. Many more were sinking helpless, and the work not nearly done. It will ever be the most eventful year in my life! this little diary will keep it in remembrance. There is much tautology and egotism, but that could not be well avoided in keeping a correct book. At times, I had no pen, ink, or paper. With a pencil, and on the fly-leaves of Russian books which I found scattered about, I made my memoranda, leaving nothing to chance or idle reports. What one sees and feels and hears is truth, and the great truth is and must be confessed with gratitude, that I owe my life and preservation to the Lord Jehovah, and to Him be all the honour and the glory.

CHAPTER
21

Quebec and Montreal

I TOOK up my appointment at York, and removed from thence to Liverpool, and remained there as Inspecting Field Officer, until I became a Major-General, and here I met and made some very kind and hospitable friends, particularly at the Uplands. The hospitality of Mr. and Mrs. R——d W——s was boundless for years. I was now released and had nothing to do. A life of idleness to me was a life of slavery. I placed myself at the disposal of the Horse Guards, and applied for employment at home or abroad, no matter where. I volunteered to go to India, to China—anywhere—but all in vain. I bethought me of my old friend, who said, 'You wrote a letter in *The Times*, and you'll get nothing', and he was a true prophet. I had no home, not ten yards of ground in all England to pitch my tent, so I went abroad, and travelled about for some years, and kept my journal, even in St. Peter's at Rome, and on the pebbly beach at St. Paul's Bay, in Malta, on Swiss lakes and on battlefields.

On the 27th June 1861 we left the Old World, and many kind and generous friends on the landing-stage, at Liverpool, who saw us away in the steamer *North Britain*, an iron ship of 2,200 tons, Captain B——. Good accommodation and a most excellent table. Some thirty-five first-class passengers, most of them second-class people. The watchful skipper rough as a bear, but always with his weather-eye open, and porridge and treacle for breakfast. The weather was fine, and nobody thought of being sick in the sunny month of June. Young ladies a little in romance, and looking at the moon and after the *Great Eastern*, some hours in advance. Next morning found us at anchor in Lough Foyle. The steamers of Allen & Co. have a Government contract of £78,000 a year for calling at Londonderry for the mails out and home. Some Pat-landers came on board, whom I asked where was Londonderry? 'O, be dad, sir, it's over the hills there, sixteen miles away.' 'Is it so far as that, Pat?' 'Well, yer honour, it mayn't be just so wide, but the roads are bad, and we give good measure.' We had nine hours to look over the hills and far away before we got to sea, and shot round those bluff rocks, and away over the trackless deep. A head wind, and blowing fresh; and it blew fresh, with a head wind, for nine days. All the anticipated joys of a summer voyage to Canada were rolled under the pillows of helpless maidens and matrons, quite *hors-de-combat*, unhappy, weary with illness, counting the days and the hours.

On 5th July discovered the first iceberg, looking very formid-able, and fields of ice in the distance. A sharp look out. Very cold; struck an iceberg in the night; had shortened speed, and now blew off our steam to keep quiet. Next morning (6th) got into a field of ice. As far as we could see nothing but a Siberian or Arctic wilderness of ice of all shapes and sizes, mountains and molehills, of the most fantastic shapes. There were waterfalls, and great baths, and corridors where one could walk about, being shaded from the sun. The sea was rolling into caves, and the receding water making a seabeach roar that resembles a battery—see how the gun is pointed, and an officer, with a cocked hat, standing in the rear! There goes Mont Blanc, a thundering big hill. It will take years to melt him down. And there's Neptune's cradle and the Devil's Punchbowl, as hard as steel, and as high as a house. Here comes a grand platform, where a company of Volunteers might skirmish on their skates. The passengers forward are throwing their empty bottles on its wide surface, with corked-up memor-andums to distant friends. This is the Grand Post, a slow coach, but a safe letterbox as long as it lasts. There they are in thou-sands and tens of thousands—if I said millions, I should be short of the numbers—and all capped with snow. How cold it blows, ther-mometer down to 46°. All the barometers of humanity here are sinking with alarm. Here we are penned up, entirely surrounded, a very grand sight it is, no doubt, but very dangerous company. And now the night is on, thick, dark, and chilly. At 11 p.m. I joined the three lookout men at the bows, and very keen, sharp eyes they had, being more quick to discover the icebergs in the long distance than I could with my glass. We had got out of the great multitude of our enemies, and were now looking for the rearguard.

Every now and then I could see one as big as a church, meeting us, when the word passed, 'Put the helm down!' or 'Steer clear!—and ice on the starboard (or larboard) bow!' We were running half-speed all night, meeting those white mountains occasionally on our course. There are generally four-fifths of them under water. One mistake, and, like the *Canadian* the other day, our ship might have been broken up and gone down below in thirty minutes, a short time to prepare for escape or for another world. But so it was, and just hereabouts thirty-five passengers, in the wreck of that steamer, lay at the bottom. I was chilled with cold and, being satisfied that there was a good lookout forward, I retired to my crib, and found next day that we were in sight of Newfoundland, but we were much annoyed with foggy weather. Here we picked up a fair wind, but had to shorten speed, it was so very hazy, and keeping a lookout for the island of Anticosta, we groped our way up the north channel, or Straits of Belleisle.

Made Father Point on the 9th July, and telegraphed to Montreal, 'All well'.

10th. At ten a.m. arrived at Quebec, and went alongside the railway wharf, where all the passengers landed. The custom-house stands quite at hand. Baggage being passed, the people jump into the railway cars, and are put down at their different localities along the line for hundreds of miles. The railway terminus is on the right bank of the St. Lawrence, at Point Levi, opposite Quebec. A ferry steamer is always plying across. Here we found the *Great Eastern*, which made the voyage in ten days, and was disembarking the Armstrong gun battery. The horses looked very fresh, and in good condition. I saw them put into railway cars same evening for Montreal, where they arrived next day, and went into camp under a tropical rain, such as one seldom sees in Europe.

There stands Cape Diamond, the great citadel of the Canadas, as I left it seventeen years ago. My old quarters, where I was fried alive in the summer, and almost frozen to death for seven winter months. There, too, are the Falls of Montmorency, still shooting over that old rocky precipice, the water flowing out of the sloping greenwood, and falling in a perpetual torrent 230 feet. In the winter the spray from below forms a cone of great magnitude, and it is a fashion for the young ladies and gentlemen to amuse themselves sliding down from the top on little sleighs, or toboggans. They go at a most rapid pace, and many are the adventures to be told in the evening at the home fireside. The pretty island, 'Orleans' and the scenery all round Quebec, is fine. The Plains of Abraham lie on the south side of the city, where Generals Wolfe and Montcalm fell in battle, 1759. It is the parade and drill ground for the troops. That pretty village in the distance is called 'Lorette'. It belongs to the last of the masters of this territory, the aborigines of the soil, a poor Indian tribe who live by making moccasins and little ornaments of bark work. They have a small annual donation of money and blankets from Government. But their generation is gone—the firewater introduced by the white men has nearly extinguished their tribes.

The weather is now very comfortably warm. Four score in the shade, and a glaring sun; but we have plenty of ice on board—indeed, a supply *ad libitum* all the voyage.

We saw the comet on the night of the 1st of July.

11th. Left Quebec at 5 a.m., and arrived at Montreal at 7.30 p.m., having stuck to the ship all the way. At half-past eight took up our quarters with those so dear, in a charming residence a mile and a half from town. The distance from Quebec is 169 miles by rail, and the river steamers, with passengers and goods, pass up and down every night.

Montreal is well grown in fine streets, and fine houses, and population, since my first acquaintance with it in 1837, when the rebellion first broke out, and the province was saved, mainly by my regiment. It is now a fine city of 100,000 people, and chief of all the Canadas. Let me introduce it to my friends.

Situated on the great river St. Lawrence, the country is as flat as far as the eye can see, excepting 'Mount Royal', from whence the name Montreal, and a beautiful mountain it is, thickly wooded, about twelve miles in circumference at the base, with a fine turnpike road all round. The breast of the hill is well covered with elegant houses, standing in their own grounds, handsomely laid out, every one commanding a *bella vista* or *belle vue*. The style and taste of the dwellings would do credit to any country in the world. They belong chiefly to the merchants in the town. Now let us sit down under this shady maple-tree, and look about us; and if anything remarkable strikes your observation, note it as a remembrance. There lies the town at your feet, every house visible. But we had better call it a city, for there is a bishop and a cathedral, which may give it the right name. The cathedral is a fine and a handsome building, with a beautiful spire. The Right Reverend F. Fulford, D.D., is the Lord Bishop. There are twelve Protestant churches of different sects, and as many Roman Catholic. The cathedral, you see, with its double towers, stands conspicuous in the middle of the city. It is represented by a bishop, and a host of priests. See how the sun glitters on all those spires and housetops! They look like polished silver, but it is only tin; or, as Paddy from Cork said, 'Sure the houses in this country are all slated with tin'.

That very large building, like a barrack, is a Jesuit college, where the light of the gospel never enters — a place where they would cook their salmon with our Bible on Fridays.

That is McGill College and University. There are professors here of arts and sciences of all sorts, where young gentlemen may receive a first-class education. The bank of Montreal is a fine building, and a prosperous one, with a capital of six million dollars, paying shareholders 8 per cent. interest. There are seven or eight other banks, all doing a good business, and many other handsome public buildings. The streets are long and wide, and, according to law, the houses are built of stone or brick, and double rows of trees shade many streets. There are some fountains, too, and miniature squares, and good shops, but very expensive. The market is a very fine, large covered building, and well supplied.

There flows the great St. Lawrence, carrying down with it the waters of five inland seas, which are forever dashing over the Niagara Falls. It is spanned, you see, by the Victoria Bridge — a wonder of itself, even in this enlightened age. This bridge cost 6,300,000 dollars. Its length is one mile and three-quarters; the tube 6,600 feet; height of centre tubes, 22 feet; width of tubes, 16 feet; length of side span, 242 feet; centre span, 330 feet; number of spans, 25. There it is. You see all before you, stretching across like the great sea-serpent. The terminus is on this side, at a most inconvenient distance from the town. The road or way to it is the most atrocious break-neck Balaclava mud passage that I ever saw in a civilised country. It is a disgrace to the mayor and corporation, who ought to mend their ways before making any other improvements. But they are all Canadians, and love to see the streets in the eastern style of Constantinople. There are good hotels, a fine post-office, and many newspapers — one of the best is printed at one cent. That island opposite the town, so like an English park, is 'St. Helen's'. You see the tents under the shady trees; part of the 47th Regiment, lately arrived from Ireland, are encamped there — the remainder on this side. Very cool quarters — for we generally have a thunderstorm, with tropical rain, every night. The next island above the bridge is 'Nuns' Island', the property of those ladies who have a convent and reside there. One half is well wooded; the rest pasture and farm. It lies so low, the flood carried off all their cows last winter, and the sisterhood had a narrow escape from being drowned. There is no end to nuns and nunneries in this Lower Canada; they are indigenous to the soil, and are very wealthy. They increase and multiply, and are always adding to their property, chiefly in lands.

That tank, on the breast of the hill below, is the reservoir which supplies all the town with fresh water. It is forced up by steam power, from the river, and the supply is inexhaustible. This is the place where human harvests grow—the cemetery, or God's acre, what a lovely resting, retired, holy ground, overshadowed by the mountain-brow. All here is shadow—all above is substance—yet everything recoils at death. But there is no remedy: we must die, all must yield to the stroke of death. Let me die by degrees, like Jacob, and see my candle burn down to the socket, so that I may see the time drawing nigh—the approach of death before I feel it. It is not far from any of us. Let us go higher up now, and have another view from the opposite side, taking in the whole optic circle. Did you ever see anything more extensively grand and beautiful? The St. Lawrence on one side, and the Ottawa, or Grand River, 800 miles in length, known by the Indians as the Kitchisippi, on the other, washing this island of Montreal. What little towns and villages, châteaux, farms, and dark forests are scattered over the great surface; the glittering church spires, peeping from amongst the trees, discover the locality of some lonely village, happy in its simplicity, and far removed from the troubles, anxieties, and turmoils of the busy, speculative world. There's a sky above of azure blue, a bright sun, the corn taking the yellow tinge, the earth loaded with abundance, the cattle in thousands in green pastures, and man at his labour. 'In the sweat of thy brow shalt thou eat bread, till thou return unto the ground'—and they do sweat in this country, not so much from hard work as from the heat of summer. A few months more, and all this scene will be a Siberia—a very wilderness of snow. You have heard of timber, or lumber-rafts, and how they come from the Far West. They are large wooden platforms of great pine timber, fastened together with wooden pins and chains, amounting at times to thousands of pounds value. There is one, you see, far away, coming down the stream. Let us drive down to the Ottawa, and see it shoot the rapids there—the distance is six miles, but our horses in Canada go like the wind. Here we are at the 'Saut', under a hickory-tree facing the rapids, and there it comes, increasing in its descent, passing round that wooded island to keep a middle course. It is one of the great pine-rafts, thirty men on board—fifteen at each end—plying their great rough oars, just hewn out of the trees. How they pull together to keep the raft in the centre, and from being twirled round by the rush of waters! There are five shanties or little wooden houses on the raft, where the people live. It is now caught by the current, and away it flies down with the gushing and boiling and gurgling waters. This is the last of many dangerous rapids, 169 miles more will leave all in Wolfe's Cove, at Quebec, from whence the timber is shipped to England.

It is now getting late, and a threatening storm gathers round the mountain—there is thunder and lightning in those clouds. I never liked to be exposed to lightning since my friend M—— was killed by my side. His body formed part of the lightning's path to the earth, and it passed through him. It is dangerous to be near a tree or lofty building, or a river, or running water. A tall object like a tree or spire will frequently discharge a lightning cloud, and if anyone were standing near, the lightning might diverge from the tree, and pass through the fluids of the human body. It runs down a tree between the bark and the wood, where the sap is most abundant. Water is a good conductor—it is therefore dangerous to be near it during a thunderstorm—the lightning might make the man its conductor to the water. Never lean against a wall in a thunderstorm, the electric fluid will sometimes run down a wall, and as man is a better conductor, would leave the wall and run down the man. Never ring a bell in a thunderstorm—bellwire is an excellent conductor. Never bar a shutter, never be in a crowd—a mass of people forms a better conductor than an individual; the vapour arising increases the conducting power. A bed, or mattress, or hearthrug are non-conductors, and lightning would not choose them for its path. People who are alarmed about lightning would be in security lying on them in the middle of a room, even more so than in an iron house, or on an iron bedstead, for the lightning would be attracted by the iron, as a better conductor than the animal fluid. But the clouds have passed away for the moment. It will rain soon, for the horses are stretching their necks and snuffing up the air—they smell the odour of plants and new hay, and sniff their fragrance. Let us go.

That huge building, like a great barrack for 5,000 men, is the latest constructed nunnery. The women seem to have a great weakness for indulging in this idle sort of existence. I would be inclined to turn them out to the haymaking, and make them generally useful. I visited at the house of a French-Canadian gentleman, about eighteen years ago, when their child was a baby. She was educated partly in a convent, and grew up very beautiful. I inquired for the family the other day, and was told they were quite heartbroken, their daughter having been persuaded by those idle women to take the veil, and enter their house of darkness. They made such an impression on the tender, youthful mind of this poor girl, she left her father and mother for a life of seclusion.

This country captivates people arriving about the middle of May. If they are for settlers, they go to work at once rejoicing, everything collected for the little farm, all now *couleur-de-rose*, and the first fruits of their labour are sweet to the taste. But there are drawbacks, and how few, if they are not of the working-class, can rough it, wield an axe, handle the pick and spade, till the ground, split wood, milk the cow, plant and dig potatoes, reap and sow, drive the waggon, and go to the mill. There must be a help-mate, of course, and she will find enough to do. The children are all useful after seven years old. The better class of people who can afford to pay servants and keep them may be more independent, but they have more cares and more trouble, and must work, and watch to get a living. They generally enjoy good health, and a good appetite—two essential blessings which may not always be found in the house of Dives. Things are pretty well balanced in life, if the people could only see, hear, and understand. When the prison of the soul is broken up in the family of a back-settler, the neighbours bury the dead under an apple or a maple tree, and there I have seen them lie in peace and security, and yet the ground not consecrated.

I think I may say in truth that Montreal is celebrated for pretty women and fine horses. Sir F. Williams, of Kars, made the same remark to me the other day, and I think him a good judge! Our horses go like the wind in harness, or under the saddle, and are thoroughly educated. The people won't put up with pipeclay water for new milk here, as they do in London. I see a cow attached to almost every good house in the west-end, all under the charge of one herdsman. He drives them into town every morning and evening, to be milked at their respective homes. As he passes each door he blows his horn, the gate opens and the milker knows her crib. In like manner he collects them by sound of his horn for the field, not over a mile from the city—all very primitive. The priests have large property about the town, and most valuable. They let their pasture for cattle at eight or ten dollars each for the season of six months, and make a great profit. They are the worst farmers or land-masters in the world. They never lay out any money on the improvement of land, and so it becomes nearly use-less and overgrown with weeds and thistles. One always may know a Canadian from an English farm, the former a neglected, bad, barren soil, out of condition, worn-out, and seldom or ever drained or manured; the latter in good heart, fenced and flourishing.

August 12th. I have been here a month living in clover; re-turned all our visits, and now as idle as a scythe in frost; I must go into the United States and look for their grand army that made such a fine race at 'Bull's Run', if I can find them, and form my own opinion of Yankee troopers, who are such braggarts. Of the Southern army we hear but little. They seem to be hermetically sealed from public view. From the North we have the most flaming accounts of success; almost every day there is a great victory, 'total rout of the rebels', and with a long list of killed, wounded, and missing; capture of prisoners, ammunition, waggons, horses, arms, etc., etc., and all other incidents with which success is generally crowned. The North raised an army of 250,000. They planned a great expedition to overcome Virginia and drive the rebels to Charleston. The grand army marched some thirty-five miles into the bowels of the land, and ran back again to the original starting-point, mostly disbanding themselves, and leaving the capital in danger. Jonathan's Bull's Run will not easily be forgotten in the New World for many a long year, win or lose.

The settlement of this war is not likely to be speedy. It is melancholy to find here in deadly strife brother against brother, and father against son. The victory will be a hollow one, whoever wins or gains the ascendancy. I think the Southerners are quite as determined to fight it out, and will never yield unless to a mutual compromise, which is desirable. The country is already thrown back half a century—that is admitted. And although the State has sanctioned an army of 500,000 men to be raised for the North, how the means may be found to pay and feed them is rather dubious— *Nous verrons.* Discipline is the sure means of conquering; bravery is useless without discipline.

Walked all over Mount Royal and did not see a grouse! But I saw the finest and most splendid view in Canada. I had never been over this mountain before, although I was stationed here for two years. It is the correct place to see the town and country, the lakes and rivers, woods and forests, and all the beautiful houses being built. Such a panorama!

The priests and the nuns are the wealthiest people about, and enjoy all the freedom and security they can desire; although when I was campaigning in this country twenty years ago they were very disloyal, almost to a man. We had to hunt them down at times, march over the country, and live at free quarters in their respective towns to show them the terrors of war, and what they might expect by contending against the law. We did all our work in the winter, while the snow lay deep on the ground, the sky blue and bright, and the fresh pure air sharpening one's appetite on those distant foraging parties.

I am now here once more after roving for twenty years, and find the country prosperous, loyal, and free. Labour and good pay for the million, bread for everyone, and land cheap enough for those who can buy. People whom I left here twenty years past poor and dependent on their two able hands, are now residing in elegant

U

houses, elegantly furnished, are wealthy and independent. It is to
be hoped that they will have the wisdom to be content, and not
lose all by speculating—a too common occurrence at home and
abroad.

The Montreal Protestant Cemetery is the most beautiful, most
romantic charming resting-place for the dead, who live to die no
more. It lies embosomed in the heart of a mountain forest; tastefully laid out, and elegantly arranged are those 124 of God's acres.
The tombs are all of white or grey marble; a common stone is not
introduced here. Every ground varies in size and form, chaste
railings or chains, or pretty fancy fences gently guard, while beautiful flowers perfume, the hallowed spot. The people do, indeed,
pay respect and honour to the dust, and display fine taste in recording the memory of the past. Every family has its own lot of
ground, large or small, as they choose to purchase. The grounds
are laid out with carriage-drives, and it is pleasure to ride, or drive,
or walk in this beautiful retreat. It commands a grand view also,
and is but two miles from the town of Montreal.

There comes a thunderstorm, I said, as we galloped away round
the mountain. Well, what is thunder? It is the noise made by the
concussion of the air when it closes again after it has been parted
by the lightning flash. It is sometimes one vast crash, because the
lightning cloud is near the earth, and all the vibrations of the air
reach the ear at the same moment. You always hear the thunder
some moments after a flash of lightning, because it has a long way
to come. Lightning travels a million times quicker than thunder:
its speed is so great that it would go 480 times round the earth in
one minute. There now, what a flash of lightning, and followed
by such pouring rain, because a change has been produced in the
physical condition of the air, which renders it unable to hold so
much water, and down it will come in a flood before we get home.
We have fine horses, let's try their speed; and so we let them go.
No lady could ride a horse better or bolder than my own dear Mary,
but we lost our chance by three or four minutes. The cloud burst,
the horses threw back their ears as the tornado dashed into their
eyes. All was nearly darkness, the hail followed, and beat down
violently—we were nearly drowned on horseback!

An open carriage passed into our grounds just before us and
drove up to the door. Seeing us alight on the steps they moved on
to the stables, and jumped out, running under cover, where a door
was found open. To let them remain there amongst horses and
dogs would have been inhospitable and unkind. So I went to their
rescue, half drowned as I was, and got them all into our château
one by one under the cover of cloaks of oilskin. They got some

changes of dress; their outside garments dried, refreshments, and a welcome. Stayed over an hour and a half until the storm passed away. Left their cards, and expressed themselves so much obliged, etc. They seemed to be high-caste people, an American family from New York travelling for pleasure. Papa, mamma, two nice girls, daughters, and a gentleman friend. Mr. C—— was a well-informed, intelligent, gentlemanlike man. He deplored the state of his country, and condemned the civil war. Said America was already thrown back half a century, and trade was paralyzed; the country was being over-taxed, and prospects very dark indeed. I had mentioned that I purposed going to Washington to see the army of the North.

Some ten or fourteen days afterwards I received such a nice letter from Mr. C—— inclosing me letters of introduction to the Secretary of State, General Scott, and General McClellan at Washington, with a hope that we would all visit his family at New York. I hope to do so, and to see more of all those good people hereafter.

August 22nd. A dinner-party at Mr. Moffat's. Met some acquaintances of the olden time. People seem to keep well in this climate. Twenty years have given the autumnal tint to the head, but no other change, and so I am very strongly pressed to pitch my tent here.

23rd. Dinner-party at home to meet a gathering of old friends come to see a live General.

24th. Got a ticket-of-leave to pass over or through the Victoria Bridge, two miles long, less 150 feet, from shore to shore. There is a side-walk for foot passengers along the single line of rail, but no thoroughfare. On each side of the central tube there is a small gallery recess, with windows looking up and down the river and to both sides, the span being 330 feet. Three rafts pass under, downwards, of course, at a good pace, while a steamboat slowly stemmed the current on to Laprairie. It is a long, dreary, dark tunnel walk, over this wonderful specimen of man's ingenuity completed by Messrs. Peto, Brassey & Co., and opened by the Prince of Wales on this day last year. Just as I emerged from the long cave, I was met by a tornado of hail, rain, thunder and lightning; the hard, white hail as large as bullets. The brilliant sun was darkened, nor could I now see 100 yards before me. The train now dashed by at full speed, and disappeared in the long tube. The rattling hailstones on the tin-covered bridge roof made more noise than the musketry at Bull's Run, with all their guns, dragoons, bullets, bombs, and thunder. Very few hard knocks, but a good deal of plunder. This Bull Run has created a new war amongst people and parties. It has taken the polish off the North side of American Independence, and

may give poor Canada a wee bit longer time to make up her
accounts before she resigns herself into the hands of those victorious
warriors (to be). Hear how they bellow through the press of New
York. 'Both England and Spain may rest assured that just retribu-
tion will be visited upon them for the outrage offered in the Queen's
proclamation, the United States will possess itself of Canada, and
her Catholic Majesty will have to pay with the sacrifice of Cuba.'
How very considerate to pass over England! Brag is a good dog,
but Holdfast is a better.

August 27th. Our party had a kind invitation to pass a couple
of days at Beauharnois with Mr. and Mrs. K——th. Started by
rail to Lachine, then by steamer *en route*, to dine at seven. Always
in luck! The small steamer had gone astray, and we took to a big
one with many passengers bound via De Chatageau. Quite out of
our way. In serpentining up that pretty river, so very close to
both banks, we stuck in the mud tight for two hours; the usual
remedies for ungrounding a ship were of course in full play. A
batch of idle nuns sat at their temple-gate waiting the vesper bells
and looking at us with complacency. It was late, and the dinner
was just being served, and what had become of us, I could hear
them say. Darkness came over the woods and the water. The
bells in the nuns' tower had ceased to chime. The thunder bel-
lowed as it knows how to do after a hot day; the lightning flashed
all about, darting down in zig-zag fashion, and this was all the light
we had. Two tables had been served with a tea-supper, i.e. tea and
coffee, cold meats, toast, and iced butter, with apple sauce for
Yankee-doodles. I confess I was a little too vexed to join this
party, although now late for iced champagne and claret at B——
house. She floats! Hurrah! But must now try back, and so we
did, counter-marching and crawling and feeling our way out of the
C. River into St. Lawrence. At ten p.m. we got alongside the old
wooden pier and found our host with a big lantern in hand looking
for us, and his carriage in waiting. All right at last, but the dinner-
party had passed away. However, we had dinner, tea, and supper,
tria juncta in uno; an hour of music and singing, and to roost at
eleven-thirty, as they say on the rail.

28th. Order of the day: Sailing and fishing and picnicking until
six p.m., dinner to be at seven-thirty. Our party at the house, Mr.
K—— and his pretty young wife, ourselves, Sir W. Fenwick
Williams of Kars, Commander-in-Chief in Canada; Colonel Hawley
and Captain Curtis, 60th Rifles; Mrs. Price and Miss G. S——. We
all embarked in Sir Fenwick's yacht, eleven of us and the crew. We
sailed about on the Lake St. Lewis in the usual way; anchored off
Horse Island, beautifully feathered with green trees to the water's

edge. What a squadron of rafts going down. There's one like an island, and with nineteen houses on it—quite a little colony. And now for the fishing. Launched three boats and got out the tackle —all kinds of the most inviting dishes for the finny tribe. Having refreshed and fortified the inward man with iced wines and beer, after sundry different dishes, the fishers tried their luck trolling, and did catch some black bass.

I went off in a shell by myself, with a pair of oars, to the edge of the Cedar rapids. I just touched the foam, and danced along the boiling current, too brisk for my coble, so I made for a curling smoke in the island, rising through the trees. There was an Indian bivouac, one young man in the *cuisine* boiling a large pot of salt pork, a 'bucket' of rice being already prepared. A long blanket thrown or stretched over a pole resting on two forked sticks, was the nocturnal dwelling, cool and simple. The party here were of the half-caste Canadian Indians, who find employment taking the rafts down the rapids.

Canoes may be seen scattered over the lakes fishing for logs! Rafts are often broken up in the rapids, and the great logs or trees, fifty, eighty, or a hundred feet long, and thick in proportion, are scattered far and wide. They are picked up by the canoes and towed ashore as prize. Part of a raft lay here in a cove—twenty-one logs of great length and thickness. The day was most brilliant and enjoyable. Bluepeter up, all hands on board the *Wanderer*; just enough wind to waft us home to a capital dinner. Mr. K. has a large house here, commanding a fine view of the lake and some nineteen islands. He manages the seigniory for Mr. Ellice, the proprietor of 30,000 acres—a little farm of eighteen square miles!

29th. Our little party broke up today at three p.m. After lunch we returned by steamer twenty-seven miles, and shot the rapids at Lachine. The fall gradually begins at Caughnawaga, and increases in speed to the boiling leap. Here everyone stands aghast, with nervous eye and clutch, deeply excited, and some with trembling limbs. The vessel now speeds on with all the waters of Niagara at her heels, dashing and foaming, rumbling, grumbling, and tumbling down to the abyss. Baptiste, a noble Indian pilot, with his calm countenance and bright eye, guides the bark down this foaming gulf, aided by three other men, but he alone can do it. Four men at the wheel, their eyes fixed on one object—the narrow, winding, rocky channel. Well trained, they act in concert, and safely guide the ship. A mistake, a snap of the rudder chain, a yard out of the narrow course, and all would be engulfed, lost, swept away with the mighty torrent. I don't think many other countrymen would have the nerve to do such a bold adventure. I rather like an adventure myself, but found them at times very dangerous. Now steered outside Nuns' Island, and away under the centre span of the Great Bridge, and to our own landing. Found the carriage waiting, and the two incomparably dear children full of joy to meet us. A trip up the river is promised by my friend of Kars, Bart., a kind, amiable man, and a very gallant soldier, as everyone knows.

30th. Taking up a newspaper today, I was shocked and grieved to see recorded the early death of a very amiable and lovely young friend of ours, the much-loved wife of Richard Watt, Esq., of Speke Hall, Lancashire. Poor dear, kind, generous Ada Watt! how many happy days we passed in your noble mansion, where all received such a warm welcome from your kind self and him who loved you so dearly—a truly generous and attached husband, devoted to yourself [1] and only child, sweet Ada, at five years old bereaved of a darling mother, the tender tie of childhood. Alas! for the living— grief for the dead; but she lives to die no more. This world, indeed, is only a training school for the next. God often takes those soonest whom He loves best, and the time they lose on earth is gained in Heaven.

[1] Poor Mr. W. soon followed his wife, aged thirty.

CHAPTER
22

The American Civil War

SEPTEMBER 2nd 1861. Left Montreal at 4 p.m., crossed by the steam ferry, and took the rail for Boston — 332 miles. Reached Rouse's Point in two hours — the land of stars and stripes! A very rickety old wooden bridge, built on piles, upwards of a mile long, conveys a very long train across the Lake Champlain. From its appearance I would not like to drive a waggon over it, but the Yankee nerves, strung like harp-strings, are always in good tone and in concert pitch until the snap comes. Here I took a sleeping car, i.e. a long carriage in which beds are fitted up in a few minutes, at half a dollar a head. I had a picnic supper in my bag, thanks to my Mary, some nice brandy, plenty of iced water in the cabin, and so I fared very well before turning into my berth. I could not help sleeping by starts, but the galloping motion all night was more like a waggon on a corduroy road. Up at six, and found the train tearing along the bank of the Merrimac. Country of a sandy soil, but well cultivated. The houses are neat, and with every appearance of comfort — a century before the old French-Canadians, who never improve. In this sleeping car, as it is called, there is a stove (for cold weather), a washstand, a curtain in the centre divides the crockery and china, and if the carriage only rolled along smoothly, it would be a most agreeable night journey and saving of time.

Arrived at the 'Revere' Hotel at nine a.m. Boston is a fine old English-like town, full of trade, good shops and newspapers for the million. From the cupola of the State House is the finest view of the city, harbour, public buildings, and surrounding country. It is almost an island. Several islands stand across the entrance of the harbour, two of them fortified. I would think the town itself might be made strong enough to secure it from any enemy, but it lies open at present.

Went out with Mr. Isaac C. Bates to his country-house on Jamaica Plains, five miles. He drove me about for two hours, and a more charming country I never saw. No end to the beautiful houses, villas, and châteaux, all detached in their own grounds. There are pleasure-gardens, orchards, and green fields and all in the finest taste. The country is undulating and well-wooded, roads very good, and here and there a pretty church spire shoots high above the greenwood trees. There is a very nice lake, too, they call Jamaica Pond. American lakes are so extensive, this pretty sheet of water is not supposed to class beyond a fishpond; it would be venerated in Lancashire.

We dined at half-past six; a nice dinner, and best of wines— amongst them Madeira sixty years in bottle. Mrs. B. is a charming, highly-informed, nice person, very pretty, hospitable, and most agreeable—nothing Yankeeish about herself or her kind husband.

Boston is gay with flags. They float over every house, across all streets; every stall in the long market building is decorated with the stars and stripes. The youths are drumming and drilling on the roadsides and in the avenues, all bitten by the same mad dog!

There is a noble harbour here, and no end to fish of all kinds, which are easily preserved, and sent coastwise. I saw a waggon-load of great blocks of ice tossed down to a fishing boat, to preserve the enormous heads of the halibut, which may be considered a dainty, but which are very ugly to look on. The Post-office is beautifully arranged, and the great granite pillars of the Customs-house are wonderful blocks of one single stone in each column.

The Americans are really a wonderful people for invention and going ahead at everything. They have started a very beautiful new sort of coffin. Some are oblong, no angles. Some have a hinge on the lid, others rounded at the ends, with plate-glass tops, and lined with quilted white silk, all of the handsomest polished woods. Mr. Lewis Jones is a man of refined taste in his trade. I wrote his epitaph:

Lewis Jones
His bones.

September 5th. Left old Boston at half-past eight this morning, by rail, and arrived in New York five o'clock p.m.—236 miles in eight hours and a half! I have no particular desire to ride upon a rail at such a pace any more. At times I expected the cars would have jumped into the air, or away off the line. It was impossible to read, or stand on one's legs. The cars are very long, each one carrying about forty people. There is a passage and communication up the centre through all the train, doors at each end and seats on either side for two, bay windows at each seat, so that one can see the country as he flies along.

Entered the City of New York, or, as the people take pride in always calling it, 'New York City', just in time for dinner at the Fifth Avenue Hotel, the largest and finest hotel, perhaps, in the Old and New World. This country is on an enlarged scale, or goes by steam. Pitman, a celebrated and favourite railway contractor, had his nuptial knot tied the other day in the railway carriage moving at its topmost speed. Characteristic of the man, never taking a holiday, or neglecting business. He had no time for a twelve o'clock ceremony in a church.

There are 24,000 miles of railways in America, built at a cost of one thousand millions of dollars. About half of this enormous treasure was lost to the original proprietors. This is in answer to an Englishman of standing in his own country who asked if there were any railways in America! It is but thirty-two years ago since the first railway was opened by Brother Jonathan.

6th. Dined with our friends who were caught in the storm at our house in Montreal. Very kind, good people; very glad to see and give me a hearty welcome. He is a wealthy merchant, has a noble house, and is a most intelligent gentleman. All so very grateful for our reception of them during the tornado.

Everything quiet, and free from military parade here. A sprinkling of officers at the hotels, and some detachments of recruits passing to join their depôts, is all I have seen. A great number of military waggons packed in a square, and a large camp at Newhaven, which I passed at railway speed, is hardly worth recording. I must march on.

Went to the Scotch Kirk with my friend, Mr. C——. A very handsome church, with a good organ, and good singing too. But what would the gude wives in Auld Reekie think o' a' them fiddlesticks? There are some very handsome churches, and some very high ones in the city, next-of-kin to the Romans. But this is a Protestant country, although all religions are freely tolerated. I dined, and passed a day with Mr. T——, on Staten Island. He drove me nearly all over it. The roads are rough and dusty; the views are very fine, and there are some handsome country seats, and very many pretty villas. Distance by steam-ferry, six miles.

The island is nine miles by eighteen. A baronet lives here, who was lately raised to that dignity for driving some steamboats across the Atlantic, and making his fortune. It is not often we hear of a gallant soldier being so distinguished for losing a fortune, and losing a limb in the service of his country; but everything goes by steam nowadays. There is Long Island, across the Bay, 120 miles in length. And there is Sandy Hook, and the big prison Lafayette, full of state prisoners just now. The fashion is to show kindness to any gentleman suspected of plotting mischief against the State, and to shut him up in the old style of the Doge of Venice. Some ladies, too, have lost their liberty for backing up their Southern friends: so that this land of liberty is not so free as it was a year gone by.

The Americans are an extravagant people, and wish to make it the fashion. A house was pointed out to me today that cost 200,000 dollars. The average rent of houses in the Fifth Avenue (two miles long) is £600 a year; but people are beginning to pull up. They feel the war taxes, but most of all the depression in trade. The wages of servants in this hotel have been cut down nearly one-third, and the ladies are giving up their hoops. But this may be from some other cause. I see the bustle behind coming into play again. Indeed, ladies at times come to dinner without stays—I suppose to indulge the appetite, as they get five meals a day here for their money. I cannot say much for their beauty, and that vile fashion of cramming a knife into the mouth makes one nervous at dinner. I can excuse them picking corn off the stick with their teeth, like a squirrel, as it is becoming general amongst *los Engleses* in Canada, but it looks funny.

Every servant-maid in this hotel is Irish. They work best, are honest, and cheerful, while American girls are too idle and independent, being generally brought up to some trade or business, and would rather be served than bow to a master.

Visited two of the most remarkable houses in New York; that of Mr. Stewart, commonly called a dry goods store, an immense establishment. You may have a pair of gloves or a million dollars' worth of carpets, silks of the richest manufacture, at any price, or coarse towels for your kitchen, damasks of all kinds, and of all prices—everything and anything that can be made or stored away in a most elegant mansion of seven floors. There are four hundred clerks employed in this house, and they sell from ten to twelve millions of dollars' worth of goods yearly. Mr. Stewart started as a petty hawker, and made his way to very great wealth in thirty-five years. He is a gentlemanly person, with very good address, and looks quite fresh. He was so obliging and sent one of his people to show us everything, and introduced me to Governor Morgan, of

New York State, who was sitting with him in his office, and with whom I had some talk about the war, the topic of all conversation.

Our next visit was to Ball, Black & Co., 587 Broadway, the great jewellers, gold and silver smiths. Here were heaps of wealth in diamonds alone, beyond anything I had ever seen. The house itself is beautiful, and arranged in three storeys, one apartment on each flat. Above these are two flats for the working gold and silver smiths. They talk of dollars as we do of shillings in England. The Prince of Wales made a handsome purchase here for the gentleman who entertained him for three days' shooting in the prairies, which afforded him joyful pleasure. Mr. Black was mourning over the war, and said some of his best and most liberal customers were secessionists. Everybody seems to feel the change for the worse, but army contractors! I am very much indebted to my friend Mr. Corning for all his disinterested attention to me.

The omnibus companies are better managed here than in England. They dispense with conductors; the passenger steps in, rings a bell, and hands out of a hole behind the driver the regulated fare of six cents, which will take him on for six miles or more, if he likes. When he wishes to stop, he pulls a strap attached to the driver, and he pulls up. They drive very slow, and save the poor horses. The 'bus is clean and roomy. There are 800 of them in the streets.

We have shop-walkers at home to catch everyone they can, and grab his money. We have *salle-à-manger* walkers here at the hotels, to see that you are properly attended, and get plenty to eat.

September 10th. Left New York at eight-thirty; crossed the ferry in the great steam-float to Jersey City, and took the rail to Philadelphia, ninety miles. It was a slow coach. Arrived at two-thirty p.m., and drove some four miles through ugly suburbs before setting down at the Continental Hotel, an enormous building, much like the one I left in New York, and carried on in the same style. The waiters are all black fellows, smart, obliging, and good-humoured. But I don't fancy the house, it is too large, and seems a little gloomy after the cheerful place I left. There are fine shady trees in the streets; the weeping willow tops all others. This is the place of its nativity, and here it flourishes. The country not interesting, excepting on the banks of the Delaware; all a flat from the St. Lawrence, and well adapted for the *chemin-de-fer*.

Very unwell all last night, something like cholera, and still a little *hors-de-combat*. I attribute this shake to total abstinence; the iced water is so good and refreshing. I followed the crowd too much, but the weather is warm. Beautiful bouquets of white and red roses here for sale in the streets; melons, peaches, and plantains in abundance. I am going into another summer, but I won't pitch my tent in America. There is no music, no sweetness in the voice of the people. There go the firebells and engines rattling away under my window, a very long way to look down, and there are people three pair higher up. One street is a journey to walk, and then such a getting-up stairs—too much for humanity.

The pretty grey squirrels are enjoying life in the squares amongst the grass, and showing their agility chasing each other up the trees; no one disturbs them in their gambols.

The omnibus here runs on a rail through all the principal streets, a very great convenience for the public. The people have a considerable notion of comfort in their way, but are a century behind Old England. The tobacco-squirting gents that one meets with in cars, i.e. railway carriages, are disgusting, and there is no escape; all one class of cars on this road. So much of equality and so independent. But this war, and its taxes, will do them good in the end. On this evening the commodious bathrooms and the most luxurious shaving-rooms are all full of visitors, anxious to enjoy themselves. That yellow fellow there, with a beard like a whinbush, is getting it trimmed. He reclines back in a velvet armchair, with his legs up and his eyes shut, and perfumes lying all around on the table. But the everlasting cigar is to him the sweetest of all perfumes.

See what a rush there is at the third edition of some newspaper, as full of lies as it can cram. Every lady and gentleman has a copy of every paper, I believe, that comes into light, but there is no reliance to be placed on any of them, flimsy lying rags! O! for an honest English newspaper. What a bedlam of voices—'Washington—comparison of generals—Bull's Run—Harper's Ferry'—and 'I guess you're goin' down South'. 'We'll whip them next time.' 'Is Jeff Davis dead?' 'Well, I can't be sure, but if he is they keep him 'bove ground, and that beats creation.'—'Old fuss and feathers wouldn't be enough for him dead or alive.'   What a clatter while I ascend to my very comfortable apartments.

September 11th. Up at six-thirty, breakfast, and to the bar to pay my bill; offered an introductory note to 'Willard's', the house in Washington, from the house in Philadelphia—not customary at home, but very useful abroad. It serves three parties without any expense.

Left by the eight-thirty train for Baltimore, ninety-eight miles. Pretty country along the Delaware. Crossed a branch of Chesapeake Bay, at Havre-de-Grace in a steam ferryboat, as big as a small island, a railway on the top deck, where all the baggage-cars were run on. There were two long tables below covered with fruit and refreshments, the peach and melon in great abundance. There was a guard of soldiers, i.e. some ragged fellows with arms, to protect the ferry; a camp in the distance, with a multitude of army waggons and horses, the latter all loose in a meadow sloping down to the bay. Crossed Bush River Bridge, lately burned by the rebels—a single line of rail a mile and half long. This beautiful Susquehanna Bay is celebrated for the canvas-back duck. Guards are now at all the ferries. Baltimore at two p.m., an hour late, and a long drive to Barnum's. Did not warm to the town. Grass grew in all the private streets, although the houses were fine and lofty in general, with marble steps leading up to the doors. The streets were wide and long, and at right angles, and intersected by tramways. Fort McHenry commands the entrance, situated on a branch of Chesapeake Bay. It was in this town the rebels showed themselves by attacking the troops in the rail cars going to Washington, and got themselves placed under martial law. There are some monuments in the city of battles fought, and won of course!

I had two letters of introduction here, but the town looked dull and deserted-like, so I took my departure, letters and all, three-thirty for the capital—thirty-eight miles. Passed through several encampments along the forest line, picturesque and cheerful. I was glad to see a tented field again, and the raw material being drilled into a military sort of discipline.

The unfinished dome of the Capitol caught my eye about dusk as we rolled up to the terminus, two hours after time. There was the usual or unusual number of bus-cabs and cars in waiting, everyone bellowing and bawling to take you everywhere. With much hard pressure I elbowed through the crowd and called for 'Willard's' bus, which put me down here at seven o'clock in the dark, and I don't know yet where I am. I put my name and rank in the book, handed the two notes to the proprietor (one was from the great hotel at New York). I was instantly attended to, and got a nice front room on the first floor, while the house, lobbies, halls, and corridors were jammed up with creation! Generals, Colonels, Captains, Volunteers, travellers from all parts of this wide-world continent, all talking together, smoking, chawin, and spitting, and restless. The marble-tile floors in a swim of tobacco expectoration! Tobacco's cheap, and Virginia grows it. A cavalry regiment has just passed under my window, but I can't see them, and now to roost.

12th. Up at six-thirty; fine morning after hard rain last night, and for a fortnight past. It did not come in my way, all sunshine since I left Montreal. I see part of the dessert for the dinner today being delivered at the door, viz. thirteen hampers of peaches, one being as much as a man can lift! What a scramble to get any breakfast, abundance of everything, but the multitude to provide for is most disagreeably on the increase and the waiters, who are of the white race here, dislike their business, and are very badly dressed. What are all those officers doing in the city, and in the hotels, and at the bars? None under the rank of a Captain fit for anything I'm told, how could they be fit for command or warfare: in from the plough but yesterday, surely 'tis hardly fair to criticise their ability or their uniform if they fight but for their flag. Bull's Run has opened the eye of the Union, and they are profiting by the race. Beauregard lost his chance, and will never get such another. Washington was his own had he chased the Bull some miles further. Great preparations are being made here to carry on the war with activity and system. There is a fine corps of army waggons for commissariat and ambulance, each drawn by four fine horses or mules; the drivers are inferior to the cattle. All is bustle and business — warlike. The crowds of inquiring people for news from the field, yesterday, after a bit of skirmish, reminded one of Brussels after the 'Waterloo', only there were no killed or wounded! The newspapers lie systematically, and depend for their reports on what they hear in the crowd. However, they must live, and they give you such a heap of lies for two cents one can't grumble at the price! Young horses for the cavalry are coming into town in great numbers, 3,000 a day. And the raw material of creation is coming in squads from the country in charge of drill sergeants to begin a new trade, all with their little carpet bags or bundles, looking very dull, cheerless, and jaded.

Called on General Scott. He was tired and lying down, and could not see me. It was but eleven o'clock — seventy-five can't do the work he wishes to perform. He sent me a pass with his compliments, and will be glad to see me after dinner. I dine today with Lord Lyons, our ambassador, at seven o'clock, which may be after General Scott has gone to bed — I will inquire.

I called on the Honourable W. H. Seward, Secretary of State: not at home; returned my call. People all very alert and busy at his office, not forgetting the tobac.; small *tubs* were arranged along the galleries to save the floors! White House, the residence of the President for the time being, reminds me of the Vice-Regal Lodge in the Phoenix Park, Dublin. Across the avenue there is a handsome square, planted with shady trees and green grass-plots, with seats for the weary. In the centre, on a large marble block, stands a fine bronze statue of General Jackson on horseback. The Treasury is a handsome building, but not yet finished. It shows thirty fine fluted columns to the front, and when the other wing is added it will be remarkable as a public building, and will do honour to the city.

Called to see Russell of *The Times*. Found him fat and jolly,
all alive, eating his breakfast as if he was not going to be paid off by
Judge Lynch and Co.! But he's not afraid: he says their bark is
worse than their bite. Although they have promised to hang him,
I would say from his jolly appearance, that he is in more danger
from a vertical sun. And the sun is very hot just now, even under
the shady trees along the street. What a luxury those shady trees
are in climates so hot as this at 39° latitude.

At four p.m., I accompanied General McClellan to visit his outposts, with all his staff and an escort of cavalry. We made a great
flourish out of the city, crossing the long bridge. I was well
mounted, but did not know where I was going, until I found myself
so far away amongst the different encampments, I began to quake
for my dinner at the British Ambassador's at seven o'clock. Eight,
and nine, and ten o'clock came at a furious pace, when we all dismounted at the tent of General Blenken, to refresh with cigars and
champagne, having previously stopped at the headquarter tent of
General Franklyn an hour before, to pay him a visit and to be introduced. Blenken is a German, a fine fellow, and a good soldier—so
is Franklyn. Blenken's band was playing very sweetly before his
tent. We had a long and agreeable conversation, and parted mutual
friends. I was introduced to all the officers of any note by
McClellan, until my right hand was squeezed to death. He has
right well fortified his position for miles along the right banks and
heights of the Potomac, and I think made it perfectly safe from any
attack of the enemy, and is carrying on his works with vigour. We
got to within three and a half miles of the Southern outposts, but
they are so hermetically sealed up there is no approaching near
without the chance of a welcome from a cannon-shot, and none of
our lives insured. The Federal army is increasing every day in
strength and discipline, the men are strong, stout, and healthy, in
fine feather, and ready to prime and load. McClellan is the very
man to lead them—young, vigilant, quiet in manner and address—
popular and with a kind word for everyone. He is always in the
saddle, and greeting his soldiers with an encouraging look and
address as he rides over the tented fields. He was extremely kind,
courteous, and friendly to me, without the least reserve in conversation. He has thrown up a great many strong redoubts in the most
commanding positions, covering the country for many miles in
front of the enemy, having first cleared his ground by felling the
forest in all directions, and spoiling many a beautiful place, as he
said, 'with great regret', but the necessity demanded the sacrifice.
The troops are very comfortably tented, plenty of fuel, and water,
with a most abundant supply of good rations, more than they can

consume. Their pay, besides, is fifteen dollars a month per man, and the officer's pay is double that of the English service—that of a Major-General is 500 dollars a month. I got home after a twenty-five miles' ride at half-past ten, too late for his lordship's good dinner, and must explain tomorrow.

From all I can see and learn, the Federal army are now in the ascendant, and will win the day. There is money at command, the capital secure, an increasing army, and good commissariat, learning their new trade, and united heart and voice. Coming home we were challenged by sentries along the whole line, and could not pass without giving the countersign, which was done by an aide-de-camp, in advance, dismounting from his horse, and whispering the word to the sentinel. I never saw more precaution. General McClellan is a man about thirty-five, fresh complexion, black hair, and sandy moustache, well-built, and about five feet eight inches and a half, with a mild and pleasing expression. He learned something in the Crimea, and has written a report of that campaign for his Government, being out there as commissioner, by order. He was educated at West Point Military School, and understands his profession as an engineer and artillery officer.

One o'clock in the morning, and now for a seven hours' snooze, in spite of the mosquitoes.

13th. Dined with General Winfield Scott, Commander-in-Chief of the United States army: a nice dinner and most superb wines. A most hospitable fine old soldier of seventy-five years, feeble on his legs, but bright and clear in intellect. His three aides-de-camp were at dinner, all Colonels and young men. Colonel Hamilton had seen service in Mexico, with the General, and had been wounded on two occasions. I had some long and agreeable conversation with the General. He told me of his being made prisoner when wounded at Lundies Lane, in Canada, 1814, and how he was well treated by all but Sir Charles Provost, the Governor. He talked of my services, and knew them all from the records. He said he had much conversation with the young Prince of Wales, a fine young fellow, who told him that he was a Colonel in the army; that our Queen was a most excellent and most exemplary sovereign. He had invited General McClellan to meet me at dinner, but, always in the saddle, he had not come up to time. If I could remain a few days longer, he would have some nice people to meet me again at dinner. He is a well-informed, unprejudiced, fine old soldier, with a kind and courteous manner. He retires soon after dinner, takes a few hours' rest, and up to work again.

The town today looks warlike—dragoons, orderlies, staff officers, and waggons tearing away through the streets, droves of young horses coming in for the cavalry, artillery, and army waggons. They are put into harness at once—some are gentle, and others kick themselves out of the traces most furiously. But they are just kicked back into the shafts again until they become gentle and tame to work. Passed the evening with *The Times* Russell, and went over the Crimean campaign afresh, and the many incidents of that war.

14th. Called at White House, and had a shake hands with President Lincoln. I went upstairs, and looked about for a state-room of reception, and someone to hand in my card. But no one in the shape of an aide-de-camp or messenger to be seen. After some turnings, I saw a lady and gentleman standing in a hall, look-ing into a room where several people were assembled. I asked where I could find the President. 'Oh, that's he, up there, writing at the table, with spectacles.' So I advanced, free and easy, as is the United States custom, up to his table, to hear him speak, and look well into his dark features. He wore a common loose, white light duster, and a pair of big shoes (easy for corns). He is about six feet in height, stoops, is thin and wiry, with black hair and beard, very kindly and familiar in his manner to all, but a very common-place looking man.

A lady sat beside him, pleading for some appointment for her son. He told her several times that he could not promise success, but she stuck to him like a brick. 'Well,' he said, 'what you want is this—just for me to pass your son over the heads of so many on a list above him.' 'But, sir, my son, you know, holds an appoint-ment,' etc., and there she sat like a woman determined to win, and she did so far, for he wrote a letter then and there to the Naval Department, and asked her if she would present it herself, or if he should send it. The lady consulted a friend beside her, and then asked the President to forward it. He got up, and took an official envelope from his bureau, inclosed it, and placed it on the letter-table, and got rid of this visitor.

The next was a gentleman introduced to ask a favour under trying circumstances. It was to pass through the lines of the Con-federate army to his home to bring back his family. This could not be granted on any terms. He had left these matters in the hands of his Generals, and all communication was entirely closed between the two armies and the ground they occupied. This clinched my expectations to pass that way, and so I gave it up.

All this private, or intended private, conference was like an open court. At times the President laughed at odd sayings, and the company joined with him. I got tired waiting and now handed him my card, saying that I had called to pay my respects, and wish

x

his cause success.   He looked at my card and read, Major-General
—George—Bell,—C.B.,—British—Army.   Then, stretching out his
long arm and a big claw, gave me a shake with, 'How is Old
England?'   'Flourishing, and friendly, sir, to the Stars and Stripes.'
The White House is always white, and now being painted white
afresh gives it a sickly white paint smell.   There is a garden behind
and hot-houses.   But all houses are hot just now, inside and out—a
melting heat.   Called to see General Scott, and found him as busy
as a bee in his office.   McClellan away to the front looking after
his defences.

The Post-Office is a noble building, the finest, perhaps, in the
world, and the Patent Office is almost equally grand.   There is an
advantage for equestrians perhaps living in this great city, that is,
they may be out in the country or in the forest from any part of the
town in ten minutes.

Passed the evening with Captain L'Amy Russell, and some nice
fellows of the American army.   One of them presented me with
his picture, an excellent likeness.   We read in a North paper just
come in—'A British Major-General who was out in a reconnaissance the other evening with Major-General McClellan, stated that
Washington was safe from any attack of the enemy.'   I was the
Britisher of course.   Someone heard me make the remark, and as
it was so favourable to the cause, it was telegraphed to New York,
and appeared in the *Herald* next day in Washington.   Smart practice!   General Mansfield, U.S.A., called on me, as he said to pay his
respects and make my acquaintance, having heard from General
Scott that I had been a distinguished officer.   I rather astonished
General Scott when I told him the liberal retirement of distinguished
General officers in the army of England.   His retiring pay will be
15,000 dollars a year!

Went to church, asked for a seat.   'Take a seat, sir, in any pew
that you like', and they were all alike, very handsome, with crimson cushions, carpets, and books.   I never felt the heat more
oppressive in India.

Everything here is in the rough; the beginning of a new creation;
men and women, different people from Brother Sam at Boston.
The crockery part live on tobacco and destroy one's comfort in
public places.   The china are not beautiful, and have begun to drop
the crinoline.   The harness, saddle, and all horse gear coarse and
common.   Great streets unfinished, extending far away into the
woods and forests.   Stand on the highest street in Washington and
you will see green forest at each end miles apart.   The Senate
House, built of white marble, is unfinished, and is perhaps the finest
specimen of architecture in the world.   It will be always white

and clean, no coal-smoke to dirty and darken its exterior. There is a little green park in its front, with a fine marble statue of Washington, and another green shady park in the rear open to the people. The Post-Office, too, is of white marble, most elegant, tasteful, and elaborate. That big one of ours in London is but a coarse, low-caste building in comparison, and our House of Lords and Commons is tumbling to dust and black as a sweep. The Americans are an inventive, ingenious, industrious, skilful, boasting, unpolished people, with good and bad in the ranks like most nations.

15th. Dined with Lord Lyons at the Embassy, a kind and hospitable, clever diplomatist. The dinner was in the style of an English nobleman, which you seldom see in this country. Russell was there, and lively in conversation as usual. Stepped into Mr. Riggs, the banker, in the evening, and had some small chat and refreshment. He is reported to be very wealthy, and has a very handsome house.

16th. Not so hot today. Went to the top of the Capitol from whence the grand panorama, the city of magnificent distances, as sometimes called, is now encircled with encampments. Two regiments were resting on the road below, on the line of march across the river to take ground on Arlington Heights. A regiment of cavalry like mice were crawling over the long bridge. There you see the white canvas towns peeping out of the woods, and the smoke of many distant camps. That highest point in the far away distance is Munson's Hill, one of the posts of the rebel army. Down below in that creek is the naval yard. Those are all the public buildings. You have under your eye at once the whole plan of the town that is to be a grand city in a hundred years.

I would not take a Block to pitch my tent here.

When is this vast and magnificent building to be finished? The dome is not covered in, but the interior has been long in use. The Lords and Commons here meet to transact the business of the U.S. as we do in London. They are not sitting at present.

Looked at the two regiments halted below — 3rd New Hampshire, and 8th Maine. Rightly sturdy, able men, about an average of twenty-eight years old, comfortably dressed, long loose blue jackets, and sky-blue pants; an excellent cap, light, and waterproof they told me, with a peak behind and before — no stiffness in it. They had water-bottles of different patterns, knapsacks, well shod, and firearms rifled. Ugly customers to meet when they get riled, or the dander up.

Dined with Doctor Russell. A very agreeable party of six. We agreed to march tomorrow, *en route* to Chicago, unless those people (who have such a burning desire to kill each other) get up a

fight, which I don't expect, although it is much talked of, and there
is a great military buzz — galloping of officers and orderly dragoons,
moving of troops, and rattling of waggons all day. I don't see
where they can fight, unless in the woods where they are encamped.
However, I stay no longer.

17th. Left Washington at half-past five p.m. Passed through
several encampments of the Federal army, and met many trains
coming in, crowded with soldiers. They were packed even on the
top of the cars, cheering as they shot along the iron road. Baltimore at eight p.m. We, i.e. Mr. Russell, Captain L'Amy, and
myself, put up at the Eutaw House, a very fine hotel. Baltimore
has a population of 260,000, a vast number of whom are ready and
willing to join the rebel side, and would do so were it not for the
strong military force here. Left at half-past eight a.m. for Pittsburgh, 332 miles. Having checked our baggage, i.e. a brass number,
say 346, is tied to a trunk, you receive a duplicate, and you have
nothing more to say to your traps until you arrive at your station.
Your baggage is then delivered, when you give up your ticket, and
to no one else.

We had to make a long *détour* to keep clear of the Confederate
army. Our route lay through Harper's Ferry, but they had possession. This Harper's Ferry had something to remind the Union
of their first great national grief — their first experience of the vanity
of boasting. War, grim servile war, hangs over them now, and an
expensive game to play they will find it; but they have some game
cocks on their side. I spoke to one in the streets of the capital,
who told me he was an old revolutionary soldier, now seventy-eight
years of age, and had walked seventy miles to offer his services to
General Scott. I know this is quite true, not from his own tale.

We bowled along the banks of the beautiful Susquehanna, a
crooked river 500 miles long, into Harrisburgh, crossing a tubular
bridge nearly as long as the Victoria at Montreal, but more wonderful. Public conveyances go through the tunnel part; there is a
rail on the top along the roof for the railway trains, but without
any parapet at all. I happened to be in the last seat of the hindmost car, and stepped out on the platform, and saw this frightful
mode of crossing a wide river. A deep chasm on either side; the
slightest mistake any day or night, and all is lost. About the middle
there is a long, wide gap, where you see the water, the bridge itself
being connected by long beams, with a continuation of the iron rail
laid into them. This is to provide against fire, that one-half might
be saved in case of a blaze some day. I confess I was very nervous,
and held on like a brick, for the pace was rapid.

Harrisburgh is beautifully situated in a fertile valley, surrounded with wooded mountains. It is the capital of Pennsylvania, on the east bank of the Susquehanna, 106 miles from Philadelphia. There are many bridges, and many picturesque islands, and it is encircled by the Kittatinny mountains, showing a fine gorge to the west. Several regiments were passing down to Washington. About fourteen miles on, we left Susquehanna river, and followed the banks of the Juniata for about 100 miles to the base of the Alleghanies, the canal keeping the road and river company most of the way. Twelve pieces of artillery passed, and loads of horses for the army. Some fine orchards, and beautiful apples, showed themselves as we flew past. At all the stations little boys and girls had baskets of pears and peaches for sale. A lady passenger, with five healthy children, was returning to her home from Philadelphia. She was the wife of an officer going to the wars, and lamenting over the sad state of things. 'The best government in the world,' she said 'was placed in jeopardy by a set of rebels; that her kindred were on the other side, and now they would all be killing each other—brother against brother, uncle against nephew.'

Arrived at Logan House Hotel, Altoona, at half-past seven, and missed all our baggage; all left behind where we changed cars. No fault of ours. A telegram was despatched, and it all came safely by the next morning in the train by which we went on our way.

Altoona is a rising little town. Nine years ago there was but one farm-house. There are great ironworks, now the grand depôt of this great Pennsylvania R.R., and a teetotal hotel as big as a barrack—the dining room 156 feet long, and tables laid out five times a day for 100 people. The trains stop to breakfast, dine, and sup here. A person stands at the grand entrance-door, with a table before him, with small change, and each person pays his half-dollar as he passes out. The meals are good, substantial, and liberal.

Up at six. Toilet easily made. Eat a most wonderful breakfast. The country mountain air sharpens our appetite, even at dawn; and now for the Alleghanies. A few miles, and we get into the hills serpentining along the sides, the fog below like a calm sea. There is a remarkable horse-shoe bend of some miles. While we were running along one side of the curve, a train on the opposite side was coming down the hill, with all the brakes on. We met, and passed at the toe of the shoe, and our engines laboured hard to drag us up to the tunnel, 3,612 feet long, and 2,200 feet above the level of the sea. Those great inclined plains are a marvel of art and of nature. They told me that the Prince of Wales, whilst crossing the Alleghanies, sat on the engine to have a full view of the country. So did my two friends today, Captain L'Amy and

Russell. But my seat behind was the best for the *belle vue*. I sat
in a chair outside, on the tail car platform, all the journey. The
hills, dales, valleys, woods, and forests, are beautiful, all serpentining, and the curves so sharp an English carriage would be jerked off
in no time. As it was, there was too much oscillating and curveting
in the rapid movement, but those Americans drive like Jehu! Only
yesterday a train went smash through a bridge, and some hundred
soldiers were killed and wounded.

Pittsburgh at twelve noon; on the Ohio river at the confluence
of the Alleghany and Monongahela. There are many fine bridges
across these rivers, and some very fine and handsome country-
houses in the distance, and much need to be in the distance, for
this great, straggling town is as black and as dirty as the worst part
of Sheffield. There is a Birmingham suburb, and a Manchester, two
miles down on the Ohio. No end to coal-mines, and manufac-
tories in iron and glass are numerous. About eighty places of
religious worship, and a population of 120,000. There are twenty-
five steamboats now lying opposite this Monongahela Hotel,
trading on the Ohio, principally with Cincinnati, of about 500 tons
each, propelled by a paddle-wheel at the stern. I went on board
two of them, and confess I would rather not try a voyage down
river to the sea of two days and two nights, at any price, although
anxious to make a *détour* to get in rear of the Southern army, and
work up to see them. I know that General Beauregard, commanding, would receive me as a neutral friend, but the time and long
distance have changed my desire, and I give it up. Weather very
hot.

20th. Left at 12.30 for Cleveland, on Lake Erie — 150 miles.
Kept the course of the Ohio for about forty miles, and saw the big
steamers paddling against the current up from Cincinnati. Russell
and I were disturbed in pleasant, but, I might say, not a joyous
conversation, when the rail-whistle sounded the disperse. Here at
Rochester station we parted company, he for Chicago, and myself
for Canada. Our chat was about the battle of the Alma, and this
was its anniversary. We were both there, but in different departments — one for fighting, the other for writing all about the fighting.

A great number of oil-wells along the line of our march, yield-
ing a fabulous quantity, and a source of great wealth. We crossed
two trestle bridges, high and long, merely a rail laid upon the beams.
They were temporary, the originals being swept away in a moun-
tain torrents. The heat today is as great as ever I found it in India.
They do manage things well in this country. When we approached
Cleveland, a person belonging to the train came and asked where
I was going — to Detroit! He gave me a ticket, for which I paid a

shilling, and for which I got a carriage from the station to the
steamboat, and found my passage there, which I received by giving
up my ticket.   And here I am on board, to pass a bright moonlight
night, bound for home, sweet home.

21st.   Up at six, and found myself in the Detroit River, and far
away from being in time to catch the morning train from Windsor
to London, C.W., where I hoped to breakfast (110 miles).   Was told
it blew so hard in the night the steamer had to take a longer course
for safety in this great fresh-water sea.   When we landed, I saw the
train going off on the Canada side, a most disagreeable sight to one
in a hurry.   This Lake Erie is 564 feet above the sea-level, and
eighteen fathoms deep; in circumference, 600 miles; and fifty miles
wide.   There are three or four steam ferry-boats, always crossing.
You may ride or drive on board, and never dismount.   I was soon
over, and clear of the stars and stripes, and all the struggle and
excitement of war.   Had a good breakfast, and got away in a slow
train at 11.30, which took seven hours and a half to reach London,
110 miles.   The day was cold, and the morning damp and drizzling.
The country inundated, being almost on a level with Lake St. Clair,
which looked rough and angry, dashing its waves into the forest
along the beach.

Here there is a dismal swamp for some twenty miles by ten, the
grand depôt for all the wild ducks in America.   One could shoot
them from the rail, but you would never see them again.   Ran
along the lake shore for three hours; this is also a small sea.   A
telescope could not bring the opposite side in view.   Plenty of
large steamers and small ships bowling up to Lake Huron (595 feet
above the sea, and 75 fathoms deep), and Georgian Bay, Michigan,
and Lake Superior—a most wonderful country for inland seas.
The rail from Windsor to London is a straight line all the way, and
the express runs it in about three hours.   It seems so odd that
Windsor and London have come to dwell in Western Canada,
amongst the woods and the forest, and the stumps; and that the
Thames should have made a race here also, and have Blackfriars
Bridge pitched over it as an old remembrance.

I found a big hotel, called Tecumseh House, close to the nice
station where I am at anchor.   Took a walk by gaslight into the
city, but could not recognise a house or a street in the little village
where I was stationed for two years, when the stumps of the forest
trees were still fast in the short wide streets.   I was informed that
in the valley of the Ohio there is a settlement of a singular class of
people calling themselves Economists.   They have all things
common; they work together in the fields, have their own parson.
They are moral and religious Christian people, and neither marry

nor are given in marriage, and are a wealthy, happy, and contented community. I sometimes almost shudder when I look back upon some of my galloping tours. Crossing arms of the sea with frightful rapidity on two iron rails suspended over an abyss, the depth below astounding, and so they rattle along, everyone now at full speed in the disUnited States. A young, active fellow at Baltimore celebrated for running, a three months' service man, whose time was up, came home, and assembling his companions, got up on a stump to give an account of the battle of the Bull's Run. 'Now,' he said, 'I guess you all know that I am a smart lad about the heels, and that I can run a bit faster than time, and win your money for you, but never vinture another cent on my legs. You all heared I ran well at the great race, when we started all in a ruck, but if ever you vinture on me again you're gone coons, for my colonel beat me on to the long bridge at Washington by half an hour, and that's sure as creation!'

The Railway Station here in London I find stands in my old garden. I went to the kirk, where at the same time a poor old nigger had his shanty in the woods. A village stands on our old steeplechase ground, a Bank and the General Post Office, fine buildings, occupy the place where my cow used to feed when I could keep her at home. But she broke away so often, and returned to her birthplace sixteen miles off, I found it inconvenient to send for her more than twice, so we parted company altogether! The old wooden Barrack in *statu-quo*, and the parade ground which we formed by rooting up the stumps (the work of defaulters), where are they? And where are all the officers and men who were so jolly at all the games got up to amuse the people? How gallantly some rode at the ring, and carried it off on top of the spear (G. B. won the prize). Their bones were left in India west, in Greece and Turkey, committed to the deep, or rest in the shallow graves where tens of thousands fell on Sebastopol's hills. This London is becoming a great place, the people call it a city. I find one of our old parsons (Cronin), a bishop, and bishops have their headquarters in cities. I have ranged over all the old places, what charming ground to ride over! If your horse drops a shoe no matter, all the highways and by-ways, sand and soft green sward. There is Westminster Bridge and Covent Garden Market, and a Palace just finished for the exhibition of provincial manufactures, cattle, vegetables, and everything that is Canadian, to open tomorrow. I must stay and see it. Here is a fine welcome from a lady friend. Twenty years have passed away since we met, and Mrs. H. is still a buxom wife, and full of the kindness and simplicity of her adopted country. 'Oh, tell me how is Mrs. B.? Does she still ride on horseback?

She was the best horsewoman I ever saw, a picture to see her gallop along our roads on her beautiful horse "Rory O'Moore". I forget nothing of those bright days. Tell me all about her, I loved her so much, so kind to me, so good and amiable. You will stop with us as long as you can, you must not pass our door. Twenty years have heaped up so many stories. You saw so much, and you will come and tell us all.' I was not very well, and did go into the bonnie cottage, and had a couple of days rest, which I required.

There is a fine Covent Garden Market, and so well supplied and so reasonable: a very big cock turkey, 6s.; fine fowls, 1s. a couple; beef and lamb best quality, 3½d. a pound; eggs, 6d. a dozen; geese, 1s. each; ducks, 1s. 8d. a pair; a melon, 5d.; oats a bushel, 34 lbs., 9d.; and so on. Very hot day, and a bad headache.

24th. Those homely domestic people the geese continue to live happy and contented in the heart of the city. There is hardly a street that may not claim its own flock, and as the streets are generally of grass and sand, they pick up a living!

Went to the exhibition in the Crystal Palace, twenty-three acres of ground enclosed for the purpose, adjoining the barracks. I found two of my old Sebastopol friends keeping guard there; both had been wounded by our shot—they are 32-pounders.

The fair, as it was called, was most creditable to this section of Canada, and many things would have gained prizes in England or France. The cattle, sheep, poultry, and some furniture of black walnut—particularly an invalid bed, or one adapted for any purpose, or for lying in any position. By pulling a cord gently (which dropped down to the pillow), the upper part of the bed was raised to any position, or lowered as easily. It was beautifully finished, and made of the feathered black walnut. The man had a patent —price £20 and 18 dollars. On show were the finest and best of agricultural implements of all sorts I ever saw. Also, finest of apples and grapes, very large and ripe, in open air; boots and shoes; all sorts of cheese, two specimens weighing 1,200 lb. each! These were the greatest monsters of the kind I ever saw. Now, a most ingenious and handsome doorbell without wires; horse-shoes for any cheval; pianos; the finest honey, and the most ingenious bee-houses to keep them all alive and always working. The ducks were of noble breed, and nearly as large as geese; all sorts of cocks and hens that one could admire for beauty of plumage, shape, and graceful appearance. There were sleighs and light waggons of various shapes and sizes, and some fine trotting horses, also a hundred other most useful and ornamental nice things, not forgetting black apples. A small lake beautifies this ground, with some pretty boats to show off the ladies, who enjoy the scene from the water.

All this to be seen where a wild forest grew thirty years ago speaks well for the progress of civilisation in Canada. The shops in the town are numerous, and much better than any in Washington. The Tecumseh Hotel is full today. It is so called after the old Indian chief who fought so bravely, and fell gallantly fighting on our side against the Americans in the revolutionary war, near this place where General Scott, my Washington friend, had then a command as Brigadier.

I next visited Niagara, and had my old room at the Clifton House. I found it the same nice, comfortable hotel, after an absence of eighteen years. My bedroom opened out on a verandah, 300 yards long, and right in front is the great Horseshoe Fall, uttering its deep, deafening roar of endless melody, and shooting over its precipice, 154 feet high and 2,000 wide, one hundred million tons of water every hour. The verandah forms two sides, one looking on the Horseshoe Fall, about a mile distant (but looks close at hand), the other side faces the American Fall, 163 feet in perpendicular height and 660 feet wide. The smaller fall between Luna and Goat Island is 240 feet wide. Now draw an armchair, and be seated in the angle of this fine look-out, and you have all the falls before your eye. The doors and windows of the hotel forever quiver and shake from the vibration of the thunder of the fall, the roar of the cataract is ever in your ears, and lulls one to sleep after a long day of exercise and excitement. There below you see the ferry-boat dancing on the boiling deep, taking the tourists to and fro. It reminds me of long years past, when I came late back at night from Buffalo, found the ferry-boat drawn up on the slips, and nobody at hand. I launched the boat with the aid of two young officers of my regiment, and rowed them safely over, after dancing about in the whirl of the deep longer than a more experienced boatman would figure in such a quadrille—but it was night. The next morning the boatmen would be saying how the fairies had carried off their bark! There is Goat or Iris Island feathered to the water's edge with green, shady trees; it contains seventy acres.

The Terrapin Tower occupies a very singular and fearful position. A few scattered masses of rock lie on the very brink of the great fall, seeming as if unable to maintain their position against the tremendous rush of water. Upon these rocks the tower is built, and will be surely swept away some day. Many accidents have happened, many lives been lost, and many more there will be. As I passed along today to the Table Rock, which has nearly all fallen into the abyss, I saw a notice on the brink of an awful perpendicular fall:

> This is the spot where
> Miss Margaret R. Rugg
> lost her life by falling over the
> precipice, while plucking a flower.
> August 24, 1844.

Another melancholy accident is recorded here.   The family of Mr. Deforest, of Buffalo, visited the Falls, 21st June, 1849, along with a young man named Charles Allington.   They were about leaving, when Mr. A. playfully seized little Annette (the daughter of Mr. D.) in his arms, and held her over the edge of the bank, exclaiming, 'I am going to throw you over!'   The poor child sprung in fear from his grasp, and fell into the rushing stream.   With a loud cry of horror the young man rushed in to save her, when they both went over the falls.   The same evening the mangled remains of the child were found in the Cave of the Winds, and the young man's body some days after.   I wonder more accidents don't happen, for there is no parapet from Clifton House along to the great falls, and at every point it is frightful to look over the mighty precipice on to the jagged rocks below.   It made my head giddy, yet there is somehow an accountable prompting desire to run into every corner of danger.   An attractive influence comes over one's mind that is almost irresistible, and you are impelled forward to the very spot where most danger awaits you.   The power and majesty of the Almighty are, perhaps, more awfully exhibited and more fully realised in this stupendous waterfall than in any other scene on earth.   It is eleven o'clock at night.   I look out, and see one huge, white, cloudy extent of 100 millions of tons of water

> Pouring and roaring,
> And waving and raving,
> Tossing and crossing,
> Flowing and growing,
> Running and stunning,
> Hurrying and scurrying,
> Glittering and flittering
> Foaming and roaming,
> Heaving and cleaving,
>   With endless rebound;
> Smiting and fighting,
> A sight to delight in,
> Confounding, astounding,
> And deafening the ear
>   With its sound.

Up with the larks, and looking out on that cascade which roused
me out of my dreams very often during the night. I asked the
ferryman's daughter if the roaring waters kept her awake. 'No,'
she said, 'on the contrary. When I go from home, I seldom sleep
well.' A hot day; thermometer in shade 70°, and a strong breeze,
which lifts the steam-like spray, and scatters it like drizzling rain,
watering the roads and gardens at a quarter-mile distance. The
great majesty of the scene is not to be described by pen. From
where I now stand, in front of and under the great fall, the sun has
just struck across the point of the Shoe, and turned that part of the
torrent into a bright emerald, while both sides are flanked by the
white, foaming, endless descent of this powerful element.

Crossed in the boat to the American side. The river is here
upwards of fifty fathoms deep — 290 stairs, if you are very active
and fond of climbing, will take you up to the top. If not, step into
the rail car, and go up for five cents. I can't go along with you
in this easy chair. I must count the steps, and get alongside of the
American Fall to get a wetting. I got within three yards of it,
where it fell perpendicularly with such a terrific roar. It was
charming damp music. On to the top, shake the drizzle off your
clothes, and sit down by the very edge of the flowing torrent. You
may wash your hands in it from the very leap-over.

See how this rocky point is worn smooth by the foot of man,
and that bush hanging over has been grasped by many a nervous
hand holding a death grip, while the dizzy head must have a peep
into the frightful abyss of terrific splendour. Now look out, and
behold this broad sheet of rolling foaming waters coming down the
slope as if shooting from the skies, for you see nothing beyond.
It comes in majesty and terror as if in exultation for the terrific
leap. Doctor Hungerford lost his life here by the falling of a
portion of the rock on which he was standing!

Walk up now to the bridge leading to Goat Island, stand on
the centre of it, look and wonder. The noble river here undulating and foaming with impatience in wayward billows and breakers
gushing forward into the thundering flood below, the great power
of this broad surface of 660 feet of mad waters gathering strength
as they go headlong forward seems as if it would sweep away our
frail standing and hurl us over the dread precipice. The fall in the
rapids, a mile above this point, is sixty feet, and the tumultuous
madness of the waters to find their level baffles all description. No
one can describe Niagara — no one can paint the scene. The Suspension Bridge is a wonderful work of art. There are three fine
hotels on this American side. The Cataract House, the finest and
best, standing close upon the falls, the long verandah hanging

almost over the rapids, and commanding one of the most singularly grand views in the New World. There is a very large ballroom, a beautiful drawing-room most elegantly furnished adjoining, a grand piano, and six pier-glasses from carpet to ceiling. One may recline there on a damask couch, and enjoy from the windows a scene which people have come to see from the uttermost parts of the earth! The charge here is the usual one at all hotels, two and a half dollars a day. A nice bedroom, breakfast, dinner, tea, and supper, no extras, no servants to pay—the use of the public rooms into the bargain!

Danced across in the ferry-boat to the Canada side. Went to the top of Biddel's look-out—150 stairs, six platforms to rest as you go up, and view the majesty of the Grand Fall, over and into its boiling, mighty and sublime deep. Took views from every point. And, lastly, being a very hot day for 26th September, I had a bathe within twenty yards of the great leap. It was fearful to see the rush of a hundred millions of tons of water passing by with such rapidity, but I was all safe behind a detached rock, and yet so near the awful scene. Part of my dress was blown into the stream, and went over the falls, which was rather inconvenient! A last look into the seething abyss, with its deafening roar or endless melody. I lay flat upon the flank of the grand *saut*, head projecting over, looking down into the boiling pit. Oh, but it was a dread scene of terror. I put forward my hand, and let it be washed in the hissing torrent, crawled backwards to get clear, and left Niagara.

Flow on forever in thy glorious robe of terror and of beauty! What are all the notes that ever rung from war's vain trumpet by thy thundering side: what is all the riot man makes in his short life to thy unceasing roar?

On a former occasion, when a little more wild for adventure, I performed the feat of passing under the great Horseshoe Fall. You change your dress in a little house for a suit of oil-cloth, and go along with the guide—the spray dashing in your face—until you slide in behind this curtain of the world's wonder. There is a narrow ledge of rock running along to the middle of the Fall, with an iron bar to hold on by. You crawl along to the end of this dark and dismal recess, halt, endeavour to open your eyes on the brink of fifty fathoms, the back spray dashing in your face. To speak is useless; you hear nothing but the everlasting roar: cautiously counter-march, and get out of this slimy promenade, and now you may whistle with joy:

'I'll gang na mair to yon toon.'

Your name is recorded in the book; you get your certificate from the keeper, pay your money, write to your friends, and say as I did, I can't describe this place.

Go and see Niagara. The suspension bridge spans the river, two miles below the Falls. A noble and stupendous structure, forming the communication between Canada and the United States.

We enjoyed a whole year's visit, near to Montreal, with our little Indian interpreter, who has now herself a son in H.M.S. — a very fine-looking, dashing young fellow, in for everything where there is a chance of a scrimmage. He volunteered for China, and won his medal at the capture of Pekin.

I never liked cold weather. We had a wall of snow round our house sixteen feet high, with a tunnel cut through it, and although the houses are generally far more comfortable inside in winter than any in England, the cold outside, particularly in an east wind, is too much for humanity. Everything is frozen as hard as a stone; the fish are cut with a saw. Artillery practice on the rapid St. Lawrence. Nothing to be seen in the country but chimney-tops and pine-trees — the merry sleigh bells always chiming, picnic parties by day and balls at night, plenty of frolic and fun for those who like it. The skating rink always crowded with charming girls perfect in this science, really dancing quadrilles to the music of a regimental band. And so the winter passes.

I was now bound for home. The choice was between two steamers, down the lakes to see the Thousand Islands which I saw before, or roll away on the rail, and get home a day sooner. The Grand Trunk Railway carried me off, equinox overtook us, the two steamers were wrecked, and the train was most providentially saved from a similar fate. Wind and rain terrific, sleepers washed away, and all the foundation. Some kind person living near saw the break-up, and saw what the terrible consequences of dashing into this gulf would come to. He got a light, and walked up the rail two miles to meet and stop the train. 'Twas done at the proper time. We pulled up on the brink of the chasm, and when daylight came the passengers walked on to the next station, and had a car sent back for the baggage. Here we had breakfast, and after four hours' delay travelled on in fresh cars at increased speed to make up time. Home to dinner at six, all well and joyful, and all's well that ends well.

During my little tour I met nought but civility, kindness, and attention from Brother Jonathan. I never heard any high-class people say an offensive word against England. It is true that many do foolishly brag overmuch, and talk about 'whipping the Britishers', etc., and it is too true that in old times the British army was always unsuccessful in America. The fact of Burgoyne, in

1777, surrendering at Saratoga, and Lord Cornwallis surrendering his army on October 19th, 1781, to General Washington, whose name is held in reverence, are circumstances kept up fresh in the memory of generations, and it would be the same with ourselves. But the great tragedy is being now played on their own broad stage. They are whipping themselves, and few sympathise with them, or are willing to interfere in their quarrels. I regret all this unholy suicidal war myself, and would fain hope it may soon be amicably arranged. It may probably end in a division of territory or a change of government, but the contending parties are desperate and uncompromising enemies just now.

Providence has hitherto smiled on this great country. When one looks back to see what has been done by perseverance and industry in two hundred years, it is quite wonderful. Look at the towns, the villages, and cities scattered over the country, the hills and valleys, covered with cattle, fruit trees, gardens, orchards, and abundant harvests of all sorts of the best. Look at the immense steamboats ploughing the grandest rivers in the world, canals bearing along the treasures of the earth, thousands of miles of railway conveying millions of people trading through the land. See New York City itself peopled by some 400,000 inhabitants, its beautiful streets, squares, churches, public buildings, and elegant houses. There are hotels not to be equalled in the world; shops containing merchandise from China, Java, Hindostan, Arabia, and all parts of the world. Harbours all crowded with ships and steamers coming and going like bees on a sunny day. Sail up the Hudson. Visit Troy, Albany, Buffalo, Lakes Erie, Superior, and Huron, the Ohio, and a thousand prosperous and thriving towns that beautify the land where wild forests and jungle grew fifty years ago. The rapid increase of wealth, the progress of refinement, and the multiplication of inhabitants must strike any traveller on his way through this most interesting world.